The LEXICON
For Ethics, Integrity & Aptitude

Catering to Evolving Trends in GS Paper-IV

|| Read and Recommended by Every Topper since 2014 ||

Editor

N. N. Ojha

Research, Written & Presented By

Niraj Kumar & Chronicle Editorial Team

www.chronicleindia.in

CHRONICLE BOOKS

The Book Division of
Chronicle Publications Pvt. Ltd.

The LEXICON
For Ethics, Integrity & Aptitude

First Edition	2013
Second Edition	2015
Third Edition	2016
Fourth Edition	2018
Fifth Edition	2019
Sixth Edition	**2020**

Price: Rs. 395.00

ISBN- 978-81-942048-2-4

Publisher

CHRONICLE BOOKS
(A Division of Chronicle Publications (P) Ltd.)

Corporate Office : A-27D, Sector-16, Noida (UP), Ph. : 0120-2514611-12
E-mail : circulation@chronicleindia.in

Registered Office : H-31, G.P. Extn., New Delhi - 110016

Printer

First Impression, Corporate Services Pvt. Ltd., NOIDA - 201301

Preface

In the present transforming society there is a need of good public administration. Over the period of time, the role of public administration (service) has transformed depending upon the evolution of governance but, the one which is eternal and long lasting is the ethical values behind the service.

Ethics is a multidimensional term that is used to describe what human should do based on rights, obligations, fairness, virtues, etc. Ethics and values forms the cornerstone of public administration system, which provides the answer to the question, **"Why Should I Be Moral".**

A recent example of this, is the arrest of an IPS officer who was on probation, for cheating during the civil services examination. It raises the question about the level of honesty and the dedication on part of the civil servant. Can such issues be only resolved with penal actions? Maybe not, and here lies the importance of ethical values, morals, integrity, attitude empathy, etc. which comes into play. Ultimately it is the moral fibre of an individual officer or public servant that counts.

Realizing the need of the hour, UPSC has taken an initiative to inculcate the ethical and moral values and thoughts for incoming new civil servants so that they feel the need of the society with empathy and serve accordingly.

The GS paper IV "Ethics Paper" of civil services examinations is the litmus test of an individual, that is not only based on a theoretical syllabus but also scrutinizes the individual from inside through judging his personal moral conducts.

This book in a pedagogical manner enlightens an individual about ethics and all its related concepts. This book is not just about the definitions, thoughts, quotations, concepts but, it is about the discussions, role play, application of thoughts and underlying cases, etc. that are useful to any individual (not only for civil service aspirants) for moral conduct.

This new **Sixth Edition of Lexicon For Ethics, Integrity & Aptitude Book** includes newly written chapters namely **'Lexicon of Case Study'** and **'Ethical Issues';** first one is focused on the different types of case studies and its solving and also the solutions of case studies asked in UPSC examinations; whereas the other one is dedicated to the ethical issues involved in practical life in different dimensions of Social, Economic, Environment, Polity and Governance and so on. For easy understanding of the small concepts in ethics 'Glossary' is also included at the end of the book.

To sum up here, we can observe that the crux of ethical behaviour does not lie in bold words, platitudes and expressions enshrined as standards, but rather in their adoption in action in sanctions against their violations. It lies in putting in place competent disciplinary bodies to investigate allegations of violations and impose sanctions quickly and promoting a culture of integrity. As rightly put by, Albert Schweitzer,

"Ethics is nothing else than reverence for life"

♦♦□□♦♦

Acknowledgement

A book is always a culmination of some loaded experiences and this book is not an exception. As 'The Lexicon for Ethics, Integrity and Aptitude' is a conspectus of ethics and so blessed with input from many learned fellows.

In the building of this book many publications and websites were very helpful and deserve the mention like Economic and Political Weekly (EPW), BBC, Financial Times, The Economist, IIPA, Harvard Business Review (HBR) and so on and also Wikipedia is as helpful as always.

The Second Administrative Reforms Commission (SARC) Report stayed as a prime mover force for this qualitative content and made this book stick to the ground of being always relevant and not to be taken far-off while dealing with highly metaphorical content.

And, a special mention to Chronicle Publications (P) Ltd. for bringing out this book, without its contribution and support it would not have been possible. Finally, thanks to all the aspirants and the readers, who always put the writer on the edge and inspire to write such qualitative content.

HOW TO USE THIS BOOK

This book 'The Lexicon for Ethics, Intergrity & Aptitude is a compendium that touches all the dimensions of ethics and related concepts. This book completely justifies the syllabus of UPSC and other examinations where ethics is dynamic subject which oscillates between morality and ethicality. This book is highly engaging with its in-depth concepts of normative ethics, meta-ethics, applied ethics and other related concepts and their related case studies given at the end of each concepts.

Wealth of real life examples, ethical dilemmas, illuminations of complexities with different ethical approaches interweaved with vivid style of writing leaves a deep-rooted impression upon a reader.

To derive, the maximum benefit from this book, a reader must be focused on the topics and study it thoroughly and after completion analyze the given case studies at the end of the chapters and try to apply the concepts on the given situational dilemmas.

During the initial reading of this book; the reader must be focused on important concepts and their relevance in real-world environment conditions/ situations.

Do not try to solve the case at the very first instance. First, study the topics, try to differentiate between the similar topics and focus yourself on the key definitions.

Now, proceed towards the given cases and assume yourself present in the given particular situation and delve into the possible solutions on the basis of the ethical concepts you have studied earlier.

The second reading should be more in-depth and the reader should try to read between the lines written and inculcate the concepts and memorize the keywords. This will help make you comfortable in the world of ethics.

Now, apply these studied concepts into previous years' case-studies and update it with the real world examples.

Hope, you will enjoy this Book!!

GENERAL STUDIES PAPER-IV

Syllabus as mentioned on the UPSC website

Ethics, Integrity, and Aptitude

This paper will include questions to test the candidate's attitude and approach to issues relating to integrity, probity in public life and his problem solving approach to various issues and conflicts faced by him in dealing with society. Questions may utilize the case study approach to determine these aspects. The following broad areas will be covered:

- **Ethics and Human Interface:** Essence, determinants and consequences of Ethics in human actions; dimensions of ethics; ethics in private and public relationships. **Human Values** - lessons from the lives and teachings of great leaders, reformers and administrators; role of family, society and educational institutions in inculcating values.
- **Attitude:** Content, structure, function; its influence and relation with thought and behavior; moral and political attitudes; social influence and persuasion.
- **Aptitude and Foundational Values for Civil Service:** Integrity, impartiality and non-partisanship, objectivity, dedication to public service, empathy, tolerance and compassion towards the weaker-sections.
- **Emotional Intelligence:** Concepts, and their utilities and application in administration and governance.
- **Contributions of Moral Thinkers and Philosophers:** From India and World.
- **Public/Civil Service Values and Ethics in Public Administration:** Status and problems; ethical concerns and dilemmas in government and private institutions; laws, rules, regulations and conscience as sources of ethical guidance; accountability and ethical governance; strengthening of ethical and moral values in governance; ethical issues in international relations and funding; corporate governance.
- **Probity in Governance:** Concept of public service; Philosophical basis of governance and probity; Information sharing and transparency in government, Right to Information, Codes of Ethics, Codes of Conduct, Citizen's Charters, Work culture, Quality of service delivery, Utilization of public funds, challenges of corruption.
- **Case Studies:** On the above issues.

CONTENT

1

LEXICON OF CASE-STUDY

The Concepts Discussed in this Unit

- What is a Case Study?
- Types of Case Studies
- A Brief on Case Studies
- Practical Approach for Solving Case Studies
- Stakeholders Involved in the Case Studies
- A Brief on Case Study – Questions @ Mains

In the following section, we have tried to present in an objective manner, how to look at the Case-Study questions, as Case-Study is said to be pedagogy of management fraternity. Apart from this, some selected write-ups, which goes a long way in enriching the optimal manner in which one can negotiate Case-Study questions has also been given.

What is Case Study?

A case study is an account of an activity, event or problem that contains a real or hypothetical situation and includes the complexities one would encounter in the workplace. Case studies are used to help you see how the complexities of real life influence decisions.

Analysing a case study requires you to practice applying your knowledge and thinking skills to a real situation. To learn from a case study analysis you will be "analysing, applying knowledge, reasoning and drawing conclusions" (Kardos & Smith 1979).

According to Kardos and Smith (1979) a good case has the following features:

- It is taken from real life (true identities may be concealed).
- It consists of many parts and each part usually ends with problems and points for discussion. There may not be a clear cut-off point to the situation.
- It includes sufficient information for the reader to treat problems and issues.
- It is believable for the reader (the case contains the setting, personalities, sequence of events, problems and conflicts).

So, in a nutshell; a case study gives you an opportunity to "participate" rather than be passive. It calls for a more engaged approach from the examinees and at the same time it is the best methodology at the hands of the examiner where he can test the probability of the presence/absence of the potential within the candidate beyond what is available in a plain answer/question type exam.

Types of Case Studies

In the Civil Services Examination, General Studies Paper IV is dedicated to Ethics that includes Case Studies section and carries more than hundred marks. Case studies are one of the major scoring areas for the aspirants and therefore, understandings of the case studies are very important aspects of the preparation. This basic understanding will direct on how to approach the case to solve the given dilemmas. The case studies asked by UPSC are unique in the sense that they are meant to check the attributes that are expected from a civil servant.

By contextual analyses of the case studies we may find that they are fundamentally 'a genuine' or 'invented' situation where an individual is exposed to moral problems or ethical dilemmas. Some of the cases may have multi-layers of ethical dilemmas, where the authorized person is exposed to several levels his upper subordinates. Such dilemmas demand strong moral standards to tackle such situations with multidimensional intellect. Also, some of the ethics cases are based on certain kinds of goals and objectives; these cases are solved by standard ethical practices. Different cases require different strategies to handle, and therefore, which type of cases are given and what approach should be followed to tackle the ethical dilemmas, calls for - firstly identification of type of case study and the dilemma involved is necessary.

In any case, a case study may take one of the four different forms:

- Illustrative case studies,
- Exploratory case studies,
- Cumulative case studies, and
- Critical case studies.

1. **Illustrative case studies** are descriptive in nature and designed to shed light on a particular situation, set of circumstances, and the social relations and processes that are embedded in them. These case studies are mainly based on one or two specific events or instances exposing a person to a certain situation. They are useful in bringing to light something about which most people are not aware of.

Example of Illustrative Case Studies: Conflict of Interest

Case: The Delhi and District Cricket Association's (DDCA) director (Cricket) Sanjay Bhardwaj has written to the ombudsman/ethics officer (retd.) Justice Badar Durrez Ahmed alleging that appointment of members of the Cricket Improvement Committee (CIC) and selectors was in violation of Conflict of Interest norms.

In his letter to the DDCA ombudsman, Bhardwaj has alleged that former India opener Virender Sehwag, who is part of the three-member CIC, runs cricket academies and that Sehwag is also the cricket operations chief of IPL team Kings XI Punjab.

The DDCA director has also alleged in his letter that Sehwag is an expert on India TV, a channel of which DDCA President Rajat Sharma is the editor-in-chief. The DDCA director also questioned the appointment of former Delhi all-rounder Mayank Tehlan to the junior selection committee. Tehlan, according to Bhardwaj, is the cousin of Sehwag. The CIC picked the senior and junior selection committees of the DDCA.

Bhardwaj has also written to the ombudsman stating that the appointments of both Aakash Chopra and Rahul Sanghvi, former cricketers, are in violation of conflict of interest norms. Chopra runs cricket academies, while Sanghvi is engaged with Mumbai Indians (team manager), Bhardwaj's letter states.

Opener Gautam Gambhir, who is an active cricketer, is also a special invitee to the committee, Bhardwaj said during a media interaction.

The DDCA director also alleged that chairman of the senior selection Committee of the DDCA Amit Bhandari and member of the committee Sukhwinder Singh both run cricket academies and fall foul of the conflict of interest norms.

How can such Conflict of Interest be Removed?

When faced with a potential conflict of interest, there are three appropriate responses - avoid, disclose, and recuse.

A. It is best to avoid situations that could result in conflicts of interest whenever possible. In commercial and financial matters, avoidance does not mean that absolutely no non-wage benefits may be accepted. It does mean that some are prohibited and that all should be carefully scrutinized. Audiologists, speech-language pathologists, and speech, language, and hearing scientists should not accept gifts or benefits unless it can be clearly demonstrated that such gifts or benefits:

- primarily contribute to the welfare of persons served professionally;
- do not reasonably appear to bias professional judgment;
- enhance one's professional knowledge and skills; and/or
- do not diminish the dignity or autonomy of the professions.

B. Disclosure is essentially a self-initiated action, with the intent to be honest and complete, to provide personal and professional information in order to remain ethically compliant with the Code. The act of disclosure is a process of transparency. Foundation to proper, professional, and ethical conduct is the intent to be honest, accurate, and complete. Disclosure of both financial and nonfinancial relationships is inherent in assumed ethical conduct. Many clinical, research, and teaching scenarios can potentially foster a natural tension between professional obligation and personal preference/gain. Misrepresentation by both errors of omission and commission can create ethical violations.

C. Recusal is the action of withdrawing from situations when one's participation creates bias that could adversely influence the decision. As an example, when one sits on a committee or board that makes decision about the advancement of others or about the distribution of resources and benefits to others, a conflict of interest may require that the professional recuses himself. Recusal may occur because of the professional's financial interests in or personal ties to one or more of the parties. By disclosing the nature of the association and by stepping out of the decision-making process, the professional ensures that any personal preferences or biases they may have will not unfairly influence the deliberations.

2. **Exploratory case studies** are such case studies which focus on preliminary investigation or actions before implementing large-scale actions or investigations on the matter. This type of case studies are typically used when one wants to identify some smaller methods of study for a large or complex study. They are useful for clarifying the process. Exploratory case studies are also often known as 'pilot studies'.

Example of Exploratory Case Studies: On Disaster Management (CSE 2015)

There is a disaster-prone state having frequent landslides, forest fires, cloudbursts, flash floods and earthquakes, etc. Some of these are seasonal and often unpredictable. The magnitude of the disaster is always unanticipated. During one of the seasons a cloudburst caused devastating floods and landslides leading to high casualties. There was major damage to infrastructure like roads, bridges and power generating units. This led to more than 100000 pilgrims, tourists and other locals trapped across different routes and locations. The people trapped in your area of responsibility includes senior citizens, patients in hospitals, women and children, hikers, tourists, ruling party's regional president along with his family, additional chief secretary of the neighbouring State and prisoners in jail.

As a civil services officer of the State, what would be the order in which you would rescue these people and why? Give Justifications (200 Words)

This case comes under

- Ethics and Human Interface
- Ethics in Public Administration
- Emotional Intelligence
- Moral Values and Compassion

Premise: The case deals with the moral understanding of the civil servant and compassion towards the common mass. The decision (mainly on the priority basis, based on compassion) of the civil servant can deal the situation with least damage of people's life.

Answer: The approach for the answer would be-

Based on the different principle like the virtue approach, common good approach, principle of utilitarianism, etc., the answer must deal with the situation and corrective action with the supportive arguments.

For example-

I will opt for the following sequence towards rescue operation-

(i) Patients in Hospitals

- They are highly vulnerable during disasters, because of their in-ability to take care of themselves. They are less in number with position known.

(ii) Senior citizens

- They are valuable members of society, and cannot be left without

help for too long. They are also vulnerable because of their old age and physical handicap.

(iii) Women and Children

- Women and Children are highly vulnerable during disasters, not just physically but emotionally as well. Children lead a generation forward, so, they must be rescued first of all.

(iv) Prisoners in Jail

- Since they are in jail, so their mobility is highly restricted. This makes them vulnerable in disaster situation. They cannot help themselves and hence need quick attention.

(v) Tourists

- They know very less about the local conditions and may be without any nutritional and life support substances.

(vi) Ruling Party's Regional President and his Family

- Since he has political linkages, he can make temporary arrangements for safety of his family till other vulnerable people are rescued. He has a family with him, so early rescue is desirable.

(vii) Chief Secretary of the other State

- He has been well trained to handle such situations. So, he can wait till others are rescued.

(viii) Hikers

- I will rescue them at last, as they have both the training as well as equipments with them, to deal with challenging terrain. They can easily wait till others are rescued.

So, I will conduct the rescue operation according to the above mentioned priority list. However, in some cases, simultaneous rescue mission can be launched for different categories as they are not mutually exclusive.

3. **Cumulative case studies** are the successive case studies to make use of earlier studies or similar situations. They are useful to make generalization from studies that have something in common. In such case studies the questioned case pulls together collections of already completed case studies on a particular topic.

Example of Cumulative Case Studies: Whistle-blowing and Vyapam Case

What is Vyapam?

According to its official website, the MPPEB (Madhya Pradesh Professional Examination Board), commonly known by its Hindi acronym, Vyapam (Vyavsayik Pariksha Mandal) claims to be "the only institute of its kind in the Country that organizes competitive tests for entrance to various professional courses every year on a very large scale". Besides common entrance tests (CETs) for professional courses such as medicine and engineering, Vyapam also conducts recruitment examinations for "different state level posts which are not to be filled through the Public Service Commission".

What is the scam all about?

The malpractices in the examinations conducted by Vyapam. The modus operandi included bribing officials, forging answer sheets, impersonating candidates and even manipulating seating arrangements. The scam also involves the accused employing imposters to write papers on the candidate's behalf. According to reports, the scam took place between 2008 and 2013.

When did it first come to light?

An Indore-based doctor and activist Dr. Anand Rai filed a Public Interest Litigation in the Madhya Pradesh High Court. The PIL led to Chief Minister Shivraj Singh Chouhan setting up an inquiry committee, which submitted its report in 2011. Two years later, in 2013, whistleblower Rai made startling revelations - said many candidates had procured admission to medical colleges in the state through fraudulent practices, including impersonation and bribery. The investigation was then handed over to a Special Task Force (STF). Since then, over 2000 people, including students, middlemen, businessmen, public officials and politicians have been arrested for their role in the scam.

How many people have died during the investigation?

Nearly 50 people have died since 2009, when the Vyapam scam was first unearthed. With more facts coming to light, deaths became murkier. Nearly half of the people died under mysterious circumstances like road mishaps and disappearances. In 2015 alone, eight people have died.

What about the whistleblowers?

The scam has seen a range of activists coming out and exposing the rot within Madhya Pradesh's professional examination board. Besides Dr. Anand Rai, whistleblowers in the case included Ashish Chaturvedi, a social activist from Gwalior and Prashant Pandey, a former IT consultant hired by the STF. All of them have complained of police harassment and constant threats to their lives for their role in exposing the scam.

4. **Critical instance case studies** are the cases based on situational conditions for an individual. These cases are unique and situational and the individual have to solve such dilemmas on the basis of his self-learning because of limited precedence.

Example of Critical Instance Case Studies: To Whistle-blow Against Polluting Industry or Not? (CSE 2016)

A fresh engineering graduate gets a job in a prestigious chemical industry. She likes the work. The salary is also good. However, after a few months, she accidentally discovers that a highly toxic waste is being secretly discharged into a river nearby. This is causing health problems to the villagers downstream who depend on the river for their water needs. She is perturbed and mentions her concern to her colleagues who have been with the company for longer periods. They advise her to keep quiet as anyone who mentions the topic is summarily dismissed. She cannot risk losing her job as she is the sole bread-winner for her family and has to support her ailing parents and siblings.

At first, she thinks that if her seniors are keeping quiet, why should she stick out her neck. But, her conscience pricks her to do something to save the river and the people who depend upon it. At heart she feels that the advice of silence given by her friends is not correct though she cannot give reasons for it. She thinks you are a wise person and seeks your advice.

A. What arguments can you advance to show her that keeping quiet is not morally right?

B. What course of action would you advise her to adopt and why?

This case comes under

- Ethics and Human Interface

- Why should I be moral?
- Conscience as a source of ethical guidance
- Morality

Premise: This question shows an internal fight between inner conscience and the need of physical real world. The graduate lacks confidence that she may easily get another job and blow the whistle against the firm. The dependants on her will also get impacted with her decision.

Answer: The approach for the answer would be-

After discussing the basics of above topics you may provide different options with supportive suggestions as-

- She should keep quiet. Private company engineers are not protected under Article 311, unlike IAS. If she is kicked out of here, may not get another job elsewhere because there is too much competition due to mushrooming of self-financed engineering colleges which are producing several engineers.
- She may approach to different NGOs (and may act as a whistle blower) and request them to produce agitation against the company without taking name of her.

Like these, there may be more different options like - she has to believe herself and try for other jobs and then quit the current one, etc., and at last, you submit the answer with conclusive statement that in such different options, I would choose this.

An **ethical dilemma** or **ethical paradox** is a decision-making problem between two possible moral imperatives, neither of which is unambiguously acceptable or preferable. The complexity arises out of the situational conflict in which obeying one would result in transgressing another.

The case studies basically involve dilemmas for choosing one accurate action from the given two or more options available. The case studies have different types of ethical dilemmas that include-

- choosing between options with conflicting merits and costs,
- the values of intended beneficiaries clash with those of humanitarian institutions, and
- ethical conflicts perceived within a hierarchy of moral obligations.

A Brief on Case-Study Format

Learning through case-study model is basically to understand the "dynamicity" of the concepts and appreciate its practical part. Case studies are in-depth investigations of a single person, group, event or community. Typically, data are gathered from a variety of sources and by using several different methods (e.g. observations & interviews).

Starting of case based study: The case study research method originated in clinical medicine (the case history, i.e. the patient's personal history). In psychology, case studies are often confined to the study of a particular individual. The information is mainly biographical and relates to events in the individual's past (i.e. retrospective), as well as to significant events which are currently occurring in his or her everyday life.

The case study is not itself a research method, but researchers select methods of data collection and analysis that will generate material suitable for case studies. This makes it clear that the case study is a method that is used by a psychologist, therapist or psychiatrist, i.e. someone with a professional qualification.

With the passage of time the case study based testing crossed the border of psychology and now these techniques are being applied in many fields. In the governance and public administration also now many case study based testing is started and therefore UPSC is focusing more on such pattern of questions.

Strengths of Case Studies

- Provides detailed (rich qualitative) information.
- Provides insight for further research.
- Permitting investigation of otherwise impractical (or unethical) situations.

Case studies allow a researcher to investigate a topic in far more detail than might be possible if they were trying to deal with a large number of research participants (nomothetic approach) with the aim of 'averaging'. Because of their in-depth, multi-sided approach case studies often shed light on aspects of human thinking and behavior that would be unethical or impractical to study in other ways.

Limitations of Case Studies

- Can't generalize the results to the wider population.
- Researchers' own subjective feeling may influence the case study (researcher bias).
- Difficult to replicate.
- Time-consuming.

Because a case study deals with only one person/event/group we can never be sure whether the conclusions drawn from this particular case apply elsewhere. The results of the study are not generalizable because we can never know whether the case we have investigated is representative of the wider body of "similar" instances. There is a lot of scope for observer bias and it could be that the subjective opinions of the psychologist intrude in the assessment of what the data means.

With India evolving from an emerging economy to a matured economy in the hyper-globalised world; the "pulls" and "pressure" on the public servant is more than ever. Keeping this in mind and also appreciating the limitations of the theoretical pedagogy, UPSC has decided to go with the best and latest international practices of testing the acumen that would be required from a serving 'public-servant'.

Practical Approach for Solving Case Studies

There may not be any single definitive approach to tackle a case study; but there can be some common steps that most approaches recommend to be followed in tackling a case study. In the civil services examinations, all the cases revolve around some key concepts of ethics, either directly or in an implicit way. Therefore, the basic understandings of some ethics concepts are necessary to be familiar and to remember. Such concepts and theories help to counter the case studies with relevant approaches. The ideal approach to solve the case studies directs to follow a balanced approach. But, in real life incidences or any real life case studies, civil servants or an actor of the case study, adopts the most relevant, lawful and viable alternative to tackle the given situation.

Common Stages for Solving Case Studies

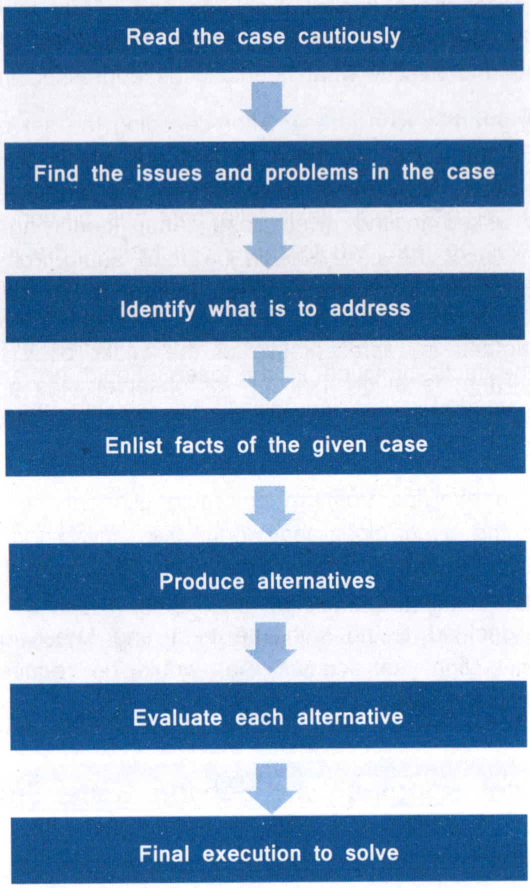

- **Read the Case Cautiously:** At first instance, during the reading of the given case, two things to be noted that what the whole case study is given for (what is the case all about); and what are the important keywords and situations given in the case.
- **Find the Issues and Problems in the Case:** Then, find the issues and problems given in the case. It is important to recognize in the beginning whether there is an ethical issue in the given situation. If the problems are directly given in the case then the problems must be comprehended accurately

that what is the actual demand of the given case. Otherwise, many cases have implicit problems and needs to be marked out. The decoded problem statement should be a clear and concise, and exactly what needs to be addressed in the case.

- **Identify what is to Address:** After decoding the set of problems given in the case, we have to find out which problem is to be resolved. Now focus must be on the particular problem that is asked in the given case. After identifying the exact problem, now the case should be read again from the point of view of the particular problem that is to be solved.

- **Enlist Facts of the Given Case:** While reading the case this time, the facts provided in the case should be enlisted that will be needed as an ingredient while solving and writing the answer of the given case. For example,

  - Who are the stakeholders in the given case? Who are involved in the particular case like civil servants, political executives, government, citizens or society at large, etc.?
  - Who is affected most by this issues? Like in the cases related to sexual harassment, it is the female employees of any organization are affected most.
  - What is cause and effect for the problems identified?
  - What is the dilemma involved?
  - Who is victim and who is responsible for the action required?
  - What Is the larger message the given case wants to convey?
  - What are the constraints and opportunities implicit to the situation? And so on.

- **Produce Alternatives:** This is very important aspect of the case solving. The problems given in the case, stakeholders involved in the case and the enlisted facts from the case are now culminated into the probable alternatives that can be executed to tackle the case give and bring a supposed ideal solution. Here only in mind or on a rough paper the possible alternatives should be written down that what actions cab be taken in the given conditions. The alternatives proposed should be related to the given case and the possibilities involved. The alternative should be realistic and pragmatic. Also, the selected alternatives should be the solutions of the cases given itself and do not require any further action for the same problem.

- **Evaluate Each Alternative and Final Execution:** Now the theories and concepts of ethics come into play. The proposed alternatives of the previous steps are now analysed here. Each alternative are now tested on the principles and concepts of ethics and then validated and rejected on the basis of such principles. Apply all the tools to discuss the merits and demerits of the entire alternative to select the most appropriate one. Every alternative should be analysed in the same manner. And finally, the culmination of all steps is concluded at the end of the case study. Even the most appropriate alternative will have some drawbacks. But it is practically impossible to produce an ideal solution to any case but approximation towards ideal solution can be delivered.

Stakeholders Involved in Case Study

Stakeholder identification process usually takes place through several stages. In the process, one has to consider the technical, political, and ethical rationality. The process has to address some important questions about legitimacy, representation, and credibility. Stakeholders are included when their involvement can influence the process. Clearly, the choices of whom to include, how, when, and why are dependent on their effectiveness and value.

Who is a stakeholder and under what situations their role is needed? Stakeholders are identified based on many factors which include:

- The interest and influence in the system or a resource and the related issues
- Knowledge about the system or resource
- Networks the stakeholder is involved within the case study area

The amount of power in any form that a stakeholder can mobilize can be included as **formal and informal influence**.

- **Formal:** This is an influence based on rules or rights, as laid down in legislation applicable to a particular region. For example, government agencies are empowered with law and rights to enforce the law; and private organizations/individuals with certain (user) rights, for example, land use rights, fishing rights.

- **Informal:** This is an influence, based on other factors than rules or rights laid down in law. For example, in the case of an interest group or non-governmental organization, if they are able to mobilize media, use resources, or lobby to put pressure on the political system.

In the given case, for solution, always specific people or groups who have a stake in the outcome of the case or given situation are termed as stakeholders. In the ethics paper in the civil services examination, stakeholders normally are related to the government and its functioning. The stakeholders may be within the government body or its executive divisions like politicians, administrators, bureaucrats, ministers, etc. They may be from the civil offices like CBI, CVC, Election Commission, etc. (any employee, officer, his superior, or even the whole department or organization). They may be common citizens, community groups, or society at large, etc.

Some of the most common stakeholders involved in case studies given in the examination can be listed as:

Civil Servants: The civil servants are the element of permanent bureaucracy of Indian government (accountable to the President of India). Often working in the public sector, an employee of the civil service is basically employed by the government to impartially implement their policies and laws. As a result, civil service employees often work in areas that highly affect people's everyday life. As the civil servants are the main elements for the policy execution they must be ethical and moral persons and compassionate with the public.

The civil servant is the main stakeholder in the case studies and he is responsible for several other stakeholders like -

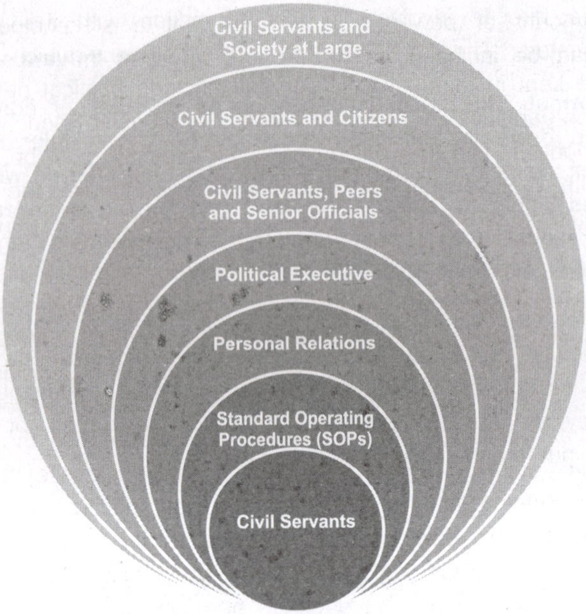

- **Civil Servants and Standard Operating Procedures (SOPs):** The civil servants are law executing elements of the government therefore they have to follow different Standard Operating Procedures (SOPs) enlisted in various codes like- Codes of Conduct, Civil Services Codes, Ethical Codes of Conduct, etc. Many instances exist where the civil servants have to opt 'out of the box' thinking and complete the given task. At this point, ethical character of the civil servants, guide them to act as per the demand and restricts them from violating the standard procedures and maintains the integrity of their office.

- **Civil Servants and their Personal Relations:** The relatives, especially the family members of the civil servants, are considered as one of the most common stakeholders. Because, in any case, there are chances of misuse of power or threat to life or safety because of actions against powerful lobbies. Here the civil servant is tested on his integrity towards his work. A pragmatic approach should be adopted by the civil servant to tackle the given dilemmas.

- **Civil Servants and Political Executive:** The civil servants are directly involved in the interaction with the political masters. Therefore, the main considerations which should be kept in mind by civil servants include political neutrality, non-partisanship, with a cordial relationship and well-set priorities. The civil officer in his all capacity must be honest with the service and suggest his opinion to the policy makers as he has a ground execution level experience.

- **Civil Services and Peers:** The colleagues, either directly or indirectly, become key stakeholders in almost every decision or step taken by a civil servant in his official capacity. An ethical conduct helps in boosting confidence, productivity or building team-spirit, professionalism with the promotion of accountable and transparent work culture. At the same time, unethical conduct can cause conflicts at the personal or professional level, wastage of public funds, resources or promote ethical lapses/misconduct.
- **Civil Services and Senior Officials:** Either directly or indirectly civil servants are affected by their officers in their official capacity. In many situations, the civil servants are given the dilemma to work against the will of their officers and that requires integrity, morality and high standards of ethics towards their work. The ethical aspect of the duty teaches the civil servants that even if the situations are adverse and officers are not at the right direction or involved in any political nexus, they must stand with truth and honesty with high moral will. These aspects give birth to the whistleblowers.
- **Civil Servants and Citizens:** The common citizens are the core of any policy execution by the civil servants and through their work touch the lives of almost every citizen. Delivery of essential services, registration of some event, business organizations or help and rescue efforts in calamities, etc. are some common processes that relates civil servants to the citizens. And therefore, the responsibility of the officers with the civil capacity is always at a high stake. So, for the service delivery by the civil servants, respect for the law of land and compassion towards common citizen must be mingled with transparency, accountability, the spirit of service, conviction, etc.

– **Civil Servants and Society at Large:** We are living in a society where everyone has some responsibility towards the society. When it comes to responsible posts and functions of civil servants, the responsibility towards the society becomes much more, making the whole society as a stakeholder in all decisions, actions and inactions of a civil servant.

Illustration of a Case Study

Case Study I: Proceed Cautiously

Rajit Kumar noticed that there was a problem brewing with two of his peers. It wasn't overt – no yelling or banging tables – but Rajit saw that they often avoided each other and started to sit apart in meetings. The tension was affecting his team's work so he wanted to get to the bottom of it. "I knew both of them reasonably well and I knew they were sensible, mature professionals," he says, so "I tried to understand the issue first." He invited one of them out for a drink and learned through casual conversation that the problems didn't stem from one incident but a mix of things:

"There was a great deal of misunderstanding that snowballed and led to mistrust and dislike towards each other," he explains.

Over the next several months, Rajit talked to both parties about what had happened. "I had at least three or four discussions with each of them to understand the real nature of conflict," he says. These conversations gave him the confidence to agree when the two people asked him to serve as a formal mediator.

"We had a good discussion but I didn't focus on the conflict or their personalities or behaviors" he says. "I focused on our common goal of being an effective team". He also suggested that the three of them continue to meet casually so they could work on building trust. It took time but eventually the two repaired their relationship, allowing the whole team to work well together again.

Case Study II: Defuse a Tense Situation

Nirja was sitting at her desk one day when she heard loud voices coming from another part of the office. Two of her co-workers – let's call them Shayam and Mohan – were having a heated arguments. "They were very loud. Some people gathered around them and began to watch," she says. "I didn't know the specific reason for the fight but I knew there was a lot of tension at that time." The firm, which offered legal advice and services to people and companies in debt, was in financial trouble, and there had been sporadic conflicts between Shayam and Mohan but nothing this serious.

Everyone else was frozen. "I realized that no one knew what to do and no one else was going to intervene," Nirja said. So, she took action. "I slowly approached them and asked them to follow me," she says. At first, they continued to yell but then she gently put a hand on each of their arms and repeated her request. The three of them went to a private corridor. "I didn't ask anything at first. They were still too excited. I just offered them a glass of water," she says. Once things were calmer, Nirja pointed out that the overall situation at the company was tense. "I described the conflict from my point of view to give them awareness of the tone in which they spoke. Then I told them that regardless of the reason for their fight they could deal with the issue in a different way," she says. She also suggested that they might talk to the department head if there was a problem that couldn't be resolved. "They did not react aggressively towards me. On the contrary, they realized that they had lost control," she says. They thanked Nirja and apologized to one another.

Principles to Remember

Do's

- Allow your co-workers to vent
- Empathize without taking sides
- Refer them to someone else if you feel you can't help

Don'ts

- Throw your two cents in without checking that your advice is wanted
- Try to play peacekeeper if you don't have the skills or the time
- Go to your co-workers' boss unless the argument is untenable and disrupting work

A Brief on Case-Study Questions @ UPSC Mains

Within this paper only the broader contours of the questions has been taken and certainly this cannot be treated as 'Model' answer as what is 'Model' for UPSC always remains shrouded in mystery and subject to varied interpretations. But, still this can be one of the approaches which you can anchor yourself-in while attempting for this paper.

An important observation, and this has already been reiterated, is that never ever take a high moral or absolute ethical standards which seems highly impractical or undoable while you are asked to solve any question related to dilemmas - ethical or moral or both - or Case Study. Maintain a fine and subtle balance between basic human traits and higher humane values without that your answer would become highly theoretical. Getting trapped into theoretical aspects is a trap in which UPSC wants you to lead. Writing such conventional answer would get you average marks but you cannot and should not expect any extra-ordinary rewards from the examiner who is looking into the honesty of your answer. Not to forget, there is a trait that is called "Relative Morality" and how much you tilt in favour of "Relative" on the one side and "Morality" on the other shows the ingenuity and truthfulness in your answer.

In the paper of 2019, there were mainly six case studies consisting 120 marks as previous papers. The length of the Case Study questions were smaller compared to the previous year questions (2018). Each Case Study required deep understanding of basic concepts of ethics and their practical application on the given dilemma situations. Though the cases were small in their appearance, they cannot be solved only by reading the given cases. Some previous knowledge and proper understanding of syllabus is essential to write the answer. It can be said that now UPSC is testing not only the theoretical knowledge but also its application on 'situation based' case studies.

Case Study: Assault of some rescue workers during the rescue operation in severely impacted natural calamity areas. (2019)

This case includes the concepts of -

- Ethics and Human Interface

- Disaster Management Ethics
- Emotional Intelligence

Ethical Dilemma: Office Duty vs. Self-protection, Integrity, Honesty and Compassion.

Premise: Floods and droughts are common feature of some Indian territories and the civil servants performing in such areas encounter such given issues in their daily routine work. This case shows the aftermath impacts of a disaster and the problems encountered by the civil servants and the rescue operators. This situation demands understanding of the ground-level situation and emotionally strong person who can act patiently after analyzing the whole situation.

Approach: In the first part of the answer, list out some qualities that are required by the public servant in such situations like compassion, integrity, kindness, empathy, etc. Then, in the answer, after analyzing the given situation, produce some alternatives like - how to convince the homeless public that the officers are there to help them and such behaviours by them will not help; motivate the rescue workers to continue work for the homeless; take some administrative help to control the irrelevant behaviours of the public, etc. The answer should be practical and not very idealistic or extreme.

Case Study: Prosecution of civil servants on their bona fide mistakes. (2019)

This case includes the concepts of -

- Foundational Values for Civil Services
- Probity in Governance
- Moral and Ethical Values in Governance
- Emotional Intelligence

Ethical Dilemma: Honesty, Uprightness, Integrity, Accountability vs. Decision Making, etc.

Premise: During the execution of duties there comes many situations, where the code of conduct is either unavailable or silent and the civil servant in the given situation performs with his own conscience. These actions are impersonal and impromptu.

Sometimes such decisions result negatively and these mistakes are termed as bona fide mistakes (or unintentional mistakes). Many civil servants get discouraged if any such mistakes are found punishable in the eyes of law.

Approach: The answer demands complete understanding about the execution - function of the civil servants. Bona fide mistakes should be defined at the beginning. Then point out some negative and positive impacts of the prosecution of the civil servants for their bona fide mistakes - like, how it can discourage others as well as the whole work culture will go defensive in mechanism. Also, throw some light on the corrective actions from the government's side and what alternative actions government can take while responding towards bona fide mistakes. In the end, there may be some dedicated lines - that, if all mechanism will go defensive then there will be perpetual status quo for the occurring situation.

Case Study: Complain against a marketing executive, indulging in sexual harassment case in an apparel manufacturing company having large number of women employees. (2019)

This case includes the concepts of -

- Ethics and Human Interface
- Sexual Harassment at Workplace for Women
- Empathy and Compassion

Ethical Dilemma: Choose between Means vs. Ends, Personal Interest and Personal Ethics.

Premise: The Company was making a loss; the management by any means wanted to make profit as well as to save the life and jobs of their employees. If the company would not be able to make profit, it may have to be closed and many would become jobless. The women are respected in any means and their dignity (or any employee's dignity) should not be compromised to make benefits. In this case, it is visible that, the management had not taken any action until the FIR was lodged; this shows the neglect of the ethical duty towards the employees.

Approach: This case is a classic example of sexual harassment at workplace for women. Very often such incidents are reported in the news. Direct answering that management is wrong will not suffice here, the company is making loss is also a matter of concern. In this, you need to identify the ethical issues involved and options available for the victim to get justice and how to prevent them in future. Also, the alternatives must be practical and lies on the ethical standards. Then, also suggest some corrective measures for short and long terms so that women can get the confidence and get back to the work with full zeal.

Case Study: Relation between Permanent Executives and Political Executive and politicization of bureaucracy. (2019)

This case includes the concepts of -

- Probity in Governance
- Ethics in Public Administration
- Conflict of Interest and Moral Duty

Ethical Dilemma: Code of Conduct vs. Code of Ethics, Integrity to the Office, Moral Duty and Political Advantage.

Premise: This case study travel a long journey from Independence of the country to till date and throws light on political interference in bureaucracy with the advancement of time and its impacts on bureaucrats. The case mentions about politicisation of bureaucracy, that refers to undue political influence in the governance due to nexus between bureaucracy and politics - resulting on one hand - government appointing their own people to senior and sensitive public service positions, and defaming politicization and on the other hand - it refers to the substitution of political criteria for merit based criteria.

Approach: This case is not a case study in reality but the understanding of bureaucracy in India since independence. The answer here cannot be 'black and white' but the mixture of both - positive and negative - consequences of cordial relation between political and permanent bureaucrats. For example, in positive sense, it can be written that when the ideological thoughts of both will be same and cordial, the making and execution of particular policies will be easier and similarly, If they both formed a nexus, it will increase the corruption and disadvantage to the citizens. Since, it is a real life case of India, there must be some real incidences quoted in the answer like Coal Scam, 2G spectrum scam, CBI called as 'Caged - parrot', etc. At the end, transparency and accountability should be discussed on a positive note.

Case Study: A woman police officer, appointed as superintendent of police in the district of a frontier state where, narcotics menace and dominance of drug mafias has been rampant. (2019)

This case includes the concepts of -

- Ethics in Public Administration
- Emotional Intelligence
- Management and Leadership
- Probity in Governance

Ethical Dilemma: Code of Conduct vs. Personal Ethics, Integrity to the Office, Leadership Management, Integrity and Attitude towards the Job.

Premise: The menace of narcotics and drug circulations is a threat to any society and it must be banned in any case. But some officials, politicians, police officers, etc. are themselves are indulged in the nexus - with the drug distributors for some personal gains, without paying attention on what its impacts on the youth and how they are ruining their life. When whole system is corrupted and channels are involved for personal gains, no single officer can fight with the whole system. But, in his official capacity, he/she can take corrective actions and promote awareness against drug use and try to reform the system itself.

Approach: The approach for the answer must be started with finding the stakeholders impacted with the situation, who are involved and the risks involved of drug abuse like - you as a police officer (SP), whole youth/society, drug distributors/peddlers, children of the society, official and local politicians, etc.

After this, there should be analysis of roots of this drug supply and reasons of rampant narcotics abuse (like money laundering, arms smuggling, drug addiction, personal gains, etc.). The issues involved should be enlisted, and their impact (merits/demerits can be listed). Then, corrective action can be produced that are available to the Superintendent of Police in his official capacity. There must be involvement of local intellectuals (and villagers) and social reformers to identify the disturbing elements, help the officers to catch them, and also towards awareness programs to check drug addiction.

Case Study: An increasing concern in India to develop effective civil service ethics, code of conduct, transparency measures, ethics and integrity systems and anti-corruption agencies. (2019)

This case includes the concepts of -

- Foundational Values for Civil Services
- Ethics in Public Administration
- Probity in Governance

Ethical Dilemma: Ethical Standards, Ethical Competence, Integrity for the Service, Civil Services Reforms.

Premise: This is not actually a case study but the analysis of the present situation of declining ethical standards among the civil servants and measures to control it. The administration is focused on internalizing the ethical conducts among the civil servants and therefore found three approaches (to promote) - ethical values, competence, and ethical standards to them. The case study itself has identified the issues and is asking in the question to focus on three specific areas which need urgent attention. Also, this case study throws light on the issues of civil service reforms.

Approach: This case study requires deep understanding about the ethical concepts (like ethical standards, ethical competence, ethical values, integrity, probity, civil services ethics, code of conducts, etc.) and cannot be answered at surfacial level without knowing the difference between the topics. At first instance, define some concepts as marked in the question and also mark the need of that concept in the civil service duty.

Then, as per the demand of the question, show how present civil service activity is declining in integrity towards the office and involved in the nexus and unethical conducts. After this, explain each three points mentioned in the question individually and application of such topics in civil conduct. Here some institutional measures can also be suggested for improvement; like reforms mentioned by Second Administrative Reforms Commission (2nd ARC), etc.

Case-Study: Ineligible beneficiary under Health-Scheme and Duty of an Officer. (2018)

This case includes the concepts of -

- Ethics and Human Interface
- Empathy and Compassion
- Attitude and Moral Values

Premise: This case is an example of improvisation/execution of a visionary thoughts into the real world. This case requires the empathy and compassion towards the needy with the logical/ rational decision making.

Approach: The answer must have the basic understanding of the situation and provide possible alternatives with rational arguments and finally suggest that what the officer should choose with supportive statement.

Case-Study: Compassion of Income Tax Officer for a Philanthropic Doctor. (2018)

This case includes the concepts of -

- Ethics in Public Administration
- Ethics and Human Interface
- Probity in Governance
- Conflict of Interests and Moral Duty

Premise: The case given, tests the ability of an officer to either follow the words of the rule or implement the spirit of the rule formed. It requires the attitude along with the aptitude to deal with the situation given.

Approach: The question itself is suggesting the alternatives available to perform in the situation. The answer must include both, the positive and negative side of the given option along with the basic concepts of ethics and then at the end you must choose one of them by quoting valid arguments in favour.

Case-Study: Prohibition of liquor in backward area and maintenance of law and order. (2018)

This case includes the concepts of -

- Ethics and Human Interface
- Aptitude

- Emotional Intelligence
- Management and Leadership

Premise: The case given is unique in nature as rather than creating a dilemma into a particular situation the case demands some reformative measure with empathy from the civil servant. The civil servant is not only there to follow the rule-book to tackle the situation but also provide some innovative measures to benefit the larger mass.

Approach: The answer should be balanced in nature with providing other corrective action for law and order and also suggestive measure for the improvement of irrigation facility of the place. For corrective action, the SP can consult with the senior officials and also explain them about actual problem in the region and may approach reformative rather than deterrence in the region.

As a Superintendent of Police in a district, the officer has a limited hand with the creation activity and formation of irrigation infrastructure or anything else, but as a responsible civil servant he can act accordingly for the benefit of the people by explaining the situation to District Magistrate or inform to the concerned MLA or MP of the constituency by also suggesting some of the reformative actions.

Case-Study: Closing of a Polluting factory, which is leading to unemployment. (2018)

This case includes the concepts of -

- Ethics in Public Administration
- Probity in Governance
- Conflict of Interests and Emotional Intelligence
- Environmental Ethics

Premise: The case demands the calculative action for the benefit of the people as well as the State order to follow (that may pose a conflict of interests) in this particular situation. It is always easy to choose between right and wrong, but it is always difficult to choose between the grey shades of either right or dark.

Approach: In this answer particularly, the cost benefit analysis can be performed and then the alternatives can be suggested. Each alternatives should be practically possible and must benefit to the larger extent of the people. Like there may be alternative of shifting of chemical plant suggesting a recycle plant and provide employment to the needy and so on.

Case-Study: A Minister's ill wishes for land-deal and Officer's Response. (2018)

This case includes the concepts of -

- Ethics in Public Administration
- Probity in Governance
- Conflict of Interests & Conflict in Administration
- Moral Values

Premise: This case demands the higher moral values and probity. The civil servant is deliberately drawn into the situation, to choose between personal advantage and ethical conduct. The acceptance of unethical conduct may lead him to neglection of inner conscience and unstability of mind and denial may drag him into troubled water where the dominance of political leaders and corrupted officers may harm the official (with also the loss of personal lucrative gain).

Approach: The answer requires the critical analysis of the available alternatives to the officer. Each alternative should have positive and negative outcomes. For example, the officer may go with his ethical conduct and execute as it is to the proposed road project.

In such situation, there will be benefit to the larger people and least loss of productive agricultural fields and green trees, but with this action the concerned minister may act in a harsh manner and remove the officer from the project and transfer him into far hinterland areas and so on.

Case-Study: An analysis on Snowden's whistleblowing. (2018)

This case includes the concepts of -

- Conflict of Interest & Conflict in Administration
- Transparency & Accountability and Whistleblowing
- Aptitude and Moral Values
- Emotional Intelligence

Premise: The case is based on the true event and demands in depth understanding and the opinion on the topic. The question can only be answered when the whole event is clear in mind. The case shows the battle between inner conscience and moral duty with the rule-book duty and illicit practices.

Approach: In this answer, there must be some facts to be quoted in both of the options provided either agree or not agree with the act performed by Edward Snowden. The basics also be discussed to clarify your statements. Then submit if you are agree and give valid arguments like it is the moral duty of an officer to perform accordingly with his inner conscience and righteous act and blow the whistle against breaching the privacy of the people.

If not agree, quote the example of integrity towards the nation and nothing can be compromised against which. Some related examples from the world also be cited to strengthen your arguments.

◆♦❐❐♦◆

2

ETHICS & HUMAN INTERFACE

The Concepts Discussed in this Unit

- Ethics and its Scope
- Branches of Ethics
- Bio-Ethics
- Ethical Standards
- Making Decisions
- Environmental Ethics
- Determinants of Ethical Behaviour
- Ethics in Human Actions
- Values
- Ethics in Public Administration
- Ethics of Violence, Terrorism and Public Relations
- What Makes a Leader?
- Human Values-Lessons from Lives of Great Leaders, Administrators & Reformers
- Personal Ethical Policy

Ethics

Ethics may be defined as the systematic study of human actions from the point of view of their rightfulness or wrongfulness, as means for the attainment of the ultimate happiness. It is the reflective study of what is good or bad in that part of human conduct for which human has some personal responsibility.

In other words, Ethics is a set of standards that a society places on itself and which helps guide behaviour, choices and actions.

Ethics is integral to public administration. In public administration, ethics focuses on how the public administrator should question and reflect in order to be able to act responsibly.

Etymologically the term "ethics" correspond to the Greek word "ethos" which means character, habit, customs, ways of behaviour etc. Ethics is also called "moral philosophy". The word "moral" comes from Latin word "mores" which signifies customs, character, behaviour etc. It is the reflective study of what is good or bad in that part of human conduct for which human has some personal responsibility.

Ethics is one of the branches of philosophy. As a philosophical discipline, ethics is the study of the values and guidelines by which we live. It also involves the justification of these values and guidelines. It is not merely following a tradition or custom. Instead it requires analysis and evaluation of these guidelines in light of universal principles. As moral philosophy, ethics is the philosophical thinking about morality, moral problems, and moral judgments.

Socio-Political Evolution of Ethics

Ethics is as old as humanity. The first ethical precepts were certainly passed down by word of mouth by parents and elders, but as societies learned to use the written word, they began to set down their ethical beliefs. These records constitute the first historical evidence of the origins of ethics. In the Western Philosophy, the history of ethics can be traced back to the fifth century B.C with the appearance of Socrates. As a philosopher among the Greeks his mission was to awaken his fellow humans to the need for rational criticism of their beliefs and practices.

Plato's theory of forms could be seen as the first attempt at defending moral realism and offering an objective ground for moral truths. While Plato was the fountainhead of religious and idealistic ethics, Aristotle engendered the naturalistic tradition. Aristotle's ethical writings (i.e. Eudemian Ethics, the Nicomachean Ethics, and the Politics) constitute the first systematic investigation into the foundations of ethics. Aristotle's account of the virtues could be seen as one of the first sustained inquiries in normative ethics. It was a clear mixture of Greco-Roman thought with Judaism and elements of other Middle Eastern religions.

The medieval period was dominated by the thoughts of Christian philosophers and theologians like Augustine and Thomas Aquinas. The influence of Christianity dominated the ethical scenario. So much so, that during this period philosophy and religion were nearly indistinguishable. The rise of Christian philosophy produced a new era of history of ethics. In St. Augustine, the most prominent philosopher of the early medieval period, ethics became a blend of the pursuit of earthly well-being with preparation of the soul for eternal salvation. The next towering figure of medieval philosophy is Thomas Aquinas. He brought about a true reconciliation between Aristotelian science and philosophy with Augustinian theology. Aquinas greatly succeeded in proving the compatibility of Aristotelian naturalism with Christian dogma and constructing a unified view of nature, human, and God.

The social and political changes that characterized the end of medieval period and the rise of modern age of industrial democracy gave rise to a new wave of thinking in the ethical field. The development of commerce and industry, the discovery of new regions of the world, the Reformation, the Copernican and Galilean revolutions in science, and the rise of strong secular governments demanded new principles of individual conduct and social organization.

Some of the modern philosophers who contributed to the great changes in ethical thinking were Francis Bacon, René Descartes, Thomas Hobbes, Gottfried Wilhelm Leibniz, Benedict de Spinoza, John Locke, David Hume, Immanuel Kant, John Stuart Mill and Friedrich Nietzsche. Further developments in ethical thinking in the West came with Karl Marx and Sigmund Freud. Here, it is not intended to give a detailed analysis of their contribution to ethics.

However, the most influential ethical thought during this period were the Utilitarianism, dominated by British and French Philosophy (e.g. Locke, Hume, Bentham, Stuart Mill) and Idealistic ethics in Germany and Italy (e.g. Kant, Hegel, Nietzsche).

The contemporary ethical scenario is a further complex area of study. The contemporary European ethics in the broadest sense attempts to cover a generous range of philosophies running from phenomenology to theories of communicative action. The conditions of contemporary civilization forced philosophers to seek for a genuine ground for ethics and moral life. In much of the English speaking world G.E. Moore's Principia Ethica (1903) is taken to be the starting point of contemporary ethical theory. Others like Martin Buber, Gabriel Marcel, Emmanuel Levinas, Max Scheler, Franz Brentano and John Dewey too have made significant contributions to the ethical thinking in other parts of the world.

Scope of Ethics

Ethics deals with voluntary actions. We can distinguish between human actions and actions of human: human actions are those actions that are done by human consciously, deliberately and in view of an end. Actions of human may not be wilfully, voluntarily, consciously and deliberately done but all the same they are done by human (e.g. sleeping, walking, etc.). It is the intention which makes the difference between human action and action of human. In ethics we deal only with human actions.

What Ethics is Not?

Ethics is not morality. Morality can be an individual set of commitments even when they are rejected by others. But, one cannot be ethical alone. Ethics brings other people for the realization of the self. Morality does not demand acquiescence from others the way ethics does. It is possible to be moral alone. A moralist can say I do not believe in war, so what if everyone else does.

Ethics is not religion. Many people are not religious, but ethics applies to everyone. Most religions do advocate high ethical standards but sometimes do not address all the types of problems we face.

Ethics is not following the law. In law, a man is guilty when he violates the rights of another. In ethics, he is guilty if he thinks of doing so (Immanuel Kant). A good system of law does incorporate many ethical standards, but law can deviate from what is ethical. Law may have a difficult time designing or enforcing standards in some important areas, and may be slow to address new problems.

Ethics is not following culturally accepted norms. Some cultures are quite ethical, but others become corrupt or blind to certain ethical concerns (United States was to slavery before the Civil War; caste system in India). "When in Rome, do as the Romans do" is not a satisfactory ethical standard.

Why be Moral?

Not few are the people who ask this question: Why should we be moral? Why should we take part in the moral institution of life? Why should we adopt a moral point of view?

In every human person there is a deep desire for good. Human being, by nature tend to good - summum bonum. Each man/woman desires what is best for himself/herself. The ethical principles and moral practices help one to attain what is best. It helps a person to perfect himself/herself as a moral being. Morality has to do more with one's interior self than the practice of some customs or set rules. Viewed from this point, morality is a deep down desire in human person and is something to do with the very nature of human person. The rational nature of human person makes him/her aware of certain fundamental principles of logical and moral reasoning. This means that there is not only a subjective aspect to every human action but also an objective one that prompts human person to base himself/herself on certain common principles.

We also find that for the functioning of any society we need certain rules and regulations. The conditions of a satisfactory human life for people living in groups could hardly obtain otherwise (neither a "state of nature" nor a "totalitarian state"). The institutions which are designed to make life easier and better for humankind, cannot function without certain moral principles. However, here the question of individual freedom can also come in. How far the society can go on demanding? Shouldn't it respect the freedom of the individual? Is morality made for man or man is made for morality?

Morality is a lot like nutrition. Most of us have never had a course in nutrition or even read much about it. Yet many of us do have some general knowledge of the field, of what we need to eat and what not. However, we also make mistakes about these things. Often thinking of the good, a particular diet can do in the long run for our health, we may go for it although it may bring no immediate satisfaction. So, too is our moral life. While nutrition focuses on our physical health, morality is concerned about our moral health. It seeks to help us determine what will nourish our moral life and what will poison it. It seeks to enhance our lives, to help us to live better lives. Morality aims to provide us with a common point of view from which we can come to agreement about what all of us ought to do. It tries to discover a more objective standpoint of evaluation than that of purely personal preference.

Ethics and Other Sciences

In our analysis of the definition and nature of ethics, we have seen that ethics as a science is concerned with an end or ideal or standard. Most sciences, instead, are concerned with certain uniformities of our experience - with the ways in which certain classes of objects (such as rocks or plants) are found to exist, or with the ways in which certain classes of events (such as phenomena of sound or electricity) are found to occur. These sciences have no direct reference to any end that is to be achieved or to any ideal by reference to which the facts are judged.

Ethics is distinguished from the natural sciences, in as much as, it has a direct reference to an end that human persons desire to attain. Although ethics is sometimes regarded as a practical science, it is not a 'practical science' as medicine, engineering or architecture in as much as it is not directed towards the realization of a definite result. Ethics is often said to be the fruit of all the sciences since it ultimately perfects human person, by ordering all other sciences and all things else in respect to an ultimate end that is absolutely supreme.

	Other Sciences	Ethics
Psychology	How a man behaves (a descriptive science)	How a man must behave (a normative science)
Anthropology	Nature of human	How man's beings and its activity actions ought to be
Social and political Sciences	Deals with the organization of man's social and political life	How man's social and life must or ought to be organized in order to be moral
Economics	Concerned with goods, i.e. with those objects which are the means of satisfying any human want	Deals with those acts which are the conditions of the attainment of the highest end of life

Branches of Ethics

A. DESCRIPTIVE ETHICS

It gives us a general pattern or a way of life of people in different types of communities. Descriptive ethics studies the history and evolution of ethics. It gives a record of certain taboos, customs or conventions. For example, it states the history of various institutions like family or marriage. Lawrence Kohlberg's theory of moral consciousness is an example of Descriptive Ethics (See Unit 5 for Kohlberg's theory).

Descriptive ethics investigates people's ethical ideals or what actions are condemned in a society. It aims to find out people's beliefs about values, which actions are right and wrong and which characteristics of a moral agent are virtuous. Descriptive ethics seeks the explanation of actual choices made by moral agents in practice. It tries to examine the ethical codes applied by various groups. Descriptive Ethics is a value-free approach to ethics. It is empirical investigation of people's moral beliefs.

B. NORMATIVE ETHICS

Normative ethics involves arriving at moral standards that regulate right and wrong conduct. In a sense, it is a search for an ideal litmus test of proper behaviour.

Normative ethics is also called as prescriptive ethics. It is the study of ethical theories that prescribe how people ought to act. It examines standards for the rightness and wrongness of actions. Normative ethics suggests punishment when a person deviates from the path of ideals. It provides justification for punishing a person who disturbs social and moral order. It tries to establish certain theories on the guidelines of some norms. Normative ethics offer the moral principles used to resolve difficult moral decisions.

Aristotle's virtue ethics, Kant's deontological ethics, Mill's Consequentialism (Utilitarianism) and the Bhagwad Gita's Nishkam Karmayoga are the theories in Normative Ethics (these have been explained later-on in Unit-5).

The Golden Rule is a classic example of a normative principle: "We should do to others what we would want others to do to us". Since one would want people to feed him if he was starving, then he should help feed starving people. Using this same reasoning, we can theoretically determine whether any possible action is right or wrong. So, based on the Golden Rule, it would also be wrong for a person to lie to, harass, victimize, assault, or kill others. The Golden Rule is an example of a normative theory that establishes a single principle against which we judge all actions. Other normative theories focus on a set of foundational principles, or a set of good character traits.

C. META ETHICS

Meta ethics is defined as the study of the origin and meaning of ethical concepts. The term "meta" means after or beyond, and, consequently, the notion of Meta ethics involves a removed, or bird's eye view of the entire project of ethics.

In Meta ethics, two issues are prominent: (1) Metaphysical issues concerning whether morality exists independently of humans, and (2) Psychological issues concerning the underlying mental basis of our moral judgements and conduct.

In other words, Meta ethics is the study of what ethical terms and theories actually refer to. It determines the validity of theories advanced in Normative Ethics. We use certain moral concepts such as right, wrong, good or bad to evaluate human actions. These moral concepts are used as tools in passing moral judgements. Meta ethics analyses ethical concepts. It studies the meaning of moral language and the metaphysics of moral facts. Meta ethics seeks to understand the nature of ethical properties and evaluations.

Meta ethics deals with the questions such as 'What is the meaning of moral terms or judgements?', 'What is the nature of moral judgements?', 'How may moral judgements be supported or defended?"

D. APPLIED ETHICS

Applied ethics is the branch of ethics which consists of the analysis of specific, controversial moral issues such as abortion, animal rights, or euthanasia. It helps to use knowledge of moral principles to present dilemmas. There are certain issues which arise due to newly adopted life style. Applied ethics deals with the questions such as, "Is getting an abortion immoral?" "Is euthanasia immoral?" "Is affirmative action right or wrong?" "What are human rights, and how do we determine them?" "Do animals have rights as well?" and "Do individuals have the right of self- determination?"

Two features are necessary for an issue to be considered an 'applied ethical issue'. First, the issue needs to be controversial in the sense that there are significant groups of people both for and against the issue at hand. The second requirement for an issue to be an applied ethical issue is that it must be a distinctly moral issue and not just a social controversy. Ethical issues concerned with the biological aspects of life and how and when it starts is included in Bio-Ethics which comes under applied ethics.

Bio-Ethics

Bio-ethics should be understood as a study of morality as it concerns issues dealing with the biological issues and facts concerning ourselves, and our close relatives, for example, almost any non-human animal that is sentient. It can be divided into three parts: **beginning of life issues,** including abortion; **end of life issues,** for example euthanasia; and finally, **ethical concerns involving medical research, as well as availability of medical care.**

I. Beginning of Life Issues

All of the beginnings of life issue are contentious. Some of the issues like: **abortion, stem-cell procurement and research,** and **cloning.** Each of these big issues (they could be considered research fields themselves) are related to each other.

Abortion : Abortion is the process of willfully removing the foetus from the womb of the mother by one or another method. Although several countries including India have legalized abortion particularly during the first trimester, everyone knows that it is an act of willfully putting an end to the life of a helpless child in the womb of its mother. For the world community, it is an ethical issue. Although abortion has been viewed as a moral issue and a challenge to human survival in the western world, it is important for us to understand that most of the abortions take place in Asian countries for various reasons. Very often people agree to participate in abortion without knowing the what, why, and how of abortion and its lifelong impact on an individual, family and the society. The moral issue involved in the abortion is, the child has as much claim as the mother to life and should have even more claim to legal protection of its right, since it is incapable of defending itself.

Right of the Unborn Child : The UN declaration on the Rights of the child maintains that "The Child by reason of its physical and mental immaturity needs special safeguards and care including appropriate legal protection before as well as after the birth." The Anti-abortionists (particularly the Christian Conservatives and in general the Creationist who believes in an intelligent designer behind human live) claim that science has proven beyond any reasonable doubt that human life begins at fertilization and even before that it is divine. The fetus from the beginning has its own life, is a totally new human being, a new person, with a genetic code quite distinct from the genetic code of its parents. That new life is completely there at fertilization, lacking only development and growth. Abortion always takes away the innocent's already existing life.

Stem Cell Research : Stem cell research is important because it provides avenues for the development of organs and tissues that can be used to replace those that are diseased for those suffering from certain medical conditions; in theory, an entire cardiac system could be generated through stem cells, as well as through all of the research required on stem cells in order to eventually produce successful organ systems. There are various routes by which stem cell lines can be procured, and this is where things get controversial.

Human Cloning and Designer Babies : Designer babies, is defined as "a baby whose genetic makeup has been artificially selected by genetic engineering combined with in vitro fertilization to ensure the presence or absence of particular genes or characteristics". After such definition, we need to pause and ask what moral or ethical limits, if any, should apply to the selection of our children's genes or characteristics. In order to answer this, we address following questions:

- How would designer babies be made?
- Is there a moral or ethical difference between using genetic technologies to prevent disease and to enhance human capacities?
- Should we be striving to protect our humanity from genetic enhancement?
- What effect will human genetic modification have on society?

II. End of Life Issues

It includes issues concerning like euthanasia and physician-assisted suicide. There are of course other issues relevant to the end of life - for example, issues surrounding consent, often through examining the status of such things as advance directives, living wills, and DNR (Do Not Resuscitate) orders, etc.

Euthanasia: Euthanasia falls into the category of vital life issue subjects, the philosophy or study of it is extremely important. It is necessary that not only in bioethics but in every field this issue is taken up because it involves the family, the basic unit of society. Previous decisions rulings affected by modern techniques need to be addressed. There are many grey areas affecting human lives. There are instances where dying patients do not accept pain killers or sedations as they wish to be alive, to enjoy the last moments with their loved ones. Many people are there who do not have anybody to love or who do not feel needed. These are the ones who will sign the living will or put to sleep permanently.

Euthanasia Debate: Historically, the euthanasia debate has tended to focus on a number of key concerns. According to euthanasia opponent Ezekiel Emanuel (an American Bioethicist), proponents of euthanasia have presented four main arguments:

a) that people have a right to self-determination, and thus should be allowed to choose their own fate;

b) assisting a subject to die might be a better choice than requiring that they continue to suffer;

c) the distinction between passive euthanasia, which is often permitted, and active euthanasia, which is not substantive (or that the underlying principle-the doctrine of double effect-is unreasonable or unsound); and

d) permitting euthanasia will not necessarily lead to unacceptable consequences. Pro-euthanasia activists often point to countries like the Netherlands and Belgium, and states like Oregon, where euthanasia has been legalized, to argue that it is mostly unproblematic.

Similarly, Emanuel argues that there are four major arguments presented by opponents of euthanasia:

a) not all deaths are painful;

b) alternatives, such as cessation of active treatment, combined with the use of effective pain relief, are available;

c) the distinction between active and passive euthanasia is morally significant; and

d) legalising euthanasia will place society on a **slippery slope**, which will lead to unacceptable consequences.

In fact, in **Oregon**, in 2013, pain wasn't one of the top five reasons people seek euthanasia. Top reasons were a loss of dignity, and a fear of burdening others.

Euthanasia in India: Passive euthanasia is legal in India. On 7 March 2011 the Supreme Court of India legalised passive euthanasia by means of the withdrawal of life **support** to patients in a permanent vegetative state. The decision was made as part of the verdict in a case involving Aruna Shanbaug, who had been in a Persistent Vegetative State (PVS) until her death in 2015. Aruna S. a beautiful nurse from South working as a nurse in Bombay (now Mumbai) and also in love with a doctor of the same hospital; both of them intending to marry; got engrappled in a crude joke of destiny when a cleaning-boy forced himself on her which got her badly injured and she went into a vegetative state from then onwards i.e. since 1973!! It is a touching and a heart rendering story of how we all are mere 'pawns' in the hands of destiny. This must also instigate us to always be good as this whole 'journey' is transient. Probably, this could be called as the theistic morality.

Suicide: Suicide is the act of intentionally causing one's own death. Suicide is often carried out as a result of despair, the cause of which is frequently attributed to a mental disorder such as depression, bipolar disorder, schizophrenia, borderline personality disorder, alcoholism, or drug abuse, as well as stress factors such as financial difficulties, troubles with interpersonal relationships, and bullying.

A number of questions are raised within the philosophy of suicide, included what constitutes suicide, whether or not suicide can be a rational choice, and the moral permissibility of suicide. Arguments as to acceptability of suicide in moral or social terms range from the position that the act is inherently immoral and unacceptable under any circumstances to a regard for suicide as a sacrosanct right of anyone who believes they have rationally and conscientiously come to the decision to end their own lives, even if they are young and healthy.

Opponents to suicide include Christian philosophers such as Augustine of Hippo, Thomas Aquinas, Immanuel Kant, etc. Others view suicide as a legitimate matter of personal choice. Supporters of this position maintain that no one should be forced to suffer against their will, particularly from conditions such as incurable disease, mental illness, and old age, with no possibility of improvement. They reject the belief that suicide is always irrational, arguing instead that it can be a valid last resort for those enduring major pain or trauma. A stronger stance would argue that people should be allowed to autonomously choose to die regardless of whether they are suffering. Notable supporters of this school of thought include Scottish empiricist David Hume and American bioethicist Jacob Appel.

Legal Status of Suicide in India (Mental Healthcare Act 2017)

As per the new Mental Healthcare Act, 2017 notified by the Health Ministry in May, 2017-

- **Manner of treatment:** Every person would have the right to specify how he would like to be treated for mental illness in the event of a mental health situation. An individual will also specify who will be the person responsible for taking decisions with regard to the treatment, his admission into a hospital, etc.
- **Access to public health care:** It guarantees every person the right to access mental health care and treatment from the government. This right includes affordable, good quality, easy access to services such as minimum mental health services in every district. Persons with mental illness also have the right to equality of treatment and protection from inhuman and degrading treatment.
- **Suicide decriminalised:** Attempting suicide is no more a crime in India and there will be no more electric shocks for mentally ill children. Notwithstanding anything contained in Section 309 of the Indian Penal Code, any person who attempts to commit suicide shall be presumed, unless proved otherwise, to have severe stress and shall not be tried and punished under the said Code.
- **Insurance:** It requires that every insurance company shall provide medical insurance for mentally ill persons on the same basis as is available for physical illnesses.

The new law aims for social inclusion of persons with mental illness by emphasising that treatment and care is to be provided in a way that enables these persons to live with their families in their own community. However, there are certain challenges in its implementation.

III. Research, Patients, Population and Access

Access to, and quality of, health care is a very real concern. A good health care system is based on a number of things, one being medicine and delivery systems based on research. But research requires, at least to some extent, the use of subjects that are human beings. As such, one can see that ethical concerns arise here. Furthermore, certain populations of people may be more vulnerable to risky research than others. As such, there is another category of moral concern. There is also a basic question concerning how to finance such health care systems.

Following are the concerns in this research ethics

Randomized Clinical Trials: Randomized Clinical Trials (RCT's) are such that the participants of such studies don't know whether they are obtaining the promising (but not yet certified) treatment for their condition. Informed consent is usually obtained and assumed in addressing the ethicality of RCT's. Notice, though, that if the promising treatment is life-saving, and the standard treatment received by the control group is inadequate, then there is a basis for criticism of RCT's.

Beneficiaries of Research: Another case that affects large numbers of people is that, certain medications can be tested on a certain population of people and yet benefits those outside the population used for testing. So, take a certain medication that can reverse HIV transmission to fetuses from mothers. This medication needs to be tested. If you go to an underdeveloped country in Africa to test it, then what kinds of obligations does the pharmaceutical company have to those participating in the

Military Ethics

Military ethics are concerned with questions regarding the application of force and the ethos of the soldier and are often understood as applied professional ethics. Just war theory is generally seen to set the background terms of military ethics. However, individual countries and traditions have different fields of attention.

Military ethics involves multiple sub-areas, including the following among others:

- What, if any, should be the laws of war
- Justification for the initiation of military force
- Decisions about who may be targeted in warfare
- Decisions on choice of weaponry, and what collateral effects such weaponry may have
- Standards for handling military prisoners and the refugees created by such wars - this issue has become the bone of contention in the past few months due to Syrian Refugees crisis which has in a way also instigated the far-right movements in Western Europe as an anti-thesis to a flexible approach shown by the respective European nation towards the plight of the refuges coming to their nation illegally through the Mediterranean Sea
- Methods of dealing with violations of the laws of war

study and those at large in the country upon making it available to those in developed nations like the U.S? If availability to those in the research country is not feasible, is it permissible in the first place to conduct the study? These are just some of the questions that arise in the production of pharmaceutical and medical services in a global context.

Ethical Standards

Why Identifying Ethical Standards is Hard?

There are two fundamental problems in identifying the ethical standards we are to follow:

1. On what do we base our ethical standards?
2. How do those standards get applied to specific situations we face?

If our ethics are not based on feelings, religion, law, accepted social practice, or science, what are they based on? Many philosophers and ethicists have helped us answer this critical question. They have suggested at least five different sources of ethical standards we should use.

Five Sources of Ethical Standards

1. The Utilitarian Approach : Some ethicists emphasize that the ethical action is the one that provides the most good or does the least harm, or, to put it another way, produces the greatest balance of good over harm. The ethical corporate action, then, is the one that produces the greatest good and does the least harm for all who are affected-customers, employees, shareholders, the community, and the environment. Ethical warfare balances the good achieved in ending terrorism with the harm done to all parties through death, injuries, and destruction. The utilitarian approach deals with consequences; it tries both to increase the good done and to reduce the harm done.

2. The Rights Approach: Other philosophers and ethicists suggest that the ethical action is the one that best protects and respects the moral rights of those affected. This approach starts from the belief that humans have a dignity based on their human nature per se or on their ability to choose freely what they do with their lives. On the basis of such dignity, they have a right to be treated as ends and not merely as means to other ends. The list of moral rights -including the rights to make one's own choices about what kind of life to lead, to be told the truth, not to be injured, to a degree of privacy, and so on - is widely debated; some now argue that non-humans have rights, too. Also, it is often said that rights imply duties-in particular, the duty to respect others' rights.

3. The Fairness or Justice Approach: Aristotle and other Greek philosophers have contributed the idea that all equals should be treated equally. Today, we use this idea to say that ethical actions treat all human beings equally - or if unequally, then fairly based on some standard that is defensible. We pay people more based on their harder work or the greater amount that they contribute to an organization, and say that is fair. But, there is a debate over CEO salaries that are hundreds of times larger than the pay of others; many ask whether the huge disparity is based on a defensible standard or whether it is the result of an imbalance of power and hence is unfair.

4. The Common Good Approach: The Greek philosophers have also contributed the notion that life in community is a good in itself and our actions should contribute to that life. This approach suggests that the interlocking relationships of society are the basis of ethical reasoning and that respect and compassion for all others - especially the vulnerable - are requirements of such reasoning. This approach also calls attention to the common conditions that are important to the welfare of everyone. This may be a system of laws, effective police and fire departments, health care, a public educational system, or even public recreational areas.

5. The Virtue Approach: A very ancient approach to ethics is that ethical actions ought to be consistent with certain ideal virtues that provide for the full development of our humanity. These virtues are dispositions and habits that enable us to act according to the highest potential of our character and on behalf of values like truth and beauty. Honesty, courage, compassion, generosity, tolerance, love, fidelity, integrity, fairness, self-control, and prudence are all examples of virtues. Virtue ethics asks of any action, "What kind of person will I become if I do this?" or "Is this action consistent with my acting at my best?"

Putting the Approaches Together

Each of the approaches helps us determine what standards of behavior can be considered ethical. There are still problems to be solved, however. The first problem is that we may not agree on the content of some of these specific approaches. We may not all agree to the same set of human and civil rights. We may not agree on what constitutes the common good. We may not even agree on what is a good and what is a harm.

The second problem is that, the different approaches may not answer the question "What is ethical?" in the same way. Nonetheless, each approach gives us important information with which to determine what is ethical in a particular circumstance. And much more often than not, the different approaches do lead to similar answers.

Making Decisions

Making good ethical decisions requires a trained sensitivity to ethical issues and a practiced method for exploring the ethical aspects of a decision and weighing the considerations that should impact our choice of a course of action. Having a method for ethical decision making is absolutely essential. When practiced regularly, the method becomes so familiar that we work through it automatically without consulting the specific steps.

The more novel and difficult the ethical choice we face, the more we need to rely on discussion and dialogue with others about the dilemma. Only by careful exploration of the problem, aided by the insights and different perspectives of others, can we make good ethical choices in such situations.

We have found the following framework for ethical decision making a useful method for exploring ethical dilemmas and identifying ethical courses of action.

Recognize an Ethical Issue

- Could this decision or situation be damaging to someone or to some group? Does this decision involve a choice between a good and bad alternative, or perhaps between two "goods" or between two "bads"?

- Is this issue about more than what is legal or what is most efficient? If so, how?

Get the Facts

- What are the relevant facts of the case? What facts are not known? Can I learn more about the situation? Do I know enough to make a decision?
- What individuals and groups have an important stake in the outcome? Are some concerns more important? Why?
- What are the options for acting? Have all the relevant persons and groups been consulted? Have I identified creative options?

Evaluate Alternative Actions

Evaluate the options by asking the following questions:

- Which option will produce the most good and do the least harm? (The Utilitarian Approach)
- Which option best respects the rights of all who have a stake? (The Rights Approach)
- Which option treats people equally or proportionately? (The Justice Approach)
- Which option best serves the community as a whole, not just some members? (The Common Good Approach)
- Which option leads me to act as the sort of person I want to be? (The Virtue Approach)

Make a Decision and Test It

- Considering all these approaches, which option best addresses the situation?
- If I told someone I respect - or told a television audience - which option I have chosen, what would they say?

Act and Reflect on the Outcome

- How can my decision be implemented with the greatest care and attention to the concerns of all stakeholders?
- How did my decision turn out and what have I learned from this specific situation?

Moral Luck

Moral luck describes circumstances whereby a moral agent is assigned moral blame or praise for an action or its consequences even if it is clear that said agent did not have full control over either the action or its consequences. This term, introduced by Bernard Williams, has been developed, along with its significance to a coherent moral theory, by Williams and Thomas Nagel in their respective essays on the subject.

Moral Authority

Moral authority is authority premised on principles, or fundamental truths, which are independent of written, or positive, laws. As such, moral authority necessitates the existence of and adherence to truth. Because truth does not change, the principles of moral authority are immutable or unchangeable, although as applied to individual circumstances the dictates of moral authority for action may vary due to the exigencies of human life. These principles, which can be of metaphysical and/or religious in nature, are considered normative for behavior, whether they are or are not also embodied in written laws, and even if the community is ignoring or violating them. Therefore, the authoritativeness or force of moral authority is applied to the conscience of each individual, who is free to act according to or against its dictates.

Moral authority has thus also been defined as the "fundamental assumptions that guide our perceptions of the world".

Moral Responsibility

In philosophy, moral responsibility is the status of morally deserving praise, blame, reward, or *punishment* for an act or omission, in accordance with one's moral obligations. Deciding what (if anything) counts as "morally obligatory" is a principal concern of ethics.

Philosophers refer to people who have moral responsibility for an action as moral agents. Agents have the capability to reflect on their situation, to form intentions about how they will act, and then to carry out that action. The notion of free will has become an important issue in the debate on whether individuals are ever morally responsible for their actions and, if so, in what sense. Incompatibilists regard determinism as at odds with free will, whereas compatibilists think the two can coexists.a

Moral responsibility does not necessarily equate to legal responsibility. A person is legally responsible for an event when a legal system is liable to penalise that person for that event. Although it may often be the case that when a person is morally responsible for an act, they are also legally responsible for it, the two states do not always coincide.

Given the notion of equating moral responsibility with voluntary action, however, moral luck becomes a problem. This problem is illustrated by an example that many moral luck philosophers employ - that of a traffic accident.

There are two people driving cars, Driver A, and Driver B. They are alike in every way. Driver A is driving down a road, and, in a moment of inattention, runs a red light as a child is crossing the street. Driver A slams the brakes, swerves, in short does everything to try to avoid hitting the child - alas, the car hits and kills the child. Driver B, in the meantime, also runs a red light but, since no one is crossing, gets a traffic ticket but nothing more.

If a bystander were asked to morally evaluate Drivers A and B, there is very good reason to expect them to say that Driver A is due more moral blame than Driver B. After all, Driver A's course of action resulted in a death, whereas the course of action taken by Driver B was quite uneventful. However, there are absolutely no differences in the controllable actions performed by Drivers A and B. The only disparity is that in the case of Driver A, an external uncontrollable event occurred, whereas it did not in the case of Driver B. The external uncontrollable event, of course, is the child crossing the street. There is no difference at all in what the two of them could have done - however, one seems clearly more to blame than the other. How does this occur?

This is the problem of moral luck. If it is given that moral responsibility should only be relevant when the agent voluntarily performed or failed to perform some action, Drivers A and B should be blamed equally, or praised equally, as may be the case. At the same time, this is at least intuitively problematic, as - whatever the external circumstances are - one situation resulted in a death, and the other did not. Moral Luck is a concept that could be applied to establish the locus of culpability based on intention. As in the foreword itself it has been discussed about the importance of intention of an act rather than the act itself. I the arena of law it is called as actus reus and mens rea which means respectively the action and the intention behind that action. In the evolved jurisprudence; more stress is given on the mens rea even if the actus reus had been devoid of what we had discussed in the concept of moral luck.

When Two of Your Co-workers are Fighting

People disagree at work. That's a given. But what if there's an all-out war between two of your co-workers? What's the right way to respond? If the people fighting are your direct reports, you have a duty to intervene, but what if they're your peers? Should you play the role of peacekeeper? Or should you just stay out of it?

What the Experts Say

Whether or not you get involved will depend on how enmeshed you are in the situation. If either person approaches you to complain or to enlist your help, you have to respond in some way. And while you may not be their manager, you have a responsibility to make sure work gets done. "If it's getting in the way of teamwork, then talk to them," says Anna Ranieri, a career counselor, executive coach, and co-author of 'How Can I Help?'

But intervening is not always a straightforward prospect. "Peer-to-peer conflict is often fuzzy," says Roderick Kramer, a social psychologist and the William R. Kimball Professor of Organizational Behavior at the Stanford Graduate School of Business. It's not always clear who's responsible and you may not know what to do. "People often find themselves in over their head. They think they can intervene, make suggestions, feel good about themselves, and move the conflict forward in a constructive way. But that's not always possible," says Kramer. Here's how to respond next time you find yourself in the middle of a co-worker battle.

Allow Venting

It can be hard to listen to people complain but sometimes that's exactly what they need. "Allowing colleagues the space and time to talk it out is a real luxury in workplaces," says Ranieri.

"People often just want a safe place to vent and in doing so, may figure out on their own what they want to do." Kramer agrees: "There are times that people are just frustrated and need to express that. Venting isn't an effective long-term strategy. "Encourage people not to get caught in the trap of venting, ruminating, and gossiping about the situation," says Kramer, because that won't move things forward. "But there's nothing wrong with tolerating a few complaints in the short term." If you're worried that by hearing one person out, you'll upset the other (on small teams, it's often obvious who's talking to whom) make an effort to get both sides of the story. "At a minimum, you should keep a cordial relationship with the other person, but a better strategy is to demonstrate that you're fully open to all your colleagues," says Ranieri.

Empathize

While listening to your colleague, show that you understand how hard the situation is. You can say, "I'm sorry this is happening," or "It's tough when two people can't see eye to eye." But you don't have to – and shouldn't – take sides. "Don't endorse one person's point of view," says Ranieri. Stay neutral instead and speak from your own experience. Offer observations like, "It seemed like Jane was stressed out and didn't mean what she said," or "I know that Joe is a direct person and can sometimes come off as harsh." The key, Ranieri says, is to "show that you know where your colleague is coming from but not go as far to say, 'You're right and he's wrong." If you're being pushed to choose a perspective, make it clear that you won't: "You seem hurt but I can't take sides because I have to work with both of you."

Explain the Impact of their Fighting

After you've demonstrated your concern, make clear how the fighting is affecting the team. Ranieri suggests something like, "You two not getting along is hard for everyone and it's preventing us from doing good work." Help both parties see how the skirmish is hurting others so they are motivated to do something productive about it.

Offer Advice Cautiously

Before you give your two cents, ask your coworkers if they want your help. "We tend to offer unsolicited advice because we think we know better," says Ranieri. But people might not want your opinion, so start by saying something like: "Would it be helpful if I suggested some ways to work this out?" Remember too that your particular perspective may not be helpful. "Maybe you've been through a workplace fight and the way you resolved it worked for you but it may not work for this situation," Ranieri explains.

Problem-Solve Together

If your colleagues do want your advice, focus on making observations about what they might do, rather than concrete suggestions. Kramer suggests you think with each of them, or just the person confiding in you, about all the possible options and lay out a decision tree. "You should be more in problem-solving mode than gossip mode and together you can decide on the right intervention," he says.

Broker a Détente

Don't rush to sit them down together however, "getting people into a room and letting them duke it out is not responsible," says Kramer. "There are likely be asymmetries in their power or their abilities and you risk causing further damage to the relationship." Of course, if the conflict has reached a crescendo – perhaps people are yelling – then you may have no option but to pull them into a meeting and quickly get to the root of the problem.

Beware Resistance

Ranieri points out that there are some people that can't and won't be helped. She says that psychotherapists call these "Yes, but" clients. "Yes, I could approach Jane but I think she should approach me first." "Yes, I want things to be better, but that will never work." So despite your best attempts, you may not see progress. If one person insists she's right or refuses help, it may be time to retreat. In those cases, you can push back the next time she approaches you: "We've talked about this multiple times and it doesn't seem like you're ready to resolve it, so I guess it is what it is right now."

Don't Escalate

Kramer and Ranieri agree that it's rarely a good idea to involve the sparring co-workers' boss (or bosses) unless the problem is truly intractable and impeding work. "That would escalate the situation and possibly make one or both people feel like a victim," says Kramer. Also, once you've raised it to other people, you may now be seen as part of the problem in their eyes, though you might consider approaching your own superior for advice as a last resort.

Know your Limits

"Remember that you aren't a psychologist or a mediator," says Kramer. "If the situation is outside your comfort zone or you think the disagreement is juvenile, there's nothing wrong with saying, 'This is not my problem.' Adds Ranieri: "When you're in the helping role, you need to make sure you take care of yourself. You don't have to be an unpaid referee." But always give one or both of your co-workers a next step to take. You may want to say, "I'm not sure I'm the right person to help you with this but you might want sit down together or find someone else." Suggest a dispassionate third party who's not part of the team hierarchy, perhaps an ombudsman, or someone from HR.

Environmental Ethics

Environmental ethics is the part of environmental philosophy which considers extending the traditional boundaries of ethics from solely including humans to including the non-human world. There are many ethical decisions that human beings make with respect to the environment. For example:

- Should we continue to clear cut forests for the sake of human consumption?
- Why should we continue to propagate our species, and life itself?
- Should we continue to make gasoline powered vehicles?
- What environmental obligations do we need to keep for future generations?
- Is it right for humans to knowingly cause the extinction of a species for the convenience of humanity?
- How should we best use and conserve the space environment to secure and expand life?

Following issues occupies environmental ethics:

- **Ecocentrism**

It is a term used to denote a nature-centered, as opposed to human-centered, system of values. The justification for ecocentrism usually consists in an ontological belief and subsequent ethical claim. The ontological belief denies that there are any existential divisions between human and non-human nature sufficient to claim that humans are, either; the sole bearers of intrinsic value, or; possess greater intrinsic value than non-human nature. Thus the subsequent ethical claim is for an equality of intrinsic value across human and non-human nature, or 'biospherical egalitarianism'.

- **Biocentrism**

Biocentrism in a political and ecological sense is an ethical point of view that extends inherent value to all living things. It is an understanding of how the earth works; particularly as it relates to biodiversity. It stands in contrast to anthropocentrism which centers on the value of humans.

Biocentrism does not imply the idea of equality among the animal kingdom for no such notion can be observed in nature. Biocentric thought is nature based, not human based.

Advocates of biocentrism often promote the preservation of biodiversity, animal rights, and environmental protection. The term has also been employed by advocates of "left biocentrism", which combines deep ecology with an "anti-industrial and anti-capitalist" position.

- **Anthropocentrism**

It is the belief that human beings are the central or most significant species on the planet (In the sense that they are considered to have a moral status or value higher than that of all other organisms), or the assessment of reality through an exclusively human perspective. The term can be used interchangeably with humanocentrism, and some refer to the concept as human supremacy or human exceptionalism.

- **Intrinsic Value (Animal Ethics)**

The intrinsic value of an animal refers to the value it possesses in its own right, as an end-in-itself, as opposed to its instrumental value, its value to other animals (including human beings). The phrase (often used synonymously with inherent value) has been adopted by animal rights advocates. The Dutch Animal Health and Welfare Act referred to it in 1981: "Acknowledgment of the intrinsic value of animals means that animals have value in their own right and as a consequence their interests are no longer automatically subordinate to man's interests". This acknowledgment has stirred a debate on what it entails in the context of animal husbandry, animal breeding, vivisection, animal testing and biotechnology.

- **Conservation Ethics**

It is an ethics of resource use, allocation, and protection. Its primary focus is upon maintaining the health of the natural world, its fisheries, habitats, and biological diversity. Secondary focus is on materials conservation, including non-renewable resources such as metals, minerals and fossil fuels, and energy conservation, which is important to protect the natural world. Those who follow the conservation ethic and, especially, those who advocate or work toward conservation goals are termed conservationists.

- **Climate Ethics**

Climate ethics is an area of research that focuses on the ethical dimensions of climate change (also known as global warming), and concepts such as climate justice.

Human-induced climate change raises many profound ethical questions, yet many believe that these ethical issues have not been addressed adequately in climate change policy debates or in the scientific and economic literature on climate change; and that, consequently, ethical questions are being overlooked or obscured in climate negotiations, policies and discussions. It has been pointed out that those most responsible for climate change are not the same people as those most vulnerable to its effects.

Terms such as climate justice and ecological justice ('eco justice') are used worldwide, and have been adopted by various groups.

- **Environmental Justice**

Environmental justice emerged as a concept in the United

States in the early 1980s. The term has two distinct uses. The first and more common usage describes a social movement in the United States whose focus is on the fair distribution of environmental benefits and burdens. Second, it is an interdisciplinary body of social science literature that includes (but is not limited to) theories of the environment, theories of justice, environmental law and governance, environmental policy and planning, development, sustainability, and political ecology.

Indian environmentalism has, for the most part, been about social justice. During the 1970s and 1980s, it was concerned with differential access to natural assets and ecosystem services. The Bhopal Gas Disaster of 1984 raised new issues, pertaining to industrial risk and safety.

- **Environmental Racism**

Environmental racism is a form of environmental injustice in which the impacts are identified as falling primarily on people of color. The term was coined in a 1987 study drawing together US census data and government data on the location of toxic waste sites; the study documented "clear patterns which show that communities with greater minority percentages of the population are more likely to be the sites of commercial hazardous waste facilities."

- **Eco-Justice**

Eco-Justice holds together commitments for ecological sustainability and human justice. It sees environmental issues and justice issues not as competing agendas, but as intertwined elements of how humans are called to relate to God's creation. It asserts that it is not possible to care for the earth without also caring for humanity, and that seeking human justice must involve care for the environment.

- **Stewardship**

Stewardship expresses the human obligation to care for God's creation. It is grounded in the proclamation that "the Earth is the Lord's" and sees humanity as caretakers, not owners, of the earth.

Stewardship has been given a wide range of interpretations. At one extreme, where humans are seen as separate from the rest

Ethics and Natural Reason

By exercising the natural reason, a person can arrive at a conclusion concerning the kind of life fitting for human beings. Ethicists argue that there is an inherent faculty of rational judgment concerned with choosing the right way of acting. Excellence in the exercise of this power constitutes the intellectual virtue of practical wisdom, prudential, and conduct in accord with its deliverances is moral virtue.

The idea of an innate power of moral knowledge is open to at least two interpretations. On the first, human beings are endowed with a capacity for rational thought, and starting from certain premises, knowledge of which is not dependent on revelation, they can arrive at conclusions about right conduct. On the second interpretation, the relevant endowment is one of a faculty of moral sense by which they can simply intuit what it is right or wrong to do. These views may be described as 'rationalist' and 'intuitionist' respectively.

of creation, stewardship is strongly colored by ideas of dominion, control and management. At the other extreme, where humans are seen as part of creation, stewardship is a way of expressing how humans might interact gently and responsibly with the rest of creation, and is a rejection of dominion.

Determinants of Ethical Behaviour

There are three main influences that determine the ethical behaviour and decisions-

- Individual personality traits: individual value system, upbringing, education, religious beliefs, experiences, etc.
- Culture/country of an individual,
- Organisation/industry: prevailing ethics of the organisation/industry an individual works for.

Personal Ethics

It is generally accepted principles of right and wrong governing the conduct of individuals.

- Our personal ethical code exerts a profound influence on the way we behave as business people.
- The first step to establishing a strong sense of business ethics is for a society to emphasize strong personal ethics.
- Expatriate managers may experience more than the usual degree of pressure to violate their personal ethics.

Decision-Making Processes

- Several studies of unethical behavior in business have concluded that business people sometimes do not realize they are behaving unethically primarily because they simple fail to ask........ "Is this decision or action ethical?"
- Often the result of applying straight-forward business calculus to a decision without considering important ethical issues.

Organization Culture

- The climate in some businesses does not encourage people to think through the ethical consequences of business decisions.
- Result of an organizational culture that deemphasizes business ethics, reducing all decisions to be purely economic.

Unrealistic Performance Expectations

- Pressure from the parent company to meet unrealistic goals that can only be attained by cutting corners or acting in an unethical manner.
- This often results in managers will, violating their own personal ethics and engage in unethical behavior.
- An organizational culture with values that reinforce ethical behavior is an essential ethical component.

Leadership

- Leaders help to establish thc culture and values of an organization, and they set the example that others follow.

The Ethical Mind

How does an ethical mind think?

- "What kind of a person, worker, and citizen do I want to be?
- Should I be supporting my close friend, even though I know he is wrong?
- Is my job and personal comfort more important than the suffering of larger society using my company's adulterated food products?"

An ethical mind is more community-oriented. Ethical mind is not equivalent to a respectful mind, which aids you to understand and form relationships with other human beings. It's important to clarify the distinction between the respectful and the ethical mind, because we assume that one who is respectful is ethical and vice versa. You can be respectful without understanding why: As a child, you might have respected your parents and grandparents because you were taught to. But ethical conceptions and behaviors demand a certain capacity to go beyond your own experience as an individual person. Once you have developed an ethical mind, you become more like an impartial spectator of the team, the organization, the citizenry, the world. And you may have to sacrifice respect for another person if your role as a citizen or worker calls on you to do damage control to protect an idea or institution you believe in.

Whistle-blowers Display Ethical Minds

Many people might see a top management doing something unethical, but they won't do anything about it because they want to keep their jobs, and they feel that they must respect the boss. A whistle-blower steps back from those concerns and considers the nature of work and the community in a larger way. He takes a mental leap past daily doings; his allegiance is to the workplace or the profession. He acts ethically even though it may cost him his respectful relation to his supervisor and, ultimately, his job and relation to his colleagues. He is able to do this because his own momentary well-being is less important than the broader mission he has endorsed.

Situations Ethics

In situation ethics, right and wrong depend upon the situation. There are no universal moral rules or rights - each case is unique and deserves a unique solution. Situation ethics rejects 'prefabricated decisions and prescriptive rules'. It teaches that ethical decisions should follow flexible guidelines rather than absolute rules, and be taken on a case by case basis.

So a person who practices situation ethics approaches ethical problems with some general moral principles rather than a rigorous set of ethical laws and is prepared to give up even those principles if doing so will lead to a greater good.

Social Ethics

Social ethics are the philosophical or moral principles that, in one way or another, represent the collective experience of people and cultures. This sort of ethics often acts as a sort of "code of conduct" that governs what is and is not acceptable, as well as providing a framework for ensuring that all members of the community are cared for. Standard ethics are typically driven by individual morals that determine right or wrong. Within a society, the focus is usually more on what may be considered appropriate behavior for people as a whole. People perceive things differently, however, and various cultures share often wildly opposing beliefs; as such, what is deemed "right" for one group may not necessarily be consistent universally – and defining social ethics as an absolute is often very difficult.

So, social ethics can also be referred to as a methodology of applying moral principles to social issues. The purpose is to clarify the moral principles and social goals inherent in social issues and public initiatives. It asserts that the relative strength of various moral claims can only be compared within the contexts of a particular social issue.

Social ethics has always been used in a relative context dependent upon the spatio-temporal milieu. What was socially ethical yesterday may not be acceptable today. Similarly, what is appreciative in one part of the world may be considered abhorrent in the other part. Take for example, the evolving issue of gay rights which in some nations and particularly in present times is considered as normal as compared to it being social anathema earlier.

Perhaps some not-as-controversial (compared to earlier times) topics that fall within social ethics are affirmative action and smoking bans. The discussions involved with these topics are rich in discussion of such moral notions as fairness, benefits, appropriation of scarce resources, liberty, property rights, paternalism, and consent.

Other issues have to do with appropriating the still very real gender differences in wealth, responsibilities, social roles, and employment opportunities. How are these differences to be understood? Obviously not because such differences are deserved. Given this, such differences need to either be morally justified (doubtful) or morally rectified, and so, if they can't be justified, then such differences should be morally eliminated/rectified. Very good work can be done on understanding how to do this in a way that does not create further moral problems.

Additionally, work on the visibility of transgendered persons is important, and how transgendered persons can be incorporated into the modern life of working in corporations, government, education, or industry, living in predominantly non-transgendered communities and networks of families with more typical gender narratives, and doing this all in a way that respects the personhood of transgendered persons.

Recently, India also, though being behind the social evolution tangent, has made some phenomenal advances in rectifying some of the fossilized social wrongs. In Tamil Nadu, we have seen first transgender becoming sub-inspector and exemplify the openness of our will to revisit some of the social-wrongs which were 'considered' right then.

Difference between Non-Moral, Immoral, and Amoral

Non-Moral Actions

Non-moral actions or events are those areas of interest where moral categories cannot be applied. Almost all examples involving human intentions, volition or behavior are described in terms of moral categories, ceteris paribus - with other things remaining same - such examples involve the possibility of helping or harming oneself or others. For example, wondering whether one should eat grapefruit, wear socks of a specific shade of color, or part your hair on the left side of the head are all usually considered non-moral issues. Yet, there are circumstances where such actions could have moral consequences. Generally speaking, statements in the sciences (so-called "factual statements") are considered to be about non-moral issues as well.

Immoral Actions

Immoral actions or events are those areas of interest where moral categories do apply and of are such a kind as to be evil, sinful, or wrong according to some code or theory of ethics. An immoral action then can be defined as a violation of a rule or code of ethics. Strictly speaking, on the one hand, an action could be considered immoral on the basis of one rule, code, or theory and, on the other hand, be considered moral or even non-moral on the another rule, code, or theory. Such examples are common from the point of view of sociological or moral relativism.

Amoral Actions

Amoral actions or events are those areas of interest exhibiting indifference to and not abiding by the moral rules or codes of society. For example, a sociopath, sometimes called a person without a conscience, and a very young child are called "amoral" because such people have no feeling or understanding of the concept of right or wrong.

Ethics in Human Actions

Humans are said to be evaluative in nature. Whenever a person does something we find others analysing his/her behaviour and commenting that it was good, bad or at times indifferent. Ethics is said to be a philosophical treatise which studies human behaviour and tries to determine whether the act performed was morally right or wrong. It cannot content itself with simply registering facts; it attempts to reflect on the meaningfulness or meaninglessness of such facts, establish or reject them on a rational basis, understand their implications, draw relevant consequences and, above all, intuit their ultimate cause.

Understanding of Human Act

There is a difference between 'Acts of Man/Human' and 'Human Acts' respectively. Not every act that a human being does is a typically human act. Human activities, like the circulation of blood, heartbeat, over which normal people in general have no control are not classified as human acts. Such acts which are beyond the control of humans and those which they share in common with animals are called as 'Acts of Humans'. Acts of humans, then, are involuntary and therefore, not morally responsible for them.

On the other hand a 'Human Act' is one which proceeds from knowledge and from consent of free will. Or, in other words, it is an act which emanates from the will with knowledge of the end or goal to which the act leads. The Human act is to be distinguished from acts of humans which are performed without intervention of intellect and free will.

The Constituent Elements of Human Action

Constituent elements of the human act refer to the inner causes or the constituting elements which generate a human person to undertake a certain act. The understanding of the human act indicates that there are two essential elements which constitute a human act:

- The Intellectual Element (knowledge) and;
- The Volitive Element (free will).

Impediments for Human Acts

In the process of performing a human act the individual might encounter certain obstacles which though may not nullify the human act and make it involuntary but they may reduce the imputability or culpability of the individual, thereby making him less responsible for the particular act. Some of the main impediments which might affect either the intellectual or the volitive constituent (or both together) of the human action are ignorance, passion, habit and fear.

Factors determining the Morality of Human Actions

Analyzing the morality of the human act is said to be a complex enterprise since it is affected by so many conditions which are within and without. Most of the moralists agree that to judge the goodness or badness of any particular human act, three elements must be weighed from which every act derives its morality. They are:

- the Object of the act;
- the Circumstances surrounding the act, and;
- the End or Intention that the one performing the act has in mind.

Bona fide Mistake

'Bona fide' is a Latin word and used to mean "in good faith." It is commonly used as a legal term if a party fails to follow the law in attempting to collect a debt. In its simplest definition, bona fide mistake is defined as an honest mistake that when rectified quickly requires no punishment. Bona fide mistake is a legal term referring to an unintentional mistake or oversight that may be corrected promptly to avoid exposure to legal action.

An example of a creditor claiming a bona fide error might be continuing to attempt to collect a debt that had already been paid. If the payoff had not been recorded properly because of a clerical or systems error, or because incorrect information was received from a prior creditor, the debt collector might claim a bona fide error to defend against prosecution. A mistake in legal judgment, however, is not ordinarily considered a bona fide mistake.

Determinism and In-determinism

The question of free will or human freedom in the matter of making a moral choice has been an issue which is discussed and deliberated by philosophers down the centuries. And the complexity of problem makes it rather difficult to take a stand in the category of 'Either; Or'. The problem is formulated thus: Determinism versus In-determinism.

Determinism is a theory which explains that all human action is conditioned entirely by preceding events, and not by the faculty of the Will. In-determinism is a theory, though not denying the influence of behavioural patterns and certain extrinsic forces on human actions, insists on the reality of free will or the capacity of the humans to make a free choice. This view asserts that humans are an exception to the rigid determinism that occurs in nature.

Determinants of Ethics in Governance

The levels of ethics in governance are dependent on the social, economic, political, cultural, legal-judicial and historical contexts of the country. These specific factors influence ethics in public administrative systems. Ethics, whether in an entire society, or in a social sub-system, evolves over a long period of time and is influenced, during its nurturance and growth, by a variety of environmental factors, such as, historical, socio-cultural, legal-judicial, political and economical.

Public Vs Private Ethics

Public ethics are the moral principle that ought to govern different areas of law and policy making, and about the ethically proper conduct of elected officials, government agents, and ordinary citizens.

It has often been said, "What happens in privacy does not hurt anyone." Does it get carried out by other means? Is anything truly secret? The implication of the two mottos above suggests that any indiscreet behavior that transpires in the privacy of a hotel room will not become publicly known and bring irreversible harm or affect that individual or the community. Accordingly, a person can be assured that there will be no public exposure of private indiscretions.

This raises the following issues;

- Do private ethics have no bearing on public life or social ethics?
- Does what occurs in the privacy of a public official's home or office have no influence on public or social policy decisions?
- Can private ethical behavior be separated from social ethics without consequences?
- Can there be public or social ethics without underlying personal ethics?
- Is there a legitimate bifurcation between private and public ethics?

These questions go to the heart of law, the extent of morality, relationships development, the inner life and its outward expression, and public and social policy development.

One ethicist said that "It is impossible to maintain a clear and precise distinction between social ethics and personal (individual) ethics. No individual behavior is without social implications. No social situation or problem is without individual repercussions." Further she said that the public policy and social ethics are intertwined. Public policy, politics, economics, war, poverty, education, racism, ecology, and crime: these are examples of the subject of social ethics. All of the social institutions she identifies encompass a vast range of issues in every segment of society and cannot exist apart from individuals. Business, education, temple, professional associations, and government all involve people as they interact, exchange ideas, trade goods and services, and make decisions. They influence one another during these interchanges and affect the structure and moral environment of society.

Values

Values are the individual principles or qualities that guide judgement and behaviour of a person or a group. Values are like an anchor in a ship. When a storm comes, a ship is not swept away by strong currents but remains anchored to the shore. A person with strong values or character sticks to his principles and is not swept away, in crisis or under pressure.

Values flow from the highest of our own self. For each one of us, there are values rooted in the finest part of the self from where we radiate outwards. These values are an inbuilt mechanism, which distinguishes the right from the wrong, the Do's and Don'ts of any action, even when no one is looking. Values are concerned with character and conduct of a person and evaluate the voluntary and habitual actions of individuals with reference to their being right or wrong.

There is another view on the values, that this self managing mechanism is not intuitive, but it is acquired from the environment by continuous teaching and the behaviour of others, especially the superior in age and statues, as perceived by an individual. We cannot deny the impact of environment, society and family on an individual for the values he imbibes. At the same time, we cannot deny the fact that the source of values is within, which guides one in making choice in acquisition of learning from the environment. We can say that there are uniform (Universal) values inbuilt in each one of us. They flow out of the highest of our own self, our ultimate holistic potential. They refer to our intrinsic humanness. Individual or personal values vary to the extent one is conscious towards this inner source and the extent to which one tends to compromise with it in the given cultural environment and other compulsions. Thus, both the source 'within' and the 'cultural environment' are important for inculcation of values.

Intrinsic Values and Extrinsic Values

Values can be viewed from the standpoint of their importance. All values are experiences of different degrees of importance in the development of individuality. So, we classify values on the basis of importance these values have.

An intrinsic value is one which has worth in its own right. It is an End-in-itself. Truth, Beauty, Goodness, Temperance, Courage, etc. are considered as intrinsic values. They are good not because of their consequences but because they are good in themselves. These values retain even if they were to exist completely alone. Intrinsic values are said to be Absolute values.

An Extrinsic value is one which is a means to some other value. It is of instrumental worth only. A pair of spectacles is good only if there are eyes behind spectacles to see through them. The spectacles have instrumental value. Extrinsic or Instrumental values are the part of larger whole. They are means to an End. Wealth, fame, physical fitness, etc. borrow their worth from something extraneous to them.

The terms Extrinsic and Intrinsic are used relatively. They are not always mutually exclusive or fixed. What is valued by one person for its own sake may be valued by another person as a means to an end.

Values can be graded as Positive Values and Negative Values, Productive Values and Unproductive values; Permanent Values and Transient Values. In general, Intrinsic Values are rated higher than Extrinsic Values. Positive Values are preferred to Negative Values. The locus of values is human mind. It is a special sort of reaction to the environment. Human mind has three psychical functions (aspects)–thinking, feeling and willing. The values corresponding to these functions are Intellectual Values (Truth), Aesthetic Values (Beauty) and Moral Values (Goodness). Truth, Beauty and Good are Universal Values.

Moral Character

Moral character or character is an evaluation of a particular individual's stable moral qualities. The concept of character can imply a variety of attributes including the existence or lack of **virtues** such as **empathy, courage, fortitude, honesty**, and **loyalty**, or of good behaviors or **habits**. Moral character primarily refers to the assemblage of qualities that distinguish one individual from another – although on a cultural level, the set of moral behaviors to which a social group adheres can be said to unite and define it culturally as distinct from others. Psychologist Lawrence Pervin defines moral character as "a disposition to express behavior in consistent patterns of functions across a range of situations".

The word "character" is derived from the Ancient Greek word "charaktêr", referring to a mark impressed upon a coin. Later it came to mean a point by which one thing was told apart from others. There are two approaches when dealing with moral character: **Normative ethics** involve moral standards that exhibit right and wrong conduct. It is a test of proper behavior and determining what is right and wrong. **Applied ethics** involve specific and **controversial** issues along with a moral choice, and tend to involve situations where people are either for or against the issue.

In 1982 **V. Campbell** and **R. Bond** proposed the following as major sources in influencing character and moral development: **heredity**, early childhood experience, **modeling** by important adults and older youth, **peer influence**, the general **physical** and **social environment**, the **communications media**, the teachings of **schools** and other institutions, and specific situations and roles that elicit corresponding behavior.

Morality and Ethics

Moral is related to issues of right or wrong and to how individuals should behave. Therefore Morality means standards of conduct that are accepted as right or proper. It is based on personal conscience rather than what the law says. Ethics and morals seem to appear similar on the face of it, but if one analyzes deeply, there is a subtle difference. Ethics define the code that a society or group of people adhere to, while morality delves into the right and wrong at a much deeper level, both personal and spiritual. Morals define personal character, while ethics stress a social system in which those morals are applied.

Ethics, Values and Morals

Ethics can also be defined as prepositional statements (standards) that are used by members of a profession or group to determine what the right course of action in a situation is. Ethics rely on logical and rational criteria to reach a decision, an essentially cognitive process.

Values, on the other hand, describe ideas that we value or prize. To value something means that we hold it dear and feel it has worth to us. As such, there is often a feeling or affective component associated with values. Often, values are ideas that we aspire to achieve, like equality and social justice.

Morals describe a behavioural code of conduct to which an individual ascribes. They are used to negotiate, support, and strengthen our relationships with others.

Value System

Values constitute an important aspect of self-concept and serve as guiding principles for an individual. Considered together, values form 'values systems'. A 'value system' is an enduring organisation of beliefs concerning preferable modes of conduct or end-states of existence along a continuum of importance. Thus, the importance of different values co-varies with the importance of others in the value system. For e.g. one may value 'honesty' over 'success'.

Ethics in Public Administration

The notion of ethics has expanded itself to involve all major realms of human existence. Here, an attempt is made to outline certain salient aspects of ethics in public administration. Broadly, they could be summarized as following maxims:

- **Maxim of Legality and Rationality:** An administrator will follow the law and rules that are framed to govern and guide various categories of policies and decisions.
- **Maxim of Responsibility and Accountability:** An administrator would not hesitate to accept responsibility for his decision and actions. He would hold himself morally responsible for his actions and for the use of his discretion while making decisions. Moreover, he would be willing to be held accountable to higher authorities of governance and even to the people who are the ultimate beneficiaries of his decisions and actions.
- **Maxim of Work Commitment:** An administrator would be committed to his duties and perform his work with involvement, intelligence and dexterity as Swami Vivekananda had observed: "Every duty is holy and devotion to duty is the highest form of worship". This would also entail a respect for time, punctuality and fulfilment of promises made. Work is considered not as a burden but as an opportunity to serve and constructively contribute to society.

- **Maxim of Excellence:** An administrator would ensure the highest standards of quality in administrative decisions and actions and would not compromise with standards because of convenience or complacency. In a competitive international environment, an administrative system should faithfully adhere to the requisites of Total Quality Management.
- **Maxim of Fusion:** An administrator would rationally bring about a fusion of individual, organisational and social goals to help evolve unison of ideals and imbibe in his behaviour a commitment to such a fusion. In situation of conflicting goals, a concern for ethics should govern the choices made.
- **Maxim of Responsiveness and Resilience:** An administrator would respond effectively to the demands and challenges from the external as well as internal environment. He would adapt to environmental transformation and yet sustain the ethical norms of conduct. In situations of deviation from the prescribed ethical norms, the administrative system would show resilience and bounce back into the accepted ethical mould at the earliest opportunity.
- **Maxim of Utilitarianism:** While making and implementing policies and decisions, an administrator will ensure that these lead to the greatest good (happiness, benefits) of the greatest number.
- **Maxim of Compassion:** An administrator, without violating the prescribed laws and rules, would demonstrate compassion for the poor, the disabled and the weak while using his discretion in making decisions. At least, he would not grant any benefits to the stronger section of society only because they are strong and would not deny the due consideration to the weak, despite their weakness.
- **Maxim of National Interest:** Though universalistic in orientation and liberal in outlook, a civil servant, while performing his duties, would keep in view the impact of his action on his nation's strength and prestige. The Japanese, the Koreans, the Germans and the Chinese citizens (including civil servants), while performing their official roles, have at the back of their mind a concern and respect for their nation. This automatically raises the level of service rendered and the products delivered.
- **Maxim of Justice:** Those responsible for formulation and execution of policies and decisions of governance would ensure that respect is shown to the principles of equality, equity, fairness,

impartiality and objectivity and no special favours are doled out on the criteria of status, position, power, gender, class, caste or wealth.

- **Maxim of Transparency:** An administrator will make decisions and implement them in a transparent manner so that those affected by the decisions and those who wish to evaluate their rationale, will be able to understand the reasons behind such decisions and the sources of information on which these decisions were made.
- **Maxim of Integrity:** An administrator would undertake an administrative action on the basis of honesty and not use his power, position and discretion to serve his personal interest and the illegitimate interests of other individuals or groups.

Violence

The word 'violence' is derived from the Latin word 'violentia' which comes from the root 'vis' which means force. Usually 'violence' denotes great force, excessive or constraint. The first two meanings: force and excessive force are taken from the stand-point of an agent's activity. The third meaning: constraint is taken from that of a passive principle affected adversely by the activity of the agent. In defining violence, we may point out two principles: the constraining and the constrained. The latter, though always passive in relation to the agent inflicting violence, may suffer violence either as an active or as a passive principle.

A casual look at our society will tell us the untold miseries existing and how this violence is perpetuated under various shades. There is cultural violence, religious violence, economic violence, media violence, group violence, sexual violence, political violence and the types of violence could be inexhaustive.

Life is being threatened by innumerable kinds of violence and we feel powerless and helpless at the intensity and the gravity of the matter. Something has gone wrong somewhere. It is the personal and collective responsibility to get on the right track of life and not on the violent one. Violence can only beget violence and not peace. Moral laxity is one of the causes of violence, others being lack of education, unemployment, caste system, poor planning and deep corruption, etc.

Moral laws are finest fabric which knits together the different persons in the society into a whole. The moral laws safeguards the inter-personal relationship and builds up a better and strong society. Whenever the moral laws of the land was tampered with and less attention was given to it, respect for life and value of life had dwindled. Laxity in moral standard of life will clearly reflect in the attitude towards life. There are already visible signs of this danger in the way human beings are treated. Human life has become the least valuable things where as the lives of other animals and birds get a better attention. This easy-go mentality may lead one to lose one's own conscience or inner voice and would end up in violence and crime against humanity.

Terrorism

The Oxford Advanced Dictionary defines terrorism as the use of violent action in order to achieve political aims or to force a government to act. The terrorists use various methods to cause panic and fear among people. Some of these methods include hostage taking, hijacking, political assassination, kidnapping, bombing, and explosions. Terrorism has several objectives, such as, to advertise the movement or to give publicity to the ideology and strength of the movement; to mobilize mass support and urge sympathizers to greater militancy; to eliminate opponents and informers and thus remove obstacles to the growth of the movement; to demonstrate the inability of the government to support the people and maintain order; to destroy internal stability and create a feeling of fear and insecurity among the public; and to ensure the allegiance and obedience of the followers.

Terrorism and Social Ethics

Terrorism has turned out over the years to be a method of dehumanizing the entire spectrum of human beings. The principles of the terrorists are rooted in destruction and dehumanization. Consequently, they take control of the ethical supervision of a society and fabricate the citizens of a substandard conscience and a splintered morality. Terror is not merely a rational phenomenon. It envelops people, body, mind, and spirit. It leaves people paralyzed by anxiety and fear. Terrorism in all its forms is always wrong. Terrorism violates human rights, including the basic right to be treated as a moral person.

Gandhian Pacifism to Cull Violence

Universal pacifists are morally opposed to all kinds of violence, not just to killing. Certainly, the most interesting and defective pacifist of the twentieth century was Mahatma Gandhi. He developed his doctrine of non-violence which proved to be very effective in the Indian freedom struggle, which he led from the front. As world citizens, everyone should be encouraged to follow the example of Mahatma Gandhi, who had a philosophy of life blended with the jewels of truth and non-violence. He led a bloodless struggle for the freedom of a nation, and of love, peace and everlasting joy in the hearts of millions of humans. Sarvodaya (welfare of all) was his secret.

Terrorist groups mostly have some disgruntlement with the streamline flow of State, Society and Economy. In popular parlance it is said that is needs sound of a blast to make the deaf hear. Actually, without eulogizing the terrorism and the violence they inculcate in, the terror and here I certainly do not mean mindless terrorism in the name of religion and geopolitical gameplan, is a symptom which needs proper treatment and not counter attack with the same sets of 'tools' they use to shout at the Society which has long lost connection with them. I know that this step is slow and always presents with the enticement of being succumbed-with but this could probably be the only way-out of this menace called violence which has engulfed the psyche of the general populace.

Terrorism as a phenomenon does raise a few ethical questions for our study and reflection. The growing hate campaigns against groups, regions and countries affect the normal morale of the society. Terrorism can thus be a threat to the civilization of the world. For, behaving ethically is a part of being civilized. The terrorists, however, are devoid of any love and benevolence and are disinterested in truth of life. They do not like to cultivate any art, literature and music. They prefer darkness of nights to the light of the day. They like their hiding places more than one loves one's home. They often kidnap children for claiming ransom. They have no qualms of conscience to make married women suddenly widows even after a few hours of marriage.

Public Relations

Public Relations have now become a vital function affecting management decisions and influencing public opinion in every public or private organisation. Today, it is indispensable for any organisation. The reasons for it being so are as follows:

- Recognition of right of expression and freedom of information
- Advance in telecommunication and transport.
- Opening up of traditionally closed societies and increasing globalisation.
- Governments employing Public Relation practice for staying in power, for development task, etc.
- Growth in business, amalgamations, collaborations, operating with subsidiaries, spreading across national boundaries and in different cultures

Ethics in Public Relations

Public Relations recognize a long-term responsibility and seek to persuade and to achieve mutual understanding by securing the willing acceptance of attitudes and ideas. It can succeed only when the basic policy is ethical, and the means used as truthful. In Public Relations, the ends can never justify the use of false, harmful or questionable means.

However, it is a difficult task to describe what is ethical and what is unethical. It would be simpler to state it as a matter of choosing between the right and wrong options in keeping with conscience. Anything that causes dissonance in the mind brings about a feeling of guilt and dishonesty. And dishonest communication cannot be an aid to cementing relationships. Public are also not to be underestimated as fools. As Abraham Lincoln said, 'you can fool some people all the time, and all of the people some of the time, but you cannot fool all the people all of the time'.

There are a number of acts that could be classified as unethical, ranging from suppressing of news to misleading the audience. Unethical act in public relations may include:

- Suppressing unfavourable news,
- Misrepresenting facts,
- Postponing to serve a cause but actually serving some other interest,
- Promising results that cannot be obtained,
- Use of undesirable method towards pressurising editors for carrying publicity material.

With increasing education, the consumers and public have became aware of their rights and a Public Relations person may have to deal with pressure groups like trade unions, consumer protection groups, environment protection activities, etc. Therefore, it is imperative for a Public Relations practitioner to be self regulating, ethical as also be careful about the legal aspects of communication.

Values in Public Relationships

The importance of articulating ethics and the values that define and underpin the public service, cannot be underscored. This is seen as critical to providing both public officials and the public with a common frame of reference regarding the principles and standards to be applied and in assisting public officials to develop an appreciation of the ethical issues involved in effective and efficient public service delivery.

An example of the importance attached to the above-mentioned ethical principles is found in the "Seven Principles of Public Life" given by the Nolan Committee in the United Kingdom.

Human Values

The values according to or against which we act are the unavoidable and essential element of all important decisions in the human arena. Values are the link that ties together personal perceptions and judgements, motives and actions. The same applies in understanding social and political life. A make-or-break idea is that values or precepts - and their various practical consequences in life - are at least as fundamental to understanding man and society as are the much-vaunted physical necessities. They are also essential in improving man and society too.

The great predominance of violence, war, hate and crime in most societies and eras of history may seem to refute the universality of human values. However, the values do go back to the earliest recorded human societies and religions and have somehow persisted throughout all the eras and all cultures. In this sense they are universal, added to which is the evolutionary nature of the human being and civilisation, whereby the assertion of these values becomes eventually more and more secure, and now on an interactive global scale through international laws and practices.

What do Human Values consist of?

Human values can be formulated or expressed in many ways: anything from practical examples to moral principles at the highest levels of generality. However, genuine human values are not abstract principles developed by academics or preachers, but life-embedded ideas and precepts, along with their various justifications. Because they are human, values are not divinely ordained rules of behaviour - not commandments set in stone. They are related to differing cultures, unique persons and situations and are developed and expressed in human terms for the human aims they collectively represent.

Basic Human Values

Human Values which have wide common appeal - possibly even a universal relevance - are:

- Truth
- Love-Caring
- Peace
- Responsibility
- Justice

Truth

The truth in any matter does not depend upon the will or wish of the individual, but is independent of desires and their related interests and opinions. Evidence that truth is an inherent value in the human psyche is found in the fact that no-one likes to be called a liar, not even most liars. Further, it is much harder to sustain a lie than to maintain the truth, because one lie leads to another until the complexity is unmanageable.

Love-Caring

The word 'love' should be taken in the very wide sense of 'care' or 'concern for'. This can be taken as a basic category or general human value which relates to concern and respect for others and the environment. The word 'love' is here used in a broader sense than in common parlance where personal and/or erotic love is the common interpretation. Its essence can be characterised by the words "Love is unselfish care and concern for the well-being of others and the world at large. The less selfish it is, the more it enriches life". Being neither a sensation, an emotion nor a mere conception, but being identifiable only at the heart or core of the human consciousness, love in this universal sense is the characteristic par excellence of the human soul or psyche. It is common to include altruism, understanding and forgiveness under the more encompassing (but vague and ambiguous) word 'love'.

Peace

As a universally-accepted positive value, peace refers to the experience of harmony, a balanced but nevertheless dynamic mental condition. Peacefulness in a person's life, in society and in world terms, is a product of all positive values working together sufficiently. Without truth, caring concern (or 'love') and justice, conflicts arise and peace is endangered or lost. While peace is the absence of disturbance, violence, war and wrongdoing generally, it is tangible present when experienced individually as peace of mind, the mutual respect and pleasure of friendliness and tolerance.

Peace of mind is individual, but peace in society is the result of positive acts, which are not violent or destructive but tolerant and constructive.

Responsibility

The human value of doing one's duty is closely related to non-violence. This is the reasonable tendency to wish to avoid harm to creatures or their environment wherever avoidable. Respecting the integral nature of eco-systems or of a social-natural environment as against the destructive influences of pollution, misuse and excessive exploitation exemplify the spirit of non-violence (the Hindu concept of 'Ahimsa' as well-developed by Gandhi). It is the inherently-sensed value that prompts us to draw back from unethical meddling in life processes.

Knowledge of what is true combined with insight into what is good, are the basis of duty, also conceived as 'acting rightly'. Behind any conscious act lies the thought. If the thought is fed by the will towards the true and the good - in contrast to purely selfish aims - the act is 'right'. This is also found in the Eastern concept of 'dharma' or action in accordance with the universal laws of nature (both physical and human nature).

Justice

The European tradition has long embraced justice as one among the higher human values, even as the highest (Socrates and Plato). The idea of justice is difficult to define satisfactorily. It is based on fairness, where the equality of every individual before the law is fundamental. As such it is a social value in that it aims to resolve and reduce conflict, guided by the principles of care and non-violence (involving the minimum use of force required). The aim to achieve social justice for the perceived common good has certainly a long pre-history as a central idea in all human societies. The Classical Greek idea of justice eventually gave rise to that of 'human rights', first formalised in the Charter of the 1948 Geneva Convention, which is continually undergoing further development and extension.

The human value justice also has wide-ranging political relevancy, such as in the strivings of egalitarianism in political democracy and other systems of rule. As such, justice is a major human value that embraces most aspects of social life. This value is to be understood in the deep Vedic sense of 'Ahimsa', being universal in implying respect for all living beings.

What Makes a Leader?

It was Daniel Goleman who first brought the term "emotional intelligence" to a wide audience with his 1995 book of that name. Goleman found that while the qualities traditionally associated with leadership–such as intelligence, toughness, determination, and vision–are required for success, they are insufficient. Truly effective leaders are also distinguished by a high degree of emotional intelligence, which includes self-awareness, self-regulation, motivation, empathy, and social skill.

These qualities may sound "soft" and unbusinesslike, but Goleman found direct ties between emotional intelligence and measurable business results. While emotional intelligence's relevance to business has continued to spark debate over the past two decades, Goleman's article remains the definitive reference on the subject, with a description of each component of emotional intelligence and a detailed discussion of how to recognize it in potential leaders, how and why it connects to performance, and how it can be learned.

The Five Components of Emotional Intelligence at Work

	Definition	Hallmarks
Self-Awareness	The ability to recognize and understand your moods, emotions, and drives, as well as their effect on others	Self-confidence, realistic self-assessment, self-deprecating sense of humor
Self-Regulation	The ability to control or redirect disruptive impulses and moods the propensity to suspend judgement-to think before acting	Trustworthiness and integrity, comfort with ambiguity, openness to change
Motivation	A passion to work for reasons that go beyond money or status a propensity to pursue goals with energy and persistence	Strong drive to achieve, optimism, even in the face of failure, organizational commitment
Empathy	The ability to understand the emotional makeup of other people skill in treating people according to their emotional reactions	Expertise in building and retaining talent, cross-cultural sensitivity, service to clients and customers
Social Skill	Proficiency in managing relationships and building networks an ability to find common ground and build rapport	Effectiveness in leading change, persuasiveness, expertise in building and leading teams

Every business person knows a story about a highly intelligent, highly skilled executive who was promoted into a leadership position only to fail at the job. And they also know a story about someone with solid–but not extraordinary–intellectual abilities and technical skills who was promoted into a similar position and then soared.

Such anecdotes support the widespread belief that identifying individuals with the “right stuff” to be leaders is more art than science. After all, the personal styles of superb leaders vary: Some leaders are subdued and analytical; others shout their manifestos from the mountaintops. And just as important, different situations call for different types of leadership. Most mergers need a sensitive negotiator at the helm, whereas many turnarounds require a more forceful authority.

However, the most effective leaders are alike in one crucial way: They all have a high degree of what has come to be known as emotional intelligence. It's not that IQ and technical skills are irrelevant. They do matter, but mainly as "threshold capabilities"; that is, they are the entry-level requirements for executive positions.

But the research, along with other recent studies, clearly shows that emotional intelligence is the sine qua non of leadership. Without it, a person can have the best training in the world, an incisive, analytical mind, and an endless supply of smart ideas, but he still won't make a great leader.

Self-Awareness

Self-awareness is the first component of emotional intelligence–which makes sense when one considers that the Delphic oracle gave the advice to "know thyself" thousands of years ago. Self-awareness means having a deep understanding of one's emotions, strengths, weaknesses, needs, and drives. People with strong self-awareness are neither overly critical nor unrealistically hopeful. Rather, they are honest–with themselves and with others.

People who have a high degree of self-awareness recognize how their feelings affect them, other people, and their job performance. Thus, a self-aware person who knows that tight deadlines bring out the worst in him plans his time carefully and gets his work done well in advance. Another person with high self-awareness will be able to work with a demanding client. She will understand the client's impact on her moods and the deeper reasons for her frustration. "Their trivial demands take us away from the real work that needs to be done," she might explain. And she will go one step further and turn her anger into something constructive.

Self-awareness extends to a person's understanding of his or her values and goals. Someone who is highly self-aware knows where he is headed and why; so, for example, he will be able to be firm in turning down a job offer that is tempting financially but does not fit with his principles or long-term goals. A person who lacks self-awareness is apt to make decisions that bring on inner turmoil by treading on buried values. "The money looked good so I signed on," someone might say two years into a job, "but the work means so little to me that I'm constantly bored." The decisions of self-aware people mesh with their values; consequently, they often find work to be energizing.

How can one recognize self-awareness? First and foremost, it shows itself as candor and an ability to assess oneself realistically. People with high self-awareness are able to speak accurately and openly–although not necessarily effusively or confessionally–about their emotions and the impact they have on their work. For instance, one manager was skeptical about a new personal-shopper service that her company, a major department-store chain, was about to introduce. Without prompting from her team or her boss, she offered them an explanation: "It's hard for me to get behind the rollout of this service," she admitted, "because I really wanted to run the project, but I wasn't selected. Bear with me while I deal with that." The manager did indeed examine her feelings; a week later, she was supporting the project fully.

Such self-knowledge often shows itself in the hiring process. Ask a candidate to describe a time he got carried away by his feelings and did something he later regretted. Self-aware candidates will be frank in admitting to failure – and will often tell their tales with a smile. One of the hallmarks of self-awareness is a self-deprecating sense of humor.

Self-awareness can also be identified during performance reviews. Self-aware people know – and are comfortable talking about – their limitations and strengths, and they often demonstrate a thirst for constructive criticism. By contrast, people with low self-awareness interpret the message that they need to improve as a threat or a sign of failure.

Self-aware people can also be recognized by their self-confidence. They have a firm grasp of their capabilities and are less likely to set themselves up to fail by, for example, overstretching on assignments. They know, too, when to ask for help. And the risks they take on the job are calculated. They won't ask for a challenge that they know they can't handle alone. They'll play to their strengths.

Consider the actions of a mid - level employee who was invited to sit in on a strategy meeting with her company's top executives. Although she was the most junior person in the room, she did not sit there quietly, listening in awestruck or fearful silence. She knew she had a head for clear logic and the skill to present ideas persuasively, and she offered cogent suggestions about the company's strategy. At the same time, her self-awareness stopped her from wandering into territory where she knew she was weak.

Despite the value of having self-aware people in the workplace, the research indicates that senior executives don't often give self-awareness the credit it deserves when they look for potential leaders. Many executives mistake candor about feelings for "wimpiness" and fail to give due respect to employees who openly acknowledge their shortcomings. Such people are too readily dismissed as "not tough enough" to lead others.

In fact, the opposite is true. In the first place, people generally admire and respect candor. Furthermore, leaders are constantly required to make judgment calls that require a candid assessment of capabilities–their own and those of others. Do we have the management expertise to acquire a competitor? Can we launch a new product within six months? People who assess themselves honestly–that is, self-aware people–are well suited to do the same for the organizations they run.

Self-Regulation

Biological impulses drive our emotions. We cannot do away with them–but we can do much to manage them. Self-regulation, which is like an ongoing inner conversation, is the component of emotional intelligence that frees us from being prisoners of our feelings. People engaged in such a conversation feel bad moods and emotional impulses just as everyone else does, but they find ways to control them and even to channel them in useful ways.

Imagine an executive who has just watched a team of his employees present a botched analysis to the company's board of directors. In the gloom that follows, the executive might find himself tempted to pound on the table in anger or kick over a chair. He could leap up and scream at the group. Or, he might maintain a grim silence, glaring at everyone before stalking off.

But, if he had a gift for self-regulation, he would choose a different approach. He would pick his words carefully, acknowledging the team's poor performance without rushing to any hasty judgment. He would then step back to consider the reasons for the failure. Are they personal – a lack of effort? Are there any mitigating factors? What was his role in the debacle? After considering these questions, he would call the team together, lay out the incident's consequences, and offer his feelings about it. He would then present his analysis of the problem and a well-considered solution.

Why does self-regulation matter so much for leaders? First of all, people who are in control of their feelings and impulses – that is, people who are reasonable – are able to create an environment of trust and fairness. In such an environment, politics and infighting are sharply reduced and productivity is high. Talented people flock to the organization and aren't tempted to leave. And self-regulation has a trickle-down effect. No one wants to be known as a hothead when the boss is known for her calm approach. Fewer bad moods at the top mean fewer throughout the organization.

Second, self-regulation is important for competitive reasons. Everyone knows that business today is rife with ambiguity and change. Companies merge and break apart regularly. Technology transforms work at a dizzying pace. People who have mastered their emotions are able to roll with the changes. When a new program is announced, they don't panic; instead, they are able to suspend judgment, seek out information, and listen to the executives as they explain the new program. As the initiative moves forward, these people are able to move with it.

Sometimes they even lead the way. Consider the case of a manager at a large manufacturing company. Like her colleagues, she had used a certain software program for five years. The program drove how she collected and reported data and how she thought about the company's strategy. One day, senior executives announced that a new program was to be installed that would radically change how information was gathered and assessed within the organization. While many people in the company complained bitterly about how disruptive the change would be, the manager mulled over the reasons for the new program and was convinced of its potential to improve performance. She eagerly attended training sessions–some of her colleagues refused to do so – and was eventually promoted to run several divisions, in part because she used the new technology so effectively.

Many of the bad things that happen in companies are a function of impulsive behavior. People rarely plan to exaggerate profits, pad expense accounts, dip into the till, or abuse power for selfish ends. Instead, an opportunity presents itself, and people with low impulse control just say yes.

By contrast, consider the behavior of the senior executive at a large food company. The executive was scrupulously honest in his negotiations with local distributors. He would routinely lay out his cost structure in detail, thereby giving the distributors a realistic understanding of the company's pricing. This approach meant the executive couldn't always drive a hard bargain. Now, on occasion, he felt the urge to increase profits by withholding information about the company's costs. But he challenged that impulse – he saw that it made more sense in the long run to counteract it. His emotional self-regulation paid off in strong, lasting relationships with distributors that benefited the company more than any short-term financial gains would have.

The signs of emotional self-regulation, therefore, are easy to see: a propensity for reflection and thoughtfulness; comfort with ambiguity and change; and integrity–an ability to say no to impulsive urges.

Like self-awareness, self-regulation often does not get its due. People who can master their emotions are sometimes seen as cold fish – their considered responses are taken as a lack of passion. People with fiery temperaments are frequently thought of as "classic" leaders – their outbursts are considered hallmarks of charisma and power. But, when such people make it to the top, their impulsiveness often works against them. In my research, extreme displays of negative emotion have never emerged as a driver of good leadership.

Motivation

If there is one trait that virtually all effective leaders have, it is motivation. They are driven to achieve beyond expectations

– their own and everyone else's. The key word here is 'achieve'. Plenty of people are motivated by external factors, such as a big salary or the status that comes from having an impressive title or being part of a prestigious company. By contrast, those with leadership potential are motivated by a deeply embedded desire to achieve for the sake of achievement.

In a nutshell, we can say that leaders do not need externalities to get motivated. Infact, they are motivated by their internal ecology of a deep desire and faith that they are 'here' to really make a change.

Empathy

Of all the dimensions of emotional intelligence, empathy is the most easily recognized. We have all felt the empathy of a sensitive teacher or friend; we have all been struck by its absence in an unfeeling coach or boss. But when it comes to business, we rarely hear people praised, let alone rewarded, for their empathy. The very word seems unbusinesslike, out of place amid the tough realities of the marketplace.

But, empathy doesn't mean a kind of "I'm OK, you're OK" mushiness. For a leader, that is, it doesn't mean adopting other people's emotions as one's own and trying to please everybody. That would be a nightmare – it would make action impossible. Rather, empathy means thoughtfully considering employees' feelings – along with other factors – in the process of making intelligent decisions.

For an example of empathy in action, consider what happened when two giant brokerage companies merged, creating redundant jobs in all their divisions. One division manager called his people together and gave a gloomy speech that emphasized the number of people who would soon be fired. The manager of another division gave his people a different kind of speech. He was up-front about his own worry and confusion, and he promised to keep people informed and to treat everyone fairly.

The difference between these two managers was empathy. The first manager was too worried about his own fate to consider the feelings of his anxiety-stricken colleagues. The second knew intuitively what his people were feeling, and he acknowledged their fears with his words. Is it any surprise that the first manager saw his division sink as many demoralized people, especially the most talented, departed? By contrast, the second manager continued to be a strong leader, his best people stayed, and his division remained as productive as ever.

Empathy is particularly important today as a component of leadership for at least three reasons: the increasing use of teams; the rapid pace of globalization; and the growing need to retain talent.

Consider the challenge of leading a team. As anyone who has ever been a part of one can attest, teams are cauldrons of bubbling emotions. They are often charged with reaching a consensus – which is hard enough with two people and much more difficult as the numbers increase. Even in groups with as few as four or five members, alliances form and clashing agendas get set. A team's leader must be able to sense and understand the viewpoints of everyone around the table.

That's exactly what a marketing manager at a large information technology company was able to do when she was appointed to lead a troubled team. The group was in turmoil, overloaded by work and missing deadlines. Tensions were high among the members. Tinkering with procedures was not enough to bring the group together and make it an effective part of the company.

So, the manager took several steps. In a series of one-on-one sessions, she took the time to listen to everyone in the group – what was frustrating them, how they rated their colleagues, whether they felt they had been ignored. And then she directed the team in a way that brought it together: She encouraged people to speak more openly about their frustrations, and she helped people raise constructive complaints during meetings. In short, her empathy allowed her to understand her team's emotional makeup. The result was not just heightened collaboration among members but also added business, as the team was called on for help by a wider range of internal clients.

Globalization is another reason for the rising importance of empathy for business leaders. Cross-cultural dialogue can easily lead to miscues and misunderstandings. Empathy is an antidote. People who have it are attuned to subtleties in body language; they can hear the message beneath the words being spoken. Beyond that, they have a deep understanding of both the existence and the importance of cultural and ethnic differences.

Finally, empathy plays a key role in the retention of talent, particularly in today's information economy. Leaders have always needed empathy to develop and keep good people, but today the stakes are higher. When good people leave, they take the company's knowledge with them.

That's where coaching and mentoring come in. It has repeatedly been shown that coaching and mentoring pay off not just in better performance but also in increased job satisfaction and decreased turnover. But what makes coaching and mentoring work best is the nature of the relationship. Outstanding coaches and mentors get inside the heads of the people they are helping. They sense how to give effective feedback. They know when to push for better performance and when to hold back. In the way they motivate their protégés, they demonstrate empathy in action.

Social Skill

The first three components of emotional intelligence are self-management skills. The last two, empathy and social skill, concerns a person's ability to manage relationships with others. As a component of emotional intelligence, social skill is not as simple as it sounds. It's not just a matter of friendliness, although people with high levels of social skills are rarely mean-spirited. Social skills, rather, is friendliness with a purpose: moving people in the direction you desire, whether that's agreement on a new marketing strategy or enthusiasm about a new product.

Socially skilled people tend to have a wide circle of acquaintances, and they have a knack for finding common ground with people of all kinds – a knack for building rapport. That doesn't mean they socialize continually; it means they work according to the assumption that nothing important gets done alone. Such people have a network in place when the time for action comes.

Social skill is the culmination of the other dimensions of emotional intelligence. People tend to be very effective at managing relationships when they can understand and control their own emotions and can empathize with the feelings of others. Even motivation contributes to social skill. Remember that people who are driven to achieve tend to be optimistic, even in the face of setbacks or failure. When people are upbeat, their "glow" is cast upon conversations and other social encounters. They are popular, and for good reason.

Because it is the outcome of the other dimensions of emotional intelligence, social skill is recognizable on the job in many ways that will by now sound familiar. Socially skilled people, for instance, are adept at managing teams – that's their empathy at work. Likewise, they are expert persuaders – a manifestation of self-awareness, self-regulation, and empathy combined. Given those skills, good persuaders know when to make an emotional plea, for instance, and when an appeal to reason will work better. And motivation, when publicly visible, makes such people excellent collaborators; their passion for the work spreads to others, and they are driven to find solutions.

Socially skilled people, however, don't think it makes sense to arbitrarily limit the scope of their relationships. They build bonds widely because they know that in these fluid times, they may need help someday from people they are just getting to know today.

Is social skill considered a key leadership capability in most companies? The answer is yes, especially when compared with the other components of emotional intelligence. People seem to know intuitively that leaders need to manage relationships effectively; no leader is an island. After all, the leader's task is to get work done through other people, and social skill makes that possible. A leader who cannot express her empathy may as well not have it at all. And a leader's motivation will be useless if he cannot communicate his passion to the organization. Social skill allows leaders to put their emotional intelligence to work.

It would be foolish to assert that good-old-fashioned IQ and technical ability are not important ingredients in strong leadership. But the recipe would not be complete without emotional intelligence. It was once thought that the components of emotional intelligence were "nice to have" in business leaders. But now we know that, for the sake of performance, these are ingredients that leaders "need to have."

Evaluating Emotional Intelligence

Most large companies today have employed trained psychologists to develop what are known as "competency models" to aid them in identifying, training, and promoting likely stars in the leadership firmament. The psychologists have also developed such models for lower-level positions.

The objective of the recent researches was to determine which personal capabilities drove outstanding performance within these organizations, and to what degree they did so. The capabilities was grouped into three categories: purely technical skills like accounting and business planning; cognitive abilities like analytical reasoning; and competencies demonstrating emotional intelligence, such as the ability to work with others and effectiveness in leading change.

Analysing the data, produced some dramatic results. To be sure, intellect was a driver of outstanding performance. Cognitive skills such as big-picture thinking and long-term vision were particularly important. But when it was calculated - the ratio of technical skills, IQ, and emotional intelligence as ingredients of excellent performance, emotional intelligence proved to be twice as important as the others for jobs at all levels.

Moreover, the analysis showed that emotional intelligence played an increasingly important role at the highest levels of the company, where differences in technical skills are of negligible importance. In other words, the higher the rank of a person considered to be a star performer, the more emotional intelligence capabilities showed up as the reason for his or her effectiveness. When star performers were compared with average ones in senior leadership positions, nearly 90% of the difference in their profiles was attributable to emotional intelligence factors rather than cognitive abilities.

Other researchers have confirmed that emotional intelligence not only distinguishes outstanding leaders but can also be linked to strong performance. The findings of the late David McClelland, the renowned researcher in human and organizational behavior, are a good example. In a 1996 study of a global food and beverage company, McClelland found that when senior managers had a critical mass of emotional intelligence capabilities, their divisions outperformed yearly earnings goals by 20%. Meanwhile, division leaders without that critical mass underperformed by almost the same amount. McClelland's findings, interestingly, held as true in the company's U.S. divisions as in its divisions in Asia and Europe.

In short, the numbers are beginning to tell us a persuasive story about the link between a company's success and the emotional intelligence of its leaders. And just as important, research is also demonstrating that people can, if they take the right approach, develop their emotional intelligence.

Human Values- Lessons from Lives of Great Leaders, Administrators & Reformers

This section has been dealt with by first giving the names of some great leaders, administrators and reformers and then by mentioning the basic human values which they possessed and practiced throughout their personal and public life.

Leader and Administrator: Meaning and Differences

Administration is defined as a process of working with and through others to accomplish the agreed goals efficiently. An administrator then is one who is responsible for carrying out this process. Administrative theorists describe the essential roles and tasks of administration as planning, organizing, leading and controlling. Management is also concerned with tasks such as planning, coordinating, directing, defining objectives, supporting the work of others, and evaluating performance. Thus a similarity exists between administration and management.

However, leadership is the exercise of high level conceptual skills and decisiveness. It is envisioning mission, developing strategy, inspiring people, and changing culture.

Administrators are appointed. They have a legitimate power base and can reward and punish. Their ability to influence is based upon the formal authority inherent in their positions. In contrast, leaders may either be appointed or emerge from within a group. Leaders can influence others to perform beyond the actions dictated by formal authority. In this sense, managers/administrators get other people to do, but leaders get other people to want to do.

Another distinguishing factor between leaders and administrators is that leaders initiate new structures or procedures to achieve organizational goals or objectives, whereas administrators utilize existing structures or procedures for this purpose. In other words, administrators are concerned with shaping existing structures and processes of the organization to produce desired results, whereas leaders have a commitment or vision and shape people around their commitment or vision. An administrator is concerned with carrying out policies, while a leader formulates policies. An administrator does the thing right, while a leader does the right thing.

Reformer

A reformer is a person who wants to improve the prevailing conditions in society by bringing about reforms in any area of human activity e.g., politics, social customs and religion.

A social reformer is a disputant who advocates for reforms to discard the social evils like child marriage, untouchability, female-foeticide, etc. Examples of social reformers include Dr. B.R. Ambedkar, Raja Rammohan Roy and Ishwar Chandra Vidyasagar. These people have been able to make an impact on the people with their philosophy and great work for the society.

A political reformer is one who promises voters that he will address poor practices or questionable activities in government. Some of the main issues addressed to by the political reformers are like corruption in government offices, right of equality to all, transparency and accountability in government activities.

A religious reformer is someone who feels that a certain religion has overstepped its bounds or has lost its original message, purpose or goal, and who attempts to bring it back to its pure state.

Leader, Administrator and Reformer: Common Values

Though they may require different attitudes, skills and traits, but all great leaders, administrators and reformers share certain values which they adhered to even in their toughest time. An attitude to serve the people, uplifting the downtrodden, impartiality and integrity, benevolence and compassion - they all became the hallmark of their personality and character. In the next section, the same has been duly elaborated.

Human Values- Lessons from the Lives of Great Leaders

There have been many great leaders over the world like Mahatma Gandhi, Abraham Lincoln, Martin Luther King Jr., Nelson Mandela, Vaclav Havel, Aung San Su Ki and Mother Teresa and ohers who lived and did all the things on the basis of basic human values. Some of these human values which manifested from their works and lives are as follows-

- Love for Justice
- Selflessness
- Respect for Humanity
- Dignity for All
- Loving and caring behaviour
- Peace loving (non-violence)
- Benevolence
- Compassion

Human Values- Lessons from the Lives of Great Administrators

Our generation has been fortunate enough to have some of the best administrators in the world. Some of them are as follows- Verghese Kurien, M.S. Swaminathan, Sam Pitroda, E. Sreedharan, C.D. Deshmukh, I.G. Patel, V.P. Menon and GVG Krishnamurthy. From the work of these administrators, it is evident that they have been guided by various professional and human values throughout their lives. Here, we mention some of the professional and human values which have been the source of their guidance in the field of administration-

- Integrity
- Non-discrimination
- Discipline
- Citizenly-duty
- Social Equality
- Lawfulness
- Sense of ethical accountability

- Loyalty
- Courage
- Solidarity and respect

Human Values- Lessons from the lives of Great Reformers

In India, there have been many social reformers like Kabir, Guru Nanak Dev, Raja Rammohan Roy, Ishwar Chandra Vidyasagar, Swami Vivekananda, etc. who challenged the prevailing evil customs and enlightened the society on various social and religious matters. We observe that their lives exhibit following values-

- Respect for Humanity
- Dignity for all
- Humanism
- Reason and Inquiry for seeking the truth
- Kindness and compassion
- Contentment
- Social Equality

Inculcating Values- Role of Family

Family being the first and major agency of socialization has great influence and bearing on the development of the child. It has been shown by various studies that most of the children who are successful/great achievers and well-adjusted come from the families where sustaining wholesome relationships exist. Therefore, it is the home, which sets the pattern for the child's attitude towards people and society, aids intellectual growth in the child and supports his aspirations and good values.

Inculcating Values- Role of Society

Administrative morality is a part and parcel of the general morality of the community. Finer said, "The ethics of every profession will be found, on close analysis, to be not much higher and not much lower than the general decency of the nation as a whole. Their nature, at the best, is powerfully moulded by the level of the surrounding and prevailing civilization."

The success of any government depends upon the effective collaboration of its citizens. All the books of civics would emphasise civic consciousness for the progress of the country. This is possible only if our educational system and mass media are reoriented to character-building among the people. People's character is the ultimate source which can supply kinetic energy for modernisation and development.

There is a great need to infuse civic consciousness, patriotism and discipline among the citizens through education, adult education and functional literacy. The members of all the communities would then cooperate with the personnel in the public services. And the personnel in the public services would work hard to bring about all round development of the people.

Inculcating Values- Role of Educational Institutes

Education is a process of initiating the learners into a form of life that is considered as desirable to preserve and promote. Education necessarily involves transmission of values. However, these changes are to be brought about employing such procedures as do not violate the freedom and autonomy of the learner.

The different aims of education-development of the human personality, pursuit of knowledge, preservation of culture, development of character, promotion of social justice, scientific temper, democracy, secularism and so on are just so many varied educational expressions of the constituents of the good life. It is through education that society seeks to preserve and promote its cherished values.

Global Standard of Ethical Behavior

Harems may still be a popular culture in Islamic countries like Turkey, Saudi Arabia or Egypt, but in countries like India and U.S., it is considered illegal. In a conservative Indian society, an Indian man having an intimate relationship with any woman other than his legally wedded wife is looked down upon and considered unethical and immoral. Similarly, while very low wages may be considered unethical in rich, advanced countries; but developing nations may be acting ethically if they encourage investment and improve living standards by accepting low wages. Likewise, when people are malnourished or starving, a government may be wise to use more fertilizer in order to improve crop yields, even though that means settling for relatively high levels of water pollution and this may qualify as an ethical practice.

Context must shape ethical practice. The theory behind such predicaments between what constitutes ethical and unethical practices is absolutism, which is based on three problematic principles. Absolutists believe -

(i) There is a single list of truths.

(ii) That these can be expressed only with one set of concepts

(iii) They call for exactly the same behavior around the world.

It clashes with many people's belief that different cultural traditions must be respected. In some cultures, loyalty to a community – family, organization, or society – is the foundation of all ethical behavior. The Japanese, for example, define business ethics in terms of loyalty to their companies, their business networks, and their nation. The Americans, for example, define business ethics in terms of liberty, the U.S. tradition of rights emphasizes equality, fairness, and individual freedom. In India, its traditional societal values hold that work is not a tool to realize one's self but a means to fulfill family and caste responsibility. It is hard to conclude that truth lies on one side or the other, but an absolutist would have us select just one. The notion of a right evolved with the rise of democracy in post-Renaissance Europe and the United States, but the term is not found in either Confucian or Buddhist traditions. We all learn ethics in the context of our particular cultures, and the power in the principles is deeply tied to the way in which they are expressed. Internationally accepted lists of moral principles, such as the United Nations' Universal Declaration of Human Rights, draw on many cultural and religious traditions. As philosopher Michael Walzer has noted, "There is no Esperanto of global ethics." There is no international consensus on standards of business conduct.

Balancing the Extremes: Three Guiding Principles

There is a need to distinguish between practices that are merely different and those that are wrong. For relativists, nothing is sacred and nothing is wrong. For absolutists, many things that are different are wrong. Neither extreme illuminates the real world of business decision making. The answer lies somewhere in-between.

When it comes to shaping ethical behavior, companies must be guided by three principles -

- Respect for core human values, which determine the absolute moral threshold for all business activities.
- Respect for local traditions.
- The belief that, context matters when deciding what is right and what is wrong.

Respecting differences is a crucial ethical practice. This is what forms the pedestal of the principle of secularism in multi-religious and multi-ethnic India. Tolerance is respecting differences in each other's religions, values, views and opinions. People often equate respect for local traditions with cultural relativism. That is incorrect. Some practices are clearly wrong. Union Carbide's tragic experience in Bhopal, India, provides one example. The company's executives seriously underestimated how much on-site management involvement was needed at the Bhopal plant to compensate for the country's poor infrastructure and regulatory capabilities. In the aftermath of the disastrous gas leak, the lesson is clear: Companies using sophisticated technology in a developing country must evaluate that country's ability to oversee its safe use.

Some activities are wrong no matter where they take place. But some practices that are unethical in one setting may be acceptable in another. For instance, the chemical EDB, a soil fungicide, is banned for use in the United States. In hot climates, however, it quickly becomes harmless through exposure to intense solar radiation and high soil temperatures. As long as the chemical is monitored, companies may be able to use EDB ethically in certain parts of the world.

How Will You Measure Your Life?

How can I be happy in my career? How can I be sure that my relationship with my family is an enduring source of happiness? And how can I live my life with integrity?

Surprisingly, the most powerful motivator isn't money; it's the opportunity to learn, grow in responsibilities, contribute, and be recognized. That's why management, if practiced well, can be the noblest of occupations; no others offer as many ways to help people find those opportunities. It isn't about buying, selling, and investing in companies, as many think.

The principles of resource allocation can help people attain happiness at home. If not managed masterfully, what emerges from a firm's resource allocation process can be very different from the strategy management intended to follow. That's true in life too: If you're not guided by a clear sense of purpose, you're likely to fritter away your time and energy on obtaining the most tangible, short-term signs of achievement, not what's really important to you.

And just as a focus on marginal costs can cause bad corporate decisions, it can lead people astray. The marginal cost of doing something wrong "just this once" always seems alluringly low. You don't see the end result to which that path leads. The key is to define what you stand for and draw the line in a safe place.

This is a personal code of ethics and in no way do I expect anyone other than myself to follow it. This is a very important distinction, because most policies are held by a community whether it be secular laws or religious morals.

As Lao Tzu said, ``Losing the way of life, men rely on goodness; losing goodness, they rely on laws."

Given below is an ideal personal ethical policy, one may adopt, to guide their life in the right direction.

Personal Ethical Policy

1. To not purposely cause harm to any other human being

This means, among other things, that one shall not fight in any war; as the saying, 'an eye for an eye makes the whole world blind'. The way to resolve issues is through knowledge, good communication, and brotherly love. One cannot take the life or freedoms of another to protect their own or promote their ideals.

2. To promote and demonstrate my ideals through my actions not through enforcing them on others

Every religion is based on the ideals of love, brotherhood and harmony. The Bible itself points out the hypocrisy in people, who profess themselves as religious and try to enforce ideals they themselves do not follow.

3. To respect the ideas, lifestyles, religions, and ideals of others

If one's own personal ideas and lifestyles are in conflict with the above stated policies, then one may not respect them, but one need not break the above policies in order to change them.

One of the greatest problems that still exist is stereotyping. People have unfavorable opinions of those who are gay, transgender, or atheists or even belonging to religion other than their own. It is through fear and not respect, that certain people and groups stand taller than others.

4. To abide by the rules, codes of conduct, and laws of the community around me as long as they are not in conflict with my higher principles

A large part of respect is doing things in acceptance with those around me. It would be rude and disrespectful to do otherwise. Governments, unfortunately sometimes, fight a never ending battle to appease both the people and the many lobbyists that try to do things that are in opposition of what is desirable by the people or healthy for society. One may choose to fight them for a higher cause.

5. To be honest and trustworthy, and to disclose my feelings

One of the main principles that allows a society to work efficiently and without violence is honesty. Hiding information by lying often causes more harm than good. One should also make good their promises to others and make sure that their words are followed by action. Included in this statement, is the need to be honest when there is something that you disagree with. Too often problems occur by hiding feeling in order to preserve temporary peace.

6. To respect the property of others as long as we have the concept of property

An important moral value is that of not stealing. That means not only stealing from others, but from nature and the commons. We live in a consumption crazed society. We have too often been caught up in the desire to consume, that through our consumption we have, in essence, promoted companies to take the lives of others and put them in sweat shops to produce for us. With more respect for what is shared, rather than hoarding what "I own," one can live at greater peace with their neighbors and global community. At the same time, one must respect what others own and hopefully through sharing through volunteerism, donations, and community service one can encourage others to see the power in this mode of thinking.

7. To promote through self-education, observation, reading, conversation, and writing the sciences or the understanding of the world around me. And to use this understanding to the benefit of myself and others through both action and sharing of knowledge.

Human progress comes through understanding, not ignorance. One can only do more damage in trying to change that which one does not understand. It is the coupling of knowledge, gained through experience, education, communication, and observation, with self-respect and love of others that will enable one to make positive contributions to society.

8. To give proper credit to others

When someone does something for someone or for a group, one should not take credit for their work. Also if one gets an idea from a source, he/she should reference it.

9. To honor confidentiality

In helping others there may be cases where they may confess certain actions or share private information with you. When they share such information, one should not spread this information except when you may find that keeping it confidential is in violation of my higher principles. For example, if someone described to me how they were going to kill someone else, one should report such a threat.

10. To promote a higher quality of life for myself and others

Probably one of the key desires of a human being is the betterment of their current situation. For some, this drives them insane to the point where this encompasses their whole being. In doing so, they diminish the lives of others through a pursuit to increase the quality of their own lives.

11. To live a healthy lifestyle and do things that will aid others in healthy living

Through exercise, good eating habits, and general good self-care, one can ease the burdens of their life and others. This includes promoting health facilities, open space, parks, hiking trails, and other public places of recreation. It also means eating right and not partaking in activities that could lead to diseases and other health problems.

12. To not have others fear me

Fear is the key to perpetuating hatred. Fear is capitalized by governments, religions, and individuals to get others to do what they want. It often leads to rebellion and war. There are much better ways to promote conformance, the best of which I found is to work together with whatever social group that surrounds me and agree through compromise and cooperation what rules should be established. It would be a great error to assume that others have the same morals as one do and that one should promote those morals with fear in order to benefit the lives of those around them.

How Personal Ethics Produce Effective Leaders

Leadership is a relationship between people. Therefore, the ability to ethically influence others is a major determinant of an effective leadership. In his book, 'Ethics and Leadership', William Hitt lists three requirements of leaders that allow them to capitalize on their ability to influence ethical conduct. These three requirements are:

(1) Achieve an understanding of ethics

(2) Serve as a role model in making ethical decisions.

(3) Develop and implement a plan of action for promoting ethical conduct on the part of his or her staff.

Ethics and effective leadership function as a cause and effect relationship Effective leadership is a result of ethical behavior. Good ethics promote all the characteristics necessary for effective leadership.

Followers must first choose to accept a leader before leadership may commence. Followers accept leaders they can trust. India chose Jawaharlal Nehru as its first Prime Minister because they trusted his ideas and vision for the independent India. Trust is considered the glue of leadership and promotes long-term success. The good ethical decision-making template adopted leads to the best decision possible under the given circumstances.

A leader with an understanding of ethics, a history of ethical decision-making and the ability to develop and execute plans of action shows stability, empathy, integrity and resolve. All of these traits shown in a leader's track record will infuse a greater sense of trust within followers. Current behavior also affects trust developed between leaders and potential followers.

After a leader is accepted, effective leadership is partially determined by the relationships a leader is able to form with others. People are unable to form true relationships with others before they understand themselves. Good ethics require a person to develop an understanding of personal beliefs. This allows a leader to identify his or her inner self and outer self. Without good ethics a person has no direct path or self knowledge. This prevents effective leadership because true relationships cease to exist.

It is unrealistic to sketch leadership as a black and white concept. Society's complexity increases the need for leadership to be seen as a 'colorful' term. One type of leadership style may be ideal for one situation, but not another. The problem with leadership today is lack of ethics. With a decrease in ethical conduct and today's increasing interactions with networks, leaders have no true direction and are less accountable for their actions. Leadership will become ethical and effective once ethics are adopted as the backbone of good leadership. It is difficult to imagine, that a change so dependent on a leader's understanding of ethics, could directly impact society's ethical conduct.

The importance of understanding ethics, motivation to act as a role model and developing a plan of action for an organization were discussed because of their importance regarding development of good leadership. These key aspects suggest personal ethics positively affecting leadership and when made a priority for leaders, will produce ethical and effective leadership.

◆◆□□◆◆

3

ATTITUDE

The Concepts Discussed in this Unit

- Attitude and its Components
- Structure and Functions of Attitude
- Cognitive Dissonance
- Social Influence
- Persuasion
- Office Politics
- Public and Administrative Attitude

Attitude

Attitude refers to a psychological tendency that is expressed by evaluating a particular object with some degree of favour or disfavour. "Object" includes people, things, events, and issues. Attitudes are the feelings and beliefs that determine the behaviour of the persons. They provide framework for responding in a particular fashion.

The attitudes may be positive or negative. The positive attitudes yield favourable behaviour and the negative attitudes yield unfavourable behaviour. Therefore all variables must be identified and analysed which help in the formation of favourable attitudes. The persons having positive attitudes towards the job and organisation may contribute their best to the organisation.

Components of Attitude- 'CAB'

There are three components of attitude, generally called CAB-

- Cognitive
- Affective
- Behavioural

A. Cognitive Component

The cognitive component of attitudes refers to the beliefs, thoughts, and attributes we associate with an object. When you form your opinion or judgment on the basis of available information and decide whether you have a favourable or unfavourable opinion on that, it is the cognitive part of an attitude we are talking about.

B. Affective Component

The affective component of attitudes refers to feelings or emotions (e.g. fear, sympathy, hate, like, pleasure) linked to an attitude object. Affect plays a very important role in attitude formation. Also, affect is a common component in attitude change, persuasion, social influence, and even decision making. How we feel about an outcome may override purely cognitive rationales.

C. Behavioural Component

The behavioural component of attitudes refers to a tendency or a predisposition to act in a certain manner. The predisposition to behave in a certain manner may be caused by affective and cognitive components. For example, the things you believe about something (for e.g. 'my boss is corrupt and is misusing company funds') and the way you feel about it (e.g. 'I can't stand working for him') may have some effect on the way you are predisposed to behave (e.g. 'I'm going to quit my present job').

Categories of Attitudes- Explicit and Implicit

Attitudes are divided into two categories as given below. The basic difference between these two types of attitudes is conscious and unconscious cognition.

- Explicit attitudes- Result of Conscious Cognition
- Implicit attitudes- Result of Unconscious Cognition

Explicit Attitudes

They are characterized as the attitudes which are the result of conscious cognition, which means person is aware of his or her attitude. Explicit attitudes are mostly affected by recent or more accessible events. These types of attitudes represent cognitive and motivational factors behind the assigning of attitude, more deliberate thinking is involved in it. Since self is involved more consciously in it so sometimes it is known as 'self reported attitude'.

Implicit Attitudes

Implicit attitudes are derived from past memories, which are rooted in unconscious cognition. Sometimes unknowingly we attribute something for object that is implicit attitude which are governed by our past memories (sometimes forgotten memories). We do not deliberately think over it. It just comes out from our self without an intention. Since cognitive part is absent in these attitudes so these are largely influenced by affective experiences and because of these experiences priming affects implicit attitudes than explicit attitudes, which means implicit attitudes are more easily accessible if there is influence of contextual factors. Since implicit attitudes are more closely related to affective experiences and the 'culture' is a collection of certain feelings and emotions, therefore, cultural biases have appreciable impact on implicit attitudes.

Formation of Attitude

Right from our birth onwards, we are exposed to a wide

variety of stimuli, both directly and indirectly, which lead to ourself acquiring particular attitudes towards the attitudinal object. It is believed that attitudes are by and large acquired as a result of various life experiences, although a small but growing body of evidence indicates that attitudes may be influenced by genetic factors, too.

A number of theories have been used to identify what lead to formation and maintenance of attitudes-

- Classical or Pavlovian Conditioning
- Instrumental Conditioning
- Observational Learning
- Genetic Factors

Classical or Pavlovian Conditioning

Classical Conditioning is a process of behaviour modification by which a subject comes to respond in a desired manner to a previously neutral stimulus that has been repeatedly presented along with an unconditioned stimulus that elicits the desired response. A stimulus is a factor that causes a response in an organism.

Conditioning is usually done by pairing the two stimuli, as in Pavlov's classic experiments. Pavlov presented dogs with a ringing bell followed by food. The food elicited salivation (unconditioned stimulus), and after repeated bell-food pairings the bell also caused the dogs to salivate. In this experiment, the unconditioned stimulus is the dog food as it produces an unconditioned response, saliva. The conditioned stimulus is the ringing bell and it produces a conditioned response of the dogs producing saliva.

Classical conditioning could play a role in establishing some of the emotional components of attitudes and prejudice. Further, through classical conditioning, people may come to have powerful attitudinal reactions to social objects even in the absence of first-hand experience. Hence, children who hear repeated pairings of words in their parents' conversations (such as say, Muslims-Aggressive, Muslims-Fundamentalists) throughout their early years of development may come to adopt such negative attitudes themselves– without even meeting them.

Instrumental Conditioning

According to this, behaviours that are followed by positive

outcomes tend to be strengthened, while those that are followed by negative outcomes are suppressed. The degree to which attitudes are verbally or non-verbally reinforced by others will affect the acquiring and maintenance of attitudes.

For example, early in your life, if your parents and teachers praised you for doing well in studies, you may have doubled your efforts and developed a positive attitude towards studies. However, if your friend's parents did not acknowledge her achievements in studies, she would have probably developed a negative attitude toward studies.

Observational Learning

The phenomenon by which a person acquires new forms of behaviour or thought simply by observing the rewards and punishments that others get is called observational learning.

Genetic Factors

Genetic factors also play a role in shaping attitudes of an individual. However, they play stronger role in shaping some attitudes than others. For example, attitudes involving gut-level preferences (say a preference for a certain kind of food) may be more strongly influenced by genetic factors than attitudes that are more cognitive in nature (say attitudes towards environment conservation).

Structure of Attitude and the Dynamic Properties of Attitude

The structure of attitudes can be examined by exploring their (CAB's) dynamic implication for information processing, retrieval and judgment. These dynamic properties of attitudes are as follows-

- Attitude Strength
- Attitude Accessibility
- Attitude Ambivalence

Attitude Strength

Attitudes differ in strength. Strong, central attitudes are attitudes that refer to important attitude objects that are strongly related to the self. These attitudes are often related to important values. Attitude strength involves several dimensions, such as - certainty, intensity and extremity, attitude origin, personal importance.

Attitude Accessibility

Attitude accessibility refers to the ease with which attitudes can be retrieved from memory, in other words how readily available is an attitude about an object, issue, or situation. Attitudes that are more accessible from memory are more predictive of behaviour, influence what messages are attended to, and how those messages are processed, and are more stable across time.

Attitude Ambivalence

People can also be conflicted or ambivalent toward an object, meaning that they simultaneously possess both positive and negative attitudes toward the object in question. Attitude ambivalence refers to the fact that our evaluations of objects, issues, events, or people are not always uniformly positive or negative; our evaluations are often mixed, consisting of both positive and negative reactions.

Attitude ambivalence may also be the result of conflicting values. For example, you may have an ambivalent attitude towards arranged marriages, because on one hand you value obedience and adherence to parents; on the other, you may value freedom and personal choice.

Moral Attitude

All humans hold and express moral attitudes. Moral attitudes include moral judgments such as "right or wrong" and "blameworthy or praiseworthy". Moral attitudes are also present when states of the world are described in terms of "good" or "bad" and "better or worse" as this tells us something about the values and worldview of the speaker. Big differences exist in what people describe as good or right. These differences in attitudes are found when comparing cultures or groups (cultural level) but also when comparing individuals within the same group of people (individual level) and when comparing the attitudes the same person expresses under different circumstances (situational level).

Moral values are the highest among all natural values. Goodness, purity, truthfulness, humility of man rank higher than genius, brilliancy, exuberant vitality, than the beauty of nature or of art, than the stability and power of a state. What is realized and what shines forth in an act of real forgiveness, in a noble and generous renunciation; in a burning and selfless love, is more significant and more noble, more important and more eternal than all cultural values. The moral values were also recognized by the great minds, such as Socrates, or Plato, who continually repeated that it is better to suffer injustice than to commit it. This pre-eminence of the moral sphere is, above all, a basic proposition of the Indian cultural ethos.

Fundamental moral attitude are–

- Reverence is a **feeling** of **respect** or **admiration** for someone or something.
- Faithfulness is the **quality** of being **faithful** to someone or something.
- Awareness of responsibility.
- Veracity is the **quality** of being **true, honest,** or **accurate.**
- Goodness is the **personal quality** of being **morally** good.

Political Attitude

An attitude is a predisposition to respond to a particular stimulus (i.e., object) in a particular manner. Political attitudes are those directed toward political objects, such as political candidates, political issues, political parties, and political institutions.

Political Attitude and Personality Traits

Scholars have acknowledged that certain personality traits influence our political leanings and orientation. In this regard, following five traits are usually mentioned-

- **Extraversion-** It implies an energetic approach to the social and material world and includes traits such as sociability, activity, assertiveness, and positive emotionality.
- **Agreeableness-** Agreeableness contrasts a pro-social and communal orientation toward others with antagonism and includes traits such as altruism, tender-mindedness, trust, and modesty.
- **Conscientiousness-** It describes socially prescribed impulse control that facilitates task and goal directed behaviour, such as thinking before acting, delaying gratification, following norms and rules, and planning, organizing, and prioritizing tasks.
- **Emotional Stability-** Emotional Stability describes even-tempered-

ness and contrasts with negative emotionality, such as feeling anxious, nervous, sad and tense.

- **Openness to Experience-** Openness to Experience (versus closed-mindedness) describes the breadth, depth, originality, and complexity of an individual's mental and experiential life.

Each trait may have different effects on our economic ideology (free market vs interventionist) as well as on our social ideology (pro-choice/pro-equality vs pro-life/pro-tradition). Four of these five traits are expected to influence our ideology. The only exception is extraversion, which is expected to influence political participation but not ideology.

> **Political Ideology**
>
> Political ideology is a certain ethical set of ideals, principles, doctrines, myths or symbols of a social movement, institution, class, or large group that explains how society should work and offers some political and cultural blueprints for a certain social order. A political ideology largely concerns itself with how to allocate power and to what ends it should be used. An ideology is a collection of ideas. Typically, each ideology contains certain ideas on what it considers to be the best form of government (e.g. democracy, theocracy, etc.) and the best economic system.

Functions of Attitude

Katz takes the view that attitudes are determined by the functions they serve for us. People hold given attitudes because these attitudes help them achieve their basic goals. The main functions of attitude are as following-

- **Utilitarian/Instrumental Function-** This function is very close to the concept of instrumental conditioning. Katz says we develop positive attitudes towards those objects that are associated with rewards and develop negative attitudes toward those that are associated with punishment.
- **Knowledge Function-** We all have a need to attain some degree of meaningful, stable, clear, and organised view of the world. Attitudes satisfy this knowledge function by providing a frame of reference for organizing our world so that it makes sense. Using such a cognitive perspective, attitudes serve as

schemas that help us in organizing and interpreting social information.

- **Ego-Defensive Function-** Some attitudes serve to protect us from acknowledging basic truths about ourselves or the harsh realities of life. These can help a person cope with emotional conflicts and protect self-esteem.
- **Value Expressive Function-** Value-expressive attitudes show who we are, and what we stand for. Hence they serve to demonstrate one's self-image to others and to express our basic values.
- **Social Identity Function-** Social identity function refers to the informativeness of attitudes for person impressions, or how much attitudes appear to convey about the people who hold them. For example, the purchase of an Indian flag on the Republic Day may be driven primarily by social identity goals.

Influence of Attitudes on Behaviour

Various research works suggested that attitudes simply influence behaviour. In fact, the earliest definitions defined attitudes largely in terms of behaviour. For example, Allport defined attitudes as tendencies or predispositions to behave in certain ways in social situations.

The most recent research works suggest that the extent of influence of attitudes on behaviour depends upon certain factors. Following are the factors, which determine degree of influence of attitudes on behaviour:

- **True versus Expressed Attitudes-** True attitude and the expressed attitudes differ because both are subject to other influences. A measured or expressed attitude may not be a person's true attitude especially when dealing with sensitive issues, contexts and situations.
- **One Instance versus Aggregate-** The effects of an attitude becomes more apparent when we look at a person's aggregate or average behaviour rather than at an individual act. For example, research shows that people's general attitude towards religion poorly predicts whether they will go and worship next weekend. That's because the weather, their mood, their health, how far the temple is from residence, alternative plans, etc.

also influence attendance. However, religious attitudes do predict quite well the total quantity of religious behaviours over a long time.

- **Level of Attitude-behaviour Specificity-** Attitude specificity, the extent to which attitudes are focused on specific objects or situations (e.g. 'Do you like to eat Mexican food?') rather than on general ones (e.g. 'Do you like to go out to eat?') is clearly an important factor in the attitude-behaviour link. Attitudes can predict behaviour if both attitudes and behaviours are measured at similar levels of specificity.
- **Self Awareness-** Another aspect that influences behaviour is the self awareness, that is, how far the individual is aware of the attitudes that he or she holds. So long as persons are not aware of their attitudes, these attitudes will tend to influence the individuals' behaviours all the more intensely. On the other hand if an individual is aware of his attitude, he or she will be quite self conscious about it and may hesitate showing it in their behaviours.
- **Attitude Strength-** The stronger the attitudes are, the greater their impact on behaviour. Attitudes formed through direct experience are stronger, and as a result, are better predictors of later behaviour. The attitudes of more personally involved individuals will be stronger predictors of behaviour than attitudes of the less involved.
- **Attitude Accessibility-** Attitude accessibility refers to the ease with which attitudes can be retrieved from memory. The more accessible attitudes can be spontaneously and automatically activated without our conscious awareness, and can guide our behaviour without us being necessarily aware of them.

Cognitive Dissonance

Cognitive dissonance is the mental stress or discomfort experienced by an individual who holds two or more contradictory beliefs, ideas, or values at the same time, performs an action that is contradictory to one or more beliefs, ideas or values, or is confronted by new information that conflicts with existing beliefs, ideas, or values. An individual who experiences inconsistency (dissonance) tends to become psychologically uncomfortable, and is motivated to try to reduce this dissonance–as well as actively avoid situations and information likely to increase it.

Social Psychology

Throughout its history, humankind has been motivated to war, terrorism, ethnic cleansing, genocide, racist hysteria, religious intolerance and extremism, mass suicide and many other forms of irrational and pathological behaviour. In order to give answers to why these atypical behaviours occur, and to understand the motivation behind people's social or political behaviour, we need to tap into the fields of social psychology.

Social psychology is defined as 'the scientific study of the ways that people's behaviour and mental processes are shaped by the real or imagined presence of others'. Social psychologists emphasise the core observation that human behaviour is a function of both the person and the situation. Accordingly, each and every individual contributes and expresses a set of distinctive personal attributes to a given situation. However, each specific situation also brings a unique set of forces to bear on an individual, compelling him or her to act in different ways in different situations.

Social Influence

Social influence is a major topic in social psychology and looks at how individual thoughts, actions and feelings are influenced by social groups.

The studies related to social Influence focus on ways in which behaviour is influenced by outside factors, and this influenced behaviour could be behaviour of a whole group or of discrete individuals. A varicty of scholars have defined ways in which individuals respond to social influences. The individual in an influential situation could comply, identify, or internalize, as defined by Professor Herbert Kelman, a well-known scholar in this subject.

'Compliance' might look like agreement with others in a social setting, but below the surface, the person has by no means been fully convinced. For instance, if in a conversation between two people, one person makes a racist comment and the other is offended and says nothing, this could be viewed as complying, so that the appearance of agreement is maintained.

Other people may 'identify' with an influential person whom they either idolize from a distance or know intimately. A person whose wardrobe choice is solely influenced by the fashion advice of a supermodel would be expressing identification. Alternately, people may 'internalize' belief systems of others. If the two conversing people in the previous example both express racist statements, they are showing they have a belief system in common, however repugnant it may be, and they have moved far past the point of compliance.

Another way of viewing these influences is to discuss the types of things that may affect the behaviour of an average person. These include the person's family, family beliefs, and family structure. Other factors, particularly as people progress to adulthood, become involved. What other people are doing in peer groups is a powerful influence.

Types of Social Influence

Social influence in general refers to how one can be influenced or affected by others. Baumeister and Bushman (2010) divided types of social influence into two major forms:

- Normative Influence
- Informative Influence

Normative Influence

Normative influence is related to the act of going along with the crowd in the effort to be liked and to be accepted. This is related to a human's fundamental need to belong to a social group thus increasing their chances to survive. By agreeing on common beliefs, values, attitudes and behaviour, there will be a higher level of acceptance and survival possibilities.

Asch's Classic Study (1955)

Asch's study showed the powerful effect of normative influence. In his experiment, participants had to judge the length of the line [which line (A, B or C) matches the first line?]. He found that people were willing to get along and make decisions consistently with the group even when the group made clear errors. Asch concluded that people would rather make wrong decisions than to suffer social rejection.

Informational Influence

In informative influence, we go along with the crowd because we think the crowd knows more than we do. This is especially during ambiguous situations when we do not have a clear idea of what to do. Two types of situations produce informational influence:

- **Ambiguous situations:** When people do not know what to do.
- **Crisis situations:** When people do not have time to think what to do.

In these situations, people follow others because they think others know what they are doing.

Principles of Social Influence

Principles of Social Influence play on fundamental human instincts and can be exploited both intentionally and unintentionally by professional influence agents. Many of these may seem like obvious tactics that advertisers and influence agents will utilize to sway our opinion. However, when we are not prepared to scrutinize and resist them, these principles will often work subliminally and quite powerfully. Thus, an important part of resisting these common influence tactics is awareness of their fundamental operating principles, contexts in which they are most easily provoked, and the best methods to avoid falling prey to them.

Following are the six principles of Social Influence-

- **Reciprocity-** This principle is based on the fact that people give back what another has given to them. It might seem obvious, and it is indeed one of the main rules of our society. Test for example yourself: smile to the people you meet, how many do reply with a smile?
- **Consistency-** This principle is based on the desire from people to be consistent with their previous actions, opinions and assertions. Combined with the idea of commitment, we can notice that people when having decided upon something, they will do whatever they can to remain to that point of view.
- **Social Proof-** This principle illustrates that people often decided what to do by looking at what similar others have done. This principle functions even better as people are in a condition of uncertainty. Uncertain people can be influenced easily.

- **Liking-** Liking is based on the principle that people are more easily influenced by those they like. It consists of several elements: physical attractiveness, similarity, praise, contact and association.
- **Authority-** The influential power of authority is undeniable. The first form is parental authority. Authority is reflected in different forms such as clothes, titles and - as it seems - automobiles.
- **Scarcity-** The rule of scarcity depicts that items and opportunities become more desirable as they are less accessible. The level of being unique or the fact they represent elsewhere unattainable advantages, are strong influential elements. Another example that speaks out for itself is censorship. The censored subjects or things are always the more interesting ones and do gain automatically in importance. "Limited editions" or "last week for sale" are slogans that have an immediate effect.

Meaning of Norms

Social norms are group-held beliefs about how members should behave in a given context. Sociologists describe norms as informal understandings that govern society's behaviours, while psychologists have adopted a more general definition, recognizing smaller group units, like a team or an office, may also endorse norms separate or in addition to cultural or societal expectations.

A norm gives a person a rule of thumb for how they should behave. However, a rational person only acts according to the rule if it is optimal for them.

Persuasion

Persuasion is an attempt to change a person's attitude and the scientific study can be traced back to Carl Hovland. He was the social psychologist from Yale University who studied the effect of films on the morale of a soldier. He and other co-researchers then studied what can be termed as "who says what to whom" as:

- **Who: the source:** The "who" component represents the source of the message.
- **Says what: the message:** The "says what" is the actual message being conveyed.

- **To whom: the audience:** The "whom" refers to the audience.

Constructs of Persuasion

They represent three things that are important in persuasion:

- The source of persuasion
- The message
- The audience

Two important criteria that can determine the effectiveness of the persuasion are credibility and likeability.

Source Credibility

A source can be viewed as credible if he/she is seen as an expert and can be trusted. Experts can be influential because people assume they know what they are talking about but at the same time they also have to be trustworthy.

Source Likeability

A source is likeable if he/she is seen as similar and attractive. The halo effect refers to the assumption that because people have desirable traits such as physical attractiveness, they may also have other desirable effects such as intelligence. This is why a message delivered by an attractive person is perceived as more powerful than a message delivered by a less attractive person.

Resisting Persuasion

There are various ways to resist persuasion:

- Attitude Inoculation
- Forewarned
- Stockpile
- Defences against Influence

Attitude Inoculation

In attitude inoculation, people who have been exposed to counter arguments have more resistance to the persuasion. This is consistent with the idea that a person becomes more resistant to diseases if he/she has been exposed to weakened doses of viruses that strengthen his/her immune system.

Forewarned

Being forewarned of the persuasion attempts can protect a person from being persuaded. When people believe someone is trying to persuade them and may take away their freedom of choice, they experience psychology reactance that motivates them to resist such attempt. This is because forewarning influences several cognitive processes that play an important role in persuasion. Forewarning gives us the opportunity to come up with counter arguments that can refute the message and gives people more time to recall relevant facts that can help refute the message. When people do the exact opposite of what they are being persuaded to do; this is called negative attitude change or a boomerang effect.

Boomerang Effect

In social psychology, the boomerang effect is "the theory of psychological reactance that is supported by experiments showing that attempts to restrict a person's freedom often produce an anti-conformity "boomerang effect". For example, in social marketing, the boomerang effect occurs as a result of attempted attitude change. If someone makes a strong attempt to change a prospect's attitude toward a subject, the prospect will counter with an equally strong response, even if, prior to the confrontation, the prospect held a weak attitude toward the subject.

Stockpile

A person with physical, cognitive and social resources is more likely to resist persuasion. In dealing with persuasion, a healthy, well-read person may be able to resist it better.

Defences against Influence Techniques

These techniques to resist persuasion are related to the techniques of social influences. If we are aware of various social influence techniques and perceive them as tricks to persuade us, we can resist them better.

Office Politics

Most of us cringe when we think about office politics. It's a disgusting, immoral mess that we try to avoid. After all, who wants to participate in backstabbing, lying, cheating, blaming, and playing people against each other? But, there may be some individuals who take a slightly less offensive view of office politics and see it as controlling agendas, building covert alliances, protecting access to key leaders, and holding "meetings before the meeting." No matter what your take, it's not surprising that honest people don't want to get involved.

But are politics at work inherently dirty?

The truth is that, just being a member of an organization is a political act. And, as a matter of fact, one influences his co-workers all the time in any organization voluntarily or involuntarily. It's how we get things done. And, to influence, we must have power, the real currency in workplaces. Most people want it. All of us need it. In healthy organizations, we "get" power, or are granted power, by virtue of our ability to inspire and provide vision. We also get power as a result of what we can do for people. In companies that value people and results, we are granted power because we help to create a vibrant climate and a resonant culture that is ripe with hope, enthusiasm, and a can-do spirit. In such companies power is used well - for the good of people and the enterprise.

Office politics is really just the art of influencing others, so we can get stuff done at work. And, despite the bad rap that politics gets, successfully engaging in politics requires the development and use of good qualities. Influencing people and getting things done requires confidence and this is grounded in self-awareness, self-management, and a desire to move people for the good of all. The combination of emotional intelligence and, what the late great David McClelland, called socialized power, can result in, influence strategies that make people enjoy working together toward common goals.

Politics can also be toxic. There may be Machiavellian-type people in your organization who indulge in lying for personal gain, self-aggrandizement, clever flattery, and people taking delight in crushing weaker team members and enemies. Such individuals tend to have lower emotional intelligence – particularly when it comes to empathy and recognizing emotions. These people are destructive, self-centered Horrors to work with. You might want to protect yourself from such influences.

But leaders must not avoid office politics. People who actively steer clear of politics don't do what the best leaders always do – build strong, positive relationships that serve a purpose beyond simple friendship. Such relationships are result of truly seeing people and valuing them for who they are. They are grounded in empathy as well as authenticity and mutual respect. In such relationships, we come to know what drives people and what they value, and can hence inspire, motivate, and influence in a way that makes them feel valued. Office politics can be seen as an art of getting along with others and of putting yourself in positions where your work will be noticed.

Public & Administrative Attitude & Governance in India

Perception, orientation and attitude of public as well as administrators play a significant role in governance of a country. Considering this, it becomes important to understand the current dynamics of public and administrative perception and attitude. This would be dealt in following sub-headings:

- Administration vis-à-vis Public
- People's perception in administration
- Administration's attitude towards people
- Reconciling of public and administration

Administration vis-à-vis Public

There is great increase in the functions and powers of administration in our times. Until the advent of the twentieth century, in the night watchman state, the role of administration vis-à-vis public was limited to maintenance of law and order, administration of justice and collection of revenue.

However, the night-watchman concept was replaced by the social service or welfare state which meant 'administration' looking after health, education, industry, agriculture and everything under the sun that affected the 'public'. In the process, the administration became, highly complex and technical and necessitated 'the specialist' - the man with expertise to perform administrative responsibilities. The task of administration via-a-vis the public in developing countries like India is still more difficult owing to the fact that vast majority of our people are poor, illiterate, tradition-minded and lack initiative necessary for the nation-building task. To overcome this and generate zeal for development is a great challenge. The Administration is expected to act as an agent of social change and economic transformation; one who motivates people and brings about their active participation in the implementation of the developmental schemes.

People's Perception in Administration

For the successful working of public administration there is a need for active citizenship and self-help. Public administration in a democracy must be based on public consent and support. In fact, it is a two-way process. People's mind must be known to the administration and at the same time, administrators' efforts must be actively supported by the people. The aspirations of the people must be taken into consideration by the administration. People will respect administration only when it responds to the aspirations of the people.

It has already been pointed out that vast majority of people in India are illiterate, poor, ignorant and apathetic towards development. To urge public to participate actively in the process of development is a challenge before the Indian administration. In order to cope up with this problem, they must know what public's attitude is towards administration.

In this regard, various studies (including studies conducted by Administrative Reform Commission) have pointed out that the citizens hold the bureaucracy in low esteem. The relationship between the citizens and public servants lack cordiality and mutual understanding. Numerous complaints are always made by the public against the civil servants regarding delays in disposal of cases, corruption, lack of proper communication, evasion of responsibility, exploitation, favouritism, arbitrary and high-handed functioning and indifferent attitude. The public is suspicious about the integrity of the public officials and regard 'right contacts', 'political pulls', 'speed money', etc. as the ways and means to get the things done. The public feels that the bureaucrats are too much rule-minded and totally devoid of any human considerations. They are reluctant in disposal of work, thus creating scope for middle-men who exploit the poor and needy people.

Administration's Attitude towards the People

The Indian bureaucracy is, by and large, urban-middle class, whereas while performing their duties they mainly deal with the rural masses that are illiterate and poor. Thus, there is a wide cultural gap between the class of administrators and the vast majority of masses. The 'administrators' find the masses indifferent and the masses view the administrators as apathetic and disinterested in the development process.

The bureaucracy points out that the people are unaware of their rights, have no understanding of the problems and make no efforts to get their grievances redressed. Further, they do not have adequate knowledge of the rules, regulations and procedure of administration. To some extent, people are pessimistic about the assistance from the bureaucracy in getting things done. The civil servants complain that there is too much interference in the administration and that the citizens try to bring pressure through local politicians. The administrators, on such occasions, find it most difficult to work honestly and freely.

Another standing complaint about the masses is that the general masses neither take keen interest in their own affairs nor do they show any initiative for bettering their own prospects. Further, they hardly support or co-operate with the civil servants who honestly try to bring about the change in the society. In fact, in a number of cases, the civil servants are looked at with contempt, suspicion, fear and distrust.

Reconciliation of Public and Administration

In the light of the divergent views held by the both the citizens and the administrators about each other, to admit the claims of both of them is difficult task. How to reconcile these mutually opposed views? Can the relationship between the two be improved? C.P. Bhambri - the educationist and professor of Political Science - opines that something more needs to be done to change apathetic attitude of the citizens and make them positive and participate in the functioning of the administration. According to him, some linkages need to be established between the citizens and administration in order to achieve the goals of mutual trust and appreciation and for this the existing hiatus between the citizen and the administration in India needs to be bridged.

As regards the linkage between the public and the administrators, public administration must be well aware as to what public thinks of the administrative acts and policies as well as what hopes and desires are entertained by the public. In this regard, a thorough rapport can be established between the administration and the public by creating an agency of public relations in the administration itself. Such an agency enables the administration to learn about the public wishes and aspirations, to advise the public about what it should think, desire and do in specific spheres of activities, to cultivate satisfactory contact between the officials and about what the administration is doing for the public.

The egalitarian goals enshrined in the Constitution of our country cannot be attained through the efforts of administration only. If the total transformation in our traditional and backward society is to take place rapidly, the tendency of our people to rely on government administration for fulfilment of each and every need will have to be abandoned. Public must shed away its negative role and adopt positive role. The aspirants of progress and prosperity cannot hold apathetic attitude towards their own issues of development. They cannot remain detached from and indifferent toward activities of the democratic government. Their initiative, interest, wholehearted support and active cooperation together with direct participation in governmental activities must be mustered behind the enormous efforts of our public administration.

The success of the administration depends upon the involvement, commitment, dedication and sacrifice with which the public servants put their efforts for the welfare of the teeming millions in the country. The administrators should see that they interact with the common people, especially those from rural areas because it is them who need the administrators most. In this regard, following has been rightly noted by Hota Committee- "Introduction of sophisticated technology alone would not make the administration people-friendly unless higher civil servants' have a proactive attitude and reach out to the common people. They must spend much more time in field visits, inspections, tours and night halts in remote and rural areas."

Case Study I

Mr. X is posted as a Deputy Commissioner of Police (DCP) in suburbs of Mumbai, Maharashtra. The shopkeepers of a nearby market complex, which lies in the area of Mr. X, are facing the problem of extortion. They have to give a fixed amount for their earning to a local goon, who extorts money from them by threatening them of dire consequences, even loss of life. The shopkeepers, due to fear, did not prefer to report the matter to the police station as they feel that police is unable to protect them and their family. Mr. X comes to know about this problem of shopkeepers through one of his sources. He also comes to know that the goon has the support of an influential politician, who belongs to the ruling party in Maharashtra. In the lack of initiatives taken by shopkeepers, it is difficult for Mr. X, to gather enough evidence against that goon. Under these circumstances what are the options available with Mr. X to deal with the issue? Is it correct for him to leave the issue unnoticed till shopkeepers come to him for registering of complain?

This case comes under the following topics:

- Moral and Political Attitudes
- Social Influence and Persuasion
- Tolerance and Compassion towards Weaker Section
- Conscience as a Source of Ethical Guidance
- Work Culture

Premise: The given case pertains to the relation between police and public. The lack of faith in the police has deterred those in problem (shopkeepers) to register the case. In the lack of evidence, it is difficult for the police officer to gather evidence against the goon as none of the shopkeepers is ready to give statement. The case also highlights the work culture of police and their ability of social persuasion. That the goon is having the support of an influential politician, the case also represents the dilemma of a police officer to act against him, especially in the lack of evidence. This also exemplifies the politicization of crime.

Answer: Police is the primary agency to maintain law and order. It has the duty to ensure that rule of law and those responsible for its violation should be brought in the court of law.

In this light, it can be clearly argued that the first and foremost role of policing is to work for a crime-free society where everyone can live with peace and harmony.

In this light, it is clear that it is the duty of Mr. X to take the issue seriously and work for the resolution of the problems faced by the shopkeepers. So it is needless to say that he can't let the issue unnoticed and wait for shopkeepers to reach him with complain. But the problem faced by him is that shopkeepers are unwilling to register the case and any suo moto interference without any evidence can invite disciplinary actions against Mr. X. Besides, his conduct can be questioned which may affect his service records. Moreover he would also face political hurdles as the goon enjoys the support of an influential politician belonging to the ruling party. Under these circumstances, the following course of action can be best suited to Mr. X:

- As an immediate step, Mr. X should deploy some police officers in the area to verify the truth of the fact, as taking any action without adequate knowledge would be against the rule of law.
- Once verified, Mr. X should meet with the Representatives of Association of Shopkeepers in that area and assure them that police is for their protection only. If possible he should try to talk with the shopkeepers directly, through the Association.
- The role of Association is important here, because the case highlights that shopkeepers lack faith in police and any attempt of direct talk may result in the failure.
- As the politician from the ruling party is involved, Mr. X should also convey the case to his superiors and take their advice on the matter that how they had dealt such cases, if any, in the past.
- The key in solving the issue lies in persuasion of shopkeepers to register the complaint against the goon, without any fear. If Mr. X is unable to do this, he should try to collect evidence with the help of some of the local persons (not shopkeepers).
- He may seek help from media but this should be done with utmost care as it may impact the image of the politician and hence the party in power. Any such attempt, without adequate evidence is detrimental to the service record of Mr. X.

- Once the evidence is gathered, he should take strict action against the goon by arresting him without fear or favour. This would establish a good reputation of police among public.
- In the long term, Mr. X should also work to enhance the police-public relations, citing the prevailing situation. A good public-police relation is key to crime-free society and effective policing.

Case Study II

You are the head of the Panchayat in a village of Haryana. A boy of lower caste, belonging to your village, has fled with the daughter of an upper caste landlord. Both were in love and wanted to marry but the caste conflict prevailing in the village was the biggest hurdle to them. Both families were at crossroads on this issue. So they planned to marry in the court of the nearby city and then came back to village. After their return to village, they met you before meeting the family members. On account of your position in village, they requested you to convince their family members. The village has witnessed many caste conflicts and honour killings in the past on account of such incidents. You know that the matter may aggravate caste related tensions. Under this circumstance, what are the possible courses of action available to you? Is it correct for you to ask the newly married couple to leave the village immediately and help them in the same? Come out with the best possible step, which you feel should be taken by you as a Village Headman.

Premise: In the given case, the dilemma faced by you is two-fold. If you choose to inform the family members of the couples about their return, the life of the couple would be under threat. On the other hand, if you try to convince the family members, your position as a village headman will be in jeopardy, given the prevailing social customs in the village. Moreover, the situation may give rise to another caste related tensions.

This case comes under the following topics:

- Morality
- Social Aptitude

- Conscience as a source of Ethical Guidance
- Human Values

Answer: A village headman is a public authority. He has a dual role to play. He has to uphold the social customs of the village community and at the same time he has to ensure that the custom of the village should not be in contravention of the rule of law. In this sense, he acts as a link between village and State authorities. In this light, it can be clearly argued that first and foremost duty of Village headman is to secure the life of the couple and provide them safe environment in village with proper dignity. He also has to ensure that, on account of this, no caste related tensions takes place. For this, he can go for following courses of actions:

- As a first step, he should call the meeting of Panchayat members along with some reputed village elders if any, discuss the issue with them and try to take them in confidence for acceptance of the couple.
- Along with members, he should decide the date to convene village assembly, where he would discuss the matter among members of village community.
- Citing the possibility of occurrence of caste related tensions, before convening the assembly, he should meet with the concerned District Collector and narrate him the entire issue. He should then ask for deployment of police force on the date of convening of assembly.
- This is necessary in order to ensure that village assembly should be convened peacefully irrespective of the final decisions taken.
- He should also ask the Collector to provide adequate security to the couple as the village has witnessed many instances of honour killings.
- He should also seek the help of local NGO, who is actively involved in the development of village and has a good reputation among members of village community. This would make it easier for him to convince the village members regarding acceptance of couple.
- Mere asking the couples to leave the village would not solve

the core problem as the case may get repeated in the future. Moreover, even if the couple leaves the village, possibilities of caste related tension would prevail in the village.

The Constitution of India guarantees liberty and equality to citizens. Putting restriction of the private decisions in the name of social customs amounts to violation of the rights conferred by the Constitution. As pointed out by the Supreme Court of India, in the absence of liberty, democracy would fail to realize its true meaning.

◆◆❐❐◆◆

4

APTITUDE & FOUNDATIONAL VALUES FOR CIVIL SERVICES

The Concepts Discussed in this Unit

- Foundational Values
- Values and Public Values
- Aptitude
- Integrity
- Uprightness
- Impartiality
- Political Neutrality
- Objectivity, Empathy and Tolerance
- Compassion and its Significance in Civil Services

Foundational Values

Why are Values Important?

Values are essential components of organisational culture and instrumental in determining, guiding and informing behaviour. For civil services, adherence to high-level public service values can generate substantial public trust and confidence. Conversely, weak application of values or promotion of inappropriate values can lead to reductions in these essential elements of democratic governance, as well as to ethical and decision-making dilemmas.

In spite of the enactment of laws, rules and regulations to ensure impartiality, honesty and devotion among the civil services, there still remains a vast area of administrative discretion which cannot be controlled by formal laws, procedures and methods. In such areas, says Otto Kircheeimer, "no supervision from above can be as effective as an automatic control on the minds of those possessing it and creating standards of efficiency as well as honesty". Any deviation from the common standards under such circumstances is likely to be discovered sooner or later and rooted out. In the words of McCanny, in all such areas "they must answer to their own conscience, to their own senses of dignity and pride, to the opinions of their fellow-men and above all, to their devotion, to their own honest effort to define the total welfare and to serve it".

Values for Civil Service

There are obvious constraints to attempts to prescribe values which public services should adopt, given the variety of historical, social and cultural forces at play in different parts of the world. But according to Second Administrative Reform Commission, integrity, dedication to public service, impartiality, political neutrality, anonymity, etc. are said to be the hallmarks of an efficient civil service. The Commission is also of the opinion that in addition to commitment to the Constitution these values should include:

a. Adherence to the highest standards of probity, integrity and conduct
b. Impartiality and non-partisanship
c. Objectivity

d. Commitment to the citizens' concerns and public good

e. Empathy for the vulnerable and weaker sections of society.

The public servant's duties today remain many, complex and often seemingly contradictory. This is reflected in the values and principles underpinning those duties - including maintaining confidentiality, acting in the public interest, providing quality advice, avoiding conflicts of interest, ensuring accountability to a range of actors and treating all colleagues equitably.

In performing each of these tasks, public servants employ a range of values as a means to guide their behaviour and to assist them in steering a course through multiple requirements. Therefore, clarity over an organisation's values is essential and the appropriateness of a particular value-system is worthy of regular consideration in the context of changing expectations and functions. Poor clarity or uncertainty about values can not only lead to ethical and decision-making dilemmas, but also affects organisational coherence by diminishing team spirit, creating organisational confusion and weak external communication.

While a core set of public service values is necessary, it is also true that different values will also apply to different parts of the public service. For example, a distinction may be made between technical, regulatory and administrative tasks, or between those parts of a bureaucracy in direct contact with the public and those which are not.

The values most commonly associated with public service are:

- Honesty and integrity
- Impartiality
- Respect for the law
- Respect for the persons
- Diligence
- Economy and effectiveness
- Responsiveness
- Accountability

Values and Public Values

The term value generally refers to the worth of something; in government, public value refers to an appraisal of what is created and sustained by government on behalf of the public. The notion of creating public value is most frequently attributed to Moore who argues that the aim of managerial work in the public sector is to create public value just as the aim of managerial work in the private sector is to create private value.

In government, public values are those values that provide normative consensus about:

- the rights, benefits, and prerogatives to which citizens should (and should not) be entitled;
- the obligations of citizens to society, the state, and one another; and
- the principles on which governments and policies should be based.

Public value is created when policy and management strategies are politically legitimate, feasible, and sustainable, operationally possible and practical, and of substantive value to the citizenry, according to Moore. In contrast, public value is destroyed when the wrong decisions are made about the needs to be satisfied, the strategies to satisfy the selected needs, and the processes to produce and deliver services.

Today, the notion of creating public value has become part of an overall managerial philosophy wherein public services are oriented toward outcomes that meet local needs and are authorized by service users and their communities.

In contrast, 'values' are complex personal judgements based on knowledge as well as an emotional reaction. They are emotion-cognitive assessments that are relatively stable and guide behaviour.

Public Values Pluralism

Public values pluralism suggests that several values and value orientations can simultaneously exist in society, all of which may be equally valid, correct, and fundamental. Moreover, incompatible values may also be incommensurable, in that they cannot be objectively measured, compared, or ordered in terms of importance. There can be little argument that public administration is characterized by a plurality of sets of values and a multiplicity of value systems that are often in conflict with one another.

For example, there are many public values and sets or clusters of public values, such as impartiality and lawfulness on the one hand, and efficiency and effectiveness on the other, that one might consider being intrinsically contradictory or even hybrid. Likewise, the pursuit of liberty can become incompatible with the pursuit of equality, the pursuit of justice with that of mercy, and the pursuit of spontaneity with that of security.

Values Training

Though the informal communication of values is of great importance, formal methods of developing values offer substantial benefits. The most well-known formal method is induction courses for new staff involving case-studies and role-play scenarios. The centrality of values to all aspects of public service work should be demonstrated and values statements analysed and expanded on.

Values seminars and workshops offer employees the opportunity to explore the meaning and practical application of values to everyday workplace scenarios. They also help to develop employees' awareness of the organisation and how it can achieve its objectives within a value-bounded framework of activity. Indeed the process of defining and examining the values of an organisation provides an opportunity for staff engagement in the development of the future direction of the organisation. The role of values should also be integrated into existing management training and development courses.

An often-overlooked element to values training is the need to demonstrate clear methods by which values conflicts can be managed or what avenues public servants should pursue in order to resolve ethical dilemmas without fear of negative personal consequences. Values conflicts should not be regarded as detrimental to an organisation and learning to cope with such conflicts is part of good public management.

Aptitude

An aptitude is a component of a competency to do a certain kind of work at a certain level, which can also be considered "talent". It is the ability to deal with aspects of the environment and to perform a particular behaviour. Aptitudes may be physical or mental.

Aptitude is also defined as the aptness or quickness to succeed in a specific field of activity. It is a present condition that is indicative of individual's potentialities for future. Thus, aptitude implies the prediction about the individual's future performance.

Attitude and Aptitude

Attitude is the manner, disposition, feeling, position, etc., with regard to a person or thing. It is the way you think about any particular person or thing. 'Aptitude' is a capability or talent innate or acquired for performing some particular task. If you have an aptitude for languages, for instance, you can learn them faster than other people.

Attitude has to do with the character and aptitude has to do with competence. Character is relatively permanent whereas aptitude can be changed and developed.

In public administration, the difference may be understood by the following example: An administrator may be very good in problem solving (aptitude part) but may have the tendency to procrastinate the decisions (attitude part). Also, an administrator may have a good aptitude in resolving the communal issues (aptitude part) but may have a negative attitude towards a particular minority (attitude part) which will naturally influence his overall decisions.

Attributes of a Good Administrator

Paul H Appleby - an important theorist of public administration in democracies - in his report (1961) 'Public Administration for a Welfare State', mentioned following attributes of a good administrator-

- Willingness to assume responsibility
- A steadily enlarging ability to deal with more problems
- A strong bent toward action
- A good listener
- Effective with people
- Capacity to build his own strength by building the competence of his organization

- Capacity to use his institutional resources
- Avoiding using power or authority for their own sake
- Welcoming reports of troublesome things
- A good team-worker
- A good initiator

Integrity

Integrity indicates soundness of moral principles, the character of uncorrupted virtues, uprightness, honesty and sincerity. According to Ministry of Personnel, "Consistently behaves in an open, fair and transparent manner, honours one's commitments and works to uphold the Public service values." Integrity in public affairs and administration is essential; and therefore there must be an insistence on it in every branch of public activity.

A fundamental rule for maintaining civil servants' integrity is to avoid situations which may give rise to a conflict of interest. The following guidelines are relevant:

A. Never use your position in the civil service to benefit yourself or your family, relatives or friends, or any other group of people with whom you have personal or social ties

B. Avoid being placed in a position of obligation to anyone by accepting excessive entertainment or favours such as free service, or indulging in games of chance with subordinates or other people with whom you have official dealings

C. Avoid putting yourself in a position that may arouse any suspicion of dishonesty, or of using your official position to benefit yourself, your family, relations or friends. For example, do not provide advice to any executive search firm if your official duties involve appointment and promotion. In procuring services or goods for your office, do not negotiate with a company in which you or your relatives hold shares. Follow prescribed tender procedures and declare an interest if necessary in the process.

D. Encourage others to consistently follow Public Service values

E. Treat people impartially, regardless of political, social, demographic, geographic, circumstances or bias

F. Enforce law, public service values and rules of conduct even in difficult situations

G. Have the courage and conviction to make and stand by the right decisions, even at significant personal cost

H. Provide honest and frank advice to uphold public interest

I. Ensure full disclosure, by sharing the political implications of the decisions being made

J. Challenge powerful and influential people, and hold them accountable to make the right decisions

K. Stand firm when dealing with unreasonable requests and demands

L. Take accountability for own actions and create a culture for others also to take accountability for their own actions

To maintain integrity of the civil service, it is important that civil servants, even after they have left the service, should continue to conduct themselves in an appropriate manner as the activities which they take up would continue to be seen by the public as a reflection of the culture and character of the civil service. Retired civil servants should act with good sense and propriety in pursuing post-service employment or business and avoid engaging themselves in activities which could be construed as being in conflict with their previous duties in the Government, or might bring the civil service into disrepute, or expose them or the Government to public controversy.

Intellectual integrity: Intellectual integrity is defined as recognition of the need to be true to one's own thinking and to hold oneself to the same standards one expects others to meet. It also means to honestly admit discrepancies and inconsistencies in one's own thought and action, and to be able to identify inconsistencies in one's own thinking.

The opposite of intellectual integrity is **intellectual hypocrisy,** a state of mind unconcerned with genuine integrity. It is often marked by deep-seated contradictions and inconsistencies.

The appearance of integrity means a lot because it affects our image with others. Therefore, hypocrisy is often implicit in the thinking and action behind human behavior as a function of natural egocentric thinking. Our hypocrisy is hidden from us. Though we expect others to adhere to standards to which we refuse to adhere, we see ourselves as fair. Though we profess certain beliefs, we often fail to behave in accordance with those beliefs.

To the extent that one has intellectual integrity, one's beliefs and actions are consistent. One practice what he/she preach, so to speak.

The establishment and maintenance of integrity in public life and public service requires a number of elements, including: legislation, regulations and codes of conduct; a society whose religious, political and social values expect honesty from politicians and officials; professionalism among officials; and a political leadership with the moral and political courage and will to take its responsibility, both public and private, seriously.

The observance of integrity is not a simple thing, if it is practiced properly and conscientiously, it will protect the society from many of its venomous ills. As Sardar V. Patel said, "You will not have a united India if you do not have a good All India Service, which has the independence to speak out its mind and which has a sense of security. I need hardly emphasize that an efficient, disciplined and contented service assured of its prospects as a result of diligent and honest work is the sine qua non of sound administration under a democratic regime, even more than under authoritarian rule". Thus, integrity needs to be given much importance especially in the public life so as to have a harmony in the society.

Integrity as a governing ethics

A strategy based on integrity holds organizations to a more robust standard. While compliance is rooted in avoiding legal sanctions, organizational integrity is based on the concept of self-governance in accordance with a set of guiding principles. From the perspective of integrity, the task of ethics management is to define and give life to an organization's guiding values, to create an environment that supports ethically sound behavior, and to instill a sense of shared accountability among employees. The need to obey the law is viewed as a positive aspect of organizational life, rather than an unwelcome constraint imposed by external authorities.

An integrity strategy is characterized by a conception of ethics as a driving force of an enterprise. Ethical values shape the search for opportunities, the design of organizational systems, and the decision-making process used by individuals and groups. They provide a common frame of reference and serve as a unifying force across different functions, lines of business, and employee groups. Organizational ethics helps define what a company is and what it stands for.

Why integrity is never easy?

All of us know cheating is a bad thing. This is one lesson that the students start learning from a young impressionable age and the principle continues to hold in one form or other, throughout our lives. Yet, a case study on the subject suggests that as many as 95% of such students admit to having engaged in some form of cheating. In hindsight, the students justify the choice as "not really cheating," "no big deal," or something that "everyone else does."

When you'll browse through the mission, vision, or value statements that corporations post on their websites, you'll notice that almost every company includes a statement about integrity. Integrity, it is said, should be the basic building block for doing business. Nobody wants to get involved with a company that lies, cheats, and misleads its customers; nor do people want to work for a company (or an administrator) that is dishonest, corrupt and unethical. Yet it's not that simple, for two reasons: First is the innate human ability to rationalize behavior. For example, when students cheat, as aforesaid, they justify and rationalize their situational behavior, and this way they can still consider themselves to be honest. The reality is that all of us (and not just students) face integrity-based choices on a regular basis. Do we reveal everything to a prospective buyer during due diligence? Is it acceptable to hide certain aspects of our background in a resume? What's considered a legitimate expense on a business trip? How honest should I be when giving feedback to my boss or subordinate? None of these situations have clear answers – and no standard procedure or policy can cover every contingency. As a result, no matter what choice we make, we can convince ourselves that it was made with integrity.

And that leads to the second reason why integrity is so difficult: Everyone defines integrity differently. Falsifying information to one person might be considered an acceptable business practice to another. This is further exacerbated by differences in culture – for example, in some business cultures people are expected to openly do favors for each other, while in other cultures those favors would be considered bribes.

The power of rationalization and the difficulties of definition reveal integrity as a subject that is neither easy nor simple. That's why solely relying on compliance functions, policies, rules, and audits – the integrity police – is usually inadequate. These mechanisms guard against gross and clearly illegal violations of integrity standards, but they do not deal with the integrity choices that we face every day. These choices require personal judgment.

Uprightness

Uprightness is defined as the quality of being honest, responsible, and moral in the perspective of ethics. Every person during their journey of social life tries to be liked and accepted by their peers as well as by themselves. This is crucial to live happily in a social life, everyone knows that without that, social standing may be affected and mental health may falter. Therefore, the quotient of moral uprightness helps in this regard.

Moral uprightness is about personality and behavior of an individual or as a civil servant. Morally upright people encounter less of a resistance socially. They are better liked and more successful because they are seen to be more trustworthy and better for the people around and society. It pays to have morals, if they are closely related to those of the people who surround an individual.

Also, when anyone grows up, they are taught, both by words and by actions, to behave in a certain way and follow certain moral code. Most people take in those rules and internalize them not only into their action but into how they view the world and how they view themselves. When a person goes against this map of morality that colours their world and personality, it causes mental pain, as well as making them dislike themselves. Most of the people try to avoid this mental pain, reinforcing again this morality. Therefore, the morally upright individual is high in his ethical character and so in his behaviour.

The Apex Court in Tarak Singh vs. Jyoti Basu, (2005) delivered by Justice C.J. Kurian Joseph, reminded "Integrity is the hallmark of judicial discipline apart from others. Integrity according to Oxford dictionary is moral uprightness; honesty. It takes in its sweep, probity, innocence, trustfulness, openness, sincerity, blamelessness, immaculacy, rectitude, uprightness, virtuousness, righteousness, goodness, cleanness, decency, honour, reputation, nobility, irreproachability, purity, respectability, genuineness, moral excellence, etc. In short, it depicts sterling character with firm adherence to a code of moral values. 'Judiciary is an integrity institution'. Therefore, Judicial Officers should possess the sterling quality of integrity."

Impartiality

Impartiality means acting solely according to the merits of the case and serving governments of different political parties and the general public equally well and in the same spirit.

Impartiality requires public servants to refrain from opinions, positions or actions that demonstrate a bias toward or against a particular cause or course of action, including the defence of government policies. In analyzing options, public servants will consider the best evidence-based knowledge. They will base their recommendations on the desired outcomes and implement the decisions lawfully taken by ministers, even if these decisions differ from the advice or recommendations provided. Apolitically impartial public service supports the government of whichever political party the electorate chooses.

Political Patronage

It refers in general to the awarding of benefits and privileges in exchange for political support. Although the individual public servant may be competent and possess the required merit criteria, political patronage refers to the awarding of benefits in exchange for political support.

Benefits and privileges can refer to a number of things, including the awarding of contracts, preferential consideration in grants and contributions, and appointments to boards and commissions. However, political patronage generally refers to political influence in hiring and promotions in the public service.

Partisanship

Partisanship is the act of supporting a party, person or cause. Partisanship refers in general to actions supporting or opposing political parties or biases. Although the primary concern for the public service is "political partisanship", other types of partisanship should not be dismissed (e.g. support for an interest group or cause that is not attached to a particular political party).

Significance of Impartiality and Non-partisanship

An impartial and non-partisan public service makes responsible, democratic government work by-

- ensuring objective and evidence-based advice which ministers can use in establishing policies and programs for general public;
- providing the information ministers need to fulfil their accountability role to Parliament and the public;
- delivering services in an effective manner;
- managing resources and programs effectively;
- ensuring a legal and constitutional transition when democratic processes result in new administrations; and
- ensuring that, once professional advice is given, there is a competent and able execution of those decisions which are lawfully made

Political Neutrality

It means that the civil service should give free and frank advice to the government impartially and without any political consideration. It also means the implementation of the decisions of the government by the civil service faithfully whether such decisions were in consonance with their advice or not.

The concept of neutrality is emphasised to generate-

- Public confidence in the administrators against political influences;
- Trust among the ministers that their orders would be faithfully carried out irrespective of their ideology; and

- Keeping an atmosphere of appraisals and promotions in the civil service which is free from political influence

However, it should be noted that complete neutrality may not be required in public affairs. The administrator should act to maximize the public interest. The administrator should be sensitive to the needs of the general public and is supposed to intervene in public matters if the proposed policy falls short of the expectations and requirements of the people at large.

Political Neutrality and Code of Conduct Rules

With the avowed purpose of maintaining integrity, discipline and political neutrality, the Civil Services Conduct Rules lay down the code of conduct for the civil servants:

- No member of the Service shall be a member of, or associated with any political party or any organization which takes part in politics, nor shall he take part in, or subscribe in aid of, or assist in any other manner, any political movement or political activity.
- It shall be the duty of every member of the Service to endeavour to prevent any member of his family from taking part in or subscribing in aid of or assisting in any other manner, any movement of, activity which is, or tends directly or indirectly to be subversive of the Government as by law established, and where a member of the Service is unable to prevent member of his family from taking part in or subscribing in aid of, or assisting in any other manner, any such movement of activity, he shall make a report to that effect to the Government.
- No member of the Service shall canvass or otherwise interfere with, or use his influence in connection with, or take part in, an election to any legislature or local authority.
- A member of the Service qualified to vote at any such election may exercise his right to vote but where he does so he shall give no indication of the manner in which he proposes to vote or has voted.
- No member of the Service shall, in any radio broadcast or communication over any public media or in any document published anonymously, pseudonymously or in his own name or in the name of any other person or in any communication to the press or in any public utterance, make any statement of fact or opinion-

- Which has the effect of an adverse criticism of any current or recent policy or action of the Central Government or a State Government; or
- Which is capable of embarrassing the relations between the Central Government and any State Government; or
- Which is capable of embarrassing the relations between the Central Government and the Government of any Foreign State

Objectivity

The principle of objectivity implies that the decisions and actions should be based on observable phenomena and should not be influenced by emotions, biases or personal prejudices. Objectivity is a central philosophical concept, related to reality and truth, which has been variously defined by sources. Generally, objectivity means the state or quality of being true even outside a subject's individual biases, interpretations, feelings, and imaginings. A proposition is generally considered objectively true (to have objective truth) when its truth conditions are met without biases caused by feelings, ideas, opinions, etc., of a sentient subject. A second, broader meaning of the term refers to the ability in any context to judge fairly, without partiality or external influence. This second meaning of objectivity is sometimes used synonymously with neutrality.

Empathy

Empathy refers to the ability to imagine oneself in another's place and understand the others' feelings, desires, ideas, and actions. In other words, empathy is about being able to accurately hear out and understand the thoughts, feelings and concerns of others, even when these are not made explicit. The ability to empathize is directly dependent on your ability to feel your own feelings and identify them. It means in order to empathize with others, we need to become aware of what we are actually feeling to acknowledge, identify, and accept our feelings. Only then we may empathize with others.

To become empathetic to others, one need to:

- Demonstrate active listening skills (such as asking probing questions, not interrupting)
- Recognise body language, facial expression, and/or tone of voice to understand the unspoken message
- Recognise unexpressed or poorly expressed thoughts, concerns, and feelings
- Pick up signals when others are not feeling comfortable and display consideration

Significance of Empathy

Empathy is widely recognized as a universal virtue, closely related to many other virtues, such as love, compassion, kindness, tolerance, respect, and acceptance. It is promoted as the empathy is the cornerstone for moral and character development. It is also essential for working towards inclusiveness in society. As an individual, we need empathy to survive and succeed in this complex world.

Sympathy and Empathy

Sympathy and empathy are separate terms with some differences. Sympathy and empathy are both acts of feeling, but with sympathy you feel for the person; you are sorry for them or pity them, but you don't specifically understand what they are feeling. However, in empathy, to an extent you are placing yourself in that person's place, have a good sense of what he feels and understand his feelings to a degree.

Tolerance

Tolerance or toleration is a fair, objective, and permissive attitude toward those whose opinions, practices, race, religion, nationality, etc., differ from one's own; freedom from bigotry. In other words, tolerance is respect, acceptance and appreciation of the rich diversity of our world's cultures, our forms of expression and ways of being human. It is fostered by knowledge, openness, communication, and freedom of thought, conscience and belief. Tolerance is harmony in difference.

Significance of Tolerance

Tolerance is the responsibility that upholds human rights, pluralism, democracy, harmony and the rule of law. It involves the rejection of dogmatism and absolutism and affirms the standards set out in international human rights instruments. Consistent with respect for human rights, the practice of tolerance does not mean toleration of social injustice or the abandonment or weakening of one's convictions. It means that one is free to adhere to one's own convictions and accepts that others adhere to theirs. It means accepting the fact that human beings, naturally diverse in their appearance, situation, speech, behaviour and values, have the right to live in peace and to be as they are. It also means that one's views are not to be imposed on others.

Compassion

Compassion is the understanding or empathy for the suffering of others. More involved than simple empathy, compassion commonly gives rise to 'an active desire to alleviate another's suffering'. Compassion involves a sense of empathy. It does not end with pity. It invokes sensibilities to understand and even feel the pain of others and motivates one to be truly helpful in overcoming this pain.

The English noun compassion, meaning 'to suffer together with', comes from Latin. Ranked as a great virtue in numerous philosophies, compassion is considered in almost all the major religious traditions as among the greatest of virtues.

Characteristics of 'compassion' can be understood by noticing that someone who is compassionate:

- Has an active desire to alleviate another's suffering.
- Helps others because he wants to, not because he has to.
- Understands the feelings of others.
- Shows empathy towards another person.
- Shows kindness without expecting anything in return.
- Recognizes and helps others that are less fortunate than him-self.

Empathy and Compassion

Empathy is a form of compassion and it is important because otherwise you could care less about what others are going through. When you can directly relate to something someone is going through, it will sometimes give you a drive and motivation to help that person especially if what you went through was also a traumatic event for you. You cannot just sit back and watch someone else go through it and possibly have the same outcome as you had. Thus, empathy is closely related to compassion, but empathy precedes compassion and is a pre-requisite for compassion.

Significance of Compassion in Civil Services

Feeling compassion is one thing; acting on it is another. Compassion is deeply rooted in human nature; it has a biological basis in the brain and body. Humans can communicate compassion through facial gesture and touch, and these displays of compassion can serve vital social functions, strongly suggesting an evolutionary basis of compassion. And when experienced, compassion overwhelms selfish concerns and motivates altruistic behavior.

The attribute of being compassionate is of immense value for a civil servant. Since a compassionate civil servant is able to deliver the services efficiently and address the concerns of weaker sections, it is considered as one of the most important attribute.

A compassionate civil servant:

- Understands the needs of the marginalised and disadvantaged, along with the needs of the wider public
- Strives to respond quickly to meet their needs in a respectful, helpful and responsive manner
- Reports issues that affect service delivery, where necessary
- Addresses all the issues of the citizens in an unbiased manner
- Ensures that levels of service are maintained - highlights risks or concerns in order to meet community requirements
- Understands the value of an affirmative action towards the marginalised and disadvantaged
- Actively seeks information from all sections of community to understand their needs and expectations

- Is accessible to all citizens and seeks their feedback to develop a clear understanding of their needs and outcomes
- Establishes mechanisms to address feedback from the community about the service provided
- Involves a diverse range of staff members, stakeholders, and delivery partners while developing implementation approaches in order to provide clarity on the benefits to the disadvantaged and to improve the quality of service provided to the citizens
- Understands issues from others' perspective, particularly the disadvantaged

Rule of Law

Rule of law indicates that no branch of government is above the law, and no public official may act arbitrarily or unilaterally outside the law. This requirement is sometimes explained with the phrase "no one is above the law".

Rule of law is also regarded as a principle of governance in which all persons, institutions and entities, public and private, including the State itself, are accountable to laws that are publicly promulgated, equally enforced and independently adjudicated. It requires, as well, measures to ensure adherence to the principles of supremacy of law, equality before the law and accountability to the law.

Equity and Equality

Equality is usually taken to mean that everyone should be treated the same (due to the fundamental equality of all persons), whereas an equity approach holds that groups and individuals should be treated according to their particular circumstances and requirements. Equity recognizes that some people have to overcome obstacles to access resources or opportunities (obstacles like illiteracy, perpetual poverty, remote areas, and place in social hierarchy). Therefore, according to equity principle, groups can be treated differently in the application of policy or the law, so as to compensate for these obstacles, and to produce just or fair outcomes.

Case Study I

You are the Director of the CBI and an allegation has been made on your conduct by an eminent person. The proof for the same is also available. The allegation relates to your meeting with some persons at your residence, which you know are quite influential and are related to the case, which is being investigated by the officers under you. You are supervising the case and are acquainted with each and every details of the case. The allegation on you put your impartiality and integrity in question. What would be your reaction? Analyse the situation by giving justification that how far it is correct for a public servant to meet the persons who are related to the case his agency is investigating?

Premise : In the given incident, the Director of the topmost investigating agency of India has been blamed of meeting the persons related to the case, which the officers junior to him are investigating. This gives rise to concern related to the conduct of civil servant. The question arises here relates to the difference in personal and professional life of a Bureaucrat, the ethical behavior of his and the impartiality in his action.

This case comes under the following topics:

- Foundational Values of Civil Services
- Impartiality
- Integrity
- Public Service Values
- Ethical Conduct

Answer: The conduct of a senior bureaucrat, like the Director (CBI), defines the working culture of the organization. Central Bureau of Investigation is the premier investigating agency of India. It investigates high profile cases, more often related to those manning the top echelon of the society and to those who define the power structure of the society. Any unethical conduct by top officer of this agency gives rise to the serious concern as it may jeopardize the neutrality of the investigation process, thereby giving a blow to criminal justice system.

In the aforesaid case, since the allegation has been made by an influential person, who is a known activist of an NGO fighting against corruption, raises the legitimacy of the case. That the proof for the same is also available makes the allegation stronger. Under these circumstances a bureaucrat, especially when he is heading such an agency, can take different course of actions.

Each and every details of the case is available with the Director-CBI. His meeting with influential person related to the case, whatever the reason may be, prima facie gives an impression of an attempt to influence the investigation process. Since the Director is at the apex of CBI, any attempt to tarnish his image is a direct attack on the agency's integrity. So, a statement clarifying the facts related to these allegations shall be issued, as a first step, from the side of Director. If needed, the Director should let an enquiry commission set up either by the government or by the judiciary, for independent investigation in the matter. Moreover, if he knows that allegation made against him are true, although his intention was not bad, he should clear the facts associated with the purpose and reasons of meeting.

The question, that to what extent the meeting of Director of CBI with these persons is justified can be better judged on the basis of existing provisions. The new government has issued a revised code of conduct for bureaucrats that require them to be politically neutral, honest, and impartial and maintain high ethical standards. The amended rules state that every member of the All India Services, which includes the IAS and IPS, shall be courteous and responsive to the public, particularly the weaker sections, and ensure accountability and transparency in discharge of his duties. The All India Services (Conduct) Amendment Rules, 2014 states, among other things, that every member of the service shall take decisions solely based on merit and in public interest and use public resources efficiently, effectively and economically.

Clearly, under these circumstances a meeting of this kind is a direct question on the ethical conduct and Impartiality of public servant. However, there is another aspect to look into the issue. CBI Director is a public authority and every citizen of India, including those related to accused has equal rights to meet with him. Such meeting may relate to the grievance of the accused or dissatisfaction from the way of investigations or other such things. Civil Services Code says that any such meeting, related to official purpose shall be done under official capacity, for which office of Director is the best suited place and not the residence. The violation of this conduct is the manifestation of misusing the position to take decisions that seek to derive financial or material benefit for himself, his family or friends.

Stressing on the need for confidentiality in key government matters, the code of conduct make civil servants liable to maintain confidentiality in performance of their duties as required by the laws, particularly where the information or disclosure may prejudicially affect the security of the State, strategic, scientific or economic interests of the State, friendly relations with foreign countries or lead to incitement of an offence or illegal or unlawful gains to any person. A civil servant is expected to perform his duties with a high degree of professionalism; uphold supremacy of the Constitution; uphold sovereignty and integrity of India, the security of the State, public order, decency and morality; maintain integrity in public service; act with fairness and impartiality and not discriminate against anyone, particularly the poor and under-privileged sections; and maintain discipline in discharge of duties and be liable to implement lawful orders duly communicated to them.

Case Study II

Chandan was a young, idealistic Chief Executive Officer (CEO) in a district panchayat. After joining his job, he carefully studied the social and economic situation in the district. He looked at various reports and materials about the problems of the district. He gathered data on the stage of development of the district, its agricultural and industrial progress and its future growth potential. He noted that as the district was covered under intensive agricultural programmes, and as it had irrigation facilities, its agricultural sector was progressive. State government schemes for incentives had led to growth of many industries in the district. Its agricultural and industrial growth created reasonable infrastructure.

The district, however, lagged in human development indicators. The birth rate was high. Unfortunately, the infant mortality rate was high. Female literacy was way below the national average. School enrolment was poor, and the drop-out ratio was high. Female sex ratio was also low. Based on these indicators, Chandan concluded that the panchayat should give the highest priority to social sector programmes in its budget.

The panchayat was an elected body. The budget is approved by its general body which consists of all its members. Chandan tried to convince the panchayat that the highest allocation in the budget should be made for social sector development. However, the general body decided to spend 40% of its budget on minor irrigation. Chandan felt that the large allocation to minor irrigation projects will benefit land owning farmers and starve other social programmes. He, therefore, asked the officers to surreptitiously divert money to social welfare programmes.

Question: In the given case, an idealistic officer after joining the job, carefully studied the socio-economic scenario of the district. He found that the economic scenario of the district was progressive as the agricultural and industrial growth had created reasonable infrastructure. But the district had very dismal social sector development. He wanted to convince the general body of the Panchayat to allocate more fund to the social sector but the Panchayat decided to spend the major portion of the fund on minor irrigation. As a result of this, the CEO took an unwarranted action. Do you think Chandan violated service code of conduct by asking his officers to allocate fund "surreptitiously"? Can service code of conduct be compromised in favour of ethical acts? What would you have done if you had been in the situation of Chandan? Do you think Chandan might have gone through ethical dilemma? If yes in what kind of ethical dilemma he might have gone?

This case comes under the following topics:

- Violation of Official Code of Conduct
- Honesty and Integrity
- Transparency
- Ethical Dilemma

Answer: Even the good ends can never justify the unethical and questionable means, though Chandan's objective was for public good however he employed questionable means by asking the officers to surreptitiously allocate the funds to social sector. In this way he not only violated his service code of conduct rules which are unambiguously do's and don'ts for every public official but also jeopardized his and subordinates' professional integrity. He presumed that allocation in agriculture would help only big land owners; here objectivity could play a vital role which Chandan did not apply. An administrator should not be carried away by his emotions, biases and personal prejudices. It is also true that an administrator should be compassionate for the weaker section of the society. But, compassion should be a good blend of integrity, empathy and objectivity. In the given case, Chandan's concern was genuine but highly prejudiced and his action was questionable.

Moreover, Chandan acted contrary to the provisions under the 73rd Constitutional Amendment Act, 1993, which attaches great importance to the capacity building of elected representatives and officials of Panchayati Raj Institutions (PRIs) as well as functionaries involved in the development programmes securing economic development and social justice in their respective areas. It is the democratically elected Panchayat who constitute planning committee and allocate the funds depending upon its priority. By asking his officers to allocate the fund surreptitiously, Chandan created a conflicting situation. Under 73rd Constitutional Amendment Act, a bureaucrat is not a policy formulating agent but a facilitating agent who is supposed to supervise the implementation of scheme.

In this situation, it is very important to create awareness and provide innovative ways to Panchayat to navigate through the crisis of poor social infrastructure. Innovative ways, informed citizenry, effective implementation and alignment of people to a goal can overcome the inadequacy of funding.

Indeed in such an undesirable situation, Chandan might have gone through ethical dilemma and had limited choices between competing sets of principle. One, as an administrator he should try to improve the educational and health standards of the weaker sections of the society. Second, as an administrator he is duty bound to follow the decisions of the elected leaders. Otherwise, his action will be considered as violation of official code of conduct.

As described in the passage, he was idealistic and was concerned about the poor performance of human development indicators and indifferent attitude of Panchayat in terms of financial adequacy to improve the situation and his futile attempt to convince the Panchayat led him to bypass service code of conduct.

He could have avoided aforesaid situation by anticipating alternate tools to improve the social infrastructure. However, he chose the way which violated service code of conduct and created suspicious working climate by involving his officers. He knew that, this is not the right way of allocating fund that is why he asked his officers to allocate funds secretly. The aforesaid logically cohesive line of thinking was in vein as he chose illegitimate, guise and unjust way; thereby Chandan was unable to bargain with his idealistic philosophy and practical feasibility of his action. He succumbed to his idealistic philosophy by assaulting on his best kept principles. Above all, the myopic view of his ability to pursue the cause on his own has further created a suspicion and jeopardized transparency in public discourse. It is point to be taken to heart that, for a public servant the foundational values like honesty, integrity and transparency are the basic ingredients of his ideological disposition to intervene in public discourse and work for common´ good.

5

EMOTIONAL INTELLIGENCE

The Concepts Discussed in this Unit

- Emotional Intelligence (EI)
- Application of EI in Administration and Governance
- Managers and Leaders
- Emotional Quotient (EQ)
- Developing EQ in Others
- How to get Employee Work
- When EI trumps IQ

Emotions

Emotion is an affective state of consciousness in which joy, sorrow, fear, hate, or the like, is experienced, as distinguished from cognitive and volitional states of consciousness.

Whereas, the term 'affective' is defined as something pertaining to feeling or emotions, especially pleasurable or unpleasurable aspects of a mental process.

Intelligence

Intelligence is a set of cognitive abilities which allow us to acquire knowledge, to learn and to solve problems.

Emotional Intelligence

Emotional intelligence is the ability to perceive emotions, to assess and generate emotions so as to assist thought, to understand emotions and emotional knowledge, and to reflectively regulate emotions so as to promote emotional and intellectual growth (Mayer and Salovey).

According to Goleman, "emotional intelligence" refers to the capacity for recognizing our own feelings and those of others, for motivating ourselves, and for managing emotions, well in ourselves and in our relationships. In simple words, emotional intelligence refers to attributes such as understanding one's feeling, empathy for others, and the regulation of emotions to enhance one's life. Aristotle wrote about emotional intelligence in 350 BC, centuries before the term became popular.

How Emotional Intelligence Became a Key Leadership Skill

The term was coined in 1990 in a research paper by two psychology professors, John D. Mayer of UNH and Peter Salovey of Yale. From a scientific (rather than a popular) standpoint, emotional intelligence is the ability to accurately perceive your own and others' emotions; to understand the signals that emotions send about relationships; and to manage your own and others' emotions. It doesn't necessarily include the qualities (like optimism, initiative, and self-confidence) that some popular definitions ascribe to it.

People who take initiative, who have a vision, and who can strategize, plan, and accomplish goals to achieve their vision are considered good leaders. But what about other kinds of skills that make up a good leader?

For leaders, having emotional intelligence is essential for success. After all, who is more likely to succeed - a leader who shouts at his team when he's under stress, or a leader who stays in control, and calmly assesses the situation?

Emotional Intelligence comes to play for the ability to accurately perceive your own and others' emotions; to understand the signals that emotions send about relationships; and to manage your own and others' emotions.

According to Daniel Goleman (in 1998 research paper), an American psychologist who helped to popularize emotional intelligence, there are five key elements to it:

- Self-awareness
- Self-regulation
- Motivation
- Empathy
- Social skills

An understanding of what exactly constitutes emotional intelligence is important not only because the capacity is so central to leadership but because people strong in some of its elements can be utterly lacking in others, sometimes to disastrous effect.

The more that you, as a leader, manage each of these areas, the higher your emotional intelligence. So, let's look at each element in more detail and examine how you can grow as a leader.

Emotional Intelligence in Leadership

1. Self-awareness

If you're self-aware, you always know how you feel, and you know how your emotions and your actions can affect the people around you. Being self-aware when you're in a leadership position also means having a clear picture of your strengths and weaknesses, and it means behaving with humility.

What can you do to improve your self-awareness?

Analyse your thoughts - If you spend just a few minutes each day writing down your thoughts, this can move you to a higher degree of self-awareness.

Slow down - When you experience anger or other strong emotions, slow down to examine why. Remember, no matter what the situation, you can always choose how you react to it.

2. Self-regulation

Leaders who regulate themselves effectively rarely verbally attack others, make rushed or emotional decisions, stereotype people, or compromise their values. Self-regulation is all about staying in control. This element of emotional intelligence, according to Goleman, also covers a leader's flexibility and commitment to personal accountability.

How can you improve your ability to self-regulate?

Know your values - Do you have a clear idea of where you absolutely will not compromise? Do you know what values are most important to you? Spend some time examining your "code of ethics." If you know what's most important to you, then you probably won't have to think twice when you face a moral or ethical decision - you'll make the right choice.

Hold yourself accountable - If you tend to blame others when something goes wrong, stop. Make a commitment to admit to your mistakes and to face the consequences, whatever they are. You'll probably sleep better at night, and you'll quickly earn the respect of those around you.

Practice being calm - The next time you're in a challenging situation, be very aware of how you act. Do you relieve your stress by shouting at someone else? Practice deep-breathing exercises to calm yourself.

3. Motivation

Self-motivated leaders work consistently toward their goals, and they have extremely high standards for the quality of their work.

How can you improve your motivation?

Re-examine why you're doing your job - It's easy to forget what you really love about your career. So, take some time to remember why you wanted this job. If you're unhappy in your role and you're struggling to remember why you wanted it, try the 'Whys technique' to find the root of the problem. Starting at the root often helps you look at your situation in a new way.

Know your stand - Determine how motivated you are to lead. Leadership Motivation Assessment can help you see clearly how motivated you are in your leadership role.

Be hopeful and find something good - Motivated leaders are usually optimistic, no matter what problems they face. Every time you face a challenge, or even a failure, try to find at least one good thing about the situation. It might be something small, like a new contact, or something with long-term effects, like an important lesson learned. But there's almost always something positive, if you look for it.

4. Empathy

For leaders, having empathy is critical to managing a successful team or organization. Leaders with empathy have the ability to put themselves in someone else's situation. They help develop the people on their team, challenge others who are acting unfairly, give constructive feedback, and listen to those who need it.

How can you improve your empathy?

Put yourself in someone else's position - It's easy to support your own point of view. After all, it's yours. But take the time to look at situations from other people's perspectives.

Pay attention to body language - Perhaps when you listen to someone, you cross your arms, move your feet back and forth, or bite your lip. This body language tells others how you really feel about a situation, and the message you're giving isn't positive! Learning to read body language can be a real asset in a leadership role, because you'll be better able to determine how someone truly feels. This gives you the opportunity to respond appropriately.

Respond to feelings - You ask your assistant to work late - again. And although he agrees, you can hear the disappointment in his voice. So, respond by addressing his feelings. Tell him you appreciate how willing he is to work extra hours, and that you're just as frustrated about working late. If possible, figure out a way for future late nights to be less of an issue (for example, give him a day off).

5. Social Skills

Leaders who do well in the social skills element of emotional intelligence are great communicators. They're just as open to hearing bad news as good news, and they're expert at getting their team to support them and be excited about a new mission or project.

Leaders who have good social skills are also good at managing change and resolving conflicts diplomatically. They're rarely satisfied with leaving things as they are, but they don't sit back and make everyone else do the work: they set an example with their own behavior.

How can you build social skills?

Learn conflict resolution - Leaders must know how to resolve conflicts between their team members, customers, or vendors. Learning conflict resolution skills is vital if you want to succeed.

Improve your communication skills - Analyze yourself that how well do you communicate. The impact of communication is large. The person at the other point must be able to comprehend you easily, and at last there must be an acknowledgement from his point to complete the process.

Learn how to praise others - As a leader, you can inspire the loyalty of your team simply by giving praise when it's earned. Learning how to praise others is a fine art, but well worth the effort.

To be effective, leaders must have a solid understanding of how their emotions and actions affect the people around them. The better a leader relates to and works with others, the more successful he or she will be.

Managers and Leaders: How Different Are They?

Abraham Zaleznik, who wrote an article centered on organizational structure and processes, provided the fundamental difference between the managers and leaders. According to him, Managerial development at the time focused exclusively on building competence, control, and the appropriate balance of power. That view, Zaleznik argued, omitted the essential leadership elements of inspiration, vision, and human passion–which drive corporate success.

The difference between managers and leaders, he wrote, lies in the conceptions they hold, deep in their psyches, of chaos and order. Managers embrace process, seek stability and control, and instinctively try to resolve problems quickly–sometimes before they fully understand a problem's significance. Leaders, in contrast, tolerate chaos and lack of structure and are willing to delay closure in order to understand the issues more fully. In this way, Zaleznik argued, business leaders have much more in common with artists, scientists, and other creative thinkers than they do with managers. Organizations need both managers and leaders to succeed, but developing both requires a reduced focus on logic and strategic exercises in favor of an environment where creativity and imagination are permitted to flourish.

What is the ideal way to develop leadership?

Every society provides its own answer to this question, and each, in groping for answers, defines its deepest concerns about the purposes, distributions, and uses of power. Business has contributed its answer to the leadership question by evolving a new breed called the manager. Simultaneously, business has established a new power ethic that favors collective over individual leadership, the cult of the group over that of personality. While ensuring the competence, control, and the balance of power among groups with the potential for rivalry, managerial leadership unfortunately does not necessarily ensure imagination, creativity, or ethical behavior in guiding the destinies of corporate enterprises.

Leadership inevitably requires using power to influence the thoughts and actions of other people. Power in the hands of an individual entails human risks: first, the risk of equating power with the ability to get immediate results; second, the risk of ignoring the many different ways people can legitimately accumulate power; and third, the risk of losing self-control in the desire for power. The need to hedge these risks accounts in part for the development of collective leadership and the managerial ethics. Consequently, an inherent conservatism dominates the culture of large organizations.

Manager vs. Leader: Personality Traits

A managerial culture emphasizes rationality and control. Whether his or her energies are directed toward goals, resources, organization structures, or people, a manager is a problem solver. The manager asks: "What problems have to be solved, and what are the best ways to achieve results so that people will continue to contribute to this organization?"

From this perspective, leadership is simply a practical effort to direct affairs; and to fulfill his or her task, a manager requires that many people operate efficiently at different levels of status and responsibility. It takes neither genius nor heroism to be a manager, but rather persistence, tough-mindedness, hard work, intelligence, analytical ability, and perhaps most important, tolerance and goodwill.

Another conception of leadership, however, attaches almost mystical beliefs to what a leader is and assumes that only great people are worthy of the drama of power and politics. Here leadership is a psychodrama in which a brilliant, lonely person must gain control of himself or herself as a precondition for controlling others. Such an expectation of leadership contrasts sharply with the mundane, practical, and yet important conception that leadership is really managing work that other people do.

If indeed problems demand greatness, then judging by past performance, the selection and development of leaders leave a great deal to chance. There are no known ways to train "great" leaders. Further, beyond what we leave to chance, there is a deeper issue in the relationship between the need for competent managers and the longing for great leaders.

What it takes to ensure a supply of people who will assume practical responsibility may inhibit the development of great leaders. On the other hand, the presence of great leaders may undermine the development of managers who typically become very anxious in the relative disorder that leaders seem to generate.

It is easy enough to dismiss the dilemma of training managers, though we may need new leaders or leaders at the expense of managers, by saying that the need is for people who can be both. But, just as a managerial culture differs from the entrepreneurial culture that develops when leaders appear in organizations, managers and leaders are very different kinds of people. They differ in motivation, personal history, and in how they think and act.

Attitudes towards Goals

Managers tend to adopt impersonal, if not passive, attitudes toward goals. Managerial goals arise out of necessities rather than desires and, therefore, are deeply embedded in their organization's history and culture.

Frederic G. Donner, Chairman and Chief Executive Officer of General Motors from 1958 to 1967, expressed this kind of attitude toward goals in defining GM's position on product development:

"To meet the challenge of the marketplace, we must recognize changes in customer needs and desires far enough ahead to have the right products in the right places at the right time and in the right quantity.

"We must balance trends in preference against the many compromises that are necessary to make a final product that is both reliable and good looking, that performs well and that sells at a competitive price in the necessary volume. We must design not just the cars we would like to build but, more important, the cars that our customers want to buy."

Nowhere in this statement is there a notion that consumer tastes and preferences arise in part as a result of what manufacturers do. In reality, through product design, advertising, and promotion, consumers learn to like what they then say they need. Few would argue that people who enjoy taking snapshots need a camera that also develops pictures. But in response to a need for novelty, convenience, and a shorter interval between acting (snapping the picture) and gaining pleasure (seeing the shot), the Polaroid camera succeeded in the marketplace. It is inconceivable that Edwin Land responded to impressions of consumer need. Instead, he translated a technology (polarization of light) into a product, which proliferated and stimulated consumers' desires.

The example of Polaroid and Land suggests how leaders

think about goals. They are active instead of reactive, shaping ideas instead of responding to them. Leaders adopt a personal and active attitude toward goals. The influence a leader exerts in altering moods, evoking images and expectations, and in establishing specific desires and objectives determines the direction a business takes. The net result of this influence changes the way people think about what is desirable, possible, and necessary.

Conceptions of Work

Managers tend to view work as an enabling process involving some combination of people and ideas interacting to establish strategies and make decisions. They help the process along by calculating the interests in opposition, planning when controversial issues should surface, and reducing tensions. In this enabling process, managers' tactics appear flexible: on one hand, they negotiate and bargain; on the other, they use rewards, punishments, and other forms of coercion.

To get people to accept solutions to problems, managers continually need to coordinate and balance opposing views. Interestingly enough, this type of work has much in common with what diplomats and mediators do, with Henry Kissinger apparently an outstanding practitioner. Managers aim to shift balances of power toward solutions acceptable as compromises among conflicting values.

Leaders work in the opposite direction. Where managers act to limit choices, leaders develop fresh approaches to long-standing problems and open issues to new options. To be effective, leaders must project their ideas onto images that excite people and only then develop choices that give those images substance.

John F. Kennedy's brief presidency shows both the strengths and weaknesses connected with the excitement leaders generate in their work. In his inaugural address he said, "Let every nation know, whether it wishes us well or ill, that we shall pay any price, bear any burden, meet any hardship, support any friend, oppose any foe, in order to assure the survival and the success of liberty."

This much-quoted statement forced people to react beyond immediate concerns and to identify with Kennedy and with important shared ideals. On closer scrutiny, however, the statement is absurd because it promises a position, which, if adopted, as in the Vietnam War, could produce disastrous results. Yet unless expectations are aroused and mobilized, with all the dangers of frustration inherent in heightened desire, new thinking and new choice can never come to light.

Leaders work from high-risk positions; indeed, they are often temperamentally disposed to seek out risk and danger, especially where the chance of opportunity and reward appears promising. From my observations, the reason one individual seeks risks while another approaches problems conservatively depends more on his or her personality and less on conscious choice. For those who become managers, a survival instinct dominates the need for risk, and with that instinct comes an ability to tolerate mundane, practical work. Leaders sometimes react to mundane work as to an affliction.

Relations with Others

Managers prefer to work with people; they avoid solitary activity because it makes them anxious. The need to seek out others with whom to work and collaborate seemed to stand out as an important characteristic of managers. When asked, for example, to write imaginative stories in response to a picture showing a single figure (a boy contemplating a violin or a man silhouetted in a state of reflection), managers populated their stories with people.

The following is an example of a manager's imaginative story about the young boy contemplating a violin:

"Mom and Dad insisted that their son take music lessons so that someday he can become a concert musician. His instrument was ordered and had just arrived. The boy is weighing the alternatives of playing football with the other kids or playing with the squeak box. He can't understand how his parents could think a violin is better than a touchdown.

"After four months of practicing the violin, the boy has had more than enough, Dad is going out of his mind, and Mom is willing to give in reluctantly to their wishes. Football season is now over, but a good third baseman will take the field next spring."

This story illustrates two themes that clarify managerial

attitudes toward human relations. The first, is to seek out activity with other people (that is, the football team), and the second is to maintain a low level of emotional involvement in those relationships. Low emotional involvement appears in the writer's use of conventional metaphors, even clichés, and in the depiction of the ready transformation of potential conflict into harmonious decisions. In this case, the boy, Mom, and Dad agree to give up the violin for sports.

These two themes may seem paradoxical, but their coexistence supports what a manager does, including reconciling differences, seeking compromises, and establishing a balance of power. The story further demonstrates that managers may lack empathy, or the capacity to sense intuitively the thoughts and feelings of others.

Managers relate to people according to the role they play in a sequence of events or in a decision-making process, while leaders, who are concerned with ideas, relate in more intuitive and empathetic ways.

The distinction is simply between a manager's attention to how things get done and a leader's to what the events and decisions mean to participants.

In recent years, managers have adopted from game theory the notion that decision-making events can be one of two types: the win-lose situation (or zero-sum game) or the win-win situation in which everybody in the action comes out ahead. Managers strive to convert win-lose into win-win situations as part of the process of reconciling differences among people and maintaining balances of power.

For those who become managers, a survival instinct dominates the need for risk, and with that instinct comes an ability to tolerate mundane, practical work.

There are undoubtedly many other tactical moves managers use to change human situations from win-lose to win-win. But the point is that such tactics focus on the decision-making process itself, and that process interests managers rather than leaders. Tactical interests involve costs as well as benefits; they make organizations fatter in bureaucratic and political intrigue and leaner in direct, hard activity and warm human relationships.

Consequently, one often hears subordinates characterize managers as inscrutable, detached, and manipulative. These adjectives arise from the subordinates' perception that they are linked together in a process whose purpose is to maintain a controlled as well as rational and equitable structure.

In contrast, one often hears leaders referred to with adjectives rich in emotional content. Leaders attract strong feelings of identity and difference or of love and hate. Human relations in leader-dominated structures often appear turbulent, intense, and at times even disorganized. Such an atmosphere intensifies individual motivation and often produces unanticipated outcomes.

Senses of Self

In 'The Varieties of Religious Experience', William James - the American thinker and philosopher who came out with his philosophy we know as Pragmatism - describes two basic personality types, "once-born" and "twice-born." People of the former personality type are those for whom adjustments to life have been straightforward and whose lives have been more or less a peaceful flow since birth. Twice-borns, on the other hand, have not had an easy time of it. Their lives are marked by a continual struggle to attain some sense of order. Unlike once-borns, they cannot take things for granted. According to James, these personalities have equally different worldviews. For a once-born personality, the sense of self as a guide to conduct and attitude derives from a feeling of being at home and in harmony with one's environment. For a twice-born, the sense of self derives from a feeling of profound separateness.

A sense of belonging or of being separate has a practical significance for the kinds of investments managers and leaders make in their careers. Managers see themselves as conservators and regulators of an existing order of affairs with which they personally identify and from which they gain rewards. A manager's sense of self-worth is enhanced by perpetuating and strengthening existing institutions: he or she is performing in a role that harmonizes with ideals of duty and responsibility. William James had this harmony in mind–this sense of self as flowing easily to and from the outer world–in defining a once-born personality.

Leaders tend to be twice-born personalities, people who feel separate from their environment. They may work in organizations, but they never belong to them. Their sense of who they are does not depend on memberships, work roles, or other social indicators of identity. And that perception of identity may form the theoretical basis for explaining why certain individuals seek opportunities for change. The methods to bring about change may be technological, political, or ideological, but the object is the same: to profoundly alter human, economic, and political relationships.

In considering the development of leadership, we have to examine two different courses of life history: (1) development through socialization, which prepares the individual to guide institutions and to maintain the existing balance of social relations; and (2) development through personal mastery, which impels an individual to struggle for psychological and social change. Society produces its managerial talent through the first line of development; leaders emerge through the second.

Development of Leadership

No one is a born leader–everyone can develop leadership skills and everyone can benefit from using them. Every person's development begins with family. Each person experiences the traumas associated with separating from his or her parents, as well as the pain that follows such a wrench. In the same vein, all individuals face the difficulties of achieving self-regulation and self-control. But for some, perhaps a majority, the fortunes of childhood provide adequate gratifications and sufficient opportunities to find substitutes for rewards no longer available. Such individuals, the "once-borns," make moderate identifications with parents and find a harmony between what they expect and what they are able to realize from life.

First, take time to honestly analyze yourself.

Learn to understand yourself. It's the first step to understanding others.

Consider these important questions:

1. What kind of leader am I? One who helps solve problems? A leader who helps people get along? How do others see me as a leader?

2. What are my goals, purposes, and expectations in working with this particular group?

Identify areas for improvement.

Ask yourself these questions:

1. Do I try to be aware of how others think and feel?
2. Do I try to help others perform to the best of their abilities?
3. Am I willing to accept responsibility?
4. Am I willing to try new ideas and new ways of doing things?
5. Am I able to communicate with others effectively?
6. Am I a good problem solver?
7. Do I accept and appreciate other perspectives and opinions?
8. Am I aware of current issues and concerns on campus or in my community?

Then--after analyzing your strengths and weaknesses--take action

Devise a strategy for upgrading your skills. Here are a few strategies to consider:

1) **Communicate effectively.** Effective communication is dialogue. Barriers are created by speaking down to people, asking closed questions that elicit yes or no answers, using excessive authority, and promoting a culture that depends on unanimity. If your focus is winning the argument or if you react defensively to criticism, you'll create fear of openness and hinder the organization's growth.

Try these steps to effective communication:

- Listen actively-ask open questions. Be genuinely interested in what other's say.
- Thank people for their openness--stress how much you value it--even if you don't like specifically what is being said.
- Point to areas of agreement before jumping on areas of disagreement-this reduces defensiveness; members won't fear being "attacked."
- Set aside your authority to create an atmosphere of partnership to reduce fear in group members.

- Promote a culture of constructive dissent-though not to the point of paralysis.
- Portray disagreement as simply a difference of opinion. Get rid of the "I'm right, you're wrong" attitude.

2) **Encourage enthusiasm and a sense of belonging**

Try to Show:

- **Friendliness:** Others will be more willing to share ideas if you're interested in them as people too.
- **Understanding:** Everyone makes mistakes. Try to be constructive, tolerant and tactful when offering criticism.
- **Fairness:** Equal treatment and equal opportunity lead to an equally good effort from all group members.
- **Integrity:** Members will take tasks more seriously if you show that you're more interested in group goals than your own personal gain.

3) **Keep everyone working toward agreed upon goals**

- Remind everyone of the group's purposes from time to time. It's easy to become too narrowly focused and lose sight of the larger goals.
- Provide encouragement and motivation, by showing your appreciation for good ideas and extra effort.
- Harmonize differences and disagreements between group members by stressing compromise and cooperation.
- Involve everyone in discussions and decisions, even if asking for opinions and ideas means a longer discussion.

4) **Get to know the people around you**

- Everyone has different abilities, wants, needs, and purpose in life. To get along with others and get results, you need to get to know them.
- Interact with group members as often as possible. The only way to get to know someone is through direct personal contact.
- Become familiar with every member of your group. Take note of each person's unique qualities and characteristics.

5) **Treat others as individuals**

Put your knowledge and understanding of each group member to work.

- **Be aware of expectations:** Everyone expects something different: recognition, a chance to learn, a chance to work with other people, etc.
- **Be creative:** A repetitious routine can cause boredom. A successful leader thinks of new and better approaches to old ways of doing things.
- **Provide rewards:** Recognition by the group is a source of personal satisfaction and positive reinforcement for a job well done.
- **Delegate responsibilities:** If everyone shares the work, everyone can share pride in the group's accomplishments. Let each member know what's expected of him/her, available resources, deadlines, etc.

6) Accept responsibility for getting things done

- **Take the initiative:** Why stand around and wait for someone else to get things started? Set an example.
- **Offer help and information:** Your unique knowledge and skills may be just what's needed.
- **Seek help and information:** Ask for advice if you need it. This will encourage group involvement and help accomplish group goals.
- **Make things happen:** By being decisive, energetic, and enthusiastic, you can and will help get things done!
- **Know when and how to say "no.":** If your time and resources are already committed, turn down extra tasks, but do it nicely.

7) Problem solving in a step-by-step way

Whether you are faced with a decision to make or a conflict to resolve, following a logical approach will help.

1. State the problem as simply and clearly as possible.
2. Gather all relevant information and available resources.
3. Brainstorm as many ideas or solutions as you can think of (with others if possible).
4. Evaluate each idea or solution and choose the best one.
5. Design a plan for using your idea or solution. Include a timetable, assigned roles, and resources to be used.
6. Follow up on your plan by asking if your idea worked and why or why not.

Great teachers take risks. They bet initially on talent they perceive in younger people. And they risk emotional involvement in working closely with their juniors. The risks do not always pay off, but the willingness to take them appears to be crucial in developing leaders.

Can Organizations Develop Leaders?

A myth about how people learn and develop that seems to have taken hold in American culture also dominates thinking in business. The myth is that people learn best from their peers. Supposedly, the threat of evaluation and even humiliation recedes in peer relations because of the tendency for mutual identification and the social restraints on authoritarian behavior among equals. Peer training in organizations occurs in various forms. The use, for example, of task forces made up of peers from several interested occupational groups (sales, production, research, and finance) supposedly removes the restraints of authority on the individual's willingness to assert and exchange ideas. As a result, so the theory goes, people interact more freely, listen more objectively to criticism and other points of view, and, finally, learn from this healthy interchange.

Another application of peer training exists in some large corporations, such as Philips N.V. in Holland, where organizational structure is built on the principle of joint responsibility of two peers, one representing the commercial end of the business and the other the technical. Formally, both hold equal responsibility for geographic operations or product groups, as the case may be. As a practical matter, it may turn out that one or the other of the peers dominates the management. Nevertheless, the main interaction is between two or more equals.

The principal question about such arrangements is whether they perpetuate the managerial orientation and preclude the formation of one-to-one relationships between senior people and potential leaders.

Aware of the possible stifling effects of peer relationships on aggressiveness and individual initiative, another company, much smaller than Philips, utilizes joint responsibility of peers for operating units, with one important difference. The Chief Executive of this company encourages competition and rivalry among peers, ultimately rewarding the one who comes out on top with increased responsibility.

These hybrid arrangements produce some unintended consequences that can be disastrous. There is no easy way to limit rivalry. Instead, it permeates all levels of the operation and opens the way for the formation of cliques in an atmosphere of intrigue.

One large, integrated oil company has accepted the importance of developing leaders through the direct influence of senior on junior executives. The Chairman and Chief Executive Officer regularly select one talented university graduate whom he appoints his special assistant, and with whom he will work closely for a year. At the end of the year, the junior executive becomes available for assignment to one of the operating divisions, where he or she will be assigned to a responsible post rather than a training position. This apprenticeship acquaints the junior executive firsthand with the use of power and with the important antidotes to the power disease called hubris--performance and integrity.

Working in one-to-one relationships, where there is a formal and recognized difference in the power of the players, takes a great deal of tolerance for emotional interchange. This interchange, inevitable in close working arrangements, probably accounts for the reluctance of many executives to become involved in such relationships.

Emotional Intelligence- Heart and Head Combined

It is important to understand that Emotional Intelligence is not the opposite of intelligence, it is not the triumph of head over heart but is the unique intersection of both. Think about the definition of emotion, intelligence, and especially, of the three parts of our mind - affect/emotion, cognition/thinking, volition/motivation. Emotional Intelligence combines affect with cognition and emotion with intelligence.

Emotional intelligence, then, is the ability to use your emotions to help you solve problems and live a more effective life. Emotional intelligence without intelligence, or intelligence without emotional intelligence, is only part of a solution. It is the head working with the heart.

Mayer & Salovey (Ability Model)

In the words of Mayer and Salovey, Emotional Intelligence is the ability to perceive emotions, to access and generate emotions so as to assist thought, to understand emotions and emotional knowledge, and to reflectively regulate emotions so as to promote emotional and intellectual growth.

There are four different areas as perceived by Mayer and Salovey in above definition-

- **Perceiving Emotions-** In order to properly understand the emotions, it is, first, necessary to accurately perceive them. In many cases, this might involve understanding non-verbal signals such as body language and facial expressions.
- **Reasoning with Emotions-** Reasoning with emotions involves using emotions to promote thinking and cognitive activity. Emotions help prioritize what we pay attention and react to; we respond emotionally to things that garner our attention.
- **Understanding Emotions-** The emotions that we perceive can carry a wide variety of meanings. If someone is expressing angry emotions, the observer must interpret the cause of their anger and what it might mean. For example, if your boss is acting angry, it might mean that he is dissatisfied with your work; or it could be because he got a speeding ticket on his way to work that morning or that he's been fighting with his wife.
- **Managing Emotions-** The ability to manage emotions effectively is a key part of emotional intelligence. Regulating emotions, responding appropriately and responding to the emotions of others are all important aspects of emotional management.

Domains of EI as Given by Daniel Goleman

Goleman gave five domains that delineate the parameters of emotional intelligence:

- **Being self aware-** The ability to recognize a feeling as it is happening is fundamental to EI. If we are unable to notice our emotions, we can be overwhelmed and also flounder at the mercy of these strong feelings.
- **Managing emotions-** This rests upon self-awareness; once

aware, we need to handle our emotions. The goal is to 'balance' the emotions, i.e., neither emotional suppression nor emotional excess. It is a continuous exercise and those who can handle emotions can face life's upsets better and far more quickly than those who do not.

- **Having self-motivation-** Underlying the accomplishment of any sort of goal is the ability to marshal our emotions in pursuit of that end. For creative tasks, focus and mastery (learning to delay gratification and stifle inappropriate desires) are important skills, and emotional control is essential.
- **Recognizing the emotions of others-** 'People' skills are based on a capacity for empathy and the ability to stay tuned to the emotions of others. Empathy kindles altruism and lies at the basis of professions that deal with caring for others, such as teaching, management, and the healing arts.
- **Handling relationship-** Interpersonal effectiveness is dependent on our ability to manage the emotions of others. Brilliant projects and innovative insights are often never realized because of a lack of social competence and leadership skill.

Attributes of an Emotionally Intelligent Administrator

An emotionally intelligent administrator will possess the ability to-

- Handle conflicts constructively
- De-personalize from the angers of others
- Deal with uncertainty and change
- Identify and abide by core values and beliefs that shape the choices you make
- Understand and empathize with positions different from others
- To enrol people into his/ her vision
- Manage difficult/unreasonable persons in all situations

Relevance of Emotional Intelligence in the Current Environment of Civil Services

Civil services today work in an environment that is beset with numerous problems, challenges, and even contradictions such as-

- Fast changing social structure and values;

- Increasing regional, economic and digital divide, rising population and unemployment;
- Inadequacy of basic necessities like housing and drinking water and infrastructure and so on;
- Increased awareness of the masses as well as existence of significant number of voiceless and marginalized poor;
- Widespread application of information technology which has helped the government on one hand, but has also put pressure on the government to "appear to be performing and in control of things";
- The 73rd and 74th Constitutional Amendments have led to decentralization of decision making and created a new class of politicians over the civil services;
- There is an all pervasive demand for improved governance. A paradigm shift has occurred in the idea of governance, of what governments should do and also how they should govern. On one hand, governments are expected to move out of many areas, and on the other hand they are expected to perform multiple roles;
- There is, however, a consensus that government should perform better, be more responsive and transparent, and enhance scope for participation of people and civil society;
- Issues get politicized easily and quickly;
- There is an all pervasive and increased cynicism and contempt of politics and administration;
- Inner dissent and conflicts over policies, programmes and implementation thereof are more open and sharper;
- There is an increased tendency on part of the people to resort to agitation and aggression. The common man is no longer satisfied easily. Even a small instance can provoke people to indulge in harmful and destructive activities. Increase in the number of frustrated and disgruntled people has only added fuel to the firc;
- The administration itself is beset with many problems- political pressures, rampant corruption, obsolete and outdated methods, procedures and laws, lack of avenues for growth, over-centralizaiton, self aggrandizement and so on;

Thus, the work environment of the civil services is much

more complex, demanding and even hostile at times. And given its present state, it is in no position to handle and tackle the problems in the old ways. Even the well intending civil servants cannot do much because all their energies are exhausted in sheer survival. Herein, lies the role of Emotional Intelligence. The emotionally intelligent civil servants can achieve a lot if they are professionally competent and positive in their approach.

Can Emotional Intelligence be Learned?

For ages, people have debated if leaders are born or made. So too goes the debate about emotional intelligence. Are people born with certain levels of empathy, for example, or do they acquire empathy as a result of life's experiences? The answer is both. Scientific inquiry strongly suggests that there is a genetic component to emotional intelligence. Psychological and developmental research indicates that nurture plays a role as well. How much of each perhaps will never be known, but research and practice clearly demonstrate that emotional intelligence can be learned.

One thing is certain: Emotional intelligence increases with age. There is an old-fashioned word for the phenomenon: maturity. Yet even with maturity, some people still need training to enhance their emotional intelligence.

Unfortunately, far too many training programs that intend to build leadership skills – including emotional intelligence – are a waste of time and money. The problem is simple: They focus on the wrong part of the brain.

Emotional intelligence is born largely in the neurotransmitters of the brain's limbic system, which governs feelings, impulses, and drives. Research indicates that the limbic system learns best through motivation, extended practice, and feedback. Compare this with the kind of learning that goes on in the neocortex, which governs analytical and technical ability. The neocortex grasps concepts and logic. It is the part of the brain that figures out how to use a computer or make a sales call by reading a book. Not surprisingly – but mistakenly – it is also the part of the brain targeted by most training programs aimed at enhancing emotional intelligence. When such programs take, in effect, a neocortical approach, my research with the Consortium for Research on Emotional Intelligence in Organizations has shown they can even have a negative impact on people's job performance.

To enhance emotional intelligence, organizations must refocus their training to include the limbic system. They must help people break old behavioral habits and establish new ones. That not only takes much more time than conventional training programs, it also requires an individualized approach.

Imagine an executive who is thought to be low on empathy by her colleagues. Part of that deficit shows itself as an inability to listen; she interrupts people and doesn't pay close attention to what they're saying. To fix the problem, the executive needs to be motivated to change, and then she needs practice and feedback from others in the company. A colleague or coach could be tapped to let the executive know when she has been observed failing to listen. She would then have to replay the incident and give a better response; that is, demonstrate her ability to absorb what others are saying. And the executive could be directed to observe certain executives who listen well and to mimic their behavior.

With persistence and practice, such a process can lead to lasting results. I know one Wall Street executive who sought to improve his empathy–specifically his ability to read people's reactions and see their perspectives. Before beginning his quest, the executive's subordinates were terrified of working with him. People even went so far as to hide bad news from him. Naturally, he was shocked when finally confronted with these facts. He went home and told his family – but they only confirmed what he had heard at work. When their opinions on any given subject did not mesh with his, they, too, were frightened of him.

Enlisting the help of a coach, the executive went to work to heighten his empathy through practice and feedback. His first step was to take a vacation to a foreign country where he did not speak the language. While there, he monitored his reactions to the unfamiliar and his openness to people who were different from him.

When he returned home, humbled by his week abroad, the executive asked his coach to shadow him for parts of the day, several times a week, to critique how he treated people with new or different perspectives.

At the same time, he consciously used on-the-job interactions as opportunities to practice "hearing" ideas that differed from his. Finally, the executive had himself videotaped in meetings and asked those who worked for and with him to critique his ability to acknowledge and understand the feelings of others. It took several months, but the executive's emotional intelligence did ultimately rise, and the improvement was reflected in his overall performance on the job.

It's important to emphasize that building one's emotional

intelligence cannot – will not – happen without sincere desire and concerted effort. A brief seminar won't help; nor can one buy a how-to manual.

It is much harder to learn to empathize – to internalize empathy as a natural response to people – than it is to become adept at regression analysis. But it can be done. "Nothing great was ever achieved without enthusiasm," wrote Ralph Waldo Emerson. If your goal is to become a real leader, these words can serve as a guidepost in your efforts to develop high emotional intelligence

How can Emotional Intelligence Help Civil Services?

Emotional Intelligence (EI) can help in three ways at the workplace-

- To achieve amicable work environment
- Improvement in the behavior and performance of individual workers
- Improvement in organizational performance

Numerous organizations in public and private sectors have used EI and reported positive results. To name a few- US Air Force, US Navy, Johnson and Johnson, Motorola and so on. In India, HPCL has used EI to create an environment that fosters emotionally intelligent leadership. As an initial measure it has trained frontline leaders and provided them with opportunities to put EI into practice.

Specifically, the awareness and the application of EI helps in the following manner-

- Greater interpersonal skills (crucial for good citizen centric administration)
- Increased capacity to handle-
  - Changes in work
  - Pressures and stress
  - Conflicts
- Ability to see the long term effects of one's actions/attitudes
- Increased levels of commitment, trustworthiness and conscientiousness
- Being able to see things in a holistic manner
- Being able to bounce back from setbacks and maintain optimism

- Finding healthy ways to handle negative/extreme feelings
- Having greater motivation - achievement drive, initiative, persistence, motivating others as well
- Better ability to communicate
- Enhanced group dynamics in terms of cooperation, collaboration and building bonds
- Enhanced leadership traits, including the knowledge about when and how to lead, when to follow
- Ability to use win-win model for negotiations
- Ability to appreciate diversity and value for others
- Ability to perform multiple tasks due to better time and information management
- Greater focus
- Aware of but minimally concerned with and affected by office politics
- Not prone to aggression
- Ability to be a change catalyst

EQ: The Quantified Format of EI

In number of studies and assumptions, EI and EQ are vaguely considered as the similar terms particularly in initial studies or theories.

Precisely they are two different terms related with each other with part-whole relationship. Emotional Intelligence in simple words can be defined as the awareness of emotions in relation of self as well as of others. EI includes well defined individualistic traits such as self awareness, self management, social awareness, relationship management, etc. in special reference to emotions of self or other. It includes control, manipulation and expression of one's emotions in appropriate manner guided by rational thinking more targeted to effective and accepted response on various criterias.

Whereas, Emotional Quotient (EQ) can be defined as a part deliberately deducted by implying any Standardized Test which denotes the level of EI present in the individual on which test is conducted ie. in simple words, EQ is just a measure of one's EI in any form.

Emotional Quotient

Emotional Quotient (EQ), also called emotional intelligence quotient, is a measurement of a person's ability to monitor his or her emotions, to cope with pressures and demands, and to control his or her thoughts and actions. The ability to assess and affect situations and relationships with other people also plays a role in emotional intelligence. This measurement is intended to be a tool that is similar to Intelligence Quotient (IQ), which is a measurement of a person's intellect.

Importance of EQ

EQ is an indicator of the accomplishment in the formation, maintenance and enrichment of both personal and professional relationships which manifests through the following aspects of an individual:

Physical Health: The ability to take care of our bodies and especially to manage our stress, which has an incredible impact on our overall wellness, is heavily tied to our emotional intelligence. Only by being aware of our emotional state and our reactions to stress in our lives can we hope to manage stress and maintain good health.

Mental Well-Being: Emotional intelligence affects our attitude and outlook on life. It can also help to alleviate anxiety and avoid depression and mood swings. A high level of emotional intelligence directly correlates to a positive attitude and happier outlook on life. It results in the the ability to stay calm in stressful situations and helps deal with the negative emotions. In order to change the way one feels about a situation, one must first change the way one thinks about it.

Relationships: EQ reflects the ability to read others cues, to accurately perceive and understand others emotional, physical and verbal expressions. By better understanding and managing our emotions, we are better able to communicate our feelings in a more constructive way. We are also better able to understand and relate to those with whom we are in relationships. Understanding the needs, feelings, and responses of those we care about leads to stronger and more fulfilling relationships.

Conflict Resolution: When we can discern people's emotions and empathize with their perspective, it's much easier to resolve conflicts or possibly avoid them before they start. We are also better at negotiation due to the very nature of our ability to understand the needs and desires of others. It's easier to give people what they want if we can perceive what it is.

Success: Higher emotional intelligence helps us to be stronger internal motivators, which can reduce procrastination, increase self-confidence, and improve our ability to focus on a goal. It also allows us to create better networks of support, overcome setbacks, and persevere with a more resilient outlook. Our ability to delay gratification and see the long-term directly affects our ability to succeed.

Leadership: The ability to understand what motivates others, relate in a positive manner, and to build stronger bonds with others in the workplace inevitably makes those with higher emotional intelligence better leaders. An effective leader can recognize what the needs of his people are, so that those needs can be met in a way that encourages higher performance and workplace satisfaction. An emotionally savvy and intelligent leader is also able to build stronger teams by strategically utilizing the emotional diversity of their team members to benefit the team as a whole.

EI and EQ in the Work Place

The workplace is about people and relationships, and an employee with a high EQ as opposed to only a high IQ should be seen as a valuable asset. Goleman made strong claims about the contribution of emotional intelligence to individual success, and specifically to success in the workplace. He identified intellectual intelligence as contributing 20 per cent towards life success and intimated that the remaining 80 per cent may be attributable to emotional intelligence.

Examples of using Emotional Quotient (EQ) at work place include the following-

- **Recruitment-** EQ measurement is invaluable in selecting and recruiting desirable and high-performance workers.
- **Predicting Performance-** Some organisations are blending IQ testing with scientific measurement of EQ to predict job perfor-

mance and direct workers to jobs where they are most likely to succeed.

- **Negotiation-** Whether you're dealing with a trading partner, competitor, customer or colleague, being able to empathize and be creative in finding win-win solutions will consistently pay off.
- **Performance Management-** 360-degree feedback is a common tool for assessing EQ. Knowing how your self-perception compares with others' views about your performance provides focus for career development and positive behavioural changes.
- **Peer Relationships-** Good networking skills are a staple of job effectiveness for the average worker. Networking has too often been associated with "using" other people, but a heightened EQ ensures a mutually beneficial approach to others.

A balanced EQ among employees build conducive work relationship with colleagues and managers. Employees tend to perceive challenges optimistically, as an opportunity for betterment rather than a threat of impediment. For example, an employee with higher EQ understands that her/his manager's decision is not only her/his own opinion rather a reflection of the shared view of the entire organization. Managers understand the non verbal cues of the subordinate. Their feelings are combination of reason, logic and reality. In this environments, employees are intrinsically motivated to their work, they assume accountability of their mistakes, instead of "finger-pointing" or "passing the buck" on others.

There are three intra-personal and two interpersonal EIs that matter most in the domain of Organizational Behavior. These are:

Intra-personal

Self-Awareness: The ability to recognize and understand one's moods, emotions and drives, as well as their effect on others

Self-Regulation: The ability to control or re-direct disruptive impulses and moods and the propensity to suspend judgment and think before acting

Motivation: A passion to work for reasons and a propensity to pursue goals with energy and persistence

Inter-personal

Social Skills - A proficiency in managing relationships and building networks to move people in the desired direction

Empathy - The ability to understand the emotional make up of other people and considering other's feelings especially when making decisions

Example: How EQ can Facilitate Change Management

Change often involves a departure from the safety of the comfort zone. As humans, we enjoy routine, but can be thrown off the ground when this routine is challenged and change is inevitable. This holds true for both work and personal lives.

In the workplace and in our personal lives being emotionally intelligent is an essential component to building resilience for mental health and successfully managing change. Emotionally intelligent leaders and managers are also able to help others to manage difficult change–

- By developing emotional maturity
- By increasing social intelligence
- As a tool to avoid or manage relationship problems
- By improving interpersonal communication
- By helping manage emotions
- As a method of coping with stress
- By influencing leadership styles
- By helping leaders make business decisions about change
- By supporting managers, supervisors and staff in the workplace
- By effectively managing resistance to change

Emotional Intelligence and Work Attitude

There are certain important behavioural attitudes, behaviour and outcomes that are essential for evaluating whether one can be viewed as an effective manager and leader. Emotional Intelligence is related with following work attitude and work behaviours-

- **Job Satisfaction-** Individuals with high emotional intelligence experience continuous positive moods and feelings that generate higher levels of satisfaction and well-being.
- **Organizational Commitment-** Emotionally intelligent individuals

are "optimistic", a trait that enables them to focus on the resolution, rather than the reasoning (who is at fault). Thus, Emotional Intelligence is expected to augment a higher level of commitment to the organizations.

- **Work-Family Confict-** A high emotional intelligence would help the managers balance family interference with work. In fact, they may be more capable of preventing work-family conflict from the beginning because they have emotional insight as to how these emotions should be managed, and the ability to improve the decision-making process.
- **Job Performance-** There is a positive effect of emotional intelligence on the success of the individual at work. Through various studies, it has been showed how the aspects of emotional intelligence - appraisal and expression of emotions, use of emotion to enhance cognitive processing and decision making, knowledge about emotions and management of emotions - contribute to effective leadership.

Emotional Intelligence and Effective Leadership

Increasingly, it is noted that basic management and leadership skills are no longer enough to lead organizations successfully. Emotional intelligence is recognised as having an important role to play in management and leadership positions where differences in technical skills are of negligible importance. Consequently, emotional intelligence is becoming a sought after quality. Some authors on emotional intelligence are of the view that emotional competencies are twice more likely to contribute to organizational success and excellence than pure intellect and/or technical expertise alone. Accordingly, being aware of our emotions and how to manage them in ways that are appropriate and effective is an important skill for leadership, the organization, the team and the individual.

The Future of Emotional Intelligence in Bureaucracies

As bureaucratic processes moved more and more away from the historical concepts of dehumanization and impersonality, the notion that emotional skills are essential to job performance and customer service has gained foothold in the public administration sector. Based on the concepts of self-awareness, self-management, social awareness, and relationship management, emotional intelligence has become key to the internal organization of public agencies (e.g. leadership, co-worker collaboration) and for the external exchange with citizen customers (e.g. as a basis for relational work/emotional labour). Despite some deficiencies (e.g. difficulties in assessment and costs), emotional intelligence skills will continue to be important for bureaucratic processes since social skills in general are expected to decline due to the increased dependency on technological forms of communication.

Helping Others Develop Emotional Quotient (EQ)

If you are one of the unlucky people who must deal with a clueless colleague or a brutish boss, you're not alone. Sadly, far too many people at work lack basic emotional intelligence. They simply don't seem to have the self-awareness and the social skills that are necessary to work in our complicated multicultural and fast-moving companies. These people make life hell for the rest of us.

What can you do to turn these folks around and make work a healthier, happier, more productive place to be? Whose job is it, anyway, to fix these people?

If one of these socially awkward or downright nasty people works directly for you, it is indeed your job to do something. They ruin work teams and destroy productivity, not to mention morale. They're little time bombs that go off when you least expect it – sucking up your time and draining everyone's energy. They need to change, or they need to leave.

Here's the problem: Emotional Intelligence is difficult to develop because it is linked to psychological development and neurological pathways created over an entire lifetime. It takes a lot of effort to change long-standing habits of human interaction – not to mention foundational competencies like self-awareness and emotional self-control. People need to be invested in changing their behavior and developing their EI, or it just doesn't happen. What this means in practice is that you don't have even a remote chance of changing someone's EI unless they want to change.

Most of us assume that people will change their behavior when told to do so by a person with authority (you, the manager).

For complicated change and development, however, it is clear as clear it can be that people do not sustain change when promised incentives like good assignments or a better office. And when threatened or punished, they get downright ornery and behave really badly. Carrot and stick performance management processes and the behaviorist approach upon which they are based are deeply flawed, and yet most of us start (and end) there, even in the most innovative organizations.

What does work is-

a) helping people find a deep and very personal vision of their own future and

b) then helping them see how their current ways of operating might need a bit of work if that future is to be realized.

These are the first two steps in Richard Boyatzis' Intentional Change theory.

Here's how people really can begin and sustain change on complex abilities linked to emotional intelligence:

Find the dream: If you're coaching an employee, you must first help him or her discover what's important in life. Only then can you move on to aspects of work that are important to this person. Then, help your employee craft a clear and compelling vision of a future that includes powerful and positive relationships with family, friends, and coworkers. Notice that I'm talking about coaching your employee, not managing him. There's a big difference.

Findout what's really going on: What's the current state of person's emotional intelligence? Once a person has a powerful dream to draw strength from, he's strong enough to take the heat – to find out the truth. If you are now truly coaching him, you're trusted and he'll listen to you. Still, that's probably not enough. You will want to find a way to gather input from others, either through a 360-degree feedback instrument like the ESCI (Emotional and Social Competency Inventory), or a Leadership Self Study process which gives you the chance to talk directly to trusted friends about their EI and other skills.

Perform Gap Analysis: Once you have the dream and the reality, it's time for a gap analysis and a learning plan. Note that I did not say "performance management plan," or even "development plan." A learning plan is different in that it charts a direct path from the personal vision to what must be learned over time to get there – to actual skill development.

Learning goals are big. Take, for example, one executive though he was talented, he was in danger of being fired for his distinct lack of caring about the people around him. He wanted what he wanted, and watch out if you were in his way. He couldn't seem to change until it finally dawned on him that his bulldozer style was playing out at home too, with his children. That didn't fit at all with his dream of a happy, close-knit family, living close to one another throughout their lives. So, with a dream in hand and the ugly reality rearing its head at work and at home, he decided to work on developing empathy. As a learning goal, empathy is one of the toughest and most important competencies to develop. The capacity for emotional and cognitive empathy is laid down early in life, and then reinforced over many years. This gentleman had a good foundation for empathy in childhood, but intense schooling and a stint at an up-or-out management consulting firm drove it out of him. He needed to relearn how to read people and care about them. He was able to succeed. Yes, it took a good while, but he did it.

These sounds like a lot of hard work for your employee, and it can be. Here's where a final important piece of the theory comes into play. They – and you – can't do it alone. People need people – kind and supportive people – when embarking on a journey of self-development. Are you there for your employees? Do you help them find other supporters, In addition to yourself, who will help when their confidence wanes or when they experience inevitable setbacks?

Developing one's emotional intelligence can make the difference between success and failure in life and in work. And, if you're the one responsible for people's contributions to the team and your organization, you are actually on the hook to try to help those (many) people who are EI-challenged, deficient, and dangerous. It's your job.

But what if you're not the boss? You can still make a difference with colleagues, too. All of the same rules apply to how people change. You just need to find a different entry point, entry begins with you creating a safe space and establishing trust. Find something to like about these people and let them know it. Give them credit where credit is due, and then some (most of these folks are pretty insecure). Be kind. In other words, use your EI to help them get ready to work on theirs.

How to Get Employee Work

What keeps you up at night as a manager? Are you worried about hitting your numbers? How to boost the results of lower performers? What about how to keep top performers motivated?

It is often believed that the most effective way to respond to these concerns is to directly tell our employees what to do. Directing a team is certainly one way to achieve your goals. But while it's tried, it's also tired. Several trends suggest that it's no longer enough to lead by authority. There's an ever-increasing trust gap between leaders and employees (we are twice as likely to trust someone "just like us" than we are as a CEO), endless distractions make it harder to separate the signal from the noise, and more than 67% of employees aren't engaged at work. All of this has left people thirsting for inspiration, which means managers have to rethink how they communicate with their teams.

No one wants another checklist task that they have to complete. We want to be called to something greater. So instead of informing and directing your direct reports, aspire to inspire. When you focus on persuading them, you'll be able to turn even a corporate initiative or new product launch into a cause that becomes their own. They'll want to step up and own their results.

The challenge is how to shift someone's response from "I have to" to "I want to." After pulling together the tips the researchers shared the same with thousands of leaders from Fortune 500 companies, non-profits, and start-ups, and they developed what they call the Communicator's Roadmap.

The vertical axis measures emotional connection. This is your barometer of trust, and it's comprised of the rapport you build with others, your likability, warmth, reliability, and empathy. You can strengthen this connection by showing warmth and care. Personal stories, especially those that reveal vulnerability, can also help others relate to you. As social psychologist Amy Cuddy explains,

"Warmth is the conduit of influence: It facilitates trust and the communication and absorption of ideas."

The Communicator's Roadmap

A guide to creating the most effective message.

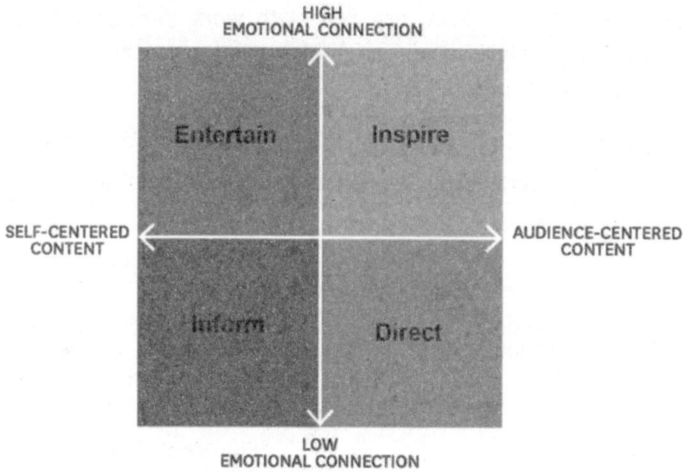

On the horizontal axis, we have content. A self-centered message, on the left side of the spectrum, is not necessarily selfish, but it's all about you – your expertise, your wisdom, your opinions, and your agenda. The right side is all about how the message relates to the other person. These are not mere facts, figures, or frameworks; they are human-scale, concrete, and actionable. If your message is not relevant to someone, it won't be persuasive.

Looking at the four quadrants, most of us default to Inform and Direct as a way to get things done. Sometimes that works - but it's not a long-term solution for retaining top talent, growing your team, or raising the bar.

Consider a hypothetical case: We worked with a client at a financial services company who had a direct report, let's call him Bill, who was not well liked. Bill was a good performer, he was effective on a stage, he got paid well – but his colleagues didn't like him. No matter how hard his manager tried to direct him, "Bill, you need to do a better job and connect with others," he wouldn't make any progress. Bill didn't care if his colleagues liked him or not.

After many dead ends, Bill's manager shifted her approach. She said to him, "I see a future for you here at our company, and I want what's best for you." Empathizing that Bill had such great potential, she made an emotional appeal to Bill's long-term goal to join the management team. She continued, "Peer relationships at that level are critical to work through others - and it's just not possible if you are not trusted and can't connect well with your colleagues."

Tailor Your Message to the Situation and Goal

When to inform, direct, entertain, or inspire your employees.

	Situation	Objective	Message
Inform	A Policy update procedure change	Simple understanding	Straightforward. 'This is process for expense reporting. the or It's due the second Friday of the month. Here are the steps...'
Entertain	A team member is nervous or uncomfortable	A personal connection	Emotional. 'I remember the first time I botched a sale pitch.... it was awful because here's what I learned....'
Direct what	Something is time-sensitive	Prioritization and specific actions	Clarity about who's doing and when. 'Maria, you're responsible for pulling the financial report together. Get it to John by Thursday at noon so he can package all the materials together.'
Inspire	Motivating someone or improving performance	Persuasion	Speak to their future using a story or analogy. 'Someone in engineering once proposed an idea, we took a risk, and it paid off. This is something I see you being able to do.'

This shift in message (toward Audience-Centered content), inspired by her confidence in him (through Emotional Connection), changed Bill's perspective. Building relationships with his colleagues was no longer something he had to do; it was something he wanted to do as part of his own goals and objectives. There was a new personal level of accountability.

Learn to become a Less Autocratic Manager – Based on a Hypothetical Situation

Mark, a ten-year veteran of the pharmaceutical R&D world with a Ph.D. in statistics, was the obvious choice to lead the SAS software and data management group of a global healthcare corporation when the current director suddenly departed. Having managed a small team of bio-statisticians successfully over three years, promoting him to director seemed like a no-brainer. Yet, within six months, despite being viewed as "high potential" by the C-suite, he had managed to alienate just about everyone.

As a team leader, he had proven himself effective – delivering results, improving processes, and directing junior staff. So why, when given the chance to manage a larger, more diverse group of top performers, would he flame out so spectacularly? The answer was simple: Mark was bossy. By the time a coach was brought in, there was an alarming downward trajectory of morale and productivity. 360 feedback suggested that although Mark was respected for his expertise, his management style wasn't working with this more experienced team. Some of his new team members matched his technical skills, and all of them were used to a great deal of autonomy.

As Mark painfully discovered, trying to run a seasoned, highly skilled group with the traditional type-A, command-and-control style is doomed to fail. Today's knowledge workers demand what leadership experts call a "post-heroic leader": one who is emotionally and intellectually agile, able to modulate their style as needed from authoritative to collaborative – and back again – in order to optimize team performance. Post-heroic leaders recognize that the key to success is not adhering to hierarchy or position power, but mastering a complex set of seemingly contradictory organizational dynamics– autonomy and shared decision-making, individuality and teamwork.

Mark's situation called for a change in mindset about what it means to be a good manager. To his credit, he was open to coaching. Yet coaxing him to become more easy-going or to let go of control was not enough. He was used to driving people hard for results.

To help him, Mark's coach re-focused the same deep desire to excel that had made him a great statistician on adjusting his style and provided a framework for change, suggesting several shifts that Mark must undertake:

From self-awareness to social awareness: This shift occurs when a manager realizes that effective leadership calls for more than just knowing one's own strengths and weaknesses. Social awareness calls for a heightened sensitivity to how one's behavior, in words and deeds, impacts others. To help build this awareness, Mark's coach asked him questions like:

- What is the impact of your management style on others?
- How do you know what others are thinking or feeling?

From directive to inquisitive: When seeking to improve processes or engender creativity from an expert group, the manager needs to shift from a stance of declaration to one of curiosity. Questions that help managers make this shift include:

- How much time do you spend listening rather than speaking?
- How do you know if you are truly listening to your people?

From power over to power with: When a manager lauds authority over subordinates, A-players tend to shut down (and look for the exit), while B-players tend to acquiesce, hide out, and fail to grow. As a result, the potential of the entire team is lost. To facilitate this important shift, a coach might ask:

- How do you stimulate the best thinking from your team?
- What is the role of your subordinates in making decisions?

From teamwork to teaming: Traditional managers tend to rely on static definitions of who is "in" and who is "out," fostering a culture of conformity and internal competitiveness. Adaptive managers evoke commitment through common values and aspirational goals, not structure. Good coaching questions include:

- How do you create a sense of belonging when the boundaries of a team are porous?
- How do you leverage diverse talents, skills, and perspectives, getting the best from everyone?

This framework gave Mark tangible guidelines to work with–not just generic admonishments to be more democratic. Coaching provided the space to acknowledge his fear of "losing his edge" and his hard-earned respect from the C-suite while exploring a different possibility: that he could have both – remaining directive when needed, but "flexing" to accommodate a variety of work styles.

Within a few weeks, he had made significant progress on two of the shifts – from power over to power with and from teamwork to teaming. The changes he made included:

1. Setting up a series of brainstorming sessions for process innovation, utilizing an outside facilitator so that he could participate as a team member – not as the boss.
2. Enlisting expert "thought partners" on his team to help make

specific decisions that impacted work flow and initiatives.

3. Pairing senior staff with junior staff for mentoring and coaching.
4. Sending a personal note to each team member, asking them to share what activity, structure, or process would support them to do their best work.
5. Holding an offsite "values summit" to explore what his people cared about most – out of which they created their own internal values statement and a list of operating principles.

Outcome:

Initially, Mark's team was skeptical about his sudden transformation, but with consistency and repetition, he earned their respect and morale improved dramatically. Encouraged by his coach to see himself not so much as "the boss" but as a role model, he began communicating with greater candor and vulnerability.

For any manager that finds herself across the table from a traditional heroic leader, like Mark – one who defaults to position power and authority – the challenge is to accelerate the shift to a more adaptive approach. Start by helping him re-connect to his aspiration to excel, not just as a functional expert but also as a leader. Then provide a framework for considering new options, a safe space for experimentation, and most important, ask thought-provoking, open-ended questions to spark his creativity. With the right kind of support, an old-fashioned manager can make the post-heroic leap, and soar.

When EI trumps IQ

Many companies and B schools still treat strategy and execution as separate beasts, despite increasing evidence that the divide does much more damage than good. A large part of the problem may be that people view strategic reasoning as a high-level executive function of the brain and tactical thought as a discrete, lower-level activity. But the two kinds of thinking are linked in an

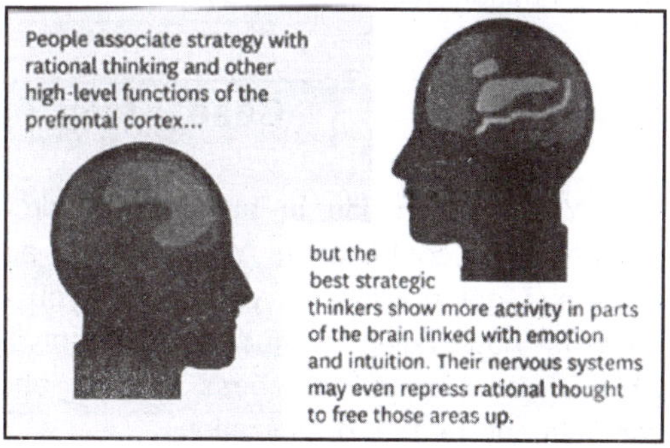

important way: They both draw considerably on social-emotional reasoning, particularly in the brains of the most adept strategic thinkers. Indeed, strategic thought entails at least as much emotional intelligence as it does IQ.

The area of the brain people tend to associate with strategic thought is the prefrontal cortex, known for its role in executive function. It allows humans to engage in anticipation, pattern recognition, probability assessment, risk appraisal, and abstract thinking. Those abilities do help managers solve problems. However, when it was examined - the best strategic performers in the sample, it was found significantly less neural activity in the prefrontal cortex than in the areas associated with "gut" responses, empathy, and emotional intelligence (that is, the insula, the anterior cingulate cortex, and the superior temporal sulcus). In other words, the conscious executive function was downplayed– while regions associated with unconscious emotion processing operated more freely.

What's more, the strongest performers' tactical reasoning relied not only on the insula (associated with emotional processing) and the anterior cingulate cortex (crucial for making new choices based on the assessment of past outcomes). It also engaged the part of the brain (the superior temporal sulcus) associated with parsing sensory stimuli and anticipating other people's thoughts and emotions – for instance, understanding how action plans would be received by the workers charged with implementing them.

Of course, IQ-based reasoning is valuable in both strategic and tactical thinking – but it's clear that managers integrate their brain processes as they become better strategists. When companies or rather the working place realize that, they may approach strategy and execution more holistically.

Case Study I

You are working in an organization and in a project which requires your coordination. You are well acquainted with your boss and have got praises for your work. You come to know that your boss is now being posted to different location. Your old boss while meeting your new boss informs about your dedication and commitment to the organization.

However, you soon realize that all is not well with the new boss. He constantly finds mistakes with your work and creates drama over it. He gives you loads of work and due to insufficiency of time, when you are not able to complete it, he gives you a hard time. Recently, over a minor mistake, he shouted over you. Your boss holds considerable power over your promotion as he is the one who will grade you annually. He also belittle your other colleagues and this has created negative vibes in the organization. You think that saying to him, will make the matters worse. Because of this, your performance is now deteriorating. How would you handle the situation?

This case comes under the following topics:

- Ethical Dilemma
- Emotional Intelligence
- Work Culture
- Empathy
- Attitude

Premise: The consequences for businesses with supervisors who belittle their direct reports or talk down to them are widely known: job performance suffers and mistakes and job migration both increase. It can even have an adverse effect on worker's health. You are suffering because your boss doesn't praise your work and instead is constantly belittling you. Here the question arises on how you can handle the situation. Your boss obviously lacks the Emotional Intelligence, which he could have used to create harmony in the organization and towards you.

Answer: Emotional Intelligence is linked to job performance. A recent study published in the Journal of Applied Psychology looked at the results of 36 separate pieces of research into the relationship between self-reported EI and job performance (measured via supervisor ratings), with an overall data set from 2,168 employed adults. Via a sophisticated bit of number crunching, the authors were able to conclude that there is a strong correlation between EI and job performance.

The ethical dilemma faced by you is that you fear negative outcomes from your boss. You are afraid that since he is your boss, he might take it as an offence and will spoil your annual performance report. However, as your performance is dwindling, he might certainly notice it and this may prove adverse to your situation.

So, let me tell you that 'Avoidance Won't Work'. No one likes dealing with unpleasantness, and as an employee who realizes the power isn't in your hands, it's easy (but not effective) to just suck it up. As a one-off response to a very occasional put-down, that may work. But if the bad behavior happens often and you don't respond, it's likely to get worse because bad bosses are often bullies with self-esteem problems–putting you down raises them up. If you don't fight back, you become an easy target.

It's best to address the problem directly without complicating elaboration. "Boss, I wish you wouldn't say that; for one thing it upsets me and then I have a hard time doing my best work." Notice that you don't say, "I wish you wouldn't say things like that," which is a generalization a bad boss may brush off. When you address the problem directly in response to a specific instance rather than generalizing the boss's response (even though he probably does say things like that quite often), it makes your boss focus on what's recently been said without accusing him of bad behavior in generalizing ways that may seem to him as if you're saying he's a bad person. Limit it to the particular instance.

The next time it happens, your response can be simply, "Boss, please!" adding, if he's not the kind of person who picks up on social cues very well, "We've talked about this and as you know, it makes giving you my best performance harder."

Timing is important, and so is understanding your boss's behavior

Bad bosses often have trigger points that set them off. Unless they're extremely toxic, they probably also have situations and environments where they're more at ease and less inclined to blow up when confronted with their misbehavior. Study the boss to find the best time to confront him.

Often, according to one study, bad bosses behave badly because they feel overloaded and/or they feel they can't take time to be nice. Another frequent response from toxic bosses is fear of being seen as weak unless they bully their reports.

This suggests two components of a responsive strategy:

confront your boss when he's calmed down and isn't giving off signs of anxiety. This might be no more than an hour or two or even less. Secondly, when you confront your boss, toss in a comment or a few sentences to reassure him that his better behavior won't make him seem weak in your eyes and also - very important! - that you're on his side. You're not bringing this up to be confrontational or to try to win a sparring contest; you're bringing it up because you want to give your boss your best performance, the one he deserves. You're addressing the behavior, but you respect your boss.

When All Else Fails...

Often a supervisor-report relationship that gets off to a bad start can change course for the better with a single good interchange. Other times, change comes slowly and you'll have to address the problem several times before there's an improvement. But, as two of the sources on dealing with a bad boss admit, in some instances there really is no cure. If it becomes clear that this is the situation, remember that you don't need to stick around and try to solve your boss's problem. While quitting in the middle of a bad boss's outburst is the worst time, with some bosses, you'll eventually need to plan your departure. If that's the case, consider your options carefully, then act strategically to leave your bad boss for a better work environment with as little drama as possible.

Case Study II

Aakash is a successful financial officer at a Mumbai-based company that recently acquired a banking institution in two southern states. Aakash will take over the recently acquired southern footprint as the new regional CEO.

The newly acquired banking institution has a long-standing reputation as a friendly institution with traditional values, and it prides itself on its exemplary customer service. The current staff has prepared a comprehensive package outlining the bank's vision and key customer success stories that demonstrate their commitment to exemplary service and low customer and employee turnover.

It is Monday morning and Aakash has called a meeting at 8 a.m. Aakash arrives at 7 a.m. and is surprised to find only a couple of employees in the building. Aakash begins the meeting at 8 a.m. sharp, and the auditorium seats are half-filled. Aakash is perplexed at the turnout but begins the meeting. "Shareholder value is what it's all about. We are the stewards of this organization, and we have a responsibility to the shareholders."

Silence echoes in Aakash ears. He continues by stating, "I expect total dedication. If you cannot commit to our new vision and strategies then this is not the right place for you. Commitment starts by being on time." Aakash motioned to the staff standing next to the auditorium doors to close the doors. "If you can't be here on time, then you can't play in our sandbox."

Later that afternoon, Aakash met with the executive team and outlined the strategies, goals, numbers, and deadlines. A meeting was held with senior staff members responsible for reporting progress. Market growth numbers were up, and new business numbers were increasing.

A quarter later Aakash had the quarterly report results. The region was on target. However, turnover increased 25 per cent. Involuntary turnover was up 10 per cent. Previous customer numbers were decreasing, and customer complaints were increasing. He reviewed the report with his staff. When he asked for input, his request was greeted with silence. He sensed an uneasy feeling in the room.

What do you think is wrong here? Do you think the leadership style by Aakash is favorable to the current condition? Comment.

This case comes under the following topics:

- Emotional Intelligence
- Work Culture
- Work Attitude
- Social Influences

Premise: The case here is conflict in the relationship between leadership skills and work attitude. It can be observed that employees in the organization are not following the top- down bottom approach. The leadership skills applied by Aakash here is not useful because it is too dominant and do not give space to other voices. As a CEO he has to strike a balance between employees and employers.

Answer: Emotional intelligence is an ability to perceive, assess, and manage the emotions of yourself and others. Daniel Goleman's groundbreaking work on emotional intelligence groups leadership competencies into four buckets: self-awareness, self-management, social awareness, and relationship management.

When employees greet Aakash with silence, it is obvious that they are fearful of him or have passive attitude. Aakash needs to change his leadership style so as to have a productive organization. And this can be done by raising EQ in himself and his employees.

The first thing that Aakash can do is that he should mitigate stress in the organisation. Stress is widely recognized as playing an important role in mental and physical health, including high blood pressure, diabetes, depression and anxiety. While the stress response is helpful when faced with an immediate crisis (such as a car coming towards you in your lane) increasing focus, respiration and visual acuity, it is too easily launched in everyday interactions. In non-emergency responses, it is disproportional and can lead to chronic health problems. EQ helps address stress by allowing us to recognize and take ameliorative action so it doesn't become chronic.

Secondly, to keep pace with changes in the workplace requires the ability to continue to learn–new technologies, evolving work relationships, and understanding emerging trends. By its nature, learning requires a degree of vulnerability: being open to making mistakes and even failure; and a willingness to stretch comfort zones while climbing the learning curve. People with high emotional intelligence have greater adaptability, demonstrate more curiosity, and are open to lessons from both successes and failures. Emotional intelligence helps lower defensiveness and negativity that blocks our ability to learn, adapt and innovate.

Another source of stress common in today's workplaces is feeling undervalued. Recent neuroscience research has revealed that this kind of psychological stress triggers the same receptors in the brain as physical pain. While activating EQ will not change all workplace dynamics, it can help to temper reactions and promote a more balanced perspective about self-worth that comes from other sources, such as family, volunteering and creative pursuits.

If employees under Aakash feel undervalued then they will work less and with no enthusiasm.

When emotions run high but are not recognized, responses often cluster at either end of a counter-productive spectrum, from paralysis on one end (being unable to respond), to impulsivity (reacting to events without full consideration) at the other extreme. Emotional intelligence allows for needed perspective, providing a wide-angle lens on problems, challenges, and opportunities to better craft informed decisions. This will help employess to make better informed decision.

Setbacks, which are an inevitable part of life, are more pronounced by instability in our workplaces and society. EQ can help us to draw on our inner strength, increase our self-confidence and widen the lens to assess difficult situations in productive ways, such as seeking advice; setting new priorities and finding ways to be resilient.

Highly effective leaders incorporate all four competencies.

♦♦❑❑♦♦

6

CONTRIBUTIONS OF MORAL THINKERS & PHILOSOPHERS

The Concepts Discussed in this Unit

- Theory of Descriptive Ethics by Lawrence Kohlberg
- Jeremy Bentham's Gross or Quantitative Utilitarianism
- Kantian Ethical Theory
- Plato's Concept of Virtues/ Cardinal Virtues
- Aristotelian Concept of Virtue
- Ethics in Indian Philosophy
- Gandhian Ethics
- Thomas Hobbes' Psychological Egoism
- Ayn Rand- Ethical Egoism
- Feminist Ethics – Carol Gilligan
- Existentialist Ethics – Jean Paul Sartre
- Theory of Punishment

Philosophy

Philosophy is the methodical work of thoughts. It is an art of life. It tries to understand the meaning and the value of life. It is an attempt to understand the Ultimate Reality. Philosophy is the study of the principles which underlie all knowledge. Philosophy tries to discover ultimate truth. It is an attempt of rational interpretation and unification of all our experiences. It tries to give a rational picture of the whole universe. The word 'philosophy' is derived from the Greek word 'philosophia' which means striving after wisdom. Philosophy is love of knowledge and philosopher is a person who seeks knowledge.

In India, Philosophy is called 'Darshan' which means 'Vision' and also the means or instruments of Vision. Indian philosophy arises out of the urge for the direct realization of ultimate Reality. We find the seeds of Indian philosophy in the Upanishads, the sacred books of Hindus.

Modern Moral Philosophy

In the 20th century, moral theories have become more complex and are no longer concerned solely with rightness and wrongness, but are interested in many different kinds of moral status. W.D. Ross for instance, argues that moral theories cannot say in general whether an action is right or wrong, but only whether it tends to be right or wrong according to a certain kind of moral duty such as beneficence, fidelity, or justice. Other philosophers have questioned whether these principles or duties can be articulated at all at a theoretical level; some have moved away from the theories and principles of normative ethics towards descriptive morality and meta-ethics. Other philosophers are still defending moral theory on the grounds that it need not be perfect in order to capture important moral insight.

Modern moral philosophy is increasingly revolving around 'claims-based' or 'rights-based ethics', which are ethical theories based on the fundamental principle of human rights and other rights or claims of the individual. Rights-based theories argue that people have a claim to certain freedoms and rights, like liberal theories which focus on people's claim to freedoms like the freedom of speech, association, religion, etc. These modern theories are focusing on people's claim to rights like human rights, civil rights, political rights and social/economic rights. One example is the Universal Declaration of Human Rights of the United Nations. Another example of rights-based theories is 'welfareism', which argues that people have a claim to a welfare state that can provide them with security, basic health services, education, jobs, housing, etc.

Development of Moral Reasoning/Consciousness- Lawrence Kohlberg (Theory of Descriptive Ethics)

Development of Moral Reasoning/Consciousness is a theory of Descriptive Ethics given by renowned psychologist Lawrence Kohlberg (refer Unit-1 for the meaning of descriptive and normative ethics). Lawrence Kohlberg started studying moral development in the 1950s. He posed hypothetical dilemmas of various types to 75 boys aged 10-13-16 and continued to question them periodically for 30 years. At the heart of each dilemma was the concept of justice. On the basis of these interviews Kohlberg concluded that how people think about moral issues reflects cognitive development and that people arrive at moral judgment on their own, rather than merely internalizing standards of parents, teachers or peers.

On the basis of thought processes shown by responses to his dilemmas, Kohlberg (1969) described three levels of moral reasoning. They are:

- Level- I: **Pre-conventional morality-** This is the most basic level of morality The Locus of control is outside the individual. People under external controls obey rules to avoid punishment or to get rewards, or act out of self interest. It is purely ego-centric approach, e.g., a child doesn't copy to avoid punishment.
- Level- II: **Morality of conventional role conformity-** As an individual grows in a complex human society he/she tends to internalize the standards of authority figures. Approval of the society is the locus of control of the moral behaviour. People at this stage of morality are concerned about being "good", pleasing others, and maintaining the social order, e.g., a secondary school goer doesn't copy because he knows his teacher and friends despise it or don't approve it at all.

- Level-III: **Morality of autonomous moral principles-** Confronted by the complexity of moral issues people now realize the conflicts between moral standards and make their own judgments, on the basis of principles of right, fairness and justice. Locus of control of moral behaviour and moral judgment is internal, e.g., a young boy doesn't copy in the competitive exams because he believes that copying defeats the purpose of the examination and therefore it is wrong.

Normative Ethics Theories

There are three important normative ethics theories-

- Virtue Ethics
- Consequentialism (prominently utilitarianism)
- Deontological Ethics (prominently Kantianism)

Virtue Ethics

Virtue ethics focuses on the 'character' of the agent rather than on the formal rules for or the consequences of actions. Virtue ethics includes an account of the purpose of human life, or the meaning of life. To Plato and Aristotle, the purpose was to live in harmony with others, and the four Cardinal Virtues were defined as-

- Prudence/ Wisdom
- Justice
- Fortitude/ Courage
- Temperance

Proponents of virtue theory sometimes argue that a central feature of a virtue is that it is universally applicable. The key elements of virtue ethical thinking are based on the approaches to ethical thinking of the ancient and medieval periods.

The roots of the Western tradition lie in the work of Plato and Aristotle, but virtues are important also in traditions of Chinese moral philosophy.

Consequentialism

This is the ethical theory that most non-religious people think

they use every day. It bases morality on the consequences of human actions and not on the actions themselves. Its emphasis, thus, is on the rightness of the 'end' rather than morality of the 'means' employed.

Thus, from a consequentialist standpoint, a morally right action is one that produces a good outcome, or consequence.

Consequentialism teaches that people should do whatever produces the greatest amount of good consequences. One famous way of putting this is 'the greatest good for the greatest number of people'.

The most common forms of consequentialism are the various versions of utilitarianism, which favour actions that produce the greatest amount of happiness. Three subdivisions of consequentialism are:

- Ethical egoism,
- Ethical altruism, and
- Utilitarianism.

Ethical Egoism

According to this perspective, an action is morally right if the consequences of that action are more favourable than unfavourable 'only to the agent' performing the action.

Ethical Altruism

According to this perspective, an action is morally right if the consequences of that action are more favourable than unfavourable 'to everyone except the agent'.

Utilitarianism

According to this perspective, an action is morally right if the consequences of that action are more favourable than unfavourable 'to everyone'.

Utilitarianism is the altruistic or universalistic form of Ethical Hedonism (where Hedonism argues that pleasure is the highest good and the supreme ideal of life). Utilitarianism maintains that the supreme ideal of life is pleasure - not the individual pleasure but universal or general happiness. The slogan of Utilitarianism is, "The greatest happiness of the greatest number".

In other words, Utilitarianism is the idea that the moral worth of an action is solely determined by its contribution to overall utility, that is, its contribution to happiness or pleasure as summed up among all persons. The more happiness or pleasure for the more people, the better. It is consequentialist because the moral worth of an action is determined by its outcome, and that the ends justify the means. This theory, thus, is in opposition to deontological ethical theory that regards some acts or types of acts as right or wrong independently of their consequences.

Utilitarianism, in normative ethics, is a tradition stemming from the late 18th and 19th century's English philosophers and economists- Jeremy Bentham and John Stuart Mill. Jeremy Bentham advocates Gross or Quantitative Utilitarianism while J.S. Mill advocates Refined or Qualitative Utilitarianism.

Deontological or Non-consequentialism Ethics

Deontology is concerned with the actions themselves and not with the consequences. It looks at the rightness or wrongness of actions themselves, as opposed to the rightness or wrongness of the consequences of those actions. It teaches that some acts are right or wrong in themselves, whatever the consequences, and people should act accordingly

Jeremy Bentham's Gross or Quantitative Utilitarianism

Bentham argues for weighing pleasures and pains in our actions. An action is right if it produces pleasure. An action is wrong if it produces pain. The worth of an action consists in its utility to produce pleasure and to avoid pain. Bentham believes that all pleasures are alike. Pleasures do not have qualitative differences. Pleasures have only quantitative differences i.e. they are more or they are less. Bentham argues that the quantity of pleasure remaining the same, pushpin (a game) is as good as poetry (i.e., there is no qualitative difference between the two).

Bentham argues that each man desires his own happiness. Each man's happiness is good for him. Therefore general happiness is good for all. Bentham asserts that by nature man is egoistic and selfish. Man can be altruistic only when, by being altruistic he satisfies his own desire too. Here Bentham suggests the moral standard of "the greatest happiness of the greatest number of people." The moral standard is not the greatest happiness of one individual but it is happiness of maximum number of people.

Mill's Refined or Qualitative Utilitarianism

The Refined or Qualitative Utilitarianism can be summarized as follows:- The moral criterion is Utility or the greatest happiness principle. Actions are right, if they promote happiness. Happiness means pleasure and the absence of pain. Actions are wrong if they produce unhappiness. Unhappiness is pain and the deprivation of pleasure. Pleasure and freedom from pain are the only desirable ends. All other things like virtue, health, love of honor, wealth, power are desired because they promote happiness.

Mill holds that qualitative distinction among pleasures is as real as quantitative distinction. Intellectual pleasures are better than sensuous pleasures. Mill believes that we ought to seek satisfaction of higher capacities.

Kantian Ethical Theory

Kantianism (or Kantian ethical theory) is deontological, revolving entirely around "duty" rather than emotional feelings or end goals. The core concept is "duty", or what one ought to do in certain situations. Kantianism states that truly moral or ethical acts are not based on self-interest or the greatest utility, but on a sense of "duty" and a sense of what is right and fair on a wider level (despite the possible consequences for the individual and their usefulness for others). Kantian theories are based on the work of the German philosopher Immanuel Kant (1724-1804).

Kant believes that moral law arises from pure will. It arises from free and rational will which is self-determined and self-legislative. A person is free when he is bound by his own will and not by the will of others. Kant regards the moral law imposed by practical reason as 'Categorical Imperative'.

Categorical Imperative is the internal law imposed by conscience upon itself. In other words, a categorical imperative denotes an absolute, unconditional requirement that exerts its authority in all circumstances, both required and justified as an end in itself.

Kant argued against utilitarianism and other moral philosophy of his day, because for example an utilitarian would say that murder is OK if it does maximize good for the greatest number of people; and he who is preoccupied with maximizing the positive outcome for himself would see murder as OK, or irrelevant.

Therefore, Kant argued, these moral systems cannot persuade moral action or be regarded as basis for moral judgments because they are based on subjective considerations. A deontological moral system was his alternative, a system based on the demands of the categorical imperative.

As an example of these categorical imperatives or duties, the philosopher W.D. Ross built upon Kant's theory and listed a few basic "duties"- One should:

- Tell the truth;
- Right the wrongs that one has done to others;
- Act justly;
- Help others in respect to virtue, intelligence, and happiness;
- Improve oneself with respect to virtue and intelligence;
- Give thanks; and
- Avoid injury to others

In Kant's words; "Act so as to treat others as ends and not merely as means".

Corruption and Ethical Theories

Virtue ethics will consider corruption as a break of several categorical imperatives, including to avoid injury and to act justly, because corruption is to favour certain people.

Likewise, deontological ethics (Kantianism) will look at your commitment to principle (and disregard the consequences of a particular act), and will argue that corruption involves deception and undermines the rational and moral capacity of those involved, and therefore deem corruption as unethical.

Consequentialist theories like utilitarianism, however, may see corruption as ethical. Some observers have argued that corruption is to "grease the wheels" and can make bureaucracies work more efficiently (which is useful to most people).

Although this argument is rarely seen today (the immediate

efficiency gain is ruined by the long-term damage made to the administrative system), the argument can exemplify a perspective from which corruption can be seen as ethical.

Virtues and Good Conduct

Virtues are good traits of character and vices are bad traits of character. Virtues as good traits of character can be and must be deliberately cultivated. They make for the survival and the well-being of the human individual and also that of the society. Good life or moral life is developed through the habitual or regular doing of good deeds or actions in changing situations.

'Character' and 'conduct' of a man are intimately related. Conduct of a man is the expression of his character in varied situations. On the contrary, moral character of a person is formed when he does good actions consistently and persistently. In this way, virtues can be cultivated and can be termed as character-values. Since virtues can be cultivated, they can also be described as the acquired dispositions of a virtuous person. Hence, virtues denote the excellence of human character, while vices are the defects of character. These virtues, in other words, refer to the inner traits of man's being. So they constitute the morality of being, while duty and good actions refer to the morality of doing. One simple but profound message of any great man is: Be good and do good, and the way to be good is through the doing of good actions consistently.

Duties are obligatory actions. A man does his duty. Virtue refers to the moral quality of a person. We, therefore, correctly say that a particular person is virtuous if he possesses good qualities. Such a virtuous person is not only good but he also does good deeds. He does not take holidays from virtues. The existence of virtues in a person is inferred from the habitual good conduct of that person. One has to choose to be virtuous and pursue the path of good and right actions. Virtues promote the well being of their possessors and also of their society, while vices run counter to the welfare of their possessors.

Virtue and Vices

The Greek term for virtue is 'arête' which was used for

excellence of any kind. But generally the excellence referred to is an excellence belonging to human person so that the virtues may be described as the forms of human excellence. 'Virtue' which comes from the Latin 'virtus' means moral excellence. A virtue is a character trait or quality valued as being good. Personal virtues are characteristics valued as promoting individual and collective well-being, and thus good by definition. The opposite of virtue is vice.

In ethics, 'virtue' is used with two somewhat different meanings:

(a) A virtue is a quality of character - a disposition to do what is right in a particular direction, or to perform one of the more universal duties;

(b) A virtue is also a habit of action corresponding to the quality of character or disposition. We may refer to the honesty of a human person, or to the honesty of his dealings equally as virtues.

Virtues can be placed into a broader context of values. Each individual has a core of underlying values that contribute to our system of beliefs, ideas and/or opinions. Integrity in the application of a value ensures its continuity and this continuity separates a value from beliefs, opinion and ideas. In this context, a value (e.g., Truth or Equality or Creed) is the core from which we operate or react. Societies have values that are shared among many of the participants in that culture. An individual's values typically are largely, but not entirely, in agreement with their culture's values. Individual virtues can be grouped into one of four categories of values: **Ethics** (virtue - vice, good - bad, moral - immoral - amoral, right - wrong, permissible - impermissible) **Aesthetics** (beautiful, ugly, unbalanced, pleasing) **Doctrinal** (political, ideological, religious or social beliefs and values) **Innate/Inborn** (inborn values such as reproduction and survival)

Vice is a practice or a habit considered immoral, depraved, and/or degrading in the associated society. In more minor usage, vice can refer to a fault, a defect, an infirmity or merely a bad habit. Synonyms for vice include fault, depravity, sin, iniquity, wickedness and corruption. The modern English term that best captures its original meaning is the word vicious, which means "full of vice". In this sense, the word 'vice' comes from the Latin word 'vitium', meaning “failing or defect”. Vice is the opposite of virtue. The term 'vice' is also popularly applied to various activities considered immoral by some: a list of these might include the abuse of alcohol and other recreational drugs, gambling, smoking, recklessness, cheating, lying and selfishness. Behaviors or attitudes going against the established virtues of the culture may also be called vices: for instance, effeminacy is considered a vice in a culture espousing masculinity as an essential element of the character of males..

Plato’s Concept of Virtues/ Cardinal Virtues

Plato (427 BC-347 BC) was a great Greek philosopher. He is known as a true disciple of Socrates. Plato’s doctrine of cardinal virtues is based on his concept of virtue. According to Plato, goodness consists of the natural and proper functioning of human nature. Besides, man is social by nature; therefore, society is a normal background of moral life of human beings. Socrates had said that virtue is knowledge. It means that insight into the nature of moral virtues is essential for becoming virtuous. Of course mere knowledge of virtue is not enough. Man has to cultivate virtues through the habit of doing obligatory and morally good actions. For Plato, good life is the life of virtues.

Plato has described four important virtues in his theory of Morality-

- Wisdom
- Courage
- Temperance
- Justice

According to him the cultivation of these four virtues constitutes a morally good life. Later on, these four virtues came to be called ‘Cardinal virtues’. The term ‘cardinal’ is derived from the word ‘Cardo’. ‘Cardo’ means a hinge or a hook which supports the door, and on which the door turns. The four virtues are cardinal because they support moral life of man in society. They are fundamental virtues. Other virtues depend upon them and are therefore subordinate to them.

According to Plato, the key to moral life is the proper

integration of the three parts of the self. The three elements or parts of human beings are:

- Passionate or Appetitive Element (Passions)
- Spirited or Dynamic & Executive Element (Will)
- Philosophical or Rational Element (Reason or Intellect)

This integration can be achieved when the spirited element helps the reason to keep the passions in check. According to Plato, the four cardinal virtues have both individual and social significance. They are found both in the individual and in the society. Human beings are rational and social animals. They have the natural tendency to live in communities. Morality of the society is the same as it is for the individual. According to Plato, society is the individual 'writ large'. For society is made up of individuals.

Aristotelian Concept of Virtue

Aristotle (384 BC to 322 BC) was also a great Greek philosopher. He was the first to write a book on ethics in the Western world. Knowledge, courage, bravery, and perseverance by themselves do not make a morally good character or man. Their ethical significance depends on the motives and the values to which they are related. Aristotle, therefore, rightly distinguishes the moral virtues from the intellectual virtues. The doctrine of the golden mean is central in Aristotle's concept of virtues.

Aristotle is also right in extending the meaning of the important virtue of justice. He considers justice as the supreme virtue. It has two forms-

- Distributive Justice
- Remedial Justice

Distributive Justice consists of the equitable distribution of wealth and honours among the citizens of the state. Remedial Justice consists of the fair transactions among the members of the community. The virtues are acquired through the development of the habit of doing virtuous actions consistently. Ability to think and ability to control one's desires and passions is the special virtue of man.

According to Aristotle, virtuous conduct consists in avoiding the extremes of excess or of deficiency. For instance, excessive indulgence is as much a vice as the excessive repression of desires. Self control, therefore, is a virtue. Likewise, courage is the mean between rashness and cowardice. For instance generosity lies between meanness and prodigality. Thus, virtue is a matter of striking a mean between two vices. Moral virtue thus is a mean state lying between two vices, viz. a vice of excess on the one side and a vice of deficiency on the other.

It is not easy to find the mean. As Sahakian has pointed out, it consists in doing the right thing, to the right person, to the right extent, with the right motive, and at the right time. For instance, the practice of generosity: give generously to the right person, at the right time, to the right extent, with the right purpose.

Ethical/Moral Relativism

Ethical relativism is the moral theory that holds that morality is relative to the norms of one's culture. That is, whether an action is right or wrong depends on the moral norms of the society in which it is practiced. The same action may be morally right in one society but be morally wrong in another. For the ethical relativist, there are no universal moral principles -- principles that can be universally applied to all peoples at all times.

Ethical relativism is a moral theory that promotes tolerance as its value.

Ethical relativists dispute the idea that there are some objective and discoverable 'super-rules' that all cultures ought to obey. They believe that relativism respects the diversity of human societies and responds to the different circumstances surrounding human acts.

Relation of Ethical Relativism to Normative Ethics

Ethical Relativism is the position that there are no objectives or universally valid moral principles, for; all moral judgments are simply a matter of human opinion.

Ethical Relativism goes one step further and makes a judgment that says the morals of the culture are right for that culture. This latter approach is a normative ethic. To further explain, given such variety in practices around the world, one is inclined to wonder who's got the right set of rules. The relativist answer is: no one does- right and wrong are relative. A normative ethic is one that asks, "What should or should not be done?"

The original advocate for this approach is Ruth Benedict, cultural anthropologist who started out trying to describe normal cultural behaviours. Her work boils down to the notion that "what is normal is moral."

Ethical/ Moral Objectivism

Ethical Objectivism is the view that there are universal and objectively valid moral principles that are relative neither to the individual nor to the society.

According to this perspective, the truth or falsity of typical moral judgments does not depend upon the beliefs or feelings of any person or group of persons. This view holds that moral propositions are analogous to propositions about chemistry, biology, or history: they describe (or fail to describe) a mind-independent reality.

When they describe it accurately, they are true–no matter what anyone believes, hopes, wishes, or feels. When they fail to describe this mind-independent moral reality, they are false–no matter what anyone believes, hopes, wishes, or feels.

Ethical/ Moral Absolutism

According to this perspective, certain principles are universal and non-overrideable and true for all situations. Moral absolutism argues that there are some moral rules that are always true, that these rules can be discovered and that these rules apply to everyone. Immoral acts- acts that break these moral rules- are wrong in themselves, regardless of the circumstances or the consequences of those acts.

Ethical/ Moral Realism

Moral realism is based on the idea that there are real objective moral facts or truths in the universe. Moral statements provide factual information about those truths.

Ethical/ Moral Subjectivism

Subjectivism teaches that moral judgments are nothing more

than statements of a person's feelings or attitudes, and that ethical statements do not contain factual truths about goodness or badness.

In more detail: subjectivists say that moral statements are statements about the feelings, attitudes and emotions that particular person or group has about a particular issue. If a person says something is good or bad they are telling us about the positive or negative feelings that they have about that something.

Ethical/ Moral Emotivism

Emotivism is the view that moral claims are no more than expressions of approval or disapproval. This sounds like subjectivism, but in emotivism a moral statement doesn't provide information about the speaker's feelings about the topic but just expresses those feelings.

Ethical/ Moral Prescriptivism

Prescriptivists think that ethical statements are instructions or recommendations. So, if I say something is good, I'm recommending you to do it, and, if I say something is bad, I'm telling you not to do it.

Ethical/ Moral Supernaturalism

Supernaturalism makes ethics inseparable from religion. It teaches that the only source of moral rules is God. So, something is good because God says it is, and the way to lead a good life is to do what God wants.

Ethical/ Moral Intuitionism

Intuitionists think that good and bad are real objective properties that can't be broken down into component parts. Something is good because it's good; its goodness doesn't need justifying or proving. Intuitionists think that goodness or badness can be detected by adults- they say that human beings have an Intuitive moral sense that enables them to detect real moral truths. They think that basic moral truths of what is good and bad are self-evident to a person who directs their mind towards moral issues. For the intuitionist, moral truths are not discovered by rational arguments.

Hedonism

Hedonism is a school of thought that argues that pleasure is the highest good, the supreme ideal of life. In simple terms, a hedonist strives to maximize net pleasure (pleasure minus pain). Ethical hedonism is the idea that all people have the right to do everything in their power to achieve the greatest amount of pleasure possible to them. It is also the idea that every person's pleasure should surpass their amount of pain.

Hedonism evaluates human actions on the basis of the consequences of actions i.e. pleasure and pain. Human conduct has a value in proportion to the amount of pleasure in it. The standard of morality for Hedonism is 'pleasure'. A right action is that which produces pleasure. A wrong action is that which produces pain.

Psychological Hedonism and Ethical Hedonism

There are two forms of Hedonism viz. Psychological Hedonism and Ethical Hedonism. Psychological Hedonism believes that pleasure is the natural object of desire. Man naturally seeks pleasure. Psychological Hedonism is a statement of fact. Ethical Hedonism believes that pleasure is the proper object desire. Man ought to seek pleasure. Ethical Hedonism is a statement of value.

Ethical Hedonism has two forms viz. Egoistic Hedonism and Universalistic Hedonism or Utilitarianism. For Egoistic Hedonism, individual's own pleasure is the highest good. And for the Universalistic Hedonism or Utilitarianism, pleasure of a number of people is the highest good. In other words, Egoistic Hedonism strives after individual's own pleasure. Universalistic Hedonism seeks general happiness and not individual pleasure.

Ethical Hedonism- Gross and Refined

Ethical Hedonism, (whether Egoistic or Universalistic) again has two varieties viz. gross and refined. Gross Hedonism gives weightage to the sensuous pleasures. All pleasures are alike and they differ only in intensity. Present pleasures are to be preferred over future pleasures. Refined Hedonism gives weightage to mental and more subtle, fine pleasures. Refined Hedonism accepts the role of reason in the attainment of pleasures.

Ethics in Indian Philosophy

In Indian view, the obligation of individual is not confined to human society only. It is extended to the whole of sentient creation. Indian philosophy holds, "Love thy neighbour as thyself and every living being is thy neighbour". Moral philosophy in India is truly speaking the art of living a good and disciplined life.

Indian view of moral philosophy is different from that of Western Philosophy. In Western philosophy ethics is an intellectual enquiry whereas in Indian view, it is the way of life to realize the ultimate reality.

Indian Schools of Philosophy

Indian Schools of Philosophy are broadly classified into Orthodox (Astika) and Heterodox (Nastika). Six chief philosophical systems viz. Mimansa, Vedanta, Sankhya, Yoga, Nyaya and Vaisheshika are Orthodox schools of Indian Philosophy. These schools accept the authority of the Vedas. So they are called as Orthodox or Astika schools. Three Chief Philosophical Systems viz. the Charvakas, the Bauddha and the Jainas are Heterodox Schools of Indian Philosophy. These schools do not accept the authority of the Vedas. So they are called as Heterodox or Nastika schools.

Features of Indian Ethics: Orthodox and Heterodox

All Indian systems of thought whether Orthodox - which follows the authority of Vedas - or Heterodox share some common features. The features of Indian Ethics can be stated as below:

- Indian ethics is the oldest moral philosophy in the history of civilization. It is difficult to ascertain the chronology of the Orthodox and the Heterodox schools (except Lord Buddha i.e., 487 BC). The remoteness of Indian ethics is responsible for making it well established in the practical life of the followers. Every school of Indian Philosophy confirms the endurance of ethical ideals which are unshaken even today.
- Indian thinkers suggest some practical means of attaining a life of perfection here in this world. The rules of conduct have been practically followed by the Yoga, the Jain and the Buddhist disciples for thousand years. The aim of Indian

moral philosophy is not only to discuss moral ideals but also to follow the path leading to the moral Ideals.

- Indian ethics has its strong and deep metaphysical foundation. Each school of philosophy, points to metaphysical ideals which are to be actually experienced. There is a synthesis of theory and practice, of intellectual understanding and direct experience of ultimate reality (Kaivalya, Nirvana, etc.) In Indian Ethics, intellectualism and moralism are two wings that help the soul in spiritual flight.
- Indian ethics is absolutistic and spiritualistic. It aims at realization of supreme reality by transcending pleasure and pain; even right and wrong and good and evil. The ideals are attainable by spiritual discipline.
- Indian Ethics is humanistic. It seeks a balance between individual's inner and outer life; individual and social life. Moral laws or code of conduct is prescribed in such a way that individual progress and social welfare will lead to harmonious living. The goal of morality is the wellbeing of humanity.
- Indian ethical thinkers preach non-violence, love, compassion and good will for all living beings. It is not limited to human beings. It includes every living beings, plants, birds, and animals, every visible and invisible form of life.
- Indian thinkers believe in the Law of Karma. Law of Karma means that all our actions good or bad produce their proper consequences into the life of an individual, who acts with a desire for fruits thereof. It is the general moral law which governs the life of all individuals. Law of Karma is the force generated by an action that has the potency of bearing fruit. It is the law of the conservation of moral values. Except Charvakas, all Indian schools accept the Law of Karma.

Purusharthas

The Indian thinkers were not only interested in knowing the Ultimate Reality but in realizing the Ultimate Reality. Philosophy is an art of living a good and fulfilling life. They prescribed Four Supreme Ends that is Purusharthas- Dharma, Artha, Kama and Moksha. The term 'Purushartha' means the goal or the end that every human being (man or woman) ought to seek. The Purusharthavada is a comprehensive Indian theory of human values.

Man is a rational, social, moral and spiritual being. His needs are to be satisfied. Good life consists in the pursuit of four Supreme Ends, namely Dharma (Virtue), Artha (Wealth), Kama (Desire) and Moksha (Liberation). Artha satisfies material needs of individual, Kama satisfies psychological needs and Moksha aims at spiritual satisfaction. Dharma accompanies throughout the life.

Dharma

The term 'Dharma' is derived from the root 'dhr' meaning to hold together, to sustain, and to nourish. Thus 'Dharma' literally means 'That which holds together.' It is the basis of harmony in individual life and order in society. Dharma is therefore the basis of social and moral order. ("Dharanat Dharma Ityahuh") Dharma as the Supreme End stands for the principles that lead to the harmony in social relationships and integrity of an individual's personality.

Among the four Purusharthas, Dharma is always mentioned first. It is given priority over others because all human pursuits have to be compatible with moral values and principles. Dharma is said to be the special characteristic of human beings. All living organism indulge in eating, sleeping, sorrow, and sex. Dharma is the distinguishing characteristic of human beings. Dharma indicates moral and reflective awareness. Man is essentially a rational and spiritual being. He is not satisfied with the mere satisfaction of biological needs of hunger, sex and safety. He has higher needs -psychological, moral and spiritual.

The Idea of Nishkama Karma (disinterested performance of duties)

The Bhagwad Gita is the most popular and the most influential religious book of the Hindus. It summarizes the important elements in Hindu philosophy. Great Indian thinkers like Shankaracharya, Ramanuja, Madhava, Dnyaneshwar, etc. have written illuminating commentaries on the Gita. Great national leaders like Lokmanya Tilak and Mahatma Gandhi have drawn inspiration from the Gita. The Gita derives its philosophical content chiefly from the Upanishads. It also synthesizes the philosophical elements from Sankhya, Yoga, etc. schools of philosophy.

The Gita preaches the path of Nishkama Karma, i.e., performing our duties in disinterested way without expecting the fruits of our actions. Our duties must be performed without selfish motive. We have to offer the fruits of our actions to the Divine. We have a right to the performance of our duties but we do not have any right to the rewards of our actions. Actions are our sphere, fruits are not our concern.

The ideal of the Gita is performance of duties in a detached spirit. The Gita teaching stands, not for renunciation of action but for renunciation in action. The Gita does not preach to renounce everything but to renounce the selfish desires and the fruits of one's actions. The individual should give up any expectation for the rewards. His actions should be the performance of his prescribed duties.

The Gita ethics is neither hedonistic nor ascetic. It condemns the wild pursuit of pleasures, as well as suppression of desires. The Gita prescribes controlled satisfaction of humanly desires. The Gita ethics promotes individual as well as social welfare.

Hinduism

Hinduism is the oldest living religion in the world. Hinduism is thought to have gotten its name from the Persian word hindu, meaning "river," used by outsiders to describe the people of the Indus River Valley. Hindus themselves refer to their religion as sanatama dharma, "eternal religion," and varnasrama dharma, a word emphasizing the fulfillment of duties (dharma) appropriate to one's class (varna) and stage of life (asrama).

Most Hindus believe in a Supreme God, whose qualities and forms are represented by the multitude of deities which emanate from him. Hindus believe that existence is a cycle of birth, death, and rebirth, governed by Karma. Hindus believe that the soul passes through a cycle of successive lives and its next incarnation is always dependent on how the previous life was lived.

Hinduism preaches optimism, because it reposes confidence in the individual. This is born out by the theory of incarnation or birth in human form of god. Whenever the universe is overwhelmed by the wicked and whenever the dharma is threatened, these incarnations take place. These periodic purges are at the basis of the Hindu division of time (Krita, Treta, Dvapara, and Kali) and the ten incarnation of Vishnu, the "Dasavataras". Those go to heaven, who have accumulated merit, the others go to hell. Hinduism also emphasizes asceticism, renunication of worldly life and non-violence, but it does not say that the life of an ascetic is the only way or the best way, to attain the desired fruits.

Other Religious Philosophies

Sikhism

The founder of Sikhism was Guru Nanak. He attem¬pted to eliminate the caste system. He was followed by nine gurus. Guru Gobind Singh was the last and tenth guru. The sacred book of Sikhism is "Guru Granth Sahib". It includes the selected works of many authors from diverse socio-economic and religious backgrounds. The religious Philosophy of Sikhism is mainly influenced by Islam and Hinduism. The principal belief in Sikhism is faith in one God - Vahiguru.

It advocates the pursuit of salvation through disciplined, personal meditation on the name and message of God. Sikhism's traditions and teachings are distinctly associated with the history, society and culture of the Indian sub-continent.

Islam

The word "Islam" means "Surrender to God". Those who submitted to this concept became Muslims. The motherland of Islam is Arabia. Arabia was inhabited by nomadic tribes called Bedouin who roamed the desert with their flocks. Each tribe was divided into clan and each clan followed its own culture. However, all of them spoke a single language and went to Mecca for pilgrimage.

Prophet Mohammed was born around 570 A.D, in Mecca. He is believed to have been a descendent of Abraham, the founder of Judaism. Mohammed received the revelation of Allah, compiled in the Quran, which is the holy and sacred book of Muslims. It gives explanation of Quranic teaching in the "Sunna", a collection of traditions. Both are reinforced by the principle of Ijma, which states the belief that a majority of Muslims cannot agree in error. The Quran, the Sunna and the Ijma are three foundations of Islam.

Islam does not profess to be a new religion for¬mulated by Prophet Mohammed but is the continuation of all former religious principles. Islam is strictly monotheistic and believes in absolute submission to God's will. Every Muslim is expected to fulfil five duties: (i) believe in Allah, the God; (ii) Do Namaz five times a day; (iii) fast during Ramzan; (iv) give alms to the poor; and (v) visit Mecca at least once in his lifetime.

There are four main bases of the Muslim social institutions - family, marriage, divorce, and institution governing inheritance. Islam has given full importance to family and laid down certain rules and regulations to maintain its order. The main objective of family is the preservation of human society and civilisation. The whole socio-cultural stru¬cture is based on it. The Quran and Shariah give basic guidelines for maintenance of social organi¬sation.

Christianity

Christianity was foun¬ded by Jesus Christ, but it has its roots in the Judaic tradition. The Bible is the sacred book of Christianity. It is divided into two books - the Old Testament and the New Testament. The Old Testament deals with the period before the birth of Jesus Christ, originally written in Hebrew and partly in Aramaic. The New Testament deals with the life and teachings of Jesus and the Acts of his Apostles which depict the formative period of Christianity, origi¬nally written in Greek and partly in Aramaic. The first four New Testament books tell the life, death and resurrection of Christ which is known as Gospels.

The Biblical concept of God is rather complex. God is one but has revealed himself in the Bible as three persons - the father, the son and the Holy Spirit. The incarnation of Jesus as man, according to the Bible, is a part of the divine plan for the atonement of the sins of mankind. Christian thought regards man as essentially sinful. Ever since Adam and Eve violated the divine will, the human race has fallen into this sinful state. In general, the religious services of Christians are mainly aimed at worshipping God in spirit and truth that is worshipping the father through Jesus and in the power of the Holy Spirit.

Zoroastrianism

Zoroastrianism is the ancient religion of Persia. It is one of the world's oldest monotheistic religions. It was founded about 3500 years ago by the prophet Zarathustra. Zarathustra preached that there was one God, whom he called Ahura Mazda. Ahura means "Lord," and Mazda means "Wise," so Zoroastrians call God the "Wise Lord."

The basic scripture of Zoroastrianism is a set of 5 poetic songs called the "Gathas," which were composed by Zarathustra himself. The Gathas are composed in a very ancient language known as Avestan, which is closely related to Sanskrit.

In the Gathas, Zarathustra preached that the One God, Ahura Mazda, is transcendent, but he is in constant relationship with human beings and the world God created through his Attributes. These Attributes are how God reaches the world, and how the world reaches God. Zarathustra did not specify a fixed number of Attributes, but soon after the Prophet they were specified into seven. These attributes are called the "Amesha Spentas," or "Bounteous Immortals." Each one of these embodies an attribute of God, as well as a human virtue. They are also symbols for the various sectors of Creation over which God watches.

Zoroastrian worship involves prayers and symbolic ceremonies said before a sacred fire. Zoroastrianism does not teach or believe in reincarnation or karma. Zoroastrianism also believes in the progress of sacred time, and the eventual end of time. Zoroastrians are roughly split into two groups: The Iranians and The Parsis.

Judaism

Judaism is the world's oldest great monotheism and the parent religion of both Christianity and Islam. The name 'Judai' derives from the Latin Judaeus and the Hebrew Yahudi, means the descendent of Judah, who was the fourth son of Jacob. Judaism recognises one god, sometimes called Elohim or Jehovah. The basic prayer of Judaism is called the Shema. The basis of Judaism is belief in the living God, who is transcendent, omnipotent and just who reveals himself to mankind. Jud¬aism is strictly monotheistic. God is the creator and absolute ruler of the universe. The emphasis in Judaism is on ethical behaviour as the true worship of God.

Judaism elaborates the system of Laws and rituals, such as dietary regulations. Jews have an ordained clergy and observe the Sabbath, which runs from the sunset of Friday to the sunset of Saturday and is observed with services of prayer in local synagogues.

Taoism

The name "Taoism" comes from Tao, the term used to represent the absolute. Knowledge of the absolute is not to be attained by study or reason, but by contemplation. The Taoists identified themselves with nature that urged the acceptance of all things in their natural state and deplored passions, unnecessary inventions, artificial ceremonies and governing activities such as war and taxation.

Taoism was founded by Lao Tse, a Chinese philospher and prominent religious leader. He worked as a record keeper in the court of the "Chou". His main work is called "Tao Te Ching", the Book of the World Law and its Power. The Taoists opposed rituals, social codes, morals and intellectualism of Confucianism. They believed that society can be reformed by returning to primitive times. In its teaching, virtue was cast in passive and feminine term. Taoism developed beliefs concerning the afterlife, which included a heaven and hell, as well as a cosmology that divided all reality into male and female principles or Yang and Yin. Taoism became concerned with magic and also provided the basis for many secret societies.

Confucianism

Confucianism was founded by Confucius, who was born in the state of Lu, Northern China in 551 B.C. Confucianism is primarily a body of ethics and can be considered as an institutional religion only; in that it requires sacrifices to the gods and ancestors. Confucianism does not restrict itself to any formalised theology. The central concept of Confucian ethics is Zen, which signifies the supreme virtue of love and goodness. There are no churches, clergy or creeds in Confucianism.

Confucianism is known to the Chinese as "Ju Chaio" (teaching of the scholars) and was the dominant force in Chinese thou¬ght, education ¬and governance for 2,000 years. Confucians generally conduct their lives according to five cardinal virtues–kindness, righteousness, decorous behaviour, wisdom and uprightness. Confucius taught that the chief ethic was benevolence and one of his prime precepts was "Treat inferiors with Propriety".

Druze

Druze is a relatively small Middle Eastern religious sect characterized by an eclectic system of doctrines and by a cohesion and loyalty among its members that have enabled them to maintain for centuries of turbulent history their close-knit identity and distinctive faith. They call themselves al-Muwahhidin ("The Monotheists").

The Druze recognize all three monotheistic religions, they believe that rituals and ceremonies have caused Jews, Christians, and Muslims to turn aside from pure faith. The Druze religion is secret and closed to converts. From the theological perspective, the secrecy derives from the tenet that the gates of the religion were open to new believers for the space of a generation when it was first revealed and everyone was invited to join.

Baha'i

The Bahá'í Faith is the youngest of the world's independent religions. Its founder, Bahá'u'lláh (1817-1892), is regarded by Bahá'ís as the most recent in the line of Messengers of God that stretches back beyond recorded time and that includes Abraham, Moses, Buddha, Krishna, Zoroaster, Christ and Muhammad.

The central theme of Bahá'u'lláh's message is that humanity is one single race and that the day has come for its unification in one global society. One of the purposes of the Bahá'í Faith is to help make this possible. A worldwide community of some five million Bahá'ís, representative of most of the nations, races and cultures on earth, is working to give Bahá'u'lláh's teachings practical effect. Their experience will be a source of encouragement to all who share their vision of humanity as one global family and the earth as one homeland.

Among the principles which the Bahá'í Faith promotes as vital to the achievement of this goal are

- the abandonment of all forms of prejudice
- assurance to women of full equality of opportunity with men
- recognition of the unity and relativity of religious truth
- the elimination of extremes of poverty and wealth
- the realization of universal education
- the responsibility of each person to independently search for truth
- the establishment of a global commonwealth of nations
- recognition that true religion is in harmony with reason and the pursuit of scientific knowledge

Yazidis

The Yazidis are Kurdish-speaking people that adhere to the religion Yazidism. Yazidism is a religion rooted in Persian religions blended with elements of pre-Islamic religious traditions, Mithraism, Christianity and Islam. In addition to the Kurdish-speaking majority, there are significant Yazidi communities that speak Arabic as their native language. Their ethnicity is obscure despite the fact that they mostly speak Kurdish. Commentators identify the Yazidis as predominately Kurds but according to some sources, they tend to regard themselves as distinct from Kurds.

Yazidis discourage marriage outside the community and even across their caste system. Their unique beliefs and practices, some are known to refrain from eating lettuce and wearing the colour blue, have often been misconstrued as satanic. Orthodox Muslims consider the peacock a demon figure and refer to Yazidis as devil worshippers.

The Yazidis are at the risk of extinction due to the onslaught of Islamist jidahists on the town of Sinjar. The Yazidis have been pushed out of houses and into the treacherous Sinjar mountains where basic necessities such as food and water have been scarce. Those who refused to move from their houses are being viciously hunted down by Islamic State.

In 2014, with the territorial gains of the Islamic State of

Iraq and the Levant (ISIS) there was much upheaval in the Iraqi Yazidi population. ISIS had previously declared the Yazidis as devil worshippers and had taken the two nearby small oil fields and the town of Zumar as part of a plan to seize Mosul's hydroelectric dam.

Buddhist Ethics

The Buddhist Ethics is compassionate and humanistic. Buddha's gospel is the gospel of love. Buddha asked for the cultivation of true love for all creation. He tried to enlighten people on the question of sorrow, its origin, its cessation and the path leading to its cessation.

The core ethical code of Buddhism is known as the five precepts, and these are the distillation of its ethical principles. The precepts are not rules or commandments, but 'principles of training', which are undertaken freely and need to be put into practice with intelligence and sensitivity.

The Buddhist tradition acknowledges that life is complex and throws up many difficulties, and it does not suggest that there is a single course of action that will be right in all circumstances. Indeed, rather than speaking of actions being right or wrong, Buddhism speaks of being skillful (kusala) or unskillful (akusala).

The Five Precepts are:

- **Not killing or causing harm to other living beings:** This is the fundamental ethical principle for Buddhism, and all the other precepts are elaborations of this. The positive counterpart of this precept is love.
- **Not taking the not-given:** Stealing is an obvious way in which one can harm others. One can also take advantage of people, exploit them, or manipulate them. The positive counterpart of this precept is generosity.
- **Avoiding sexual misconduct:** It includes avoiding breaking commitments in the area of sexual relations. The positive counterpart of this precept is contentment.
- **Avoiding false speech:** Truthfulness, the positive counterpart of this precept, is essential in an ethical life.
- **Abstaining from drink and drugs:** The positive counterpart of this precept is mindfulness, or awareness. Mindfulness is a

fundamental quality to be developed by following the Buddha's path, and experience shows that taking intoxicating drink or drugs tends to run directly counter to this.

Jaina Ethics

Jaina ethics is directed toward the liberation of the individual. Its orientation is therefore religious. Its end is the spiritualization of all areas of life in order to fit the individual for his final goal. Its primary precept applicable to king and commoner alike is, "Do your duty and do it as humanly as you can". The Jain morality and ethics are rooted in its metaphysics and its utility towards the ultimate objective of liberation. Jaina ethics evolved out of the rules for the ascetics, which are encapsulated in the Mahavratas or the five great vows:

- Ahimsa, non-violence
- Satya, truth
- Asteya, non-stealing
- Brahmacharya, celibacy
- Aparigraha, non-possession

These ethics are governed not only through the instrumentality of physical actions, but also through verbal action and thoughts. Thus, ahimsa has to be observed through mind, speech, and body. The other rules of the ascetics and laity are derived from these five major vows.

Jainism does not invoke fear of or reverence for God or conformity to the divine character as a reason for moral behaviour, and observance of the moral code is not necessary simply because it is God's will. Neither is its observance necessary simply because it is altruistic or humanistic, conducive to general welfare of the state or the community. Rather, it is an egoistic imperative aimed at self-liberation.

Charvaka Ethics or Lokayat-mat

Among all the schools of Indian Philosophy, Orthodox or Heterodox, the Charvaka School has unique position. It advocates Atheism, Materialism and Hedonism. The Charvaka views are always the object of criticism for all other schools of thought. The original work of the Charvakas is not available. We know the Charvaka view through the criticism of other philosophers. The Charvaka view is also known as 'Lokayatmat'. This school holds that only this world (Loka) exists.

Indian thinkers advocated four Supreme Ends (Purusharthas) viz. Dharma (Virtue), Artha (Wealth), Kama (Desire) and Moksha (Liberation). The Charvakas accept reality of this empirical world and the physical body as the soul. Hence, the Charvakas deny Dharma and Moksha as the supreme ends. They accept Kama as the primary goal of life. The economic values (Artha) are accepted as means to derive individual pleasures (Kama). Artha is subordinate to Kama as wealth is means to sensuous enjoyment.

The Charvakas believe that human existence is confined to the physical body and to this life. So, the physical pleasure is the only good thing one can obtain. The goal of human life is to obtain the maximum amount of pleasure and to avoid pain, in this life. **Thus, the Charvakas advocate Gross Egoistic Hedonism.** The Charvaka School is the only school in Indian tradition that advocates hedonistic ethics.

Gandhian Ethics

Gandhian philosophy is a double-edged weapon. Its objective is to transform the individual and society simultaneously, in accordance with the principles of truth and non-violence. Gandhi, as leader of Indian national movement, and as prolific writer has commented on almost every aspect of human life and society. His thoughts are multidimensional and cover political, social, economic, religious and ethical aspects of human life. He was influenced not only by Tolstoy, Carlyle and Thoreau but also by ethical principles embedded in Buddhism, Jainism, Hinduism and Christianity.

The twin cardinal principles of Gandhi's thought are truth and non-violence. His ideas are generally expressed in moral categories or terminology. Ethical theories provide the underpinnings for Gandhian thought in any sphere. Evolution of Gandhian ideas took place within a matrix of non-violent mass political struggle. In the process, they went through some twists and turns.

Gandhi is not an academic thinker, he is a mass leader. Hence, his emphasis is not on idealism but on practical idealism. Moreover, Gandhian philosophy is certainly considered as a universal and timeless philosophy. They hold that the ideals of truth and non-violence, which underpin the whole philosophy, are relevant to all humankind.

Gandhi on Moral Behaviour

According to Gandhi, an action is moral if it is volitional, intentional, universal, practical, selfless, and free from fear and compulsion simultaneously. The cultivation of calmness, wildness and tranquility of personality; fostering of good habits; observance of chastity, altruism and righteousness, etc. are the elements of moral life in Gandhian ethics. Similarly, the moral law in Gandhian ethics is a pious, universal, eternal, immutable, independent of space and time, objective, self-imposed dwells in the heart and deals with the inner being of one's personalities.

Gandhi and Non-violence

Non-violence in Gandhi's thinking was a tool that anyone could (and should) use and it was based on strongly religious thinking. Non violence, in its active sense, includes truth and fearlessness. Gandhi insists that non-violence is not a creed of inaction. Nor is it for the weak or the timid. Non-violence does not signify meek acceptance of evil. It is better to be violent than to be cowardly. Gandhi naturally feared that non-violence may become a convenient alibi for avoiding confrontation with the British rulers.

According to Gandhi, many prerequisites are necessary for persistent pursuit of ahimsa. Foremost among these are truthfulness and fearlessness. Except God, men should not fear anyone else. If men obey God, they need not worry about any human agency. From this follows the doctrine of Satyagraha which denotes fearless pursuit of truth. Satyagraha is the name which Gandhi gave to the peaceful protests against British rule in India. And the peaceful protesters are called as satyagrahis.

A close look at the instructions that Gandhi gave to followers of his satyagraha movement in India clears his concept of non-violence. The instructions are as follow:

- A satyagrahi will harbour no anger.

- He will suffer the anger of the opponent.
- In so doing, he will put up with assaults from the opponent, never retaliate; but he will not submit, out of fear of punishment or the like, to any order given in anger.
- When any person in authority seeks to arrest a civil resister, he will voluntarily submit to the arrest, and he will not resist the attachment or removal of his own property, if any, when it is sought to be confiscated by authorities.
- If a satyagrahi has any property in his possession as a trustee, he will refuse to surrender it, even though in defending it he might lose his life. He will, however, never retaliate.
- Non-retaliation excludes swearing and cursing.
- Therefore, a satyagrahi will never insult his opponent, and therefore, also not take part in many of the newly coined cries which are contrary to the spirit of ahimsa.
- A civil resister will not salute the Union Jack, nor will he insult it or officials, English or Indian.
- In the course of the struggle, if anyone insults an official or commits an assault upon him, a civil resister will protect such official or officials from the insult or attack even at the risk of his life.

Gandhi's Economic Ideas

Gandhian ethics cover economic sphere also. Gandhi says that everyone should earn his bread with his own hands or through manual labour. He calls it bread labour, and it alone gives man his right to eat. It is impossible for a few to amass wealth without exploiting the rest. Exploitation is a form of violence. As men have a right to live, they are entitled to the means of securing food, shelter and clothing.

Gandhi does not propose drastic or violent means of bringing about economic equality. Ideally, wealth should be distributed equally among all members of the society. As this is impracticable, Gandhi proposes that wealth should be shared equitably. He urges that people should reduce their wants and live a simple life. This process will release resources which can be used to help the poor.

Doctrine of Trusteeship

Gandhi has introduced a concept in which the rich are

regarded as trustees of wealth. Ultimately, as all property belongs to God, the excess or superfluous wealth which the rich possess belongs to society and should be used for supporting the poor. Wealthy people have no moral right to what is more than their proportionate share in national wealth. They simply become trustees for the disproportionate share of God's property they hold. They have to use it for helping the poor.

Seven Deadly Sins

Mahatma Gandhi said that seven things will destroy us. Notice that all of them have to do with social and political conditions. Note also that the antidote of each of these "deadly sins" is an explicit external standard or something that is based on natural principles and laws, not on social values.

- Wealth Without Work
- Pleasure Without Conscience
- Knowledge Without Character
- Commerce (Business) Without Morality (Ethics)
- Science Without Humanity
- Religion Without Sacrifice
- Politics Without Principle

In the following text the above deadly sins are being discussed with a present context and the concurrent milieu in mind.

1. Wealth Without Work

This refers to the practice of getting something for nothing - manipulating markets and assets so you don't have to work or produce added value, just manipulate people and things. Today there are professions built around making wealth without working, making much money without paying taxes, benefiting from free government programs without carrying a fair share of the financial burdens, and enjoying all the perks of citizenship of country and membership of corporation without assuming any of the risk or responsibility. How many of the fraudulent schemes that went on in the 1980s, often called the decade of greed, were basically get-rich-quick schemes or speculations promising practitioners, "You don't even have to work for it"?

Justice and judgement are inevitably inseparable, suggesting that to the degree you move away from the laws of nature, your judgement will be adversely affected. You get distorted notions. You start telling rational lies to explain why things work or why they don't. You move away from the law of "the farm" into social/political environments. When we read of organisations in trouble, we often hear the sad confessions of executives who tell of moving away from natural laws and principles for a period of time and begin overbuilding, over borrowing, and over speculating, not really reading the stream or getting objective feedback, just hearing a lot of self-talk internally. Now they have a high debt to pay. They may have to work hard just to survive - without hope of being healthy for five years or more. It's back to the basics, hand to the plow. And many of these executives, in earlier days, were critical of the conservative founders of the corporations who stayed close to the fundamentals and preferred to stay small and free of debt.

2. Pleasure Without Conscience

The chief query of the immature, greedy, selfish, and sensuous has always been, "What's in it for me? Will this please me? Will it ease me?" Lately many people seem to want these pleasures without conscience or sense of responsibility, even abandoning or utterly neglecting spouses and children in the name of doing their thing. But independence is not the most mature state of being - it's only a middle position on the way to interdependence, the most advanced and mature state. To learn to give and take, to live selflessly, to be sensitive, to be considerate, is our challenge. Otherwise there is no sense of social responsibility or accountability in our pleasurable activities. The ultimate costs of pleasures without conscience are high as measured in terms of time and money, in terms of reputation and in terms of wounding the hearts and minds of other people who are adversely affected by those who just want to indulge and gratify themselves in the short term. It's dangerous to be pulled or lulled away from natural law without conscience. Conscience is essentially the repository of timeless truths and principles - the internal monitor of natural law. A prominent, widely published psychologist worked to align people with their moral conscience in what was called "integrity therapy." He once said that he was a manic-depressive. "I knew I was getting suicidal," he said. "Therefore, I committed myself to a mental institution. I tried to work out of it, neutralize it, until I reached the point where I could leave the hospital. I don't do clinical work now because it is too stressful. I mostly do research. And through my own struggle, I discovered that integrity therapy was the only way to go. I gave up my mistress, confessed to my wife, and had peace for the first time in my life."

3. Knowledge without Character

As dangerous as a little knowledge is, even more dangerous is much knowledge without a strong, principled character. Purely intellectual development without commensurate internal character development makes as much sense as putting a high-powered sports car in the hands of a teenager who is high on drugs. Yet all too often in the academic world, that's exactly what we do by not focusing on the character development of young people. One of the reasons for advocating about taking the Seven Habits into the schools is that it is character education. Some people don't like character education because, they say, "that's your value system." But you can get a common set of values that everyone agrees on. It is not that difficult to decide, for example, that kindness, fairness, dignity, contribution, and integrity are worth keeping. No one will fight you on those. So let's start with values that are unarguable and infuse them in our education system and in our corporate training and development programs. Let's achieve a better balance between the development of character and intellect. The people who are transforming education today are doing it by building consensus around a common set of principles, values, and priorities and debunking the high degree of specialization, departmentalization, and partisan politics.

4. Commerce (Business) Without Morality (Ethics)

In his book Moral Sentiment, which preceded Wealth of Nations, Adam Smith explained how foundational to the success of our systems is the moral foundation: how we treat each other, the spirit of benevolence, of service, of contribution. If we ignore the moral foundation and allow economic systems to operate without moral foundation and without continued education, we will soon create an amoral, if not immoral, society and business. Economic and political systems are ultimately based on a moral foundation.

To Adam Smith, every business transaction is a moral challenge to see that both parties come out fairly. Fairness and benevolence in business are the underpinnings of the free enterprise system called capitalism. Our economic system comes out of a constitutional democracy where minority rights are to be attended to as well. The spirit of the Golden Rule or of win-win is a spirit of morality, of mutual benefit, of fairness for all concerned. Paraphrasing one of the mottos of the Rotary Club, "Is it fair and does it serve the interests of all the stakeholders?" That's just a moral sense of stewardship toward all of the stakeholders. I like that Smith says every economic transaction. People get in trouble when they say that most of their economic transactions are moral. That means there is something going on that is covert, hidden, secret. People keep a hidden agenda, a secret life, and they justify and rationalize their activities. They tell themselves rational lies so they don't have to adhere to natural laws. If you can get enough rationalization in a society, you can have social mores or political wills that are totally divorced from natural laws and principles. I once met a man who for five years served as the "ethics director" for a major company. He finally resigned the post in protest and considered leaving the company, even though he would lose a big salary and benefit package. He said that the executive team had their own separate set of business ethics and that they were deep into rationalization and justification. Wealth and power were big on their agendas, and they made no excuse for it anymore. They were divorced from reality even inside their own organization. They talked about serving the customer while absolutely mugging their own employees.

5. Science Without Humanity

If science becomes all technique and technology, it quickly degenerates into man against humanity. Technologies come from the paradigms of science. And if there's very little understanding of the higher human purposes that the technology is striving to serve, we become victims of our own technocracy. We see otherwise highly educated people climbing the scientific ladder of success, even though it's often missing the rung called humanity and leaning against the wrong wall. The majority of the scientists who ever lived or living today, and they have brought about a scientific and technological explosion in the world. But if all they do is superimpose technology on the same old problems, nothing basic changes. We may see an evolution, an occasional "revolution" in science, but without humanity we see precious little real human advancement. All the old inequities and injustices are still with us. About the only thing that hasn't evolved are these natural laws and principles - the true north on the compass. Science and technology have changed the face of most everything else. But the fundamental things still apply, as time goes by.

6. Religion Without Sacrifice

Without sacrifice we may become active in a temple but remain inactive in its sermons. In other words, we go for the social facade of religion and the piety of religious practices. There is no real walking with people or going the second mile or trying to deal with our social problems that may eventually undo our economic system. It takes sacrifice to serve the needs of other people - the sacrifice of our own pride and prejudice, among other things. If a temple or religion is seen as just another hierarchical system, its members won't have a sense of service or inner workship. Instead they will be into outward observances and all the visible accoutrements of religion. But they are neither God-centered nor principle-centered. The principles of three of the Seven Habits pertain to how we deal with other people, how we serve them, how we sacrifice for them, how we contribute. These are win-win interdependency, empathy, and synergy - require tremendous sacrifice.

7. Politics Without Principle

If there is no principle, there is no true north, nothing you can depend upon. The focus on the personality ethic is the instant creation of an image that sells well in the social and economic marketplace.

You see politicians spending millions of dollars to create an image, even though it's superficial, lacking substance, in order to get votes and gain office. And when it works, it leads to a political system operating independently of the natural laws that should govern - that are built into the famous speech of our first PM on the midnight of independence: "Long years ago we made a tryst with destiny, and now the time comes when we shall redeem our pledge, not wholly or in full measure, but very substantially. At the stroke of the midnight hour, when the world sleeps, India will awake to life and freedom. A moment comes, which comes but rarely in history, when we step out from the old to the new, when an age ends, and when the soul of a nation, long suppressed, finds utterance. It is fitting that at this solemn moment we take the pledge of dedication to the service of India and her people and to the still larger cause of humanity." The key to a healthy society is to get the social will, the value system, aligned with correct principles. You then have the compass needle pointing to true north - true north representing the external or the natural law - and the indicator says that is what we are building our value system on: they are aligned. But if you get a sick social will behind the political will that is independent of principle, you could have a very sick organization or society with distorted values. For instance, the professed mission and shared values of criminals who rape, rob and plunder might sound very much like many corporate mission statements, using such words as "teamwork," "cooperation," "loyalty," "profitability," "innovation," and "creativity." The problem is that their value system is not based on a natural law. Figuratively, inside many corporations with lofty mission statements, many people are being mugged in broad daylight in front of witnesses.

Principle-Centered Power

To some, these principles and the ideals they represent are readily attributable to notable leaders of distinction such as Mahatma Gandhi, but they are harder to find in the much more common experiences of everyday living. In response to this concern, Gandhi replied, "I claim to be no more than an average man with less than average ability. I am not a visionary. I claim to be a practical idealist. Nor can I claim any special merit for what I have been able to achieve with laborious research. I have not the shadow of a doubt that any man or woman can achieve what I have, if he or she would make the same effort and cultivate the same hope and faith.

A Personal Note

Gandhi emphasized: "A person cannot do right in one department whilst attempting to do wrong in another department. Life is one indivisible whole."

Or, they are being robbed of self-esteem, money, or position without due process. And if there is no social will behind the principles of due process, and if you can't get due process, you have to go to the jury of your peers and engage in counterculture sabotage. In the movie 'The Ten Commandments', Moses says to the Pharaoh, "We are to be governed by God's law, not by you." In effect he's saying, "We will not be governed by a person unless that person embodies the law." In the best societies and organizations, natural laws and principles govern - that's the Constitution - and even the top people must bow to the principle. No one is above it. The Seven Habits will help you avoid these Seven Deadly Sins.

Rational Lies

If I were sitting opposite a psychopath who had a particular sensitivity about ants, and I knew that if I told him that ants have six legs then he would jump up and start killing the surrounding people, then it would be difficult to justify telling him my wonderful fact about ants, regardless of whether I believe that ants really have six legs or not.

Or suppose I knew my friend's wife was cheating on him, but I also knew that he was terminally ill and would die within the next few weeks. The question of whether or not to inform him of my knowledge is genuinely complex, and the truth or falsity of my knowledge about his wife is only one factor in the answer. Different people may disagree about the correct course of action, but no-one would claim that the only relevant fact is the truth of the statement that his wife is cheating on him.

This is all a standard result of expected utility maximization, of course. Vocalizing or otherwise communicating a belief is itself an action, and just like any other action it has a set of possible outcomes, to which we assign probabilities as well as some utility within our value coordinates. We then average out the utilities over the possible outcomes for each action, weighted by the probability that they will actually happen, and choose the action that maximizes this expected utility.

This distinction is particularly easy to miss as the line between belief and communication becomes subtler. Suppose that a friend of mine has built a wing suit and is about to jump off the empire state building with the belief that he will fly gracefully through the sky. Since I care about my friend's well-being I try to explain to him the concepts of gravity and aerodynamics, and the effect it will have on him if he launches himself from the building. Examining my decision in detail, I have placed a high probability on his death if he jumps off the building, and calculated that, since I value his well-being, my expected utility would not be maximized by him making the leap.

But now suppose that my friend is particularly dull and unable or unwilling to grasp the concept of aerodynamics, and is hence unswayed by my argument. Having reasonably explained my beliefs to him, am I absolved of the moral responsibility to save him? Not from a utilitarian standpoint, since there are other courses of action available to me. I could, for example, tell him that his wing suit has been sabotaged by aliens --- a line of reasoning that I happen to know he'll believe given his predisposition towards X files-like conspiracy theories.

Would doing so be contrary to my committed rationalist stance? Not at all; I have rationally analysed the options available to me and rationally chosen a course of action. The conditions for the communication of a belief to be deemed rational are exactly the same decision theoretic conditions applicable to any other action: namely that of being the expected utility maximizer.

If this all sounds too close to "tell people what they need to hear" then let's ask under what specific conditions it might be rational to lie. Clearly this depends on your values. If your utility function places high value on people falling to their death then you will tend to lie about gravity and aerodynamics as much as possible.

Convincing somebody of a falsehood will, on average, lead to them making poorer decisions according to their values. My soon-to-be-airborne friend may be convinced not to leap from the building immediately, but may shortly return with a wing suit covered in protective aluminium foil to ward off those nasty interfering aliens. Nobody is exempt from the laws of rationality. To the extent that their values align with mine, convincing another of a falsehood will have at least this one negative consequence with respect to my own values. The examples above are specific situations in which other factors dominate my desire for another person to be better informed during the pursuit of their goals, but such situations are the exception rather than the rule. All other things equal, lying to an agent with similar values to mine is a bad decision.

Had I actually convinced my friend of the nature of gravity and aerodynamics rather than spinning a story about aliens then next time he may return to the rooftop with a parachute rather than a tin foil wing suit. In the example I gave, this course of action was unlikely to succeed, but again this situation is the exception rather than the rule. In general, a true statement has

When We Rationalize, We Indulge in Rational Lies

To rationalize is to give some fallacious reasoning to prove as right something that is wrong and that we know is wrong. We resort to rationalization when we are attached to getting something without paying the price for it. When we rationalize, we indulge in rational lies - we succumb to the temptation to lie and we use our intelligence for serving the temptation instead of fighting it.

The Bhagavad-Gita points to such rationalization when it declares as pretenders those who externally act as if they are sense-controlled but internally delight in sensual fantasies. Isn't this the plight of all spiritual seekers? Possibly. But the mismatch between externals and internals is not necessarily problematic - its rationalization is.

When we seek a principle-centered life, it's natural that what we profess publically may not always match with what we are able to practice privately. Though we want to live purely, impure desires still afflict us, and we may sometimes succumb to them. Such succumbing simply makes us struggling seekers, not hypocritical pretenders.

We become hypocritical pretenders when we make no efforts to purify ourselves, when we focus our energy primarily on rationalization instead of on rectification, when we continue delighting in the prestige coming from the image of being self-controlled without striving for the purity to actually become self-controlled. When we rationalize, arguing, "Those standards are, anyway, impractical. This is a fallen age, after all. I am ok the way I am," and we do nothing to rectify ourselves, then we indulge in rational lies.

The alternative to rationalization is rectification, and 'bhakti-yoga' makes rectification easy and efficacious. We can see the gap between our aspirations and our actions as a spur for purification.

the potential to improve the recipient's brain/universe entanglement and thereby improve his potential for achieving his goals, which, if his values align with my own, constitutes at least one factor in favour of truth-telling. All other things equal, telling the truth is a good decision.

This doesn't mean that telling the truth is valuable only in terms of its benefits to me. My own values include bettering the lives of others, so achieving "my goals" constitutes working towards the good of others, as well as my own.

Is there any other sense in which truth-telling may be considered a "good" in its own right? Naively one might argue that the act of uttering a truth could itself be a value in its own right, but such a utility function would be maximized by a universe tiled with tape players broadcasting mundane, true facts about the universe. It would be about as well-aligned with the values of typical human being as a paper clip maximizer.

It's a more reasonable position for rationality in others to be included among one's fundamental values. This, I feel, is more closely aligned with my own value. All other things equal, I would like those around me to be rational. Not just to live in a society of rationalists, though this is an orthogonal value. Not just to engage in interesting, stimulating discussion, though this is also an orthogonal value. And not just for others to succeed in achieving their goals, though this, again, is an orthogonal value. But to actually maximize the brain/universe entanglement of others, for its own sake.

Do you value rationality in others for its own sake? Ponder on this question to come up with a true rather than a 'rational lie'. Afterall we all have become too intellectual to conveniently rationalise our lies. Rightly said that we all are living in an era of Post-Truth.

To present the emphatical context of the concept of Rational Lies one cannot miss the excellent lyrics of an album "Circle of Dust" released in 1992.

Rational Lies – The Song (Lyrics)

Here it is again
The voice that scares my thoughts away
Demands attention for itself
Itself alone, seems so unthreatening
But promises a bitter sting
Soon my heart & mind become a battle zone

Push aside all reason
A Sailor to a Siren's call
Excuse reality for temporary lies
Sometimes I can't believe
The things I'll try to justify... only more lies again

[Chorus]
Get out of my head leave me alone
You're no longer welcome here
A voice so sweet with words that kill
A wicked whisper in my ear

In my time of weakness
Is when I see your strength displayed
Screaming silently, tickling my ear
Lie! I know who you really are
& I see your hatred masked behind your smile

[Chorus]
O' wretched man, so failure prone
Who will deliver me?
I once was lost; but now I'm found
Was blind but now I see...
I once was lost but now I'm found
Was blind but can I see?
[Chorus]

Morality of Self-Interest

Morality of self-interest is another name for **Egoistic Ethics**. There are two types of egoism:

- Psychological egoism
- Ethical egoism

According to psychological egoism man by nature strives for the satisfaction of his or her desires and fulfils one's interests. Man, by nature, is selfish. English Philosopher, Thomas Hobbes (1588 -1679) is an advocate of psychological egoism.

According to ethical egoism, one may or may not strive to fulfil one's desires. To say that one ought to practice the morality of rational self interest means that one ought to be an egoist in pursuing his or her own rational interests.

Thomas Hobbes' Psychological Egoism

Hobbes' moral thought is based on the view that what we ought to do depends greatly on the situation in which we find ourselves. According to Hobbes, where political authority exists, our duty seems to be quite straightforward i.e. to obey those in power.

Hobbes argues that society originates out of self-interest and fear, not out of natural feeling for one's fellow men. He defends as natural and reasonable the interest each man takes in his own welfare and happiness. In a state of nature the first and only rule of life is self-protection and men have a natural right to do anything which serves this end.

Hobbes establishes civil authority and law as the foundation of morality. He argues that morality requires social authority, which must be in the hands of a sovereign power whose authority is absolute. Morality is based upon-law and the law of the absolute sovereign. Moral Conduct is possible only through the institution of Government which can reward right actions and punish wrongdoing. Without civil authority it would be foolish and dangerous to follow the precepts of morality. Men are moral only if it is conducive to individual security and prime condition of security is absolute civil power.

Ayn Rand- Ethical Egoism

American thinker Ayn Rand (1905-1982) was an ardent advocate of ethical egoism in 20th century America. She vehemently stood for the virtue of rational selfishness. Rand's morality of self-interest emphasizes the values of rational choice. Freedom, personal dignity, self-reliance, self-belief, and dignity of labour are important values in her ethics.

She was of the view that we must choose our ends by reason only or we perish. According to her Human Model, man does not merely seek food but he has to do productive work also. For that purpose he has to choose actions. He has to think. He has to seek knowledge. He needs knowledge in order to live. Hence, selfishness is a virtue. Further she elaborates: Selfishness means the pursuit of one's rational self-interest. In her view, concern with one's own interests is not an evil. Rand was opposed to Altruistic Morality. Altruism orders man to sacrifice one's interest for the good of others. Altruism is possible but it is not desirable. According to her, pure altruism treats humans as sacrificial animals, and every kind of dictator advocates altruistic morality, and suppresses human rights and freedom of thought and speech.

According to Rand, there is nothing wrong in helping others. But it is not one's ethical duty to help others. One may try to reform society but it is not one's moral obligation to do so. One may choose to help others and reform society, but that is or that should be one's choice. It must be the result of one's free and rational choice.

Feminist Ethics – Carol Gilligan

Feminist Ethics is an attempt to revise, reformulate or rethink traditional Ethics. Feminists have developed a wide variety of gender-centred approaches to ethics. For ages, ethical thinkers have talked about two great moral imperatives: 'Justice' and 'love'. The concept of 'love' is replaced by the concepts of 'goodness', 'utility', etc. Carol Gilligan, like a few other feminists, has emphasized issues related to women's traits and behaviours, particularly their 'care giving ones'. Gilligan's ethical theory is essentially based on the "communal nature of women." The theory is titled as "ethic of care" as against typical conventional male oriented "ethic of justice".

Ethics of Care and Ethics of Justice

Distinction between Ethic of Care and Ethic of Justice was given by Carol Gilligan. According to Gilligan under the ethic of justice, men judge themselves guilty if they do something wrong. Whereas under the ethic of care, women are reluctant even to judge the action. This reluctance to judge itself may be the indicative of the care and concern for others. Thus, women not only define themselves in a context of human relationship but also judge themselves in terms of 'care and concern'. As a result of this a woman's judgement, her moral deliberations become very different. Gilligan further brings out the distinction between 'ethic of care' and 'ethic of justice'. In her view the quality and quantity of relationships is of great importance in both the systems. Individual rights, equality before law, fair play, a square deal - all these goals can be pursued without personal ties to others. Justice is impersonal. Whereas sensitivity towards others, loyalty, responsibility, self sacrifice and peace- making all these reflect interpersonal involvement. Care comes from connection.

Existentialist Ethics – Jean Paul Sartre

Jean Paul Sartre is one of the best known philosophers and a great existentialist of the 20th century. He is regarded as the father of Existentialist philosophy.

Existentialism is widely considered to be the philosophical and cultural movement which holds that the starting point of philosophical thinking must be the individual and the experiences of the individual. Existentialists generally believe that traditional systematic or academic philosophies are too abstract and away from concrete human experience.

A central proposition of existentialism is that "existence precedes essence", which means that the most important consideration for the individual is the fact that he or she is an individual–an independently acting and responsible conscious being ("existence")–rather than what labels, roles, stereotypes, definitions, or other preconceived categories the individual fits ("essence"). The actual life of the individual is what constitutes what could be called his or her "true essence" instead of there being an arbitrarily "attributed essence" used by others to define him or her. Thus, human beings, through their own 'consciousness', create their own values and determine a meaning to their life.

The Ethics of Authenticity

The 'ethics of authenticity' is at the very heart of existentialism. It emphasises the absolute character of the free commitment by which every man realizes himself in realizing a type of humanity. Sartre very emphatically states that "Freedom," "Choice", and "Self-Commitment.", are the three pillars on which the ethic of authenticity is erected.

It is often taken to mean that one has to "create oneself" and then live in accordance with this self. What is meant by authenticity is that in acting, one should act as oneself, not as "one" acts or as "one's genes" or any other essence requires. The authentic act is one that is in accordance with one's freedom.

The Authenticity Paradox

Authenticity has become the gold standard for leadership. But a simplistic understanding of what it means can hinder your growth and limit your impact.

Consider Vaanya, a general manager in a health care organization. Her promotion into that role increased her direct reports 10-fold and expanded the range of businesses she oversaw–and she felt a little shaky about making such a big leap. A strong believer in transparent, collaborative leadership, she bared her soul to her new employees: "I want to do this job," she said, "but it's scary, and I need your help." Her candor backfired; she lost credibility with people who wanted and needed a confident leader to take charge.

Or take George, a Malaysian executive in an auto parts company where people valued a clear chain of command and made decisions by consensus. When a Dutch multinational with a matrix structure acquired the company, George found himself working with peers who saw decision making as a freewheeling contest for the best-debated ideas. That style didn't come easily to him, and it contradicted everything he had learned about humility growing up in his country. In a 360-degree debrief, his boss told him that he needed to sell his ideas and accomplishments more aggressively. George felt he had to choose between being a failure and being a fake.

Because going against our natural inclinations can make us feel like impostors, we tend to latch on to authenticity as an excuse for sticking with what's comfortable. But few jobs allow us to do that for long. That's doubly true when we advance in our careers or when demands or expectations change, as Vaanya, George, and countless other executives have discovered.

In a research on leadership transitions, it was observed that career advances require all of us to move way beyond our comfort zones. At the same time, however, they trigger a strong countervailing impulse to protect our identities: When we are unsure of ourselves or our ability to perform well or measure up in a new setting, we often retreat to familiar behaviors and styles.

But this research also demonstrates that the moments that most challenge our sense of self are the ones that can teach us the most about leading effectively. By viewing ourselves as works in progress and evolving our professional identities through trial and error, we can develop a personal style that feels right to us and suits our organizations' changing needs.

That takes courage, because learning, by definition, starts with unnatural and often superficial behaviors that can make us feel calculating instead of genuine and spontaneous. But the only way to avoid being pigeonholed and ultimately become better leaders is to do the things that a rigidly authentic sense of self would keep us from doing.

Why Leaders Struggle with Authenticity

The word "authentic" traditionally referred to any work of art that is an original, not a copy. When used to describe leadership, of course, it has other meanings–and they can be problematic. For example, the notion of adhering to one "true self" flies in the face of much research on how people evolve with experience, discovering facets of themselves they would never have unearthed through introspection alone. And being utterly transparent–disclosing every single thought and feeling–is both unrealistic and risky.

Leaders today struggle with authenticity for several reasons. First, we make more-frequent and more-radical changes in the kinds of work we do. As we strive to improve our game, a clear and firm sense of self is a compass that helps us navigate

What is Authenticity?

A too-rigid definition of authenticity can get in the way of effective leadership. Here are three examples and the problems they pose.

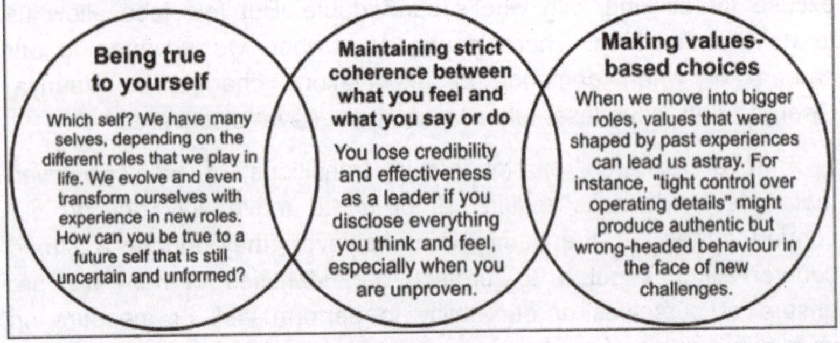

choices and progress toward our goals. But when we're looking to change our game, a too rigid self-concept becomes an anchor that keeps us from sailing forth, as it did at first with Vaanya.

Second, in global business, many of us work with people who don't share our cultural norms and have different expectations for how we should behave. It can often seem as if we have to choose between what is expected–and therefore effective–and what feels authentic. George is a case in point.

Third, identities are always on display in today's world of ubiquitous connectivity and social media. How we present ourselves–not just as executives but as people, with quirks and broader interests–has become an important aspect of leadership. Having to carefully curate a persona that's out there for all to see can clash with our private sense of self.

In dozens of interviews with talented executives facing new expectations, it is seen that they most often grapple with authenticity in the following situations:

Taking charge in an unfamiliar role

As everyone knows, the first 90 days are critical in a new leadership role. First impressions form quickly, and they matter. Depending on their personalities, leaders respond very differently to the increased visibility and performance pressure.

Psychologist Mark Snyder, of the University of Minnesota, identified two psychological profiles that inform how leaders develop their personal styles. "High self-monitors"–or chameleons, as I call them–are naturally able and willing to adapt to the demands of a situation without feeling fake. Chameleons care about managing their public image and often mask their vulnerability with bluster. They may not always get it right the first time, but they keep trying on different styles like new clothes until they find a good fit for themselves and their circumstances. Because of that flexibility, they often advance rapidly. But chameleons can run into problems when people perceive them as disingenuous or lacking a moral center–even though they're expressing their "true" chameleon nature.

"Being authentic doesn't mean that you can be held up to the light and people can see right through you."

By contrast, "true-to-selfers" (Snyder's "low self-monitors") tend to express what they really think and feel, even when it runs counter to situational demands. The danger with true-to-selfers like Vaanya and George is that they may stick too long with comfortable behavior that prevents them from meeting new requirements, instead of evolving their style as they gain insight and experience.

Vaanya hemmed herself in like this. She thought she was setting herself up for success by staying true to her highly personal, full-disclosure style of management. She asked her new team for support, openly acknowledging that she felt a bit at sea. As she scrambled to learn unfamiliar aspects of the business, she worked tirelessly to contribute to every decision and solve every problem. After a few months, she was on the verge of burnout. To make matters worse, sharing her vulnerability with her team members so early on had damaged her standing. Reflecting on her transition some years later, Vaanya said: "Being authentic doesn't mean that you can be held up to the light and people can see right through you." But at the time, that was how she saw it–and instead of building trust, she made people question her ability to do the job.

Delegating and communicating appropriately are only part of the problem in a case like this. A deeper-seated issue is finding the right mix of distance and closeness in an unfamiliar situation. Stanford psychologist Deborah Gruenfeld describes this as managing the tension between authority and approachability. To be authoritative, you privilege your knowledge, experience, and

Why Companies Are Pushing Authenticity Training

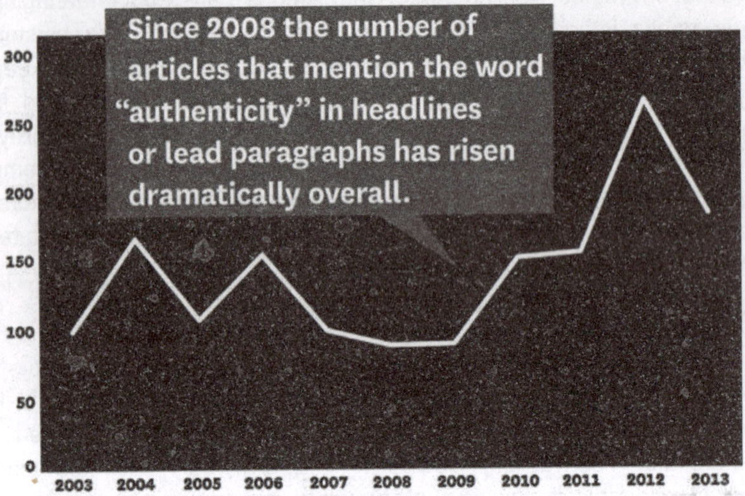

SOURCE *NEW YORK TIMES, FINANCIAL TIMES, WASHINGTON POST, ECONOMIST, FORBES, WALL STREET JOURNAL, AND HBR*

Managers can choose from countless books, articles, and executive workshops for advice on how to be more authentic at work. Two trends help explain the exploding popularity of the concept and the training industry it has fed.

First, trust in business leaders fell to an all-time low in 2012, according to the Edelman Trust Barometer. Even in 2013, when trust began to climb back up, only 18% of people reported that they trusted business leaders to tell the truth, and fewer than half trusted businesses to do the right thing.

Second, employee engagement is at a nadir. A 2013 Gallup poll found that only 13% of employees worldwide are engaged at work. Only one in eight workers–out of roughly 180 million employees studied–is psychologically committed to his or her job. In study after study, frustration, burnout, disillusionment, and misalignment with personal values are cited among the biggest reasons for career change.

At a time when public confidence and employee morale are so low, it's no surprise that companies are encouraging leaders to discover their "true" selves.

expertise over the team's, maintaining a measure of distance. To be approachable, you emphasize your relationships with people, their input, and their perspective, and you lead with empathy and warmth. Getting the balance right presents an acute authenticity crisis for true-to-selfers, who typically have a strong preference for behaving one way or the other. Vaanya made herself too approachable and vulnerable, and it undermined and drained her. In her bigger role, she needed more distance from her employees to gain their confidence and get the job done.

Selling your ideas (and yourself)

Leadership growth usually involves a shift from having good ideas to pitching them to diverse stakeholders. Inexperienced leaders, especially true-to-selfers, often find the process of getting buy-in distasteful because it feels artificial and political; they believe that their work should stand on its own merits.

Here's an example: Anne, a senior manager at a transportation company, had doubled revenue and fundamentally redesigned core processes in her unit. Despite her obvious accomplishments, however, her boss didn't consider her an inspirational leader. Anne also knew she was not communicating effectively in her role as a board member of the parent company. The chairman, a broad-brush thinker, often became impatient with her detail orientation. His feedback to her was "step up, do the vision thing." But to Anne that seemed like valuing form over substance. "For me, it is manipulation," she told me in an interview. "I can do the storytelling too, but I refuse to play on people's emotions. If the string-pulling is too obvious, I can't make myself do it." Like many aspiring leaders, she resisted crafting emotional messages to influence and inspire others because that felt less authentic to her than relying on facts, figures, and spreadsheets. As a result, she worked at cross-purposes with the board chairman, pushing hard on the facts instead of pulling him in as a valued ally.

Many managers know deep down that their good ideas and strong potential will go unnoticed if they don't do a better job of selling themselves. Still, they can't bring themselves to do it. "I try to build a network based on professionalism and what I can deliver for the business, not who I know," one manager said. "Maybe that's not smart from a career point of view. But I can't go against my beliefs....So I have been more limited in 'networking up.'"

Until we see career advancement as a way of extending our reach and increasing our impact in the organization–a collective win, not just a selfish pursuit–we have trouble feeling authentic when touting our strengths to influential people. True-to-selfers find it particularly hard to sell themselves to senior management when they most need to do so: when they are still unproven. Research shows, however, that this hesitancy disappears as people gain experience and become more certain of the value they bring.

Processing negative feedback

Many successful executives encounter serious negative feedback for the first time in their careers when they take on larger roles or responsibilities. Even when the criticisms aren't exactly new, they loom larger because the stakes are higher. But leaders often convince themselves that dysfunctional aspects of their "natural" style are the inevitable price of being effective.

Let's look at Nilesh, a food company production manager whose direct reports gave him low marks in a 360 review on emotional intelligence, team building, and empowering others. One team member wrote that it was hard for Nilesh to accept criticism. Another remarked that after an angry outburst, he'd suddenly make a joke as if nothing had happened, not realizing the destabilizing effect of his mood changes on those around him. For someone who genuinely believed that he'd built trust among his people, all this was tough to swallow.

Once the initial shock had subsided, Nilesh acknowledged that this was not the first time he'd received such criticism (some colleagues and subordinates had made similar comments a few years earlier). "I thought I'd changed my approach," he reflected, "but I haven't really changed so much since the last time." However, he quickly rationalized his behavior to his boss: "Sometimes you have to be tough in order to deliver results, and people don't like it," he said. "You have to accept that as part of the job description." Of course, he was missing the point.

Because negative feedback given to leaders often centers on style rather than skills or expertise, it can feel like a threat to their identity–as if they're being asked to give up their "secret sauce." That's how Nilesh saw it. Yes, he could be explosive–but from his point of view, his "toughness" allowed him to deliver results year after year. In reality, though, he had succeeded up to this point despite his behavior. When his role expanded and he took on greater responsibility, his intense scrutiny of subordinates

The Cultural Factor

Whatever the situation–taking charge in unfamiliar territory, selling your ideas and yourself, or processing negative feedback–finding authentic ways of being effective is even more difficult in a multicultural environment.

In one of the research done at INSEAD it was found that styles of persuading others and the kinds of arguments that people find persuasive are far from universal; they are deeply rooted in a culture's philosophical, religious, and educational assumptions. That said, prescriptions for how leaders are supposed to look and sound are rarely as diverse as the leaders themselves. And despite corporate initiatives to build understanding of cultural differences and promote diversity, the fact is that leaders are still expected to express ideas assertively, to claim credit for them, and to use charisma to motivate and inspire people.

Authenticity is supposed to be an antidote to a single model of leadership. (After all, the message is to be yourself, not what someone else expects you to be.) But as the notion has gained currency, it has, ironically, come to mean something much more limiting and culturally specific. A closer look at how leaders are taught to discover and demonstrate authenticity–by telling a personal story about a hardship they have overcome, for example–reveals a model that is, in fact, very American, based on ideals such as self-disclosure, humility, and individualistic triumph over adversity.

This amounts to a catch-22 for managers from cultures with different norms for authority, communication, and collective endeavor because they must behave inauthentically in order to conform to the strictures of "authentic" leadership.

became an even bigger obstacle because it took up time he should have been devoting to more-strategic pursuits.

A great public example of this phenomenon is Indira Gandhi. Those who worked with her knew she could be merciless if someone failed to prepare as thoroughly as she did. She was capable of humiliating a staff member in public, she was a notoriously bad listener, and she believed that compromise was cowardice. As she became known to the world as the "Iron Lady," Indira Gandhi grew more and more convinced of the rightness of her ideas and the necessity of her coercive methods. She could beat anyone into submission with the power of her rhetoric and conviction, and she only got better at it. Eventually, though, it was her undoing; the application of Emergency that she was ousted by her own party.

A Playful Frame of Mind

Such a rigid self-concept can result from too much introspection. When we look only within for answers, we inadvertently reinforce old ways of seeing the world and outdated views of ourselves. Without the benefit of what I call outsight–the valuable external perspective we get from experimenting with new leadership behaviors–habitual patterns of thought and action fence us in. To begin thinking like leaders, we must first act: plunge ourselves into new projects and activities, interact with very different kinds of people, and experiment with new ways of getting things done. Especially in times of transition and uncertainty, thinking and introspection should follow experience–not vice versa. Action changes who we are and what we believe is worth doing.

Fortunately, there are ways of increasing outsight and evolving toward an "adaptively authentic" way of leading, but they require a playful frame of mind. Think of leadership development as trying on possible selves rather than working on yourself–which, let's face it, sounds like drudgery. When we adopt a playful attitude, we're more open to possibilities. It's OK to be inconsistent from one day to the next. That's not being a fake; it's how we experiment to figure out what's right for the new challenges and circumstances we face.

One research suggests three important ways to get started:

Learn from diverse role models

Most learning necessarily involves some form of imitation–and the understanding that nothing is "original." An important part of growing as a leader is viewing authenticity not as an intrinsic state but as the ability to take elements you have learned from others' styles and behaviors and make them your own.

But don't copy just one person's leadership style; tap many diverse role models. There is a big difference between imitating someone wholesale and borrowing selectively from various people to create your own collage, which you then modify and improve. As the playwright Wilson Mizner said, copying one author is plagiarism, but copying many is research.

The importance of this approach was observed in a study of investment bankers and consultants who were advancing from analytical and project work to roles advising clients and selling new business. Though most of them felt incompetent and insecure in their new positions, the chameleons among them consciously borrowed styles and tactics from successful senior leaders–learning through emulation how to use humor to break tension in meetings, for instance, and how to shape opinion without being overbearing. Essentially, the chameleons faked it until they found what worked for them. Noticing their efforts, their managers provided coaching and mentoring and shared tacit knowledge.

As a result, the chameleons arrived much faster at an authentic but more skillful style than the true-to-selfers in the study, who continued to focus solely on demonstrating technical mastery. Often the true-to-selfers concluded that their managers were "all talk and little content" and therefore not suitable role models. In the absence of a "perfect" model they had a harder time with imitation–it felt bogus. Unfortunately, their managers perceived their inability to adapt as a lack of effort or investment and thus didn't give them as much mentoring and coaching as they gave the chameleons.

Work on getting better

Setting goals for learning (not just for performance) helps us experiment with our identities without feeling like impostors, because we don't expect to get everything right from the start. We stop trying to protect our comfortable old selves from the threats that change can bring, and start exploring what kinds of leaders we might become.

Of course, we all want to perform well in a new situation–get the right strategy in place, execute like crazy, deliver results the organization cares about. But focusing exclusively on those things makes us afraid to take risks in the service of learning. In a series of ingenious experiments, Stanford psychologist Carol Dweck has shown that concern about how we will appear to others inhibits learning on new or unfamiliar tasks. Performance goals motivate us to show others that we possess valued attributes, such as intelligence and social skill, and to prove to ourselves that we have them. By contrast, learning goals motivate us to develop valued attributes.

When we're in performance mode, leadership is about

presenting ourselves in the most favorable light. In learning mode, we can reconcile our yearning for authenticity in how we work and lead with an equally powerful desire to grow. One leader I met was highly effective in small-group settings but struggled to convey openness to new ideas in larger meetings, where he often stuck to long-winded presentations for fear of getting derailed by others' comments. He set himself a "no PowerPoint" rule to develop a more relaxed, improvisational style. He surprised himself by how much he learned, not only about his own evolving preferences but also about the issues at hand.

Don't stick to "your story"

Most of us have personal narratives about defining moments that taught us important lessons. Consciously or not, we allow our stories, and the images of ourselves that they paint, to guide us in new situations. But the stories can become outdated as we grow, so sometimes it's necessary to alter them dramatically or even to throw them out and start from scratch.

That was true for Maria, a leader who saw herself as a "mother hen with her chicks all around." Her coach, former Ogilvy & Mather CEO Charlotte Beers, explains in *I'd Rather Be in Charge* that this self-image emerged from a time when Maria had to sacrifice her own goals and dreams to take care of her extended family. It eventually began to hold her back in her career: Though it had worked for her as a friendly and loyal team player and a peacekeeper, it wasn't helping her get the big leadership assignment she wanted. Together Maria and her coach looked for another defining moment to use as a touchstone–one that was more in keeping with Maria's desired future self, not who she had been in the past. They chose the time when Maria, as a young woman, had left her family to travel the world for 18 months. Acting from that bolder sense of self, she asked for–and got–a promotion that had previously been elusive.

Dan McAdams, a Northwestern psychology professor who has spent his career studying life stories, describes identity as "the internalized and evolving story that results from a person's selective appropriation of past, present and future." This isn't just academic jargon. McAdams is saying that you have to believe your story–but also embrace how it changes over time, according to what you need it to do. Try out new stories about yourself, and keep editing them, much as you would your résumé.

Again, revising one's story is both an introspective and a social process. The narratives we choose should not only sum up our experiences and aspirations but also reflect the demands we face and resonate with the audience we're trying to win over.

Countless books and advisers tell you to start your leadership journey with a clear sense of who you are. But that can be a recipe for staying stuck in the past. Your leadership identity can and should change each time you move on to bigger and better things.

The only way we grow as leaders is by stretching the limits of who we are–doing new things that make us uncomfortable but that teach us through direct experience who we want to become. Such growth doesn't require a radical personality makeover. Small changes–in the way we carry ourselves, the way we communicate, the way we interact–often make a world of difference in how effectively we lead.

Punishment and its Ethical Justification

"Punishment is the just retribution for deliberate breach of moral law". Wrongness of the act is brought home to the criminal by punishing him. If a good act deserves to be praised or rewarded, then a bad act should be punished. This is the ethical justification of punishment.

Punishment is often known as a kind of negative reward paid to the criminal. Because, if we do not punish the criminal, then there will be no harmony, equity and uniformity in society. There will remain no respect for moral laws and moral persons. Moral laws will look like a type of advice possessing no value. Therefore in order to preserve the majesty, supremacy, authority and dignity of moral laws - a criminal should be punished because an offender deliberately violates the moral law and disregards the authority and supremacy of moral laws.

Theories of Punishment

There are three main theories of punishment:

- **Deterrent (or Preventive) theory,** believes that punishment is given, so that potential criminal can learn a lesson and not commit the same crime again.
- **Retributive theory,** believes that punishment is given, because it is deserved and for no other reason.
- **Reformative (or Educative) theory,** suggests that punishment is given to reform the criminal.

Each theory has its own basic principle. The first order principle of Deterrent theory is to maximize the total amount of happiness in society by reducing the crime rate, that of Retributive theory is justice and the basic principle of Reformative theory is to make the criminal, a morally better individual.

Deterrent or Preventive Theory of Punishment

The Deterrent theory of punishment is utilitarian in nature, for it believes that man is punished, not because he has done a wrong act or committed a crime but in order that crime may not be committed. It is best expressed in the word of a judge, who famously said, "You are punished not for stealing sheep, but in order that sheep may not be stolen". By making the potential criminals realize that it does not pay to commit a crime, the Deterrent theory, hopes to control the crime rate in the society, so that people may have a feeling of security. The first order principle is maximum happiness of the maximum number of people in the society. Jeremy Bentham is the promoter of this theory.

Retributive Theory of Punishment

The Retributive theory believes that punishment must be inflicted because it is deserved and no other reason. The first principle is justice and the assumption is that if a right act has to be rewarded, a wrong act must be punished, for punishment is simply the reward of the wrong act. By punishing the wrongdoer, we are treating him as equal. Aristotle and Hegel are of the opinion that punishment is kind of negative reward paid to a criminal. Hegel says that violation of moral law is the demand for punishment and hence we should punish a criminal. Punishment follows as a fruit of his evil deeds.

Reformative or Educative Theory of Punishment

As the name suggests, punishment is given for the purpose of reforming the criminal. The supporters of this theory believe that a man commits a crime because, either he is ignorant, or because he has done a wrong, so he may be in a position to improve himself. This theory also holds that most of the crimes are due to pathological phenomenon i.e. one commits crime due to some mental deficiency or insanity or physiological defect. Therefore, the criminal ought to be cured and ought to be reformed.

Traditionally, Plato has been regarded as the father of the Reformative theory and his position can be summarized in the following three positions:

- The state is related to the delinquent as parent to a child.
- Wickedness is a mental disease.
- Punishment is a moral medicine for wicked acts, and however unpalatable it may be, it is absolutely necessary.

Global Justice

Global justice is an issue in political philosophy arising from the concern that the world at large is unjust. A theory of global justice aims to give us an account of what justice on a global scale consists of and this often includes discussion of the following components:

- identifying what should count as important problems of global justice;
- positing solutions to each identified problem;
- identifying who might have responsibilities in addressing the identified problem;
- arguing for positions about what particular agents (or collections of agents) ought to do in connection with solving each problem, and;
- providing a normative view which grounds the aforementioned

Theories of global justice aim to help us understand our world better and what our responsibilities are in it.

When is a problem a Global Justice Problem?

A problem is often considered to constitute a global justice problem when one (or more) of the following conditions obtain:

- Actions stemming from an agent, institution, practice, activity (and so on) that can be traced to one (or more) states negatively affects residents in another state.
- Institutions, practices, policies, activities (and so on) in one (or more) states could bring about a benefit or reduction in harm to those resident in another state.
- There are normative considerations that require agents in one state to take certain actions with respect to agents or entities in another. Such actions might be mediated through institutions, policies, or norms.
- We cannot solve a problem that affects residents of one or more states without co-operation from other states.

So, in general, a problem is one of global justice when the problem either affects agents resident in more than one state or the problem is unresolvable without their co-operation. For the problem to be considered genuinely global rather than regional, it should affect more than one regional area.

Following are some of the issues that arise in the field of global justice:

- War and Just Conduct
- Humanitarian Intervention
- Terrorism
- Global Economic Injustice
- Global Gender Justice
- Immigration
- Global Environmental Issues
- Global Health Issues

7

CIVIL SERVICES VALUES & ETHICS IN PUBLIC ADMINISTRATION

The Concepts Discussed in this Unit

- Concept, Characteristics, Status and Problems of Ethics in Public Administration
- Ethical Issues in Indian Civil Services
- Ethical Concerns and Dilemmas in Government and Private Institutions
- Moral Free Space
- Laws, Rules, Regulations and Conscience as Sources of Ethical Guidance
- Accountability and Ethical Governance
- Bureacratic-ness and Ethical Competence
- Strengthening of Moral and Ethical values in Governance
- Ethics and Ethical Issues in International Affairs/ Relations
- Corporate Governance and Corporate Scandals
- Principles of Public Life
- Ethical Issues in Healthcare Industry

Public Administration

Public administration is the executive branch of government. It essentially deals with the machinery and procedures of government as these are used in the effective performance of government activities. Administration has been defined as a co-operative human effort toward achieving some common goals. Public administration is that species of administration which operates within a specific political setting.

The 'public' aspect of public administration lends special character to it. The adjective can be looked at formally to mean 'government'. So, public administration is government administration, the focus being specifically on public bureaucracy.

With the growing importance of government in the wake of expanding public functions, public administration has become highly complex and more and more specialized.

Ethics and Accountability in Governance

Public administration is an activity which encompasses each and every aspect of human life. The explosion and spread of information and communication technology, the wide acceptance of democratic form of government and changing social norms enable the people to demand higher standards of ethics, transparency and accountability in the public sector. Ethical public service is considered as a prerequisite of well functioning democracy. Ethical, transparent and accountable public sector is also a precondition of good governance that ensures sustainable development and responsive public policy. It also helps to improve the performance of public sector by preventing systemic corruption.

The effectiveness of public administration depends on the understanding and cooperation between the citizens and public servants. The primary concern of the citizens in a good civil society is that their government must be fair and good. For a Government to be good it is essential that their systems and sub-systems of Governance are efficient, economical, ethical and equitable. In addition, the governing process must also be just, reasonable, fair and citizen friendly. For these and other qualities and good governance, the administrative system must also be accountable and responsive, besides promoting transparency and people's participation.

There is a great deal of alienation between the people and the public service which undermines the legitimacy, effectiveness and credibility of public administration. To bridge this gap it is necessary to create confidence in the minds of the people towards the competence, fairness, honesty, impartiality and sincerity of the public services.

The manipulation and lack of ethics in administration not only reduces the effectiveness but also has several negative effects for the society as a whole. It leads to poor administration and mismanagement of human and material resources. Several rules, regulations and laws exist to ensure impartiality, honesty and devotion among the public servants. But still, there remain a vast area of administrative activity which cannot be controlled by formal laws, procedures and methods. 'In such cases administrators are accountable only to their own conscience, their own sense of duty towards the social welfare. Along with that there is also a need to have an "ethics infrastructure" that not only provides guidance for good conduct but also administratively and legally punishes misconduct.

The "ethics infrastructure" includes measures to enhance and preserve organizational integrity, access to information that promotes transparency and accountability and prevents misuse of power by public personnel. Decision-making by administrators must be based on fairness, transparency and accountability and a sense of the public interest, as well as the careful exercise of the legal authorities delegated by Parliament.

Ethics in Public Administration

The American Society of Public Administration (ASPA) has laid down the code of Ethics for Public Administrators-

- the public servants should put the public interest above the self interest and subordinate institutional loyalties to the public good. They are committed to exercise discretionary authority to promote the public interest. Accordingly they should oppose all forms of discrimination and harassment, and promote affirmative action.

- the public servants should recognize and support the public's right to know the public's business and involve citizens in decision-making policy. The public servants should encourage the people to participate actively in the affairs of the government.
- It is the duty of the public servants to respect the Constitution and the Law that define responsibilities of public agencies, employees, and all citizens and promote constitutional principles of equality, fairness, representativeness, responsiveness and due process in protecting citizens' rights.
- the public servants are committed to perform their duties honestly and should not compromise them for advancement, honour, or personal gain. They should conduct official acts without favouritism and ensure that others receive credit for their work and contributions.
- the public officials should make every effort to strengthen organizational capabilities to apply ethics, efficiency and effectiveness in serving the public.
- the public officials should strive for Professional Excellence. They should work hard to strengthen individual capabilities and encourage the professional development of others to upgrade competence.

Characteristics of Public Administration

- It is part of executive branch of government.
- It is related with the activities of the state.
- It carries out the public policies.
- Public Administration is politically neutral.
- It realises the aspirations of the people as formulated and expressed in the laws.
- Scholars insist on the commitment and dedication to the well being of the people. Otherwise, Public Administration behaves in a mechanical, impersonal and inhuman way.

Ethics in Public Administration: Status

In spite of growing interest in ethics, the public is not convinced that there has been much improvement in bureaucratic behaviour. This may be because schools of public administration have not uniformly instituted courses on ethics. It is recognized that there is no uniform approach to developing course in or teaching of ethics in schools of public administration.

Public administration is a complex, diverse and exciting discipline involving theories, paradigms and practices often borrowed from other sciences. Many scholars have bemoaned the fact that public administration has been in a state of chaos for years. Some scholars have questioned whether it is a separate discipline at all. But regardless of these allegations, there is no question about the need for and improvement of courses in public administration. In this regard, it is noted that, if public administration itself has an identity crisis, it should not be surprising that ethics for public administrators is undergoing a worse identity crisis.

Ethics in Public Administration: Problems

Public administration's treatment of ethics involves many things, including whether to use philosophy as its foundation and, if so, whose philosophy to use. Should the works of Aristotle and St. Thomas Aquinas-involving the existence of a real, external world with objective rules, laws and regulations- be the foundation of ethics? Or should the philosophy of Plato and the German Idealists dictate the approach? Do we live in a subjective world created by human consciousness, where consciousness dictates reality? Are right and wrong things we interpret as such? Are right and wrong relative to every actor? Or maybe there is a combination of both approaches that can help in the teaching of ethics.

In this context, John Rohr and Terry Copper, while recognizing the importance of teaching ethics in schools of public administration, considers it difficult to do justice to ethics if classical or political ethics (as he calls it) is not the foundation. Yet, this situation creates a dilemma: If ethics is derived from philosophy, philosophy will likely be short-changed owing to a heavy course load for public administration students. On the other hand, if schools offer no courses in philosophy, or only "a smattering of philosophy," the students are short changed. Rohr, thus develops an ethical foundation for bureaucrats based on the U.S. Constitution and on opinions of the U.S. Supreme Court. Rohr writes:

The best educated means of preparing bureaucrats to fulfil this obligation (an oath to uphold the Constitution) is to use

Supreme Court opinions on salient 'regime values' to encourage them to reflect on how these values might best influence their decision making as persons who govern.

According to Rohr, then, the best approach is to use Supreme Court opinions on salient regime values, encouraging public servants to consider how these values best influence their decision making. Regime values are those of the political entity brought into existence by the creation of the U.S. Constitution. Rohr believes that regime values derived from studies of Supreme Court opinions reflect the public interest or the salient values of society. However, while public administrators can make ethical decisions by studying opinions of the Supreme Court, these opinions are often tedious and boring. Divergent opinions may provide a framework for decision making, but not necessarily for making the right decisions, which is the core of ethics.

Further, Rohr's reliance on the Supreme Court to guide public administrators in discretionary administrative decisions may be useful in the United States. But, it is unlikely that these opinions will be helpful to public administrators in other countries. This same criticism is applicable to Immanuel Kant's argument, which claimed that obedience to law through application of the so-called Categorical Imperative made human actions ethical. Apparently something above and beyond the U.S. Constitution and the opinions of the Supreme Court is needed to guide the ethics of public administrators.

Other authors think that classical ethics is outdated, that the principles developed by human reasons and related somewhat to theology are outmoded and no longer workable, particularly for people working in the public sector. What they suggest, and what practice frequently bears out, is a so-called ethical principle that might be termed the "done thing." Adolescents are great advocates of this principle: "Everybody is doing it." The claim that everyone is doing something does not always mean that everyone is actually doing it; and if everyone is doing it, that does not necessarily mean that the executed thing is right. There must be a criterion for morality (what is right or wrong) other than the "done thing".

Business writers such as Peter Drucker, who make no distinction between public and private administration, deny that there is a separate ethics for business. By implication, public administrators do not need a separate code of ethics. Drucker writes: "But there is neither a separate ethics of business, nor is there one needed. According to Drucker, the only ethics needed for all professionals is contained in the Hippocratic Oath "primum non nocere" ("above all, not knowingly to do harm"). This oath contains a general ethical principle of natural law and is addressed in classical ethics.

Determinants of Ethics in Public Administration

The major determinants of administrative conduct in the public sector include:

- the political construct of which public administrators are a part
- the legal framework
- the administrators and public employees who are responsible for the provision of public services
- the citizens and users of public services that are a part of the civil society.

First, the determinants of ethics in public administration with regard to the individual attributes of public/civil servants include ethical decision-making skills, mental attitude, virtues and professional values. Secondly, the organizational structure dimension is explained by clear accountability, collaborative arrangements, dissent channels, and participation procedures. Third, the political organizational culture includes artefacts, beliefs and values, and assumptions. Leadership is important in the development, maintenance, and adaptation of organizational culture. Ethical behaviour is encouraged when organizations have a climate where personal standards and employee education are emphasized, where supervisors stress the truth, and where employees regularly come together to discuss ethical problems. Finally, societal expectation includes public participation, laws, and policies.

Ethical Issues in Indian Civil Services

Today the Indian Civil Services are facing a large number of ethical issues and most of them, directly or indirectly, are related to corruption. Corruption is an important manifestation of the failure of ethics. The word 'corrupts' is derived from the Latin word 'corruptus', meaning 'to break or destroy'. The word 'ethics' is from original Greek term 'ethicos', meaning 'arising from habit'. It is unfortunate that corruption has, for many, become a matter of habit, ranging from grand corruption involving persons in high places to retail corruption touching the everyday life of common people.

There are two facets to corruption:

- The institution which is highly corrupt;
- Individuals who are highly corrupt.

There is a need to work on public profiteering and also value to be attributed to the services rendered by officers. Interlocking accountability is a process by which evaluation could be done easily and accountability ensured.

Various ethical issues faced by our civil servants are:

- Asymmetric distribution and Abuse of Power
- Lack of accountability
- Political interference and Cronyism
- Lack of integrity
- Lack of action against corrupt officials
- Lack of proper protection to whistleblowers
- Lack of proper Code of Conduct for Public Servants
- Lack of transparency and sensitivity towards common man

In this regard, the Second Administrative Reform Commission (ARC) has observed as under-

- Corruption is a matter of concern particularly at the cutting edge levels of the bureaucracy.
- There is a perceptible lack of commitment in public servants towards redressal of citizens' grievances.
- Red-tapism and unnecessary complex procedures add to the hardship of citizens.
- Government servants are rarely held to account and complaints to higher authorities usually go unheeded.
- Generally the attitude of many public functionaries is one of arrogance and indifference.
- Frequent transfer of officers reduces their effectiveness and also dilutes their accountability.

- Sometimes there is "unholy" nexus between unscrupulous politicians and bureaucrats leading to poor governance.

Value Conflicts

A value conflict occurs when individuals or groups of people hold strong personal beliefs that are in disagreement within themselves or in disagreement with the institution's/ organization's values. These may include religious differences, cultural differences or differences in upbringing.

Values-based conflicts are particularly pervasive in public policy. Indeed, nearly all public (policy) controversies entail divergent beliefs about what is right and what is wrong, what is just and what is unjust. Many policy decisions are essentially choices among competing values. Simply consider how:

- Efforts to promote equal opportunity might result in conflicts among values such as efficiency, justice, equality, diversity, merit, and individual achievement;
- Crime prevention policies might trigger competition among values such as liberty, safety, due process, equity, effectiveness, access, and justice; and
- Domestic security policies might produce conflict among values such as knowledge generation, information sharing, confidentiality, privacy, civil liberties, individual rights, and safety.

Framework of Ethical Behaviour

The role of ethics in public life has many dimensions. At one end is the expression of high moral values and at the other, the specifics of action for which a public functionary can be held legally accountable. Any framework of ethical behaviour must include the following elements:

- Codifying ethical norms and practices
- Disclosing personal interest to avoid conflict between public interest and personal gain
- Creating a mechanism for enforcing the relevant codes
- Providing norms for qualifying and disqualifying a public functionary from office

Public Interest and Public Administration

The public interest refers to the "common well-being" or "general welfare". The public interest is central to policy debates, politics, democracy and the nature of government itself. Government has a universalistic character. It has to serve the common good without making any sort of distinction between man and man. The importance of a sense of public interest as a wider ethical commitment in public administration assumes significance in this context.

Philosophies of Public Interest

Philosophies of public interest fall broadly into four classes-

- Intuitionist Philosophy
- Perfectionism
- Utilitarianism
- Theory of Justice

1. Intuitionist Philosophy

It seeks to justify existing practices by pointing out that in conflicting situations, the administrator chooses an alternative by intuition. In other words, what the administrator actually does is an intuitionist solution which seems to him the right course of action under given circumstances. This philosophy does not provide any guideline for action, nor does it spell out an explicit theory of public interest.

2. Perfectionism

The administrator views public interest from the standpoint of promotion of excellence in all spheres of social activities. Public resource should be spent in such a way that the best members of the society benefit most from the expenditure. Thus seen, Perfectionism is an elitist philosophy and anti-egalitarian and is not compatible with democratic society. It favours excellence at the expense of social equality.

3. Utilitarianism

According to Utilitarian Philosophy the public interest is served when a public policy makes as many as possible better-off even though it may render a few worse-off. Public interest is judged by the augmentation of the net balance of social satisfaction.

4. Theory of Justice

This theory was propounded by the philosopher John Rawls. Rawls suggests two basic principles of justice to test public interest. The first principle is that each person is to have an equal right to the most extensive basic liberty compatible with a similar liberty for others. The other principle postulates that public policies are reasonably expected to be to everyone's advantage and public position and offices are open to all. In case of conflict between these principles, the second principle is expected to prevail and give way to the first. Rational decision-making in public administration has to have an ethical framework. These principles provide an operating logic for the determination of public interest by the decision-makers.

Human Rights

Human rights are commonly understood as "inalienable fundamental rights to which a person is inherently entitled simply because she or he is a human being." Human rights are thus conceived as universal (applicable everywhere) and egalitarian (the same for everyone). These rights may exist as natural rights or as legal rights, in local, regional, national, and international law. The doctrine of human rights in international practice, within international law, global and regional institutions, in the policies of states and in the activities of non-governmental organizations, has been a cornerstone of public policy around the world.

The main characteristics of human rights are-

- They are universal and inalienable
- They are equal and non-discriminatory

Egalitarianism

Egalitarianism is a trend of thought that favours equality for particular categories of, or for all, living entities. Egalitarian doctrines maintain that all humans are equal in fundamental worth or social status. According to the Merriam-Webster Dictionary, the term has two distinct definitions in modern English. It is defined either as a political doctrine that all people should be treated as equals and have the same political, economic, social, and civil rights, or as a social philosophy advocating the removal of economic inequalities among people or the decentralisation of power. Some sources define egalitarianism as the point of view that equality reflects the natural state of humanity.

Constitutional Morality

"Constitutional morality is not a natural sentiment. It has to be cultivated. We must realize that our people have yet to learn it. Democracy in India is only a top-dressing on an Indian soil which is essentially undemocractic". – **Dr. B.R. Ambedkar**

The strength or weakness of constitutional morality in contemporary India has to be understood in the light of a cycle of escalating demands from the people and the callous response of successive governments to those demands. In a parliamentary democracy, the obligations of constitutional morality are expected to be equally binding on the government and the opposition. In India, the same political party treats these obligations very differently when it is in office and when it is out of it. This has contributed greatly to the popular perception of our political system as being amoral.

Principle of Constitutional Morality

The concept of Constitutional Morality was first propounded by the English classicist George Grote in "A History of Greece", referring to the complex value of what the written constitution stands for.

What does Constitutional Morality mean? By Constitutional Morality, Grote meant "a paramount reverence for the forms of the Constitution, enforcing obedience to authority and acting under and within these forms, yet combined with the habit of open speech, of action subject only to definite legal control, and unrestrained censure of those very authorities as to all their public acts combined, too with a perfect confidence in the bosom of every citizen amidst the bitterness of party contest that the forms of constitution will not be less sacred in the eyes of his opponents than his own".

The principle of constitutional morality fundamentally intends to bow down to the standards of the Constitution and not to act in a way which would wind up violative of the rule of law or manifests the activity in a subjective way. It actually works at the fulcrum and guides as a laser beam in institution building. The democratic values survive and become successful where the people at large and the persons-in-charge of the institution are strictly guided by the constitutional parameters without paving the path of deviancy and reflecting in action for the primary concern to maintain institutional integrity and the requisite constitutional restraints. Commitment to the Constitution is a facet of constitutional morality.

Therefore, in Indian sense, constitutional morality is the soul of the Constitution, which is found in the Preamble of the Constitution, which declares its ideals and aspirations, and is also found in Part III of the Constitution, particularly with respect to those provisions which assure the dignity of an individual.

Different Usage of the Term 'Constitutional Morality'

In contemporary usage, Constitutional Morality has come to refer to the substantive content of a Constitution. To be governed by a Constitutional Morality, on this view, to be governed by the substantive moral implication any Constitution holds. For instance, the principle of non-discrimination is often taken to be an element of our modern Constitutional Morality. In this sense, Constitutional Morality is the morality of a Constitution.

A second usage that Dr. Ambedkar was more familiar with, in this view, Constitutional Morality refers to the conventions and protocols that govern decision-making where the Constitution vests discretionary power or is silent.

For Grote, there were only two other probable cases in which Constitutional Morality had risen. The first was the aristocratic combination of liberty and self-restraint experienced in 1688 in England; the second was American Constitutionalism.

All other attempts had failed. For DR. Ambedkar, this lesson was an important one, adding to the worry of creating democracy in a country like India, whose society was entirely lacking in democratic spirit and experience.

Understanding Constitutionalism

The Constitution is a unifying document. It captures to the extent necessary - cultural, economic, legal, political and social concepts of a society. It speaks about the constitution of a society. It establishes State institutions. But the content of constitutionalism is the manner in which institutions conduct themselves to further the very objectives of the Constitution. The theory of constitutionalism is necessary to understand the division and limitation of governmental power, the recognition and protection of certain individual rights, the protection of property and the notion of representative or democratic government.

Elements of Constitutional Morality

Freedom and Self-restraint: Self-restraint was a precondition for maintaining freedom under properly Constitutional government. The most political expression of a lack of self-restraint was revolution. Both violent revolution and passive resistance are equated as exemplifying a kind of excess and lack of self-restraint incompatible with Constitutional Morality. The understood equivalence stated between Satyagraha and violence has roots in Dr. Ambedkar's experience of Satyagraha as a form of coercion. It is a feature of Constitutional Morality that while government is subject to the full force of criticism, this criticism must, in some sense, be 'pacific' or peaceful criticism.

Recognition of Plurality: Respecting Constitutional forms is the only way in which a genuinely non-violent mode of political action can come into being. The only way of non-violent resolution amidst this fact of difference is securing some degree of unanimity on a Constitutional process, a form of adjudication that can mediate difference.

Suspicion of any Claims to Represent the Will of the People: Dr. Ambedkar was suspicious of any form of hero worship. But this suspicion of personification was part of a larger sensibility that formed a crucial element of his Constitutional Morality.

Constitutional Morality as the Essence of Constitutionalism

In addition to the obvious text of the Constitution, the sub-text and spirit of the Constitution also add force and understanding to its implementation. The essence of Constitutionalism that gives immutable feature and serves as a moral compass in the implementation and interpretation of the Constitution is the principle of Constitutional Morality.

Constitutionalism and Constitutional Morality must be viewed literally as interchangeable and possible synonymous expressions. While morality seems to have a more subjective connotation in its ordinary use, but in the understanding of a Constitution, it means literally the ethos or constitutionalism.

A simplistic approach to Constitutional Morality would be to assume that principles of fundamental rights such as the right to life and liberty, the right against discrimination and the freedom of speech are just some examples of Constitutional Morality that had been drafted into the Constitution.

This principle encourages every 'citizen' to be vigilant of not only his or her individual rights but also group rights. It poses a dilemma for every citizen, in that it expects of him to shun opportunism and distance himself from circumstances of personal gain where they conflict with national or public interest.

A similar dilemma exists for Governments which find their agenda driven programs forbidden by the principle of Constitutional Morality that does not allow its 'supreme' power to be used for a context other than for which it was granted.

Dilemma

A dilemma is a problem offering two possibilities, neither of which is practically acceptable. One in this position has been traditionally described as "being on the horns of a dilemma", neither horn being comfortable.

Ethical Dilemma

An ethical dilemma arises from a situation that necessitates a choice between competing sets of principles. Thus an ethical dilemma can be described as a circumstance that requires a choice between competing sets of principles in a given, usually undesirable or perplexing, situation. There are three conditions that must be present for a situation to be considered as ethical dilemma-

- The first condition occurs in situations when an individual, called the "agent," must make a decision about which course of action is best. Situations that are uncomfortable but that don't require a choice are not ethical dilemmas.

- The second condition for ethical dilemma is that there must be different courses of action to choose from.
- Third, in an ethical dilemma, no matter what course of action is taken, some ethical principle is compromised. In other words, there is no perfect solution.

Types of Ethical Dilemmas

Conflicts of interest are possibly the most obvious example that could place public sector leaders in an ethical dilemma. Other types of ethical dilemmas in which public servants may find themselves include conflict between: the values of public administration; justifications for the institutions; aspects of the code of conduct; personal values and supervisor or governmental directive; professional ethics and supervisor or governmental directive; personal values and professional ethics versus governmental directive; blurred or competing accountabilities; and the dimensions of ethical conduct.

These dilemmas are in three broad categories:

- **Personal Cost Ethical Dilemmas-** This dilemma arises from situations in which compliance with ethical conduct results in a significant personal cost (e.g. jeopardizing held position, missing opportunity for financial or material benefit, injuring valued relationship etc.) to the public-servant-decision-maker and/or the Agency;
- **Right-versus-Right Ethical Dilemmas-** This dilemma arises from situations of two or more conflicting sets of bona fide ethical values (e.g. public servants' responsibility of being open and accountable to citizens versus that of adhering to the Oath of Secrecy/Confidentiality etc.).
- **Conjoint Ethical Dilemmas-** This dilemma arises from situations in which a conscientious public-servant-decision-maker is exposed to a combination of the above-indicated ethical dilemmas in searching for the "right-thing-to-do".

Unavoidable Ethical Dilemmas for Public Officials

For a citizenry to retain its trust in Government, it must have confidence that those in public service are at all times acting in the best interest of the public. As stewards of the public trust, government leaders and employees have a fiduciary responsibility to act in a manner that is fair and unbiased, that is loyal to the public by putting public interest before personal gain, and that fulfills duties of competency, integrity, accountability, and transparency. In fulfilling these duties, public officials will encounter predictable ethical dilemmas which arise out of their role as public servants. These include:

Dilemmas Involving Fairness

What matters potentially influence your ability to work in the public interest and represent all constituents equally and fairly?

- Are you favoring family, friends, or neighbors over another petitioner?
- Are you favoring a campaign contributor over another constituent?
- Are you disfavoring a constituent who supported an opponent?
- Is your vote biased against a proposal of a colleague who worked against your election?
- Is your vote biased in favor of a proposal of a colleague who has promised to vote your way on another matter?
- Are you favoring the agenda of your party over a policy you believe to be good for the community?
- Are you giving all of your constituents equal access?
- Are you allowing all parties the right to be heard at public meetings?
- What is a fair process for bidders on city contracts?
- What process is fair in labor negotiations with public employees?

Dilemma's Involving Conflict between Personal Interests and Public Interests

- Do you have personal interests that conflict with your duty of loyalty to the public you have been elected to serve?
- Are there outside or future employment considerations that conflict with your public duty?
- Are there conflicts between your duty to your family that may affect your decision making?
- Is the pursuit of personal financial gains taking precedent over good governance?

- Is the interest in furthering personal, community, or political relationships conflicting with your public duties?
- Do you use the indicia of your office for personal gain?
- Do you use public resources for personal or political purposes?
- How do you deal with conflicting public duties inherent in serving both as a council member and as a member of a commission, agency, board, or district?
- Can you use confidential information learned in office for purposes outside of official business?
- Do you recuse yourself from participating in decisions involving parties with whom you have a relationship or subjects in which you have an interest?
- Have you resigned from organizations in which membership may give rise to future conflicts?
- Do you avoid the appearance of an improper conflict even if you personally believe you can act in an unbiased manner?

Dilemmas Involving the Faithful Executions of your Official Duties

- Can you competently fulfill the responsibilities of your office?
- Do you regularly participate in the decision-making process, except when you have a conflict which prohibits your participation and have you made yourself knowledgeable on all issues before you?
- Do you always exercise your independent judgment and can you personally investigate issues?
- Is it appropriate to ignore staff recommendations and substitute your own judgment?
- When, and how, can you seek outside advice or counsel on an issue?
- Is it proper to introduce sponsored legislation?
- Do your constituents deserve a public explanation from you on all decisions you have made?
- Is it ethical to delay a decision or obfuscate an opinion because of timing in an election cycle?
- Is your first commitment to consider the needs of your community, district, city, state, or nation?

Ethical Consumerism

Ethical consumerism can be defined as a type of consumer activism, which is based on the practice of purchasing products and services, produced in a way that minimizes social and/or environmental damage, while avoiding products and services deemed to have a negative impact on society or the environment.

It is a broad label for companies providing products that appeal to people's best selves. This can be as simple as buying an electronic equipment consuming less electricity or as complex as boycotting goods produced by child labour. Combining the general idea of ethics and shopping is the mainstream concept behind ethical consumerism; in hope that maybe we can shop our way to a better world.

The fact that people practice ethical consumerism is evident in that people regularly buy products which fall into the ethical category like organic products, hybrid cars, environmentally-friendly detergents, fair trade goods, energy-efficient light bulbs, electricity from renewable energy, recycled paper and wood products marked by Bureau of Indian Standards. Being an ethical consumer can also involve watching your food miles: how much energy was used getting the product to you. Ethical consumption can be a powerful tool for change, with the recent success in increasing usage of solar panels in rural as well as urban areas being a case in point. However, there is still a long way to go.

- Should you remain independent when joining a voting bloc may be more conducive to achieving your policy goals?
- Should you ever exchange promises to vote for another's proposed legislation in return for their promise to vote for yours?
- What are your obligations to subsequently follow the rule of the majority when you argued for an opposite result?
- Are you respectful of staff roles, responsibilities, and time?
- Should you be a whistle blower even if it means potentially derailing a policy objective you are pursuing?
- When you speak with the press do you distinguish between official representations and personal views?

Dilemmas Involving Acting with Integrity

- Do you conduct yourself honestly and with the integrity expected from public officials?
- Are you truthful in all your dealings with colleagues, public, and the press?

- Are you willing to speak truth to power?
- Should you employ innuendo and inference when discussing a political or governmental opponent?
- Do you have the strengths of your convictions and can you withstand pressure to influence your independent judgment?
- Can you resist temptation to take advantage of your position for personal gain?
- To what extent can you accept gifts?
- To what extent can you allow gifts to family members and others associated with you?
- Is the offer of college admission or a grant of an honorary degree to someone close to you considered a gift if you are engaging in matters that effect that educational institution?
- If your family member is offered a job by someone with official business before you, is that considered a gift to you?
- To what extent are contributions to a charity you favor considered gifts to you?
- Does it make a difference if you know that a quid pro quo is expected in return for an otherwise legally acceptable gift?

Dilemmas Involving Accountability

- To maintain the public trust do you act in a manner that is transparent and is accountable to your constituents?
- Do you comply with all public record laws and do you keep proper financial records?
- What communications are you required to keep?
- Do you frequently inform the citizenry of what is happening in your office or commission or agency?
- Are you responsive to press inquiries?
- Are conversations about public business on your private email or personal social media page part of the public record?
- Do you have an ethical duty to admit to wrong doing even if you do not have a legal duty to implicate yourself?
- Can you meet unofficially with legislative members outside of the collective bargaining process?
- Under what circumstances can you meet or communicate with developers?

- Under what circumstances can you meet with contractors bidding on public projects?
- Are closed Facebook groups where you are friends with other official decision makers considered meetings?
- Are sequential emails to individual decision makers considered meetings?
- Are comments posted on your personal, campaign, or government blog considered a meeting?
- Do you need to make your personal calendar available to the public?

Some More Examples of Ethical Dilemmas

Following are some examples of ethical dilemmas for a public administrator-

- Would he keep silent when he finds that administrative discretion is abused, or that corruption or nepotism are practiced? Or should he blow the whistle?
- Should he actively engage in pressure group activities because he sympathizes with their views?
- Should he actively participate in party politics? Or should he endeavour only to promote the public good and uphold the high standards of public office?

Resolving Ethical Dilemma

Public servants should ask themselves following questions when making ethical decisions:

- Is the action legal and consistent with Government policy?
- Is the action in line with my agency's goals and Code of Conduct?
- Do I think it's the right thing to do?
- What will be the outcomes for: the agency, my colleagues, other parties and me?
- Can I justify doing it?
- What would happen if the action was publicly scrutinised?

Moral Free Space

As Einstein is reported to have said, "Things should be as simple as possible–but no simpler." Many business practices that are considered unethical in one setting may be ethical in another. Such activities are neither black nor white but exist in what is called moral free space. In this gray zone, there are no tight prescriptions for a company's behavior. Administrators and managers must chart their own courses – as long as they do not violate core human values like respect for human dignity, respect for basic rights, and good citizenship.

Consider the following example

Some Indian government companies offer the opportunity of compassionate employment to the employees' children, in case of their untimely deaths or permanent disabilities. We are also well aware of the use of personal references and recommendations during recruitments and promotions. The Constitution, under Article 16, provides equality of opportunity for all citizens in matters relating to employment or appointment to any office under the State, but allows certain exceptions for the members of Schedules Caste (SC), Schedules Tribes (ST), Other Backward Classes (OBC), women and children. It can even make reservations in regard to a class or classes of employment or appointment to an office under the Government, on the basis of religion and residence. The companies honor these commitments even when other applicants are more qualified than an employee's child or referral candidate. Such perks are extremely valuable in a country where jobs are hard to find, and it may also reflect the Indian culture's belief that the West has gone too far in allowing economic opportunities to break up families. But in most western countries, it would be branded unacceptable nepotism. In the United States, for example, the ethical principle of equal opportunity holds that jobs should go to the applicants with the best qualifications. If a U.S. company made such promises to its employees, it would violate regulations established by the Equal Employment Opportunity Commission. Given this difference in ethical attitudes, how should U.S. managers react to Indian nepotism? Should they condemn the Indian companies, refusing to accept them as partners or suppliers until they agree to clean up their act?

Despite the obvious tension between nepotism and principles of equal opportunity, it is not right to condemn the practice for Indians. In a country, such as India, that emphasizes clan and family relationships and has catastrophic levels of unemployment, the practice must be viewed in moral free space. The decision to allow a special perk for employees and their children is not necessarily wrong – at least for members of that country. Again, providing reservations for the upliftment and advancement of certain socially and educationally backward classes in a caste-ridden Indian society has to be seen in the light of positive discrimination.

Organizational Integrity

Many administrators think of ethics as a question of personal psyche, a confidential matter between individuals and their consciences. These executives are quick to describe any wrongdoing as an isolated incident, the work of a rogue employee. The thought that the company could bear any responsibility for an individual's misdeeds never enters their minds. Ethics, after all, has nothing to do with management.

In fact, **ethics has everything to do with management.** Rarely do the character flaws of a lone actor fully explain corporate misconduct. More typically, unethical business practice involves the tacit, if not explicit, cooperation of others and reflects the values, attitudes, beliefs, language, and behavioral patterns that define an organization's operating culture.

Ethics, then, is as much an organizational as a personal issue. In fact, an organization forms when individuals with varied interests and different backgrounds unite on a common platform and work together towards predefined goals and objective. Administrators who fail to provide proper leadership and to institute systems that facilitate ethical conduct share responsibility with those who conceive, execute, and knowingly benefit from corporate misdeeds.

Administrators must acknowledge their role in shaping organizational ethics and seize this opportunity to create a climate that can strengthen the relationships and reputations on which their companies' success depends. Executives who ignore ethics run the risk of personal and corporate liability in today's increasingly tough legal environment. In addition, they deprive their organizations of the benefits available under new federal guidelines for sentencing organizations convicted of wrongdoing. These sentencing guidelines recognize for the first time the organizational and managerial roots of unlawful conduct, and base fines, partly on the extent to which companies have taken steps to prevent that misconduct.

For example, T. N. Seshan, Chief Election Commissioner of India (1990-96), managed to stamp his authority on the country's electoral system. He largely ended malpractices in elections held in the country, by introducing major reforms and redefining the status and visibility of the Election Commission of India. The Model Code of Conduct required Seshan to effectively use it to clean up the entire election process. An Indian Administrative Service officer, he earlier served as the 18th Cabinet Secretary in 1989. He won the Magsaysay award for government service in 1996.

Loyalty to a Leader

You might have heard, key to winning is to "value loyalty above all else".

Loyalty is linked with success in many people's minds because the archetypal successful leader always demands utmost loyalty and in turn this demand is linked with a special competence.

But loyalty to a leader is overrated, even dangerous.

A lot many times, we see governmental and corporate crime as stemming either from rampant greed throughout the ranks or from the solitary crimes of a few misfits, but some studies show that unethical behavior in organizations is mostly caused by belief in and too much loyalty to a "great leader" who turns out to be morally compromised. Charismatic managers first attract their employees and then start to demand more and more from them until the employees' behavior crosses an obvious moral line. Several misconceptions underlie the loyalty myth, but most important seems to be the expected link between demanding loyalty and possessing talent. A leader may demand loyalty because he simply knows best; his followers are flawed in some way that does not allow them to see the truth. In real organizations, leaders don't have all the answers, and followers have more responsibilities than just blindly submitting to whoever is at the top of the food chain. Organizations are not set up as perfect hierarchies in which a leader swoops down from on high to make declarations of brilliance which loyal employees follow (and traitorous employees oppose). Leadership does not come merely from one or two individuals located at the tops of hierarchies but from people who are spread throughout the organization. A more "transformational" leadership style, which focuses on working together with employees to produce superior work, leads to better organizational outcomes than a "heroic" leader helming a loyal crew. Allowing employees to speak up and take an active part in the decisions of organizations has been shown to be an effective strategy across industries. This strategy may be uncomfortable for a manager because it means listening to potentially negative feedback. On the other hand, it is not particularly helpful to one person who is trying to accomplish complex tasks to be expected to possess masterly powers and the ability to perform every task perfectly without input from anyone else.

Conflict of Development Vs Conflict of Tradition

How can administrators discover the limits of moral free space? That is, how can they learn to distinguish a value in tension with their own from one that is intolerable? Helping administrators develop good ethical judgment requires companies to be clear about their core values and codes of conduct. But even the most explicit set of guidelines cannot always provide answers. That is especially true in the thorniest ethical dilemmas, in which the host country's ethical standards are not only different but also seem lower than the one in home country. Administrators must recognize that when countries have different ethical standards, there are two types of conflict that commonly arise. Each type requires its own line of reasoning.

In the first type of conflict, which I call a conflict of relative development, ethical standards conflict because of the countries' different levels of economic development. Due to a relative sense of dispossession coupled with scarcity of opportunity developing countries may accept wage rates that seem inhumane to more advanced countries in order to attract investment. As economic conditions in a developing country improve, the incidence of that sort of conflict usually decreases

The second type of conflict is a conflict of cultural tradition. For example, Saudi Arabia, unlike most other countries, does not allow women to serve as corporate managers. Instead, women may work in only a few professions, such as education and health care. The prohibition stems from strongly held religious and cultural beliefs; any increase in the country's level of economic development, which is already quite high, is not likely to change the rules.

To resolve a conflict of relative development, an administrator must ask the following question: Would the practice be acceptable at home if my country were in a similar stage of economic development?

In the 1980s, the Government of India fought hard to be able to import Ciba Geigy's Entero Vioform, a drug known to be enormously effective in fighting dysentery but one that had been banned in the United States because some users experienced side effects. Although dysentery was not a big problem in the United States, in India, poor public sanitation was contributing to epidemic levels of the disease. Was it unethical to make the drug available in India after it had been banned in the United States? On the contrary, rational people should consider it unethical not to do so.

Apply our test: Would the United States, at an earlier stage of development, have used this drug despite its side effects? The answer is clearly 'Yes'. But there are many instances when the answer to similar questions is 'No'. If the dangerous side effects of a drug treatment outweigh its benefits, administrators should not accept health standards that ignore the risks. But while I write this, I am sure that there must be something more swirling in your mind. Yes, may be even if US (representing Western Democracy Model) would have been at an incipient stage of the development trajectory then also due to a relatively more importance that was always attached to every single life in that nation, it could have denied using that drug. Though, I know that this fact could be debated as how can one prove that US or for that matter Western Democracies always had this attitude of valuing human life as means and not ends. And the more important debatable question could be that how can one prove that India (representing all the 'South' nations) do not have that attitude.

Ethical Breakdown

In country like India having a very 'flexible' attitude towards corruption, ethical breakdowns is a way of life. They happen every second, in about every sector, in every corner of India. Whether that is the quacks diagnosing people or people becoming blind and dying in government medical clinics or political parties instigating communalization for political gains or misusing public funds for personal benefit, examples are galore!

Businesses which disregard the wishes of their customers fade away into oblivion, says management books. Yet, customers across all regions of India are taken for a ride by unethical business practices. At a time when businesses are trying hard to retain their customer base from losing it to competition, it makes sense to ponder how poor treatment of customers affects them or does it affect them at all? Otherwise, what is the rationale behind the ever-growing number of consumer complaints against suppliers of goods and services, from builders, brokers of financial products, retailers and travel agents to telecom service providers? What do you say of a vendor who vacillates in taking responsibility for a defective product, say a military equipment which may have its own set of drastic consequences besides extinguishing the life of the patriotic soldier using it, or refuses to refund for services not rendered, or a pharmaceutical company that introduces a drug without fully complying with guidelines of clinical trials? What are the implications of doing business without business ethics? Is it only a cost to the customers at the receiving end? Maybe 'yes' in the short run, but over a longer period, it hurts businesses in an increasingly globalised commercial environment, where customers across regions are connected through ever expanding social media. Besides, during slowdown, unsatisfied customers dump unethical businesses first and add to their miseries.

Some unethical practices which are common in India:

- **Illegal Medical Practitioners:** Poor illiterate people, who face the brunt of epidemics and diseases in their unhygienic surroundings, look for inexpensive medical treatments. They are rescued by the quacks and street dentists, who are now present in every corner of India, in spite of the Government declaring it to be an illegal business. They hardly carry any license or certificate for that case and can't be held responsible for the after-effects of a wrong treatment.
- **Food Adulteration:** This is probably the most common and unfortunately, accepted illegal business in India. The name

"Maggi" may ring a bell. Few years ago, Pepsi and Coca-Cola were found to contain unacceptably high levels of pesticide residues. Adding insult to injury and if we try to understand the gravity of it, besides being an effective poison to the human metabolism, Pepsi and Coca-Cola have been used by some farmers to combat pests because of low costs compared to conventional pesticide brands. Most recent case deals with the bread adulteration case which was brought by CSE report. Food manufacturers had been mixing potassium bromate with flour, to improve the elasticity and strength of dough. The ingredient speeds up the process of making bread and also gives baked goods a white color while the agent itself is heavily carcinogenic and is banned in Europe and US. Although, we have Food & Drug Administration and Prevention of Food Adulteration Rules, 1955 that regulates laws on food safety and decides about the permissible limits of agents/enzymes/preservatives/additives but still they are not enforced strictly at the ground level. The aftermath, every year, more than thousands of people in the country get ill or lose their life because of food adulteration.

- **Begging:** Giving money to beggars is considered as a generous act by most of us. We pity them and wonder what might have happened to them to have such a miserable life. However, the real picture is beyond one's imagination. Begging is actually a booming business for human traffickers and the beggars are part of their play to extract money from passerby. Begging is downright illegal but people hardly know about the reality and are always eager to please God by helping the 'needy'.
- **Hooch & Bootlegging:** Alcohol consumption could be injurious to health and family as well. But every city in the country now has one alcohol shop probably after every 2 kilometer. But the growing concern in the country is the increasing trade of local-made alcoholic drink or Desi Daru, as it is popularly called. This falls under illegal business, since gullible poor people consuming it dies. In June 2015, hundreds of slum dwellers died in Mumbai in one of the worst case of hooch tragedy and such incidence are much common with a frequency of one such happening every quarter and smaller cases happening every day. With the states like Bihar, Gujarat and to an extent Kerala having implemented the prohibition law on

liquor; the jury is still out whether this can be called as a governable move. It is also being witnessed that this types of prohibitory action only increases the illegal trade and rent seeking by the excise department. Moreover the liquor shops in the border states gets the added advantage where sales shoots-up. This proposition also applies to some extent on the sale of tobacco products. There is an ethical dilemma of a kind for the government between its tax collection - as the tobacco products and liquor shop allocation coupled with excise duty on it - and the concern for longevity of its subjects. Some radicalist also say that if government is so much interested in making the life and society free of such ills should altogether ban the production rather than getting onto such half-baked measures.

- **Child Labor:** According to Fundamental Rights and the Directive Principles of State Policy in India, it is a punishable act to make children less than 14 years work in factory or mines. But the problem lies in the ignorance of people about this law and continuous harassment of child in different ways.
- **Moral Turpitude in dealing with Foreign Tourist:** From airport to taxis, hotels, shops and tour guides - all try to fleece innocent foreign tourists in a country that claims to practice Atithi Devo Bhava. It has tarnished India's image as a favored tourist destination. Growing sexual assaults against women tourists worsen the already bad situation.
- **Financial Sector Scams:** Frauds like PNB Fraud case, Sharda Chit Fund scam, NSEL, where poor gullible people lost their life's savings are becoming a regular feature. Trust deficit will impede the future growth of the sector.
- **Sex Determination and Female Feticide:** Gone are the days when people used to differentiate between a girl child and a boy child. Every child brings along some specialty and is precious to their parents. While one part of India paints a picture of an open-minded and forward thinking country, the other part is gloomy and still very backward. There are nooks and corners in most of the states in India where female child is unwanted and killed while in mother's womb. The law imposes strict punishment on those who are caught practicing the illegal act of sex determination and abortion of female

child. Unfortunately, female fetus is still killed or left behind after birth to be an orphan.

- **Prostitution:** There are various models world over to control this societal menace. In Scandinavian Nordic nations it is illegal to buy sex while in nations of South America and US it is illegal to sell sex. In some countries like Germany and Gambia, prostitution is legal, but in other parts of the world, including India, it is regarded as an illegal trade. Such countries are suffering from growing red light areas. India is a victim to human trafficking, as well as growing diseases like HIV/AIDS.
- **Movies CD/DVDs Piracy Market:** Most of us don't even realize that using a pirated CD/DVD is an illegal act. We are so used to the easy availability of the pirated products that we don't want to take the hassle of waiting for the genuine CDs and DVDs to arrive in the market.
- **Counterfeiting:** The increasing population and the growing inequality among the people in India can be said to be one of the reasons behind the growing illegal business of duplicate goods. A common sight in India is that an item that is sold at Rs 1000 in a mall is available as a duplicate product and at a rate twice less than that of the former. This market is flourishing as more than half of the population in India falls under middle class and couldn't afford expensive goods.

Max Weber, in his magnum opus 'Protestant Ethic and the Spirit of Capitalism', showed that values determined social action and culture shaped economic development.

Discipline, pursuit of wealth and abiding by contracts led to growth of capitalism in the West. In India too, Marwaris, Gujaratis in North and West and Chettiars in South could succeed initially because of cultural orientation towards hard work and entrepreneurship.

Is moral degeneration in an increasingly consumerist society like ours responsible for ignoring its cultural best practices – with implications for doing business environment? Perhaps; but what about India's record on contract enforcement? India is above only Timor-Leste, when it comes to enforcing contracts.

Slower judicial decisions lead to 'de facto' ineffective enforcement of tort laws. In a welfare-oriented democratic polity like ours, the government cannot remain a mere spectator. A system of online filing of complaints will improve complaint registration and empower unorganized customers against unethical business practices. However, tough regulation alone will not be enough.

Attitudinal changes are needed if one wants value for one's money. Aggrieved customers must raise their voice against deficiency in services at all forums, starting from social media to consumer courts. Above all, businesses must realize that the key to sustained growth in top and bottom line is ethical business practice. They can ignore it at their own peril in an intensely competitive business environment.

How Organizations Shape Individuals' Behavior

The once familiar picture of ethics as individualistic, unchanging, and impervious to organizational influences has not stood up to scrutiny in recent years. Organization and leaders play an incredibly important role in shaping the moral behaviors of people within an organization. They are perceived by this group as the authorities who legitimate the rules. If leaders don't play by the codes of conduct, those at the conventional level will likely view the code of conduct as irrelevant and act in accordance.

Other individuals may feel demoralized by the context or leave the organization entirely. Individuals at this level of moral reasoning tend to believe that institutional norms cannot be changed. For example, some civil service officers leave the service because they find it difficult to work in a political environment and rampant corruption. Acknowledging the importance of organizational context in ethics does not imply forgiving individual wrongdoers.

Many people resist acknowledging the influence of organizational factors on individual behavior–especially on misconduct–for fear of diluting people's sense of personal moral responsibility.

But this fear is based on a false dichotomy between holding individual transgressors accountable and holding "the system" accountable. Acknowledging the importance of organizational context need not imply exculpating individual wrongdoers. To understand all is not to forgive all.

Laws, Rules, Regulations and Conscience as Sources of Ethical Guidance

There are two sources of guidance by which human beings can judge the morality of their actions. These sources are particularly important to public administrators and may offer clearer and more practical guidance.

One is outside the actor, and is law; the second is within the actor, and is conscience. These two impose on us an obligation to be moral- that is, to do good and avoid evil.

The Notion of Law

In ethics, law has a moral connotation. St. Thomas Aquinas defined law as "an ordinance of reason for the common good, promulgated by him who has care of the community." Aquinas explained that the word lex (Latin for "law") comes from the Latin word ligare, which means "to bind." It induces people to act or restrains them from acting. It imposes an obligation.

Law, then, sets up a course of action that must be followed. St. Thomas Aquinas said that, in drawing up a course of action, the legislator must act reasonably. What the legislator commands must be good, possible and just.

Regulation

Although law is an ordinance or a rule resulting from human reason, it is not the same as a regulation or ordinary rule. Regulations often help clarify laws, although sometimes they do not achieve that objective. Regulations focus on the individual good, whereas the purpose of a law is to promote the common good. On the basis of source, the authority to enact a law belongs to those with jurisdiction or those who are lawfully in charge of the community. The source of a regulation is any private authority, such as an organization, a superior or a head of household. On the basis of extent, a law does not ordinarily bind outside the territory of the legislator. For example, U.S. Laws do not bind in Europe, whereas a regulation may bind a person wherever he or she goes.

Divisions of Law

St. Thomas Aquinas recognized that two kinds of law exist in time:

- Natural Law
- Positive Law

Natural law developed with time or with the coming of human beings. It is based on human nature, and human reason can discover it. Positive law also developed with time. It consists of laws that depend on the free will of the legislators and are promulgated by some external sign.

Natural law provides some general guidance on what is right and wrong for human beings. While human reason is capable of discovering some principles of natural law, these principles are often vague and general. People can be invincibly ignorant of some principles of natural law.

Because of the vagueness of natural law, positive laws based on natural law are necessary to clarify at least some principles. Together natural law and positive laws provide guidance on the morality of human actions.

Qualities of Natural Law

According to St. Thomas Aquinas, natural law has two qualities:

- Universality
- Immutability

Universality means that natural law extends to all human beings. All human beings have the same human reason and can have at least some knowledge of what is right and what is wrong. A second quality of natural law is its immutability-that is, it does not change. It remains the same for human beings of all places and at all times. The reason natural law does not change is that human nature does not change.

Civil Law

A civil law is a kind of positive law. A civil law is one that a legislator freely enacts and promulgates. As the natural laws are generic and vague, civil laws aim to clarify them. To be more specific, civil laws do three things:

- They sometimes declare or repeat natural law;
- They sometimes determine or clarify what natural law contains; and
- They often concern issues not commanded or forbidden by natural law

Effects of Natural, Positive and Civil Laws

Natural law has two effects on human beings. First, natural law not only tells us what is good, it also imposes a 'moral obligation' to do good and avoid evil. A 'moral obligation' is the necessity of carrying out something commanded by law we must obey. Natural law imposes a 'moral obligation' on all human beings, regardless of race, religion or sex, to obey its principles. The second effect follows from the notion of all laws: there are penalties and sanctions attached to natural law. For obeying natural law, there are rewards; for disobeying, there are punishments.

If positive laws are based on natural law and often clarify natural law, there is an obligation to obey positive laws. This 'moral obligation' rests on the assumption that positive laws conform to natural law, or do not command what natural law forbids or forbid what natural law commands.

Conscience: A Source of Ethical Guidance

The discussion of law focused on principles of morality outside human beings. Conscience is something within human beings that determines the morality of human actions. Conscience is a special act of the mind that comes into being when the intellect passes judgment on the goodness or badness of a particular act. It is a practical judgment on particular, concrete, human actions.

From a deontological perspective, conscience is a judgment–an act of the intellect. It is not a feeling or an emotion, but, rather, an intellectual decision. It is also a decision with a view to a particular action. Conscience can make a practical judgment on the morality of either a past action or an action about to occur.

Conscience is different from law. Law states a general rule concerning actions; conscience lays down a practical rule for specific action. Conscience applies the law or rule to specific actions; therefore it is wider than law. Some have said that conscience is to law as a brush is to paint.

Obeying civil laws rests on the assumption that there is a lawful government with proper authority which enacted the law, that the lawss are contrary to natural law, that the civil laws are morally possible to obey, that they are for the common good and that the lawful authority has sufficiently promulgated it. If any of these conditions is absent, citizens need not obey a particular civil law. This is the argument favouring civil disobedience, however such disobedience may be illegal and result in punishment.

Accountability and Ethical Governance

Accountability and ethics are closely related. Effective accountability helps the achievement of ethical standards in the governance system. For example, legislative or parliamentary control through questions, debates and committees provide ample opportunity to the people's representatives to raise, among other things, issues of ethics and morality in the governance system.

"Ethics can be considered a form of self-accountability, or an `inner-check' on public administrators' conduct" (Rosenbloom and Kravchuk, 2005). Self-accountability and external accountability are interrelated for it is the latter that imposes expectations on the former. However, there are certain time-tested norms of moral conduct that determine the nature of self-accountability. These precepts of moral philosophy may be considered as internal checks. Essentially, however, it is the synthesis of external as well internal checks that determine the parameters of administrative ethics. The higher the level of ethics, the lower the need for strong instruments of external accountability and control. Conversely, lower the level of ethics, higher the need for potent external means for ensuring accountability.

Accountability

Accountability means answerability of officials for their decisions and actions. Accountability ensures that officials in public, private and voluntary sector organisations are responsible and answerable for their actions and that there is redress when duties and commitments are not met.

In other words, accountability means liability to give a

satisfactory account of the exercise of the power of discretion vested in some authority to which it is due, failing which, some kind of punishment may follow.

The strength of accountability and transparency in a programme or a system is expressed by its efficiencies and effectiveness, which in turn may be measured by the extent and quality accrued by the target beneficiaries.

Dimensions of Accountability

The core values involved in the question of accountability are democracy, efficiency and ethics. Adam Wolf acknowledges at least five dimensions in the concept of accountability:

- Legal dimensions (Rule of Law)
- Fiscal dimensions (Use of public funds)
- Policy and performance dimensions (Meeting goals, promises and expectations)
- Democratic dimensions (Informing and consulting legislatures and citizens)
- Ethical dimensions (Behaving in accordance with codes of ethics or general moral standards)

These dimensions all exist implicitly in the everyday affairs of public administration and guide behaviour even if they are not raised as explicit concerns.

Responsibility and Accountability

The term accountability should not be confused with the term responsibility. Responsibility refers to the public servant's responsiveness to the public, by methods and procedure to enforce the public will, while accountability denotes the specific method and procedure to enforce a public servant's responsibility.

World Bank's View on Accountability

World Bank has identified two broad types of accountability-

- Micro Accountability
- Macro Accountability

Micro Accountability

Micro accountability remains critical, especially in ensuring government responsiveness to the views and needs of the public for which services are intended. The concepts of 'exit' and 'voice' have been used to underscore the importance of micro accountability. For instance, competition or scope for the public to 'exit' when dissatisfied with a service, may have a salutary effect on the agency concerned by reducing its revenues and then by making the careers or pay of the staff less secure. Similarly, 'voice' in the sense of participation of the public may influence the quality or volume of a service through some form of articulation of preferences of demand. Accountability is increased, if such 'voice' makes the public agency more responsive to public demands. World Bank emphasizes to find out the ways of increasing 'exit' and 'voice' at the design stage of service delivery projects to enhance the accountability and improve the service delivery system.

Macro Accountability

World Bank has stated that the macro accountability has two dimensions-

- Financial accountability
- Accountability for overall economic performance

Financial accountability involves, as the Bank document identifies-

- A properly functioning government accounting system for effective expenditure control and cash management;
- An external audit system which reinforces expenditure control by exposure and sanctions against misspending and corruption; and
- Mechanisms to review and act on the results of audits and to ensure that follow up action is taken to remedy problems identified.

Accountability for economic performance involves

- Review of resource use in public investment programs and general strengthening of the capacity of governments to monitor and evaluate their own economic performance including proper resource use.

Exit, Voice and Loyalty Theory

This theory was given by Albert O. Hirschman. According

to this theory, members of an organization, whether a business, a nation or any other form of human grouping, have essentially two possible responses when they perceive that the organization is demonstrating a decrease in quality or benefit to the member: they can 'exit' (withdraw from the relationship); or, they can 'voice' (attempt to repair or improve the relationship through communication of the complaint, grievance or proposal for change). For example, the citizens of a country may respond to increasing political repression in two ways: emigrate or protest. Similarly, employees can choose to quit their unpleasant job, or express their concerns in an effort to improve the situation.

While both exit and voice can be used to measure a decline in an organization, 'voice' is by nature more informative in that it also provides reasons for the decline. Exit, taken alone, only provides the warning sign of decline. Exit and voice also interact in unique and sometimes unexpected ways; by providing greater opportunity for feedback and criticism, exit can be reduced; conversely, stifling of dissent leads to increased pressure for members of the organization to use the only other means available to express discontent, departure. The general principle, therefore, is that the greater the availability of exit, the less likely voice will be used. However, the interplay of loyalty can affect the cost-benefit analysis of whether to use exit or voice. Where there is loyalty to the organization (as evidenced by strong patriotism politically, or brand loyalty for consumers), exit may be reduced, especially where options to exit are not so appealing (small job market, political or financial hurdles to emigration or moving).

By understanding the relationship between exit and voice, and the interplay that loyalty has with these choices, organizations can craft the means to better address their members' concerns and issues, and thereby effect improvement. Failure to understand these competing pressures can lead to organizational decline and possible failure.

Government Accountability

Government accountability means that public officials- elected and unelected- have an obligation to explain their decisions and actions to the citizens.

Government accountability is achieved through the use of a

variety of mechanisms- political, legal and administrative- designed to prevent corruption and ensure that public officials remain answerable and accessible to the people they serve.

Government and Governance

The term governance has wider meaning and implication than the government. Government refers to the machinery and institutional arrangement of exercising the sovereign power for serving the internal and external interest of the political community, whereas governance means the process as well as result of making authoritative decisions for the benefits of the society. Government applies to ruling the people by official machinery while governance relates to serving the people.

Governance is a system in which exercise of the legitimate authority of the states doesn't become the prerogative of elected leaders or selected bureaucrats rather it seeks to ensure the active participation of people in this process in a just, transparent and accountable manner.

Philosophical Foundation for Good Governance

The term 'good governance' can actually be traced back to the ancient Greek period if we catch the essence of Aristotle's fundamental statement that "the state came into existence for the sake of mere life, but continued for the sake of good life." If we look for the answer what constitutes "good life", we will eventually be led to find the components of good governance of the present day. Good life begins with the guarantee of the protection of life, liberty and property for all, the underlying conditions of the origin of state, which Thomas Hobbes, John Locke, and Jean-Jacques Rousseau indicated in their "social contract" theories. In the words of John Locke, government shall govern "so long as they can protect the interest of the people or the trust the people have placed in them". This is how the concepts of democracy, rule by consent, and good governance came into existence in the theory and practice of government. Now, for the citizens in democratic state, it is vital that all powers of state should be exercised in a way conformable to their ideas of liberty, fair dealing and good administration. This feeling of the citizens resulted in the practice of maintaining 'rule of law', 'accountability' and 'transparency' in administration - the basic components of good governance in any democratic country.

Good Governance

There is no single and exhaustive definition of 'good governance', nor is there a delimitation of its scope that commands universal acceptance. Depending on the context and the overriding objective sought, good governance has been said at various times to encompass: full respect of human rights, the rule of law, effective participation, multi-actor partnerships, transparent and accountable processes and institutions, and attitudes and values that foster responsibility, solidarity and tolerance.

Participation

Inequalities and discriminations of various kinds like gender, race, caste, creed, place of birth etc. are addressed in the good governance by participation of various stakeholders in governance either through direct or through legitimate intermediate institutions or representatives. Informed and organized participation is emphasized. It means freedom of association and expression for all to raise their concerns.

Ethical Governance

Ethical Governance is a concept related to good governance. It requires that public officials adhere to the principle of serving others by setting a high standard of moral conduct and by considering their jobs as vocation. Vocation here means a purpose-driven life devoted to the well being of all.

Parameters of Good Governance

- Voice and accountability;
- Absence of political instability and violence;
- Government effectiveness;
- Reasonableness of the regulatory burden;
- The rule of law; and
- The absence of graft.

Of these, the last two are the most directly significant in the context of ethical governance. 'Rule of law' measures whether

Five Barriers to an Ethical Organization

Even the best-intentioned executives are often unaware of their own or their employees' unethical behavior. Here are some of the reasons and what to do about them.

	Description	Example	Remedies
Ill-conceived Goals	We set goals and incentives to promote a desired behavior, but they encourage a negative one.	The pressure to maximize billable hours in accounting, consulting, and law firms leads to unconscious padding.	Brainstorm unintended consequences when devising goals and incentives. Consider alternative goals that may be more important to reward.
Motivated Blindness	We overlook the unethical behavior of other when it's in our interest to remain ignornant.	Baseball officials failed to notice they'd created conditions that encouraged steroid use.	Root out conflicts of interest. Simply being aware of them doesn't necessarily effect on decision making.
Indirect Blindness	We hold other less accountable for unethical behavior when it's carried out through third parties.	A drug company deflects attention from a price increase by selling rights to another company, which imposes the	When handling off or outsourcing work, ask whether the assignment might invite unethical behavior and take ownership of the increase implications.
The Slippery Slope	We are less able to see other's unethical behavior when it develops gradually.	Auditors may be more likely to accept a client firm's questionable financial statements if infractions have accrued over time.	Be alert for even trivial ethical infractions and address them immediately, investigate whether a change in behavior has occurred.
Overvaluing Outcomes	We give a pass to unethical behavior if the outcome is good.	A researcher whose fraudulent clinical trial saves lives is considered more ethnical than one whose fraudulent trial leads to	Examine both 'good' and 'bad' decision for their ethical implications. Reward solid decision processes, not just good outcomes. deaths.

crime is properly punished or not; enforceability of contracts; extent of black market; enforceable rights of property; extent of tax evasion; judiciary's independence; ability of business and people to challenge government action in courts etc. 'Absence of graft' measures relative absence of corruption among government, political and bureaucratic officials; of bribes related to securing of permits and licences; of corruption in the judiciary; of corruption that scares off foreign investors.

Bureaucratic-ness

Administrative accountability should be ensured by the administrative system itself. One can have external agencies or authorities to make sure that administrator at various levels function in an accountable manner. But the routine procedures and processes of the administrative system should be such that the administration works in a more responsible manner.

In India, the British had created a system that made officers and staff accountable to the British as symbolized by the Viceroy/ Governor General, Provincial Governors and District Collectors. But many of the procedures that they had put into place are still in force thus 'ensuring' that today's government servants work for a "wrongful" objective, to say the least. This accountability mismatch not to the people of India but to follow strict procedures to "save" their 'kursi', the whole thing becomes full of time consuming red-tape and bureaucratic-ness. Bureaucratic-ness - has been put to emphasize on this mentality or shall we say the whole plethora of ambience which forms this typical work culture called bureaucratic work-culture and we all know what does its meaning imply.

Amongst the many instruments that have lost their efficacy in today's world are office inspections, whether of one's own office or of subordinate offices. Inspections are still carried out, but often more as a formality-a paper inspection-perhaps hurriedly completed towards the end of each financial year. Such inspections are often carried out merely to show that the inspection norm has been met. And if a couple of minor shortcomings have been pointed out in the inspections note, then it is considered a job well done. However, the purpose of such inspections is to enable the working of the office to be systematized and to act as a measure to ensure improvements in functioning in the future as also to identify areas where the system is performing sub-optimally. If the office functions in a smooth and proper manner then the number of issues getting sidetracked or delayed would decrease and the decision makers would receive files containing all relevant information about the cases and the related rules or laws and precedents and possible alternatives, and thus would take better and more appropriate decisions, and accordingly the office's functioning would approximate more and more to standards of accountability.

Inspection

Inspection not only help identify sections or subordinates who are weak in their performance, and who need motivation and greater supervision from the boss, but also to ensure that required procedures (and check lists for various types of examination of different types of cases) are being properly followed.

For example, it is prescribed that file movement registers should be kept at each desk - but the practice is rarely followed in many offices except at the level of the head of the department. Thus not only can certain files inadvertently get misplaced, but subordinates who are not well intentioned can deliberately delay and 'misplace' files in case they have not received 'speed money' from the citizen applicant concerned. Regular and properly conducted inspections would ensure that file movement is taking place properly and is being suitably tracked in the office. It is also prescribed that all papers received in any section should be diarized and given a receipt number and thereafter dealt with appropriately. Some clerical staff are lax in this diarization and keep stacks of loose papers in their office. It is easy for some such loose papers to get misplaced or to be deliberately delayed. Inspection can also help to put a stop to such shortcomings.

Inspections also help in ensuring that files are being properly maintained, that each file is being given a proper number as per its subject matter, that use of part files is being avoided, that each file is having its pages duly numbered, and that files are being kept in racks as per their subject matter file number next to any other related file on the same matter, etc.

Case: Be Corrupt or Give up the Aspirations for Social Work (CSE 2016)

Saraswati was a successful IT professional in USA. Moved by the patriotic sense of doing something for the country she returned to India. Together with some other likeminded friends, she formed an NGO to build a school for a poor rural community. The objective of the school was to provide the best quality modern education at a nominal cost. She soon discovered that she has to seek permission from a number of Government agencies. The rules and procedures were quite confusing and cumbersome. What frustrated her most was delays, callous attitude of officials and constant demand for bribes. Her experience and the experience of many others like her have deterred people from taking up social service projects. A measure of Government control over voluntary social work is necessary. But it should not be exercised in a coercive or corrupt manner. What measures can you suggest to ensure that due control is exercised but well meaning, honest NGO efforts are not thwarted? (300 words, 25 marks)

This case comes under

- Ethics and Human Interface
- Ethics in Public Administration
- Probity in Governance
- Conflict of Interests

Premise: The case presents the importance of NGOs in social development and also difficulty in smooth functioning of even well-meaning NGOs. This case deals the conflict with the aspiration of a person or NGO with traditional corrupt system.

Answer: The approach for the answer would be-

Discuss the basics involved in the question and then provide different alternatives.

Following steps must be taken to ensure that due control is exercised by the government over NGOs and at the same time well-meaning and honest NGOs are not prevented for cause-

i. A voluntary acceptance of a code of ethics by all NGOs.

ii. Government officials must be attached with masses with the string of empathy and compassion. This will enable them to be more responsive to social sector initiatives.

iii. Introducing the concept like "Right to Clearance" for NGOs as they play a very important role in social sector. The prior investigation and analysis regarding NGO's work must be completed in time bound manner.

iv. Involvement of local people in NGOs functioning.

v. Strict implementation of anti-corruption laws and check on demand for bribes. Grievance redressal mechanism against such cases.

vi. The trust deficit between government and NGOs must be removed. This would be the first step in making the functioning of NGOs easier. This can be done by transparency and proactive declaration of NGOs work by themselves.

vii. Work culture in government offices must be improved. Officials must be made more responsive, objective, and competent.

The tendency to downgrade the importance or sanctity of the administrative office inspection has also resulted in the practice followed by some officers of letting the accompanying inspection team prepare the inspection note and then signing it to complete the inspection - thus effectively leaving the inspection to the clerks in the inspection team. If the inspection has to fulfil its role of being a tool for improving the qualitative and quantitative output of the office and thus the office's ability to stand up to the accountability assessment, then the inspecting office, while of course taking the assistance of members of the inspection team, has to go into details of each aspect of the inspection himself going through sample files and registers and looking at the record and information storage and retrieval systems, and also to discuss the working of the office being inspected in a meeting with its officers and staff who should be asked to suggest measures to bring about improvements in the working of the office concerned.

Such a periodic review, whether linked to an inspection of one's own office, or whether separately conducted, could help to identify categories of files which could be subjected to the 'peshi' system of dealing with them. The peshi system comes from court working whereby for each court case file the Presiding Officer indicates on its order sheet the date of peshi when the file is to be resubmitted after complying with the orders recorded on the order sheet. For administrative files such a system has not been mandated. But certain important or urgent files could be identified according to the category on whose note sheet portion the officer would indicate the date on which the file is to be resubmitted for further consideration after complying with the directions as per the note sheet. Thus, the subordinate staff would be made accountable for complying with the direction by certain date and then resubmitting the file for further directions or decision. This would ensure that the files that require to be dealt with on priority are dealt within a time bound manner from one stage to another.

The 'peshi' system for dealing with important or urgent files can also be linked to a system of ensuring that necessary reminders are automatically issued after a fixed period has passed.

Periodic review of pending audit paras and draft has also been traditionally prescribed for each office or department. But the tendency has developed to remain busy with achieving important targets (physical and financial) of the department or office and dealing with the day to day correspondence and the flow of petitioners till a Public Accounts Committee (PAC) meeting gets fixed, when the pending audit matters are hurriedly pulled out and looked into with a view to facing and seeing off the PAC meeting with a minimum of adverse comments. Thus, the objectives of the audit system related to highlighting procedural lacunae that can be set right or to providing lessons for better administrative efforts in future are likely to get neglected unless regular periodic reviews trying to go into each pending audit para in details are undertaken. After all the punishing of persons who have undertaken wrong actions is a lower order objective of the audit exercise as compared to making the administrative system more accountable and efficient in future.

A word about internal audit as opposed to the independent audit by the A.G.-Internal audit should be a tool for the government to improve its working and to make it more accountable. However, this would really work if the internal audit parties were placed under the supervision of the Administrative Secretary or Executive Head of Department who are accountable for the working of their department. The trend presently in many State Governments is to have the internal audit teams attached to the Finance Department of the Ministry. This effectively make them into another tier of external audit like the AG's audit which appears to be more concerned with pointing out and fixing responsibility for lapses that have occurred (which of course is required) rather than identifying good practices and procedures which could be emulated elsewhere, or indicating procedural shortcomings which need to be set right for the future.

A regular review permits detailed and proper analysis which not only would ensure that each matter is dealt with in a better manner, but would also be conducive for steps aimed at systemic improvement. However, the tendency is for hurried reviews at the eleventh hour, when replies have to be given to Parliament/ Legislative or to higher supervisory authority, when there is no time for thorough or proper analysis to set systems right - but there is time only to deal with the particular matter raised.

For every office or department a large number of periodic (monthly, quarterly, annual) returns and statements are prescribed to be prepared and sent to supervisory authorities at the next higher level. Some such statements pertain to implementation of governmental programmes and achievement of related targets and some others to internal housekeeping or internal management of the office.

Unfortunately many officers take this as a routine matter conveniently left for subordinate staff to prepare and to send off and, except for the few statements where the superior authority of Chief Minister/Chief Secretary/PMO, etc. is known to be taking particular interest and where the department's or office's image about performance is likely to be formed in the eyes of the Government or the media. Such statements may even be signed unseen for "routinely" sending to the senior authority or head office where also the statements once ready were examined or analyzed by the head of office or head of department even for a few minutes, certain problem areas within the office/department would get highlighted (including those where the problems seem to be persistent) and thereafter steps could be taken to set systems into place to ensure efficient, responsible and accountable working at each level in the organization. That in fact is the purpose why the preparations of such statements have been prescribed in the first place.

Present Psychology

The trend today appears to be, to look to external agencies rather than to internalized efficiency for ensuring accountability. Thus if ensuring the achievement of district developmental goals is to be achieved then a Minister in-charge and/or a Secretary in-charge are designated to regularly visit the district to review and sort out implementational problems and generally to oversee the work, thus diluting the sense of responsibility of the district collector and the district level officers. If corruption is to be checked then the anti-corruption department (or agencies like CBI) and Vigilance Commissioner or audit parties are looked to rather than emphasizing the internal procedures and working of each office that could reduce opportunities for corruption. Redressal of public grievances received and forwarded from the Head Office (e.g. CMO, Chief Secretaries Office) are emphasized and strictly monitored rather than it being stressed that the offices should initially function in such a manner that fewer people need to raise grievances with higher authorities.

This brief comment is not meant to belittle the importance of special agencies or the accountability of watch dogs that government creates to oversee and ensure from the outside that each office functions in a more accountable manner. However, it is felt that sufficient attention should also be paid to the traditionally prescribed office procedures (including the system of office inspections) which should be routinely followed in an efficient and accountable manner.

Present day induction training of government officers does not pay sufficient attention to teaching the implementers about office procedures and how best to follow them or how to be effective while conducting inspections, and most of the subordinate and clerical staff rarely receive any training at all - thus they are not sufficiently familiar with office management procedures, or the conduct of effective office inspection. Nor, in the absence of such training, have they been sensitized about the rationale and importance of such procedures. (In fact a Chief Minister had once directed, to plan in such a way so that every officer and staff from the highest to the lowest level in the State Secretariat be put through a short course on use of office procedures and the proper ways of dealing with and maintaining files to ensure quick and appropriate decision making, because most persons in the Secretariat appeared to be ignorant and lacking in this regard).

Ethical Competence

Ethical competence is the quest for knowledge and action that defines right and wrong behavior. Ethical competence is a key distinguisher between simply having skills and having a true sense of professionalism. It is the stage beyond technical competence where ethical competence must be considered when extending policies to support skill and competencies to training and education for professional occupations. Competence in this sense is based on underlying knowledge and skills, as well as the ability to mobilise 'appropriate' values and attitudes.

Developing Ethical Competence

Developing 'ethical competence' among officials aims in part to promote rational commitment to appropriate civic norms and standards, through the use of reflective learning. Positive supports for the ethical competence carried out by public officials should be communicated to the client and wider public.

Some of the methodologies are developed by the researchers to inculcate ethical competence in the civil servants but that requires a more account of the specific elements related to ethical competence like -

- **Problem Identification Skills:** This set of skills cover the diagnostic and analytic skills needed to identify an ethically problematic situation in a role-relevant context, together with the ability to undertake a values-clarification process to test the proper application of relevant standards, to test assumptions, and to conclude whether further information might change the decision makers' understanding of the matter.
- **Problem-solving Skills:** This set of skills supports the task of resolving an issue to achieve an appropriate outcome, where competing and conflicting goods compete for attention. Problem-solving in this context requires both 'moral reasoning' ability and a 'systems thinking' approach to deal with reasonably foreseeable consequences of any proposed decision.
- **Integrity Skills:** This is a quality of being strong with high moral standards - to be maintained without any deviation; they must work together for good results.
- **Advocacy Skills:** The ability to advocate effectively for a principled and reasoned view of a given matter, and to argue in favour of, or against, a proposed decision and its ethical justification. Such advocacy necessarily involves different audi-

ences, such as ministers, media, involved parties, civil servants, review tribunals, and the public at large.

- **Self-awareness and Trust-building Skills:** This involves taking proper account of the legitimate rights and interests of other parties, including the state. Officials must develop ability to be disinterestedly self-critical in recognizing the merits and weaknesses of their institutional position, and of the principled positions that may be taken by other officials, individuals, and interests.
- **Subject-matter Knowledge:** All public officials need a good-enough grounding in the institutional ethics standards that apply to their specific role, and the institutional supports, such as law, policy, and processes that define that role in practice. They also require a good enough understanding of the real-world context in which they seek to perform their functions, to ensure that their decision making is relevantly grounded.
- **Attitude and Commitment:** Perhaps the most problematic area of developmental intervention in ethics is achieving commitment to the application of standards. Notoriously, knowledge of norms does not of itself guarantee conforming conduct.

These are some of the ethical competences in public official that must be developed to help them to deal in decision making by overcoming dilemmas and useful for the effective public policy making.

In the context of a democratic system of government, holders of public office are expected to recognise obligations - trust, integrity, and duty - to the extent that the question "Why should I do my duty" can have only rhetorical application. A civil servant must give his full ability to his job, he must be honest, upright, trustful, responsible, and must follow high standard of integrity. Lack of any ethical feature could result in wrong consequences

Strengthening of Moral and Ethical Values in Governance

There are several avenues through which the values can be instilled in the public service. We consider some of them here:

- Leadership
- Working environment

- Workable codes of conduct and value statements
- Professional socialisation mechanisms such as training
- Risk review
- Controls

In this context, a set of twelve recommendations/ principles have been prepared by a group of OECD countries. The objective of the recommendations is to help the countries to evaluate institutions, systems and mechanisms which they use to promote compliance with the ethical norms of public administration.

The principles may be applied at the national or at a level of lower administration. Political leaders may use the principles in evaluating the ethical management system and the extent to which the ethical norms are used in administration. These principles, in brief, are as follows:

- Ethical standards for public service should be clear
- Ethical standards should be reflected in the legal framework
- Ethical guidance should be available to public servants
- Public servants should know their rights and obligations when exposing wrongdoing
- Political commitment to ethics should reinforce the ethical conduct of public servants
- The decision-making process should be transparent and open to scrutiny
- There should be clear guidelines for interaction between the public and private sectors
- Managers should demonstrate and promote ethical conduct
- Management policies, procedures and practices should promote ethical conduct
- Public service conditions and management of human resources should promote ethical conduct
- Adequate accountability mechanisms should be in place within the public service
- Appropriate procedures and sanctions should exist to deal with misconduct

Risk Review

Values can be enhanced in administrative system by reviewing potential risk areas and developing a 'values and ethics risk management' strategy. Certain elements of public service work are more sensitive to value conflicts than others, and the OECD identifies tax, customs and justice administration, as well as the political-administrative interface, as particularly relevant in this regard. Identifying the areas which are most at risk of value (or ethical) conflicts and developing specialist codes of conduct (process manuals) for the staff working in these areas are necessary for the development of a value-based working environment.

Control as a Means to Strengthen the Values and Ethics in Governance

Prevention is better than cure. Heintzman identifies that effective controls are arguably the dominant factor in ensuring high levels of values and ethics performance in public organisations. Such controls include:

- Clear policies, procedures and controls
- Separation of duties and oversight
- Effective monitoring, audit and reporting
- Clear mechanisms for reporting wrongdoing
- Effective and transparent action when wrongdoing is discovered

Civic Society Engagements

The citizens' voice can be effectively used to expose, denounce and restrain corruption. This calls for the engagement of civil society and the media in educating citizens about the evils of corruption, raising their awareness levels and securing their participation by giving them a 'voice'. This introduces a new dimension to the concept of accountability of government to the people otherwise than through the traditional horizontal mechanisms of legislative and legal accountability of the executive and internal vertical accountability. Civil society here refers to formal as well as informal entities and includes the private sector, the media, NGOs, professional associations and informal groups of people from different walks of life.

In India, there have been many outstanding cases of civil society engagement. In fact, civil society initiatives to improve governance in India have grown in scale and content from the early 1990s. There have been efforts in different parts of country to challenge current paradigms, test alternative approaches and share the learning from these experiences. Some successful civil society engagements are:

- Public Interest Litigation by Common Cause Delhi and Consumer Education and Research Centre, Ahmedabad, the Association for Democratic Reforms of Ahmedabad;
- Report Card Survey of Public Affairs Centre, Bangalore;
- Jan Sunwai by Mazdoor Kisan Shakti Sangathan, Rajasthan and Parivartan, Delhi;
- Campaign for Electoral Reforms and Citizens' Charters by Lok Satta, Hyderabad

Integrity Pacts

Integrity Pact is a mechanism that helps in promoting transparency and creating confidence in public contracting. The term refers to an agreement between the public agency involved in procuring goods and services and the bidder for a public contract to the effect that the bidders have not paid and shall not pay any illegal gratification to secure the contract in question. For its part, the public agency calling for bids commits to ensuring a level playing field and fair play in the procurement process. An important feature of such pacts is that they often involve oversight and scrutiny by independent, outside observers.

Proactive/ Preventive Vigilance

Preventive vigilance attempts to eliminate or reduce the scope for corruption in the long run. The main emphasis in proactive vigilance has been on identifying suspected corrupt elements and then devising mechanisms to weed them out or to ensure that they do not occupy sensitive positions. In this regard, the following main tools have been evolved:-

- List of Officers of Doubtful Integrity containing the names of all officers against whom disciplinary action on some vigilance related issue is pending or who is undergoing punishment on a vigilance related matter.
- Agreed List of Suspect Officers containing the names of those officers on whom there is a strong suspicion of indulging in corruption. These officers are kept under watch.

- List of Undesirable Middlemen containing the names of middlemen, touts, etc. dealing with sensitive organizations.
- Annual Property Returns which help in identifying the suspected corrupt elements/practices.
- Vigilance Clearance is obtained from the Vigilance Commissioner for Board level appointments in PSUs and PSBs.

Ethics in International Affairs/ Relations

For this section, we define the term "ethics" as the department of study concerned with the principles of human duty. Ethics, as the term is used in the international sphere, will be defined as "the study of the nature of duties across community boundaries. It is the study of how members of 'bounded' communities, mostly nation-states, ought to treat outsiders and strangers and specifically whether it is right to make such distinctions".

It is worth mentioning that the discipline of international relations is concerned with explaining and discussing issues that are inherently ethical in nature, as evidenced by a review of some of the most commonly asked questions in the area. For instance, as Chris Brown states in International Relations Theory, the moral standing of the sovereign state is one of the major topics discussed by international theory. Mervyn Frost further identifies as election of such questions. For example, when is intervention by one state in the domestic affairs of another state justified? When may states justifiably go to war? Answers to these ethical and normative questions are central to international relations theory.

International Ethics

International ethics refers to the good that international interactions, exchanges, relations can bring to our planet earth and to all life forms and which can be harmed by unfriendly, hostile, uncooperative behaviours. Aware that the harms that one country can do to another and to the international space and relations, international ethics offers insights into how nations and other entities treat other nations and its people.

International ethics may be fruitfully defined as that which enables one to participate more actively in shaping and building good international community.

Various agencies of the UN by their presence and action in various countries, promote certain universal principles that transcend the boundaries of individual nations and the ethical principles pursued by individual nations.

Global Dimension of Ethics

When we leave home and cross our nation's boundaries, moral clarity often blurs. Without a backdrop of shared attitudes, and without familiar laws and judicial procedures that define standards of ethical conduct, certainty is elusive. Should a company invest in a foreign country where civil and political rights are violated? Should a company go along with a host country's discriminatory employment practices? If companies in developed countries shift facilities to developing nations that lack strict environmental and health regulations or if those companies choose to fill management and other top-level positions in a host nation with people from the home country, whose standards should prevail?

What works in a company's home country can fail in a country with different standards of ethical conduct. What are the principles that can help them work through the maze of cultural differences and establish codes of conduct for globally ethical business practice? How can companies answer the toughest question in global business ethics: What happens when a host country's ethical standards seem lower than the home country's?

Cultural Relativism

Cultural Relativism is the principle that an individual human's beliefs and activities should be understood by others, in terms of that individual's own culture.

According to cultural relativism, no culture's ethics are better than any other's; therefore there are no international rights and wrongs. If the people of India tolerate the bribery of their public officials, so what? Their attitude is no better or worse than that of people in Denmark or Singapore who refuse to offer or accept bribes. Then there's an old adage, "When in Rome, do as the Romans do" which is tempting, especially when failing to do as the locals do, means forfeiting business opportunities. The inadequacy of cultural relativism, however, becomes apparent when the practices in question are more damaging than petty bribery or insider trading.

Ethical Imperialism

At the other end of the spectrum from cultural relativism is ethical imperialism. This directs people to do everywhere exactly as they do at home. Consider the large U.S. computer-products company that in 1993 introduced a course on sexual harassment in its Saudi Arabian facility. Under the banner of global consistency, instructors used the same approach to train Saudi Arabian managers that they had used with U.S. managers: the participants were asked to discuss a case in which a manager makes sexually explicit remarks to a new female employee over drinks in a bar. The instructors failed to consider how the exercise would work in a culture with strict conventions governing relationships between men and women. As a result, the training sessions were ludicrous. They baffled and offended the Saudi participants, and the message to avoid coercion and sexual discrimination was lost.

For example, being a woman in USA is vastly different from being a woman in Saudi Arabia. In Saudi Arabia, women face several restrictions based entirely on gender. She can get arrested for driving a car. A woman cannot travel, attend university, work, or marry without her guardian's permission. But, recently some initiatives are visible to break this cultural-impasse. In the local body elections held in Saudi Arabia, we saw women candidate standing as contenders. Still, these are small changes. The United States, on the other hand, promotes gender equality and women's active participation in decision-making, fostering woman empowerment. In Saudi Arabia, family is the first priority; in the United States, family usually comes second (after work), parents usually take care of themselves when they become old because their children are busy with their own life. Every country has its own culture and tradition. It is not only different from one country to another, but also it is different from one city to another city in the same country.

International Ethics under various Approaches

The impact of various approaches of international affairs over international ethics may be explained under following headings-

- Realism
- Idealism
- Constructivism

- Cosmopolitanism
- Equality of Life

Realism and International Ethics

In the international realm, realism holds that the only thing that really matters is power - what power a country has. Nothing else matters - morality, ethics, law, and political systems, legal systems, cultural systems - are all irrelevant. Realism conceives the international sphere as a space where "anarchy" prevails and there are no rules.

The realist approach to international sphere or international relations is simply to deny any role for common or shared ethics, and create an ethically neutral zone or an ethics free zone which can be filled by the power of one who is dominant. Pursuing realism and realist policies will be detrimental to our common world with its common vision of a humane future for everyone.

Idealism and International Ethics

Idealism focuses on "common interests" between nations, and not necessarily at the power or power distance or at power balance. It seeks to build the international sphere on the basis of idealist values that are of common interests to nations participating in any international issues and problems.

In idealism, the international system, international order and the international sphere follow rules, laws and institutions. In idealism, thus ethics, morality, laws, legal systems, international institutions all have a central place. Thus idealism contrasts sharply with realism which emphasized only power. The world becomes less dramatic and less dangerous, even though conflicts are far from removed.

Constructivism and International Ethics

Constructivism focuses on things like foreign policy, diplomatic initiatives, etc. to shape international relations and the international sphere where a country has credible influence. In these things the focus is on domestic politics and how it shapes foreign policy with what goals in mind. Basically constructivism allows for influence of national identities and its constructions on the international sphere.

A flavour or dimension is added through identity politics into international sphere and relations. Constructivism shows that nations resist any threat to their identities, nationalism, national sovereignty that are perceived. They need not be real at all. This works against attempts to make the world a better place or to change world systems or world order.

Cosmopolitanism and International Ethics

Cosmopolitanism shares something in common with idealism, namely, do the right thing. The right thing to be done is to behave as you would want others to behave. Behave in ways that you think others should behave. It focuses on how we interact in a global community. What is relevant is the global community since we interact with people in other countries. It holds that since we interact with other countries, we have a moral duty to treat people of that country morally as moral people. Cosmopolitanism thus empowers international ethics and the development of "global values and ethics" fully.

Cosmopolitanism argues for following morally lawful behaviour. Where rules and laws do not exist, it would require that we come together and negotiate the rules and laws that are ethical to follow and follow them in our relations with people of other countries and in our interactions with people of other countries.

Equality of Life and International Ethics

Every life may be considered as having equal moral weight. In this belief, valid if one holds such beliefs, it is the global interest that count as much as domestic interests. No preference is given by governments or by anybody else to the welfare of citizens of that country. There are no differentiating factors recognized by such governments that distinguish between the welfare of its citizens and those belonging to another country. Everyone has equal rights. Everyone is treated equally in equal respect.

Respect for life should guide international ethics, in thought, word and deed. When that day comes when we respect the right to life of the unborn, it will be truly a day of universal peace. If you have to make decision about which world you want to live in, without knowing what position you will be in, you would choose a world that protects the weakest of the weak, the least advantaged. Such a world is full of meaning of life and in such a world equality of life will be an accepted principle.

Ethical Issues in International Affairs

Proponents of realism, or realpolitik, in international affairs often make the claim that there is no room for morality in state decision making. States do what they must because they are locked in a battle for survival against other states. In this way of thinking, ethics are a luxury for which leaders and states have no time. Further, thinking about doing "what is right" could be dangerous, distracting leaders from doing "what is necessary". On the other side, some liberal thinkers argue that all our acts have moral implications, nowhere starker than in the international realms of war and peace, intervention, human rights, globalization, and development. As humans, we cannot separate ourselves from the ethical repercussions of our actions.

As the interaction, competition and collaboration among the nations is continuously increasing, we find that it has raised many ethical issues in the global arena. It is observed that though the world is becoming a better place to live in terms of economic prosperity, but in terms of equality, peace, environment and human rights, there have been number of issues involving some ethical concerns also. Here we will discuss some of the ethical issues which have been cause of concern in international affairs:

- **A. Management of Common Goods-** The 'Global Commons' refers to resource domains or areas that lie outside of the political reach of any one nation State. International law identifies four global commons namely: the High Seas; the Atmosphere; Antarctica; and, Outer Space. There have been ethical issues regarding each of the 'global common' which are explained in following headings:
- **High Seas-** These areas have historically been guided by the principle of the common heritage of humankind - the open access doctrine or the mare liberum (free sea for everyone). However, now the countries have started claiming sovereignty over these High Seas considering their heavy strategic importance in geo-polity and for commercial use (though this restriction is in violation of UNCLOS provisions). This restricts the right of other countries on these resources. It raises the basic ethical question- Is claiming sovereignty over the High Seas ethically correct?

- **Antarctica-** These days we notice that Antarctica is facing rapid environmental degradation due to human pressures such as pollution, and the effects of global warming. Whether it is ethically correct for the countries to spoil the environment of the Antarctica which may have greater repercussions in coming time?
- **Climate Change-** Countries are divided on the issue of 'CBDR' (common but differential responsibilities) and on technology transfer and funding arrangements.
- **Outer Space-** More and more satellites are being launched by more and more countries in the outer space. This has created congestion in outer space risking the collision of satellites. Further, China tested its capability to destroy a satellite in outer space. This has raised ethical questions related to peaceful use of outer space.
- **B. Humanitarian Interventions-** In recent decades, American and some European countries have intervened in the internal affairs of other countries on the ground that the voice of public is not being respected and there is violations of basic human rights. Though these efforts look apparently bona fide, but it has also been argued that the intervention was mala fide and was encouraged by the geo-strategic reasons. This raises the ethical question whether it is right for a country to interfere in the internal affairs of another country and who would take the moral responsibility for the loss of human lives which always occur in these interventions?
- **C. Disarmament-** Ironically, the cause of disarmament is being promoted by those countries that have massive reserves of nuclear armaments, missiles and nuclear powered submarines. Further, countries like USA impose economic and other sanctions on countries like Iran to prevent it from developing nuclear weapons. There are unanswered questions like how it is ethical for a country to impose sanctions on others without discarding their own nuclear arsenals.
- **D. Intellectual Property Rights-** The developed countries are depriving the poor countries from accessing the new technologies by the restrictive clauses of intellectual property rights. Ironically, the same restrictive provisions are also applied on things like life-saving medicines. In this debate, it is essential

to determine whether it is justifiable for a country/ company to defend its intellectual property rights on the ground of commercial benefits, or they should ethically share the technology for the greater cause of humanity.

- **Trade Negotiations/ Doha Round-** The Doha round of World Trade Organisation is pending to reach a consensus. In this context, the basic question involved is whether the developing countries are ethically and morally correct when they demand relatively higher concessions in international trade.

In these ethical issues, the major ethical dilemma faced by a country would be to choose between the 'national interest' and 'ethical responsibility'. It has been observed that countries went on to pursue their national interest without giving weightage to their ethical responsibility (for example, countries are trying to find out new sea route across Arctic, without considering that this would be doubly harmful as the global warming is already causing melting of Arctic ice). This would, in long turn, would be detrimental not only for the other countries but for the promoter country also.

Therefore, it becomes necessary to consider the ethical grounds in international arena, as only a holistic approach can ensure equal and sustainable development for the world and its people.

Let us discuss some more ethical issues cropping up globally:

- **Dumping hazardous waste in poor countries**

Hundreds of thousands of discarded items like computers and gadgets, which under British law must be dismantled or recycled by specialist contractors, are being packaged into cargo containers and shipped to countries such as Nigeria and Ghana. Here, they are stripped off their raw metals by young men and children working on poisonous waste dumps. The Basel Convention on the Control of Trans-boundary Movements of Hazardous Wastes and their Disposal was designed to reduce the movement of hazardous waste between nations, and specifically to prevent transfer of hazardous waste from developed to less developed countries. Countries like the United States have signed the Convention but not ratified it. We may denounce governments that permit such abuses, but many countries are unable to police transnational corporations adequately, even if they want to. And in many countries, the combination of ineffective enforcement and inadequate regulations leads to behavior by unscrupulous companies that is clearly wrong. Cultural relativism is morally blind to such issues, but clearly this is an unethical practice. There are fundamental values that cross cultures, and companies must uphold them.

• Foreign Aid & Grant

Foreign aid and grants are given by foreign countries in the form of economic, development, technical, or military aid given by one nation to another for purposes of relief and rehabilitation, for economic stabilization, or for mutual defense.

The genuineness of such 'supposedly' ethical altruism is, however, widely debated. Consider this: The United States first recognized the usefulness of foreign aid as a tool of diplomacy in World War II. Such a program, policymakers believed, would fulfill three goals: it would furnish humanitarian assistance to needy people, it would promote liberal capitalist models of development in other countries, and it would enhance national security. The U.S. commitment to foreign aid since has amounted to well over $1 trillion – not counting hundreds of billions more donated through the International Monetary Fund, World Bank, and other multilateral agencies. Always a controversial program, foreign assistance drew its broadest support in the early Cold War era. At that time, the effort to undermine communism permeated all other aid considerations, including the plight of the poor, the expansion of democracy abroad, and U.S. economic goals that might be served by foreign assistance, such as stimulating private investment and opening up markets to American products.

Development aid has long been recognized as crucial to help poor developing nations grow out of poverty. But "Trade, not aid" is regarded as an important part of development promoted by some nations. Aid as a foreign policy tool caters much to aid the donor not the recipient. It has a geopolitical value for the donor countries, for example, aid increased when a Cold War had to be fought. It has been observed that, although Official Development Aid (ODA) is normally expected to provide new cash resources for recipient countries, to increase development spending, an increasing portion of ODA is spent on emergency relief in countries that donors have deemed critical for security reasons. For example, while a large amount of aid was given to Afghanistan and Iran, ODA seems to be barely increased for meeting the Millennium Development Goals (MDG). Thus, aid flows are largely dictated by geo-strategic concerns rather than by efforts to reduce poverty.

Furthermore, it has been argued that spread of effects of foreign aid is much less than its backwash effects due to various socio-political-economic and administrative reasons. Therefore, foreign aid even at concessional terms may impose burden on the developing countries and virtually retard their growth. Consequently, the capital made available is likely to be dissipated as has happened in Tanzania, Ethiopia, Bangladesh, etc. In fact, foreign aid is likely to retard the economic growth and development of the developing countries because it hampers the working of free market mechanism by encouraging government intervention, protectionism, excessive money creation, and state-created distortion, like political intervention, corruption, bureaucratic procedural delays, etc. Though foreign aid increases the resources of the recipient countries but it does not follow that it will accelerate the rate of development because the results depend on the expenditure of aid-funds, the tied or untied nature of aid and also on the repercussions of the flow of aid on the basic determinants of material progress, particularly attitudes, policies and institutions. Thus, aid has often come with a price of its own for the developing nations:

- Aid is often wasted on conditions that the recipient must use overpriced goods and services from donor countries.
- Most aid does not actually go to the poorest who would need it the most.
- Aid amounts are dwarfed by rich country protectionism that denies market access for poor country products, while rich nations use aid as a lever to open poor country markets to their products.
- Large projects or massive grand strategies often fail to help the vulnerable as money can often be embezzled away.

Recent increases in foreign aid do not tell the whole truth about rich countries' generosity, or the lack of it. There is a sharp decline in aid for agricultural development, and a rising share in total aid outlays of humanitarian aid in response to emergencies as opposed to long-term development and aid to the poorest countries. Moreover, development assistance is often of dubious quality. In many cases, aid is primarily designed to serve the strategic and economic interests of the donor countries. An aid system based on the interests of donors instead of the needs of recipients' makes development assistance inefficient.

While food aid is a very worthy cause and many do their utmost to genuinely help in this field, it may unwittingly contribute to the harm, especially the non-emergency relief, because the poor countries will remain dependent. The way the food aid programs of various rich countries are structured may be of concern. Dumping food on to poorer nations (i.e. free, subsidized, or cheap food, below market prices) undercuts local farmers, who cannot compete and are driven out of jobs and into poverty, further slanting the market share of the larger producers such as those from the US and Europe.

Beyond the crimes of imperialism, foreign aid has also been vilified for aiding and abetting despotic regimes that have done little for their people. In several African countries, governments have been so corrupt and countries so wracked by civil war that foreign aid has served only to line the pockets of dictators. While such funds have certainly helped mitigate illiteracy and disease in much of the world, their record of lifting countries out of poverty is more mixed. Foreign aid has been attacked by critics for imperialistically exploiting the Third World for Western interests, distorting economies, hurting local farmers and peasants, and consolidating the grip of local elites at the expense of the average Third World resident.

Ethical Issues in International Funding

Conditionality

Conditionality is a concept in international development, political economy and international relations which describes the use of conditions attached to a loan, debt relief, bilateral aid or membership of international organizations, typically by the international financial institutions, regional organizations or donor countries. In the context of international funding, 'conditionality' is typically employed by the International Monetary Fund, the World Bank or a donor country with respect to loans, debt relief and financial aid.

In other words, conditionality refers to policy changes which an aid donor agency stipulates a government must undertake in order to obtain, or retain, access to the donor's financial support; it is an exchange of money for policy action. It arises most frequently in connection with the 'adjustment' programmes of the International Monetary Fund and World Bank but bilateral donors have made greater use of it in recent years.

Conditionality may involve relatively uncontroversial requirements to enhance aid effectiveness, such as anti-corruption measures, but they may also involve highly controversial ones, such as austerity or the privatization of key public services, which may provoke strong political opposition in the recipient country. Other types of conditionality that often occur are aid which is tied to be used in a specific way (for example, many countries tie aid to the purchasing of products from donor countries).

Japan is under a heavy dose of Abenomics where lots of yen is being printed (you can call it quantitative easing of a kind never seen before) and the nation itself does not need that much of it. The interest earned on Yen lending inside the nation has decreased to a negative level. Thus, Japan in a way has found a reliable investment nation like India where it can give Yen at 'soft' interest rate - the 'soft' rate of return is more than what that yen could have earned in Japan - and also have some conditions attached to it like usage of Japan made metro accessories, if we are talking in the context of Delhi Metro or Japanese made coach or consultancy given by Japanese engineering company for the Ahemdabad-Mumbai bullet train track. By this, not only is Japan earning some interest money on its yen but also is able to generate employment back at home. In doing these if Japan is also gaining some good-manship of India then it is an added bonus.

Debt-Trap Diplomacy

Debt-trap diplomacy is a type of diplomacy based on debt carried out in the bilateral relations between countries. It involves one creditor country intentionally extending excessive credit to another debtor country with the alleged intention of extracting economic or political concessions from the debtor country when it becomes unable to honour its debt obligations. The conditions of the loans are often not made public and the loaned money is typically used to pay contractors from the creditor country.

The term was first used by Indian academic Brahma Chellaney to describe a number of loans given by People's Republic of China to countries in South and South East Asia.

Initiative by China

Critics of Chinese lending practices allege that many loans associated with China's Belt and Road Initiative to build infrastructure projects using Chinese contractors in strategically located developing countries are a type of debt-trap diplomacy. Critics in both the western, Indian and African media have also criticised the secretive conditions of the loans as well as their high interest rates.

Sri Lanka as an example

One of the most cited examples of alleged debt-trap diplomacy by China is a loan given to the Sri Lankan government by the Exim Bank of China to build the Magampura Mahinda Rajapaksa Port and Mattala Rajapaksa International Airport. The state-owned Chinese firms China Harbour Engineering Company and Sinohydro Corporation were hired to build the Magampura Port at a cost of US $361 million which was 85% funded by Exim Bank of China at an annual interest rate of 6.3%. Due to Sri Lanka's inability to service the debt on the port, it was leased to the Chinese state-owned China Merchants Port Holdings Company Limited on a 99-year lease in 2017. This caused concern in the United States, Japan, and India that the port might be used as a Chinese naval base to contain China's geopolitical rivals.

Issues Involved in Conditional Funding

Following issues (inherently ethical) related to conditional funding arises in international arena:

- The donors shape the policy framework and strategies through impositions, seriously undermining the rights, choices and decisions of the people to determine their own demands and actions needed for their own development.
- Local societal diversities and local ownership are ignored by conditionality.

A case for Neo-Liberalism

Neo-liberalism is promoted as the mechanism for global trade and investment supposedly for all nations to prosper and develop fairly and equitably. Neo-liberalism includes:

The rule of the market – freedom for capital, goods and services, where the market is self-regulating allowing the "trickle down" notion of wealth distribution. It also includes the deunionizing of labor forces and removals of any impediments to capital mobility, such as regulations. The freedom is from the state, or government.

- Reducing public expenditure for social services, such as health and education, by the government.
- Deregulation, to allow market forces to act as a self-regulating mechanism
- Privatization of public enterprise (things from water to even the internet).
- Changing perceptions of public and community good to individualism and individual responsibility.

At the international level then we see that this additionally translates to:

- Freedom of trade in goods and services
- Freer circulation of capital
- Freer ability to invest

The underlying assumption then is that the free markets are a good thing. They may well be, but unfortunately, reality seems different from theory. From a power perspective, "free" trade in reality is seen by many around the world as a continuation of those old policies of plunder, whether it is intended to be or not. However, we do not usually hear such discussions in the mainstream media, even though thousands have protested around the world for decades. Furthermore, as J.W. Smith argues, even though it is claimed to be Adam Smith's free trade, neoliberalism was and is mercantilism dressed up with more friendly rhetoric. Even during its prevalent times before the Second World War, neoliberalism had already started to show signs of increasing disparities between rich and poor. The Reagan and Thatcher era in particular, saw neoliberalism pushed to most parts of the globe, almost demonizing anything that was publicly owned, encouraging the privatization of anything it could, using military interventions if needed. Structural Adjustment policies were used to open up economies of poorer countries so that big businesses from the rich countries could own or access many resources cheaply.

- It is argued that aid conditionality infringes on countries' democracy and sovereignty.
- Policy conditions can interfere with the formation of an independent and mature democracy and political framework.
- It is argued that economic policy decisions, such as whether to privatize essential services or liberalize trade barriers within any given country - developing or developed - should be made by national governments and not influenced by leverage of increased external funding.
- Democratic ownership implies mutual accountability, transparency, and participation in policies and programmes, where both donors and governments feel equal, sharing responsibility and seeing Civil Society Organisations as key players. Domination by the government or the donors in the process undermines the basic principles of democratic ownership.

Ethical Issues in Funding for Clinical Trials

There is a considerable potential for ethical disputes to arise where clinical research, supported by developed countries, takes place in developing countries. Research partnerships where one partner is dominant in terms of funding an organisation, may lead to ethical standards being compromised and the possible exploitation of both researchers and research participants. The problem is exacerbated by the fact that potential research participants in some developing countries, whether patients or healthy volunteers, will often be more vulnerable to exploitation than those living in wealthy countries for a variety of reasons. These include limited access to basic healthcare, the difficulties of implementing guidance set out in international guidelines in local circumstances, consent procedures where cultural norms may conflict with developed country notions of autonomy and a relative lack of familiarity with developed country concepts of research and research procedures.

> Places such as South Africa - where mostly vulnerable poor with low literacy levels are recruited and the culture is to accept authority without question - are fertile land for ethical misconduct related to clinical research. India is another example, where a recent trial of two vaccines against the virus responsible for cervical cancer has had a lot of negative publicity after some deaths that were later shown to be unrelated to the trial, but exposed ethical irregularities in the Indian system.

In detail, following ethical and social issues arise when a developed country sponsors clinical trials in a developing or undeveloped country.

- The potential risk of harm to participants (persons on which trial is being conducted) has led to the following ethical question- To what extent should individuals in developing countries be invited to take part in research which may expose them, and the populations from which they are drawn, to a possible risk of harm, yet offer them little or no direct benefit?
- It is widely accepted in clinical research that participants must be respected and their consent sought to participate in a trial. There may be problems of language and some concepts may be difficult to explain or may be considered culturally unacceptable. Questions about whether consent is freely given also raise the issue of inducements. Access to better healthcare and payment may provide powerful incentives to participate in clinical research. Under these circumstances, it can be difficult to ensure that consent procedures are genuine and legitimate.
- What happens after the clinical trial is over? The quality of healthcare available to a trial community will probably decline at the end of a trial. Often, large-scale trials of interventions in developing countries are associated with improvements in community healthcare during the period of the trial due to better staffing and facilities. The support required for the improvement will not ordinarily continue after the trial is over. Is there an ethical obligation on somebody to maintain an improved standard of care for participants after the trial?

Ethical Issues in International Funding for Promoting Human Rights

These days, International Human Rights and Humanitarian Non-governmental Organizations (INGOs) are major players on the world stage. They fund human rights projects, actively participate in human rights and humanitarian work, and criticize human rights violations in foreign lands. They work in cooperative networks with each other, with local NGOs, and with international organizations. They consult and lobby governments and international organizations, sometimes participating in high level negotiations and diplomacy for global policy development.

Here, the important ethical concern is the issue of government funding for INGOs as many of them do accept funds from developed countries. Their independence and legitimacy is therefore suspected by the government of host countries, especially by the less-than-democratic governments. It is argued that they are operating in these countries not for the genuine concern of human rights but for increasing the trust deficit between the government and citizens, as mandated by their funding agencies.

Corporate Social Responsibility

Corporate Social Responsibility (CSR) is a phenomenon wherein organisations serve the interest of society by taking responsibility for the impact of their activities on customers, employees, shareholders, communities and the environment in all aspects of their operations.

In other words, CSR is the continuing commitment by business to behave ethically and contribute to economic development while improving the quality of life of the workforce and their families as well as of the local community and society at large.

Corporate Governance

Corporate Governance is defined as a set of systems, processes and principles which ensure that a company is governed in the best interest of all stakeholders. It is about promoting corporate fairness, transparency and accountability.

Corporate Governance in Public Enterprises

The debate on corporate governance in the public sector is of somewhat recent origin but much of what governments do in delivering public services involves running major business. Governments try to achieve through public sector a complicated array of political, social and economic objectives.

Corporate governance in the public sector involves much more complexity because it raises significant questions about government monopoly, ownership concentration, regulatory capture, and redistribution.

In view of the significant contribution of the public sector and the dominant role it would continue to play in the Indian economy, improving corporate governance in public enterprises has assumed a sense of urgency.

Considering the values at stake, it is only reasonable that governments develop their expertise as owners and improve the governance of their enterprises.

But while the gains are apparent, practicing corporate governance of state owned enterprises is a complex task. One paramount challenge is to find the right balance between the government's duties to be an active owner, while desisting from making undue political interference in the management of the company. Another challenge is to make sure that the government does not distort competition in the way it uses its regulatory and supervisory powers.

Corporate Governance: Challenges in Public Enterprises

Corporate Governance of state owned enterprises is a major challenge in many economies. A close examination reveals that the government has a massive task before it to create the enabling conditions that would improve the quality of corporate governance across the public enterprise system and in its transition to become market oriented. In this regard, some of the issues which need to be addressed are as follows:

- **Unclear Ownership Objectives:** Public Enterprises have been given a wide range of goals and objectives, e.g., price controls, output targets, employment goals and requirements to provide social services. As some of these goals happen to be conflicting, it makes it difficult for managers to proceed towards goals with conviction. Politicians may also abuse this discretion and meddle in company's affairs for political gain. Therefore, explicitly defining the goals and objectives can help reduce political interference, clarify management goals, improve performance monitoring, and reduce opportunities for corruption.
- **Weak Owners-** In a private company, owners play a key role in corporate governance. By contrast, in public enterprises, the state exercises its ownership role through weak institutions, sets inconsistent goals and does not properly monitor company performance. In present scenario of liberalization, opening of markets, shareholder activism and greater need for transpar-

ency and accountability demanded by stakeholders, it becomes mandatory for public sector companies to follow the corporate governance norms strictly.

- **Low Levels of Transparency and Disclosure-** Publicly owned enterprises lack transparency. Opacity undermines performance monitoring, limits accountability at all levels, conceals debt that can damage the financial system and creates conditions under which corruption can flourish. To improve transparency, public enterprises should increasingly be made to comply with high standards of accounting and auditing.
- **Unprofessional Board of Directors-** It has been observed that boards of public enterprises are weak and decision making is influenced by the government. Improving the boards requires many steps including increased authority, autonomy and professionalism.

Principles of Public Life

Democracy is not a state of being, it is an organic process. As part of this process, countries maturing towards democracy create more and more sophisticated notions of values and principles. In even highly developed countries, these principles can suddenly become more expansive as a society is confronted with a corruption scandal. Behavior that was previously considered acceptable is condemned as it is viewed through the lens of principle.

This lens refocuses the action often as unacceptable behavior from one who is a temporary steward of the public interest. When principles and values are the primary focus of public service, they act to provide a guide for unanticipated events.

A primary example of an Ethics Code is the Seven Principles of Public Life developed by the Committee on Standards in Public Life in Great Britain. When Prime Minister John Major created the committee in 1994 the terms of reference were sweeping: "To examine current concerns about standards of conduct of all office holders of public office, including arrangements relating to financial and commercial activities, and make recommendations as to any changes in present arrangements which might be required to ensure the highest standards of propriety in public life."

Seven Principles of Public Life

The Nolan Committee has set out 'Seven Principles of Public Life' which it believes should apply to all in the public service. These are:

Selflessness: Holders of public office should act solely in terms of the public interest. They should not do so in order to gain financial or other benefits for themselves, their family or their friends.

Integrity: Holders of public office should not place themselves under any financial or other obligation to outside individuals or organizations that might seek to influence them in the performance of their official duties.

Objectivity: In carrying out public business, including making public appointments, awarding contracts, or recommending individuals for rewards and benefits, holders of public office should make choices on merit.

Accountability: Holders of public office are accountable for their decisions and actions to the public and must submit themselves to whatever scrutiny is appropriate to their office.

Openness: Holders of public office should be as open as possible about all the decisions and actions that they take. They should give reasons for their decisions and restrict information only when the wider public interest clearly demands.

Honesty: Holders of public office have a duty to declare any private interests relating to their public duties and to take steps to resolve any conflicts arising in a way that protects the public interest.

Leadership: Holders of public office should promote and support these principles by leadership and example.

The definition of office holders was also sweeping including all elected officials and civil servants at the national and local levels.

The primary critique of ethics codes is that they are too abstract and because of that they are difficult to enforce. Although there is some truth to both of these critiques, usually the problem lies with the institutionalization of the civil service and the ability to enforce behavior in only the most narrow of areas. Some research suggests that just having a code without an institutional fabric can actually lead to greater pressure to commit misconduct than having no code at all.

Values of Public Service

The Public Service and the Public Servants shall be guided

by the following values in the discharge of their functions:

(1) Patriotism and upholding national pride
(2) Allegiance to the Constitution and the law of the nation
(3) Objectivity, impartiality, honesty, diligence, courtesy and transparency
(4) Maintain absolute integrity

Public Services Code

The Government shall promote the Public Service Values and a standard of ethics in the Public Service operations, requiring and facilitating every Public Service employee:

- To discharge official duties with competence and accountability; care and diligence; responsibility, honesty, objectivity and impartiality; without discrimination and in accordance with law
- To ensure effective management, professional growth and leadership development
- To avoid misuse of official position or information and using the public moneys with utmost care and autonomy
- Function with the objective that Public Services and Public Servants are to serve as instruments of good governance and to provide services for the betterment of the public at large; foster socio-economic development, with due regard to the diversity of the nation but without discrimination on the ground of caste, community, religion, gender or class and duly protecting the interest of poor, underprivileged and weaker sections.

The Second Administrative Reform Commission (SARC) is of the view that in addition to commitment to the Constitution the public values should include:

a. Adherence to the highest standards of probity, integrity and conduct
b. Impartiality and non-partisanship
c. Objectivity
d. Commitment to the citizens' concerns and public good
e. Empathy for the vulnerable and weaker sections of society

Business Vs Ethics: Corporate Scandals

Organizations are products of man's desire to make money. The world has been witness to the grandeur and failure of some big corporations. Individuals are not spared from scandals; more so, a corporation can get involved with allegations of unethical behavior by the people acting within or on behalf of the business entity. Oftentimes, a corporate scandal involves accounting fraud or something almost like it. Some of these corporations went to greater heights in just a short period of time and this caused suspicions to arise.

These well-regarded companies have fallen further into the ravine even when all the astute people tried to find loopholes and make use of unconventional sources in order to resuscitate the nearly-dying corporations.

With numerous corporate scandals and spectacular bankruptcies dominating headlines for many years, ethics has become an important matter both in corporate headquarters as well as in business-schools. American corporate icons such as Enron's former Chairman Kenneth Lay (who was found guilty on 25 May 2006, of ten counts against him) was once held up in classrooms and lecture halls across the various countries as examples of successful business leaders. Today, he is again discussed in business schools, but as examples of highly unethical business leaders, not, as previously, role model. The corporate scandals that have rocked the world and Indian business sector over the last few years have left an indelible impact on various levels.

1. First, they left the managerial class severely bruised with accusations of self-dealing.
2. Second, they destroyed small and large fortunes for many shareholders.
3. Third, they provided the impetus for new regulation, the most significant example being the Securities Laws (Amendment) Act, 2014.

Most important of all, however, has been the damage done on people's trust for the dual pillars of modern capitalism, the corporate enterprise and market system as mechanisms for the efficient allocation of capital and the preservation and growth of society's investable wealth. It is 'greed' that capitalism uses as an incentive to derive maximum effort from the individual. 'Greed' as an incentive to produce value based on economic efficiency works well for the individual and the society. Uncontrolled greed, on the other hand, can sacrifice both, economic efficiency and value. This happens, for example, when company managers and/or owners try to distort information so they can trade their stock holdings with and reap profits from unsuspected investors.

The corporate scandals of recent years demonstrate a clear lack of a market ethos by those that ought to have the greatest allegiance to the market, that is, top corporate executives. Instead, we have seen the display of personal and quick gratification at the expense of a higher good that is essential of the type of society we espouse.

These failures also show that Adam Smith's prescription that individual action based on self interest maintains competition and engenders economic prosperity is not entirely workable when taken to the extreme of ethical egotism, that is, when maximizing personal utility becomes the guide for one's actions. Individuals as economic agents interact within a social mechanism - the market - whose well-being is also of paramount importance. An ethos of individual utility that supplants the ethos for the common good, i.e., the market, is not a viable prescription for economic behavior.

The Indian Way

As Ratan Tata, former Chairman of the Tata Group, observed, “If you choose not to participate in corruption, you leave behind a fair amount of business.” Much has been written about the benefits of doing business in India – low input costs, easy access to labor and a massive consumer base. Less has been said about the ability of companies in India to thrive by bending rules, greasing palms and broadening ethical boundaries. At a time when the issue of corruption threatens the stability of the Indian government and scandals unearthed in sectors from sports to telecommunications total tens of billions of dollars, it is becoming increasingly critical for multinational managers to ask whether business success in India comes at an ethical cost. Following the 1991 fiscal reforms, India's growth story has entered its third decade in dramatic fashion. Annual growth bordering on double digits, a middle class set to grow eightfold in the coming two decades and more than 1034 million mobile subscribers (and growing by a million every month) are but a few highlights of the narrative that has reshaped the global business landscape. Business groups today, use the tactics of a concept known as pressure group, pioneered by America, to help the businesses gain contracts and favors through a process called lobbying.

India saw inflows of money that the country's politico-business arena had never seen before or even contemplated. Politicians saw businessmen become billionaires in a few months because of licenses the politicians had granted. This created a render unto Caesar what is Caesar's type of demand. The demand was met because the flood of money was so large. We think this decade's explosion in corruption in the Indian political-business sector was primarily due to the waves of foreign capital flooding into India.

The German firm Enercon, the world's fifth-largest wind turbine manufacturer, was forced to walk away from its US$566 million joint venture after being intimidated by authorities and failing to find legal recourse to what it termed "government-abetted theft." Even Ratan Tata admitted that officials' expectations of bribes were the reason he did not establish a domestic airline.

Below are given some infamous scandals in India:

- **2G** - The infamous "2G" scandal of 2008, in which the government granted telecommunication licenses on a first-come-first-served basis instead of through an auction, is estimated to have cost taxpayers US$40 billion (as per the prospective loss figure given in the CAG report). This resulted in bargain-basement prices for valuable assets and precluded many eligible parties from procuring licenses. This crucible prompted the chairman and founder of one of India's leading retail groups to say that in India, corruption is necessary for growth. He went on to cite the example of the "2G" scandal: Without it, had the licenses been granted by auction, mobile calls would never have fallen so quickly to two cents per minute! And this is the irony of crony capitalism and rent-seeking that has become such an indispensable part of the whole gamut of governance.
- **Satyam Computer Services** - Lax corporate governance has

also hurt investor confidence, as illustrated by the revelation of questionable accounting practices at Satyam Computer Services. This 2009 scandal, which is also called the 'Enron of India' saw US$70 million in real assets transformed into US$1 billion in imaginary assets and sent the Bombay Stock Exchange tumbling 5% in a single day. A special court under India's Central Bureau of Investigation (CBI) on April 10 held the founders and former officials of outsourcing firm, Satyam Computer Services, guilty in an accounting scam worth Rs 7,000 crore ($1.1 billion). B Ramalinga Raju, the company's former chairman, has been sentenced to seven years in jail.

- **SAHARA** - On February 26, 2014, shock waves were felt through out the country as the Supreme Court of India issued a non-bailable warrant for the arrest of Sahara India Chairman Subrata Roy. This decision attracted attention for one major, unexpected reason. One would consider investor fraud worth more than US $3 billion as incredulous under any circumstance, but corporate scandals of this nature in India have lost their propensity to amaze. Indeed, what was most surprising about this case was real consequences for the perpetrator, a rarity for corporate crimes in India. Despite immense political pressure and the regulatory body's own restrained powers, the Securities and Exchange Board of India managed to secure a landmark victory after an arduous, five-year battle against Sahara.
- **Saradha Group Chit-Fund Scam-** The Saradha Group scam of 2013 also saw as many as 1.7 million investors of a Ponzi scheme lose approximately US $5 billion when it collapsed. India has been flooded with various Ponzi schemes that take advantage of unsuspecting investors looking for alternate banking options. Lacking access to formal banks, low-income Indians often rely on informal banking. These informal banks invariably consist of money lenders who charge interest at inflated rates and were soon replaced by more sophisticated methods of conning people through disguised Ponzi schemes. Fund raising is done through legal activities such as collective investment schemes, non-convertible debentures and preference shares, as well as illegally through hoax financial instruments such as fictitious ventures in construction and tourism. The rapid spread of Ponzi schemes, especially in North India, has various causes,

not the least of which include the lack of awareness about banking norms, steadily falling interest rates, lack of legal action against such activities, and the security of political patronage. Unarguably, networks with high-ranking politicians in the state government of West Bengal allowed the Ponzi scheme to stay afloat undetected for as long as it did. Here, too, regulatory bodies like SEBI were blatantly disregarded until the scheme went bust in April 2013.

- **Few Others-** Indicative of the ubiquity of the problem, it is estimated that US$1.5 trillion in black money – an amount far exceeding India's GDP – is hidden in foreign banks. Individual cases help ground this issue in reality. Madhu Koda, the son of a tribal farmer, who rose to become chief minister of the State of Jharkhand, was discovered to have undisclosed assets of US$1 billion, including a hotel in Thailand and a coal mine in Liberia. Businessman Hasan Ali, accused of money-laundering and arms-dealing, owes the government US$16 billion in taxes.

Here is a list of some infamous corporate scandals that rocked the world.

- **Union Carbide-** Union Carbide is a chemical manufacturing company hit the news when an industrial disaster exposed more than 5 million people in Bhopal, India to methyl isocyanate gas after a leak from the pesticide plant.

  The terrible gas-leak incident in Bhopal is considered one of the worst industrial disasters of all time. The Indian Government sued the company and Union Carbide was charged with a fine of $480 million.

- **BP Oil -** The largest marine oil spill in history happened in 2010 when a massive amount of oil leaked from one of the wells into the Gulf of Mexico near the Mississippi River Delta. It was caused by a wellhead blowout during the digging process, which killed 11 people and eventually caused great harm to marine life and affecting about 800 km of American coastline.

  The company was plagued by many serious setbacks because of the spill. BP processed almost $1 million in damage claims and by far has paid the claimants close to $5 million.

- **Enron -** Enron is an American company doing business in the energy industry which was founded in 1985. It was conferred as "America's Most Innovative Company" for six consecutive years by the Fortune magazine because of its significant growth in the market.

That fame, however, changed when the Enron Scandal was brought into the limelight in 2001, making it the largest bankruptcy of all time, amounting to a whopping $63.4 billion. It led to a massive job loss in 2002. More importantly, it pioneered several policy changes to ensure that every American corporation's books are properly audited. India too had has its share of financial frauds.

The Ethics of Corporate Fraud: Should We Care?

When we think of corporate fraud, there is a tendency to imagine it as an isolated event with no real repercussions in our lives. We often look at the lofty numbers and associate the loss with an abstract, theoretical entity. In reality, the financial costs of corporate scams have deep ethical considerations and significant implications in our lives.

Many of these scams include taxpayer money that would ideally go toward improving amenities for citizens. Clearly, corporate fraud has deep financial ramifications for all of us, even if we don't see them immediately. Ethics no longer remain a matter of personal opinion and strict guidelines need to be enforced in order to clearly differentiate between right and wrong. Companies that commit fraud cross ethical lines and that has far reaching consequences.

It is quiet instigating but natural to think that every penny taken out of the "regular" economy and hoarded in the "black" economy is like artificially created "sink-holes" which 'heats' the overall economy without creating any meaningful socially relevant asset.

With a population of over 1.2 billion, more than 250 million people in India live in abject poverty. The Indian economy relies significantly on the corporate sector, and the rising number of financial scams has pertinent ethical implications now more than ever.

The Sahara and Saradha Group scandals represent the antithesis of all business ethics. Sahara, for one, has been convicted of wrongfully acquiring investor money without proper authorization.

There are also accusations of Sahara laundering black money; this is a clear breach of ethics on their part. By definition, black money includes money siphoned off by illegal means that was ideally meant to provide other services. Not only is this a blatant misuse of other people's money, it also raises serious questions about government resources that were wasted on this unnecessarily long investigation.

On the other hand, the ethical violations committed by the Saradha Group were more obvious and possibly more damaging. The schemes run by Saradha were primarily aimed at low-income people who did not have access to formal banking. Unsurprisingly, these low income investors were hit hardest by the scam. When the Ponzi scheme collapsed, it caused severe financial loss to its 1.7 million investors, but the poorer population of West Bengal bore the worst brunt. Many were bankrupted, and a great number resorted to suicide.

The Saradha case undoubtedly represents the worst kind of damage, unethical practices in business can beget. The ramifications of the actions of a few conniving businessmen and politicians can still be felt throughout rural West Bengal. There is no doubt that conning poor people into investing in a hoax scheme, only to abandon them when it collapses, falls in the far dark end of the ethical spectrum.

Therefore, corporate scams of this nature not only symbolizc the ethical and moral standards of a company but on a larger scale represent those of the country and her people. This sort of generalization can cause foreign companies to lose interest in investing in a country and could cost India (or any country, for that matter) dearly.

Ethical Issues in Healthcare Industry

The issue of ethics and economic efficiency in the provisioning and delivery of services is complex in a developing country like India, where health indicators are poor.

In recent years, the terms "bio-medical ethics", "bio-pharmaceutical ethics", and "health care ethics" are gaining importance. The term bio-medical ethics includes the issues related to reproductive biology, such as stem cell research and human cloning and the ethical dimensions arising out of these changes. The term bio-pharmaceutical ethics refers to the ethics associated with the discovery and development of the products. The term health care ethics is increasingly being used as an umbrella term to encompass ethical aspects previously included in medical, bio-medical, bio-pharmaceutical and also organizational- and business ethics of different stakeholders involved in the provisioning and delivery of health care services. Health care is a key aspect of any developing nation and the need for quality, accessible and affordable health care is a necessity.

The field of medical ethics has long existed, arising from the Hippocrates oath, and tenets of the early religious healing traditions of the West. The International Code of the World Medical Association, an organization representing physicians founded in 1947, ensures that physicians strive for the highest possible standards of ethical behavior and care at all times.

An incisive read through the below given Code of Ethics by Medical Council of India for doctors and registered medical practitioners (only the relevant portion) could be meaningful engagement. From this code only the relevant has been picked up and the same is being produced below.

1. Code of Medical Ethics

Duties and responsibilities of the Physician in general:

1.1 Character of Physician (Doctors with qualification of MBBS or MBBS with post graduate degree/ diploma or with equivalent qualification in any medical discipline):

1.1.1 A physician shall uphold the dignity and honour of his profession.

1.1.2 The prime object of the medical profession is to render service to humanity; reward or financial gain is a subordinate consideration. Whosoever chooses this profession, assumes the obligation to conduct him in accordance with its ideals. A physician should be an upright man, instructed in the art of healings. He shall keep himself pure in character and be diligent in caring for the sick; he should be modest, sober, patient, prompt in discharging his duty without anxiety; conducting himself with propriety in his profession and in all the actions of his life.

1.2 Maintaining good medical practice:

1.2.1 The Principal objective of the medical profession is to render service to humanity with full respect for the dignity of profession and man. Physicians should merit the confidence of patients entrusted to their care, rendering to each a full measure of service and devotion.

1.5 Use of Generic names of drugs: Every physician should, as far as possible, prescribe drugs with generic names and he/she shall ensure that there is a rational prescription and use of drugs.

1.8 Payment of Professional Services: The physician, engaged in the practice of medicine shall give priority to the interests of patients. The personal financial interests of a physician should not conflict with the medical interests of patients. A physician should announce his fees before rendering service and not after the operation or treatment is under way. Remuneration received for such services should be in the form and amount specifically announced to the patient at the time the service is rendered. It is unethical to enter into a contract of "no cure no payment". Physician rendering service on behalf of the state shall refrain from anticipating or accepting any consideration.

1.9 Evasion of Legal Restrictions: The physician shall observe the laws of the country in regulating the practice of medicine and shall also not assist others to evade such laws. He should be cooperative in observance and enforcement of sanitary laws and regulations in the interest of public health. A physician should observe the provisions of the State Acts like Drugs and Cosmetics Act, 1940; Pharmacy Act, 1948; Narcotic Drugs and Psychotropic Substances Act, 1985; Medical Termination of Pregnancy Act, 1971; Transplantation of Human Organ Act, 1994; Mental Health Act, 1987; Environmental Protection Act, 1986; Pre-natal Sex Determination Test Act, 1994; Drugs and Magic Remedies (Objectionable Advertisement) Act, 1954; Persons with Disabilities (Equal Opportunities and Full Participation) Act, 1995 and Bio-Medical Waste (Management and Handling) Rules, 1998 and such other Acts, Rules, Regulations made by the Central/State Governments or local Administrative Bodies or any other relevant Act relating to the protection and promotion of public health.

2. Duties of Physicians to their Patients

2.1 Obligations to the Sick

2.1.1 Though a physician is not bound to treat each and every person asking his services, he should not only be ever ready to respond to the calls of the sick and the injured, but should be mindful of the high character of his mission and the responsibility he discharges in the course of his professional duties. In his treatment, he should never forget that the health and the lives of those entrusted to his care depend on his skill and attention.

3. Duties of Physician in Consultation

3.1 Unnecessary consultations should be avoided:

3.1.1 However in case of serious illness and in doubtful or difficult conditions, the physician should request consultation, but under any circumstances such consultation should be justifiable and in the interest of the patient only and not for any other consideration.

3.1.2 Consulting pathologists/radiologists or asking for any other diagnostic Lab investigation should be done judiciously and not in a routine manner.

3.6 Patients Referred to Specialists: When a patient is referred to a specialist by the attending physician, a case summary of the patient should be given to the specialist, who should communicate his opinion in writing to the attending physician.

6. Unethical Acts

A physician shall not aid or abet or commit any of the following acts which shall be construed as unethical -

6.1 Advertising:

6.1.1 Soliciting of patients directly or indirectly, by a physician, by a group of physicians or by institutions or organizations is unethical.

6.3 Running an open shop (Dispensing of Drugs and Appliances by Physicians): - A physician should not run an open shop for sale of medicine for dispensing prescriptions prescribed by doctors other than himself or for sale of medical or surgical appliances. Drugs prescribed by a physician or brought from the market for a patient should explicitly state the proprietary formulae as well as generic name of the drug.

6.4 Rebates and Commission:

6.4.1 A physician shall not give, solicit, or receive nor shall he offer to give solicit or receive, any gift, gratuity, commission or bonus in consideration of or return for the referring, recommending or procuring of any patient for medical, surgical or other treatment. A physician shall not directly or indirectly, participate in or be a party to act of division, transference, assignment, subordination, rebating, splitting or refunding of any fee for medical, surgical or other treatment.

6.4.2 Provisions of para 6.4.1 shall apply with equal force to the referring, recommending or procuring by a physician or any person, specimen or material for diagnostic purposes or other study/ work. Nothing in this section, however, shall prohibit payment of salaries by a qualified physician to other duly qualified person rendering medical care under his supervision.

In a move to curb the unethical marketing practices of pharmaceutical companies, a recent initiative was taken by the government companies by spelling out a uniform code of conduct for the industry. Accordingly, doling out freebies, cruise tickets, paid vacations and sponsorships to educational conferences and seminars for doctors by pharmaceutical companies has been banned since January, 2015.

At present, the pharmaceutical industry follows a "self-regulatory" code that curbs unethical sales promotion and marketing expenses, bans personal gifts, and all-expenses paid junkets for doctors and their families, but there have been several instances where companies have violated the code. Industry experts say the code exists only on paper as companies try to influence prescriptions through several ways.

The code includes banning gifts, hospitality, medical samples, medical grants, and clarifies the relationship with healthcare professionals. Regarding gifts, it says "no gifts, pecuniary advantages, or benefits in kind may be supplied, offered or promised to persons qualified to prescribe or supply drugs, by a pharmaceutical company, or any of its agents including retailers, distributors or wholesalers". It says "in any seminar, conference or meeting organized by a pharmaceutical company for promoting a drug or disseminating information, if a medical practitioner participates as a delegate, it will be on his/her own cost."

Consider another news item from February 23, 2014. In a bizarre move, the Medical Council of India (MCI) – the apex regulatory body of doctors and the medical practice in the country – has decided to shrink its own jurisdiction. It has reinterpreted its code of ethics regulations as being applicable only to individual doctors and not doctors' associations.

Clause 6.8 of the Code of Medical Ethics Regulation, 2002 clearly states that it pertains to "code of conduct for doctors and professional association of doctors in their relationship with pharmaceutical and allied health sector industry". However, the executive committee of the new MCI in its meeting on February 18 decided that the term "association of doctors" be deleted from the clause. In effect, the MCI has stated that the action it took against the Indian Medical Association (IMA) for endorsing products of Pepsi and Dabur in exchanges for crores of rupees or against the Indian Academy of Pediatrics for accepting funding from pharmaceutical companies will no longer be valid. Endorsement is expressly forbidden by the code of ethics, which says that "no doctor ought to endorse any commercial product or drug or therapeutic article."

Health care services have a special moral quality. The purposes of health care services include saving lives, preventing or relieving suffering, preventing and curing disease and disability, and ameliorating the consequences of disease when it cannot be prevented or cured. Few people can be morally comfortable with the idea that some people should be denied access to healthcare that might relieve their suffering or save their lives because they cannot pay for it.

Consider an imaginary patient. Let us observe the trajectory for an imaginary patient (Patient X) traversing through the value chain in Indian health care. Patient X might be a poor farmer, an entrepreneur, or a settled professional. Patient X visits a general physician, who advises diagnostic tests, and cautionary medicines and could also refer X to a specialist. It is possible that some of the recommended tests or medicines or consultation with a specialist might not be necessary, but it is becoming a common knowledge that a doctor generally has a commission in all of the above stated steps of treatment.

Now, Patient X has bills to pay and the following options of payment: if Patient X has been treated at a public hospital she may have the option of not paying any of the bills; Patient X could approach her insurance provider if she is employed in a big company and has employer-provided insurance; Patient X could approach her insurance provider from the state if she comes from below-the-poverty-line and has state provided insurance. Despite the options, it is an arduous journey, and one hopes, without serious implications.

The above anecdote is educative of how as a patient or a consumer, one is dependent on so many stakeholders across the value chain in the Indian health care industry. These include doctors - the generalists and the specialists, medical devices companies, pharmaceutical companies, diagnostic clinics, insurance companies, clinical trial organizations, and other service providers entering the field. The inter-relationships across the actors are complex and raise several issues pertaining to conflicts of interest.

The key ethical issues concern the different players in health care- the physician, the bio-pharmaceutical industry, and the chemist.

The bio-pharmaceutical industry

a. Pricing of drugs (brand vs. generic)
b. Investments of MNCs in tropical disease drug discovery to life style
c. Advertising - information disclosure in ads; doctor-pharmaceutical firm nexus to promote certain drugs over others through samples, sponsorship and other practices, with little attention to quality
d. Availability of banned drugs and counterfeits
e. Disregard of regulations in sponsoring clinical trials
f. Private health care providers and the issue of "inappropriate care"

Physician

a. Irrational prescription of drugs

b. Prescription by brand names instead of equivalent generics

c. Commission received for referrals to diagnostic centres

d. Prescription of non-essential drugs

e. Monitoring of the Medical Council of India and its code-of-conduct

Pharmacy/Chemist

a. Use of the MRP as the price

b. Collusion by pharmacists on price

Regulation of the Healthcare/Pharmaceutical Sector

Relative to the pharmaceutical industry, no issue raises more ethical considerations in the emerging markets (or in the developed ones) than pricing.

Ethical issues in pricing cluster around two poles:

(1) Providing access to existing medicines for those who cannot pay

(2) Maintaining the incentive to continue to develop medicines that address unmet needs

Some argue that the developed world is a sufficiently large and wealthy market to bring forth innovation in medicines and that ignoring the property rights of companies in lower income countries through compulsory licensing, voiding of patents, strict price controls, or whatever mechanism can do no meaningful harm to the future flow of medicines. For medicines that treat conditions prevalent in both developed and emerging markets, it is almost certainly true that the lost sales from "free riding" in low income countries are not a large deterrent to innovation at least in the near term. However, such static effects are not the only ethical consideration.

Companies that might start selling at very low prices in lower income markets have a natural interest in moving into higher income markets, and products sold at low prices in low income countries will naturally tend to flow into higher income markets whether through legitimate channels or otherwise. Additionally, generics manufacturers seeing opportunities to challenge patents in developed countries have an incentive to turn their attention to those markets as well. Both these forces threaten to leave those with low incomes without the supply they need.

Additionally, as the emerging markets continues to grow, they become meaningful markets and larger and larger segments of their populations will have the capacity to pay for innovative medicines. Should they not? Is there no ethical responsibility for people who can afford to pay for innovative products to do so regardless of where they live? The National Pharmaceutical Pricing Authority (NPPA) which is the regulator for prices in the pharmaceutical market is located under the Department of Pharmaceuticals which is situated under the Ministry of Chemicals and Fertilizers. We are talking about health care here and the Ministry of Health and Family Welfare should have been the ministry or the custodian of the drug regulator in this case. The NPPA's motto is to serve the consumers while encouraging the pharmaceutical manufacturers to produce adequate quantity of quality products to meet the rising demand. However, we know from experience that often protecting the interests of the industry becomes a priority over protecting the interests of the consumers. For instance, if you look at the list of essential medicines, there has been a considerable reduction in the number of medicines which are covered in the National List of Essential Medicines (NLEM) over time. While at the same time more and more private companies have been given licenses to produce drugs in our country. The government has allowed pharmaceutical companies to hike rates of 509 essential medicines used for treating various ailments like diabetes, hepatitis and cancer by 3.84 per cent with effect from April 1.

The second point about regulatory enforcement is about the quality of the drugs which are available in the market and what the regulator has done in order to ensure that quality is maintained. The Central Drug Standard Control Organisation (CDSCO) which controls the in-flow of drugs into the country and oversees clinical trials is placed under the Ministry of Health and Family welfare. However, if you discuss issues with them, they say that their sole responsibility is to ensure that they provide licenses to international firms entering the market. The license for domestic drug firms is provided by the state drug controllers, who are also responsible for monitoring the performance of these firms in the market with regard to availability and quality of the drugs they produce. And studies show they are not well-equipped or skilled at doing so.

The third issue concerns marketing of prescription drugs. As in any industry, there are legitimate concerns about the incentives the seller of a good might have to distort information conveyed about their product. In health care, this concern is heightened by the fact that the ultimate consumer, the patient, is typically somewhat disconnected from the choice of medical approach to use. When the physician acts in the patient's best interest, the ethical concern about marketing is less serious. So a first step in thinking about the ethical challenge in marketing pharmaceuticals might be to consider the incentives facing the care-giving physician. Under the Indian Medical Council (Professional Conduct, Etiquette and Ethics) Regulations, 2002, pharmaceutical companies are not supposed to influence the behaviour of doctors by offering gifts/ commissions. But evidence suggests otherwise, going by the large number of complaints which have been received by the MCI about such practices. Recently there has been an attempt by the Health Ministry to come up with a Uniform Code of Pharmaceutical Marketing Practices (UCPMP). It is a voluntary guideline but the Ministry is very keen to enforce it, given the prevailing concerns related to marketing of drugs in the country.

The fourth and the last point pertaining to experiences in regulation is registration of health care institutions. The Clinical Establishment Act, 2010, which was notified earlier in May 2012, still remains a model law and is yet to be adopted and adapted across most of the states. Related to this, in terms of the performance of the health care institutions, according to the National Antibiotic Policy of 2010, the government has been toying with the idea of prescription audit to assess adherence to "rational use of drugs" (RuD) by the doctors and healthcare institutions. But there has been resistance to this suggestion, especially from the Drug Traders Associations in the country.

The ethical conduct in the domain of medicine and pharmacy including the medical practitioners has become very relevant due to growing occurrences of adulterated attitude heavily impregnated with the poison of money-making attitude among every stakeholders engaged with this fraternity.

This becomes more glaring due to the heavy asymmetric information between the customer (read patient) and those experts coupled with a vulnerability streak whenever one goes for his treatment or life saving operation.

Case Study I

You are working as a Divisional Engineer in the Department of Signals in Indian Railways. A severe train accident, which has taken place in your zone, has resulted in the death of over 50 people. According to media reports, the accident was caused due to the transmission of wrong signals, which has resulted in the coming of two trains on the same track. This occurred because of the negligence of staff in your department. The government has set up an enquiry commission to look into the issue and suggest further actions to be taken. You have been appointed as the Head of the Commission. After conducting enquiry, you come across the gross negligence of duty by Mr. A, the Station Master of the station before which accident took place. He left the office during working hours for his personal work which resulted in transmission of wrong signals. But Mr. A is a close relative of the General Manager (GM) of your Zone and you are getting constant pressure from him for manipulating the enquiry report. Your promotion as a Divisional Railway Manager (DRM) is due next month and a favorable report from GM office is essential for it. Also, the deadline set by the government for submission of report is also reaching closer. If you miss the deadline, your service record and your promotion, may get affected. What would be your reaction? Come out with an amicable solution to deal with the issue.

Premise: In this situation, a public servant faces an Ethical Dilemma. On the one hand he has to be honest with his duty, while on the other, he also has to keep his superior in confidence, the favourable report of whom is essential for his promotion to a crucial post. In simple words, his future is at stake. Here the question that arises relates to integrity of public servant, his morality, his dedication to duty and his ability to sacrifice personal gains for safeguarding national interest.

This case comes under the following topics:

- Ethical Dilemma
- Probity in Governance
- Accountability
- Work Culture
- Public Service Values

Answer: Honesty and integrity on the part for public servant are two important pillars of efficient governance. As the accident that took place caused the loss of public life, it is needed to be taken as the top priority to bring the person responsible for it, in the court of enquiry. However, undue influence from various sources deters a public servant to deal with the issue effectively.

The ethical dilemma faced by the Divisional Engineer (DE), in the given case, presents the example of above explained fact. As per the Indian Railway Act, 1989 and the rules formulated by Indian Railways, a Divisional Railway Manager (DRM) heads a division and is appointed for three years. Each division comes under a zone and DRM of different divisions report to their respective zones. A zone is headed by General Manager (GM). Hence GM of a Railway Zone occupies a crucial administrative position. Under these circumstances an unfavourable report by the GM may inhibit the appointment of a person as DRM. If the Divisional Engineer gives correct report, it would invite departmental or legal action against Mr. A, which would put him in the bad book of GM. On the other hand, if he manipulates the report, he may get benefits and rewards related to his career, but he, by doing so, is making a compromise with core values of public service. Under this circumstance he can exercise following options:

As a first step DE should politely convey his inability to follow the order of GM. As the matter pertains to life of people, manipulation of report would not solve the problem. He should explain the GM that if the responsible person is not punished, it would set a bad precedent and may lead to more accidents in future.

At the same time, DE should remain committed to his duty and must prepare correct and fair report, irrespective of any outside influence.

The Railway Board Act, 1905 provides for controlling the Administration of Railways. GMs of all the zones report to the Railway Board, which controls and coordinate their function by ensuring that they should work in public interest.

As the second step DE should inform about the incident and undue pressure he is getting from GM regarding manipulation of reports, to the Railway Board. This would provide an edge to him in his appointment as DRM, even if GM gives an adverse report.

Third step by DE should be to give adequate opportunity to Mr. A for making statement in his defence. Before recommending any departmental enquiry, the reason for the negligence caused by Mr. A must be known. This would be in consonance of the principle of Natural Justice which is enshrined as a basic feature in our Constitution.

Case Study II

You are the Prime Minister of the country A. The President of a neighboring country B is scheduled to visit your country by next week. Your country has been witnessing a long dispute related to border with the country B. The new leadership, which has been just taken over in the country B, has expressed the willingness to resolve the ongoing border issue. Hence the visit has gained a national attention and is crucial for your country. The country B is also expected to come with new investment plans. Your country has been facing the problem of poor infrastructure and is in urgent need of funds for the same. However, just ahead of one day of the visit, you have been informed by Army Chief of your country that soldiers of country B has started firing in border area, resulting in the loss of life of 5 soldiers of your country. The matter has reached to the media and is likely to form the headlines of next day's newspaper. You are aware of the national response against the incident, on one side, while the significance of the visit, on the other. How far is it correct for you to refuse to host the President of country B as a sign of showing protest to this incident? What measure would you take under such circumstances?

This case comes under the following topics:

- Ethical Concerns in International Relations
- Ethical Dilemma
- Morality
- Ethical Governance

Premise: The given case relates to the relation between two neighbouring countries, facing a border dispute for a long time. The scheduled visit of the President of one country is overshadowed by a firing incident that took place in the border area. The PM of country A faces a dilemma in his action. As a PM, he has to strike a balance between national interest and his obligations under international relations.

Answer: Diplomacy and National interest are the two important wheels on which the wagon of International Relations run. Here, if PM cancels the meeting with the President of country B, he will miss an opportunity to settle the long border dispute.

He will also forgo a significant amount of investment which could make his country prosperous by giving a boost to infrastructure sector. On the other hand, if he attends the President with gratitude after the incident which took place in the border area, he would attract a criticism and national outrage that may affect his political career in future.

It would also amount to compromising with the national pride. Under these circumstances the Prime Minister of Country A should take following actions:

Following the incident, he should immediately summon the Ambassador of the country B and seek clarifications from him on the incident. This would convey the strong objection the country A is taking against the act of Country B.

He should call a meeting of Senior Bureaucrats along with intelligence and security chiefs of the nation to decide the further moves. As the matter pertains to international relation, the decision must be taken by keeping focus on long term interest, for which a unilateral decision solely by PM may be unviable.

The international diplomacy requires a high degree of professionalism. Keeping this in view, the PM should not cancel the meeting with the President of country B. This would reflect his long term vision. This would also save the wastage of public money utilized in the preparation of visit.

At the same time he should instruct the army chief to respond any further incident with firm actions.

During the visit, he should accord a warm welcome to the President of country B and at the same time he should strongly condemn the firing incident by country B. This would reflect the high degree of professionalism in his conduct.

A statement in media from him should also be issued condemning the incident and asking the people to be calm, as the matter is needed to be resolved through diplomatic means rather than by retaliatory measures.

8

PROBITY IN GOVERNANCE

The Concepts Discussed in this Unit

- Concept of Probity and Public Service
- Philosophical Basis of Governance and Probity
- Civil Services
- Transparency and Right to Information
- The age of whistle-blower
- Code of Ethics & Codes of Conduct
- Political Ethics
- Citizens' Charter and Work Culture
- Significance of Service Delivery
- Utilization of Public Funds
- Equity & Ethics
- Corruption & Measures to check it
- Legislative Control over Administration
- Politicization of Bureaucracy and Bureaucratization of Politics
- Judicial Control over Public Administration

Public Service

The term public service carries different meanings.

The first meaning of 'public service' is in the sense of a public utility, i.e., it refers to the kind of services governments commonly provide - electricity, healthcare, maintenance of law and order, urban and rural infrastructure, etc.- where the prime criteria of success are availability, affordability and accessibility of services.

In this connection, the delivery of public service means the goods and services offered by government institutions to the public, and it includes the interface between the citizen and the administration.

Second, public service refers to all the public functionaries including all those working in the army as well as the judiciary and the executive.

Probity

Probity is the evidence of ethical behaviour in a particular process. The term probity means integrity, uprightness and honesty.

For Government employees and agencies, maintaining probity involves more than simply avoiding corrupt or dishonest conduct. It involves applying public sector values such as impartiality, accountability and transparency.

Probity is also regarded as being incorruptible. However, probity goes further than the avoidance of being dishonest because it is determined by intangibles like personal and societal values.

It is also regarded as strict adherence to a code of ethics based on undeviating honesty, especially in commercial (monetary) matters and beyond legal requirements.

Ensuring probity in public sector activities is part of every public official's duty to adopt processes, practices and behaviour that enhance and promote public sector values and interests.

Probity in Governance

"Apart from the traditional civil service values of efficiency, integrity, accountability and patriotism, it is necessary for civil servants to inculcate and adopt ethical and moral values including probity in public life, respect for human rights and compassion for the downtrodden and commitment to their welfare". (Second ARC)

Probity in governance is an essential and vital requirement for an efficient and effective system of governance and for socio-economic development. An important requisite for ensuring probity in governance is absence of corruption. The other requirements are effective laws, rules and regulations governing every aspect of public life and, more important, an effective and fair implementation of those laws, etc.

Philosophical Basis of Governance and Probity

The ethical concerns of governance have been underscored widely in Indian scriptures and other treatises such as Ramayana, Mahabharata, Bhagvad Gita, Buddha Charita, Arthashastra, Panchatantra, Manusmriti, Kural, Shukra Niti, Kadambari, Raja Tarangani, and Hitopadesh. At the same time, one cannot ignore the maxims on ethical governance provided by the Chinese philosophers such as Lao Tse, Confucius and Mencius.

In the Western philosophy, there are three eminent schools of ethics. The first, inspired by Aristotle, holds that virtues (such as justice, charity and generosity) are dispositions to act in ways that benefit the possessor of these virtues and the society of which he is a part. The second, subscribed to mainly by Immanuel Kant, makes the concept of duty central to morality: human beings are bound, from knowledge of their duty as rational beings, to obey the categorical imperative to respect other rational beings with whom they interact. The third is the utilitarian viewpoint that asserts that the guiding principle of conduct should be the greatest happiness (or benefit) of the greatest number. The Western thought is full of ethical guidelines to rulers, whether in a monarchy or a democracy. These concerns are found in the writings of Plato, Aristotle, Thomas Jefferson, Alexander Hamilton, Thomas Penn, John Stuart Mill, Edmund Burke, and others.

The gist of wisdom on administrative ethics is that the public administrators are the "guardians" of the Administrative State. Hence, they are expected to honour public trust and not violate it. Two crucial questions raised in this context are "Why should guardians be guarded?" And "Who guards the guardian?". The administrators need to be guarded against their tendency to misconceive public interest, promote self-interest, indulge in corruption and cause subversion of national interest. And they need to be guarded by the external institutions such as the judiciary, legislature, political executive, media and civil society organisations. These various modes of control become instruments of accountability.

The current discipline of public administration accords primacy to the `values' of equity, justice, humanism, human rights, gender equality and compassion. The movement of Good Governance, initiated by the World Bank in 1992, lays stress, inter alia, on the ethical and moral conduct of administrators. While the New Public Management movement is more concerned with administrative effectiveness, the New Public Administration focuses on administrative ethics in its broader manifestation. Both the movements are complementary to each other. This complementarity of foci is as truer today as it was a hundred years ago when the industrial world was experiencing the rise of Scientific Management amidst a strong acceptance of the notion of administrative responsibility. John Kennedy, during his Presidency (1961-1963) had averred: "No responsibility of government is more fundamental than the responsibility of maintaining the higher standards of ethical behaviour".

The ideal-type construction of bureaucracy, propounded by Max Weber also highlighted an ethical imperative of bureaucratic behaviour. Weber (1947) observed: In the rational type, it is a matter of principle that the members of the administrative staff should be completely separated from ownership of the means of production and administration. Officials, employees and workers attached to the administrative staff do not themselves own the non-human means of production and administration. There exists, furthermore, in principle complete separation of property belonging to the organisation, which is controlled within the sphere of office, and the personal property of the official, which is available for his own private uses.

Objective of Probity in Governance

Probity in Governance seeks to achieve the following:

- To ensure accountability in governance;
- To maintain integrity in public services;
- To ensure compliance with processes;
- To preserve public confidence in Government processes;
- To avoid the potential for misconduct, fraud and corruption.

Private Interests

The term 'private interests' includes not only the personal, professional or business interests that an officer may have, but also the personal, professional or business interests of the individuals or groups that the officer associates with.

This might include relatives, friends or even rivals and enemies. In other words, private interests are those interests that can bring either benefits or disadvantage to the officer, or to others whom the officer may wish to benefit or disadvantage.

Such interests can involve an actual or potential financial gain or loss and can involve property, shares, unpaid debts, or some form of gift or benefit - including a job opportunity or secondary employment.

Other private interests may not have a financial component, but could involve personal or family relationships or sporting, social or cultural activities that could influence an officer's judgement or decision.

Public Duty to Serve the Public Interest

The 'public interest' is the collective interest of the entire community - not the sum of individual interests or the interest of a particular group. All public sector officers have a public duty to put the public interest above their own personal or private interests when carrying out their official duties. This principle applies to anyone engaged to deliver government programs and services, whether as a full or part-time employee, casual or contract staff member, board member, consultant or volunteer.

Civil Service

Civil Service is the executive branch of a government. The term 'civil service' refers to that section of public service which is employed in the civil services of the government. Civil services thus exclude functionaries working in the army and judiciary. Thus, all civil services are public services, but all public services are not civil services.

Importance of Civil Services to Governance

Governance is the exercise of economic, political and administrative authority to manage a country's affairs at all levels. It consists of the mechanisms, processes and institutions through which citizens and groups articulate their interests, exercise their legal rights, meet their obligations and mediate their differences. Without good governance, no amount of developmental schemes can bring in improvements in the quality of life of the citizens. On the contrary, if the power of the state is abused, or exercised in weak or improper ways, those with the least power in the society are most likely to suffer. In that sense, poor governance generates and reinforces poverty and subverts all efforts to reduce it. The civil service forms an important part of the institution of the state and plays a crucial role in the administration of the country. It has to carry out task in terms of the constitutional mandate and the legal framework. If civil services perform in effective and efficient way, the people may be served in the best possible way and maximum public interest can be ensured. The importance of the Civil Service to governance stems from the following:

- Its presence throughout the country and its strong binding character;
- Administrative and managerial capacity of the services;
- Effective policy-making and regulation;
- Effective coordination between institutions of governance;
- Leadership at different levels of administration;
- Service delivery at the cutting edge level;
- Provide 'continuity and change' to the administration.

New Public Service

The New Public Service (NPS) is a new approach in public administration. The concept was initiated by Janet Denhardt and Robert Denhardt.

They have put the central role of government as 'service'. Government as they argue, 'should not be run like a business, it should be run like a democracy'. 'Public interest' and 'democratic citizenship' are the hall marks of government.

The theory gives seven broad principles to be followed by government and administration so as to fulfil their democratic responsibility and to improve the service delivery mechanism-

- Serve citizens, not customers
- Seek the public interest
- Value citizenship over entrepreneurship
- Think strategically, act democratically
- Recognize that accountability is not simple
- Serve rather than steer
- Value people, not just productivity

Development Administration

Development Administration is an 'action-oriented' and 'goal-oriented' administrative system (E. Weidner). It is about administration with a 'difference'. Its focus is on government influenced change-towards the attainment of progressive social, economic. and political objectives.

Development administration is characterized by:

- Its purposes
- Its loyalties
- Its attitudes

The purposes of development administration are to stimulate and facilitate defined programs of social and economic progress. They are purposes of change and innovation and movement as contrasted with purposes of maintaining the status quo. In terms of loyalties, the bureaucracy has to be accountable to the people and not to any vested institutional interests, nor to any king or empire. In terms of attitudes, development administration calls for positive, persuasive, and innovative stances from the bureaucracy.

The traditional norms or forms of administration must be placed by flexibility and adaptability to changing needs and situations.

Behavioural Parameters for Development Administration

Pai Panandiker and Kshirsagar, propose four behavioural parameters-

- Change orientation
- Result orientation
- Citizen participative orientation
- Commitment to work

Traditional Public Administration and Development Administration

The difference between the traditional public administration and development administration can be made out by observing and analyzing the features of both the concepts.

Features of Development Administration are as follows - change oriented, goal and result oriented, flexible and dynamic, concerned with innovative approach, believes in decentralization, stress on participation of people.

Features of traditional administration are as follows- status quo oriented, emphasis on economy and efficiency, hierarchical and rigid, concerned with routine operations, believes in centralization, resists organizational change, stress on directions from authority, not much involvement of people.

New Public Administration

New Public Administration is an anti-positivist, anti-technical, and anti-hierarchical reaction against traditional public administration. The 1960s in the USA was a time of unusual social and political turbulence and upheaval. In this context, it was observed that neither the study nor the practice of public administration was responding suitably to the escalating turmoil and the complications that arose from those conditions. NPA theory deals with the following issues-

- Democratic Citizenship
- Public Interest
- Public Policy, and
- Services to Citizens

NPA stands for four important aspects-

- **Relevance:** Traditional public administration has too little interest in contemporary problems and issues. NPA suggests that social realities must be taken into consideration and changes should be specific to the needs of the area and of the people. NPA also suggests the inclusion of rationality of the people too in the process of policy formulation.
- **Values:** NPA holds that value-neutrality in public administration is an impossibility and the public administration should explicitly espouse the cause of the disadvantaged sections in the society.
- **Social Equity:** NPA believes that the purpose of public organisation is the reduction of economic, social and psychic suffering and the enhancement of life opportunities for those inside and outside the organisation. It challenged the public administration to make it more proactive to major social issues and put the realization of social equity as the chief goal of public administration.
- **Change**: NPA shows skepticism towards the deeply rooted powers vested in permanent institutions and the status quo. It suggests for operational flexibility and organisational adaptability in the administrative system to meet the environmental changes.

NPA provides solutions for achieving these goals, popularly called 4 D's i.e. Decentalisation, Debureaucratisation, Delegation and Democratisation.

New Public Management

The 1990s saw the emergence of a new model of public sector management. This has been variously called: 'Managerialism', 'New Public Management', market-based public administration, 'Entrepreneurial Government', etc. The thrust has been toward a determined effort to implement the 3Es: Efficiency, Economy and Effectiveness.

The New Public Management (NPM) has following salient features:

- Focus on management, on performance appraisal and on efficiency.

- Desegregation of public bureaucracies into agencies which deal with each other on a user-pays basis
- Use of quasi-markets and contracting out to foster competition
- Cost-cutting
- A style of management which emphasizes output targets, limited term contracts, monetary incentives and freedom to manage.

Entrepreneurial Governments

Within the New Public Management (NPM) theme, there has been a more positive perspective given by Osborne & Gaebler in Reinventing Government (1992). They suggest a ten-point programme for what they call Entrepreneurial Governments (EGs)-

- EGs promote competition between diverse providers of goods and services.
- They empower citizens by pushing control out of bureaucracy.
- They measure performance of their agencies focusing particularly on outcomes not inputs.
- They are driven by their missions and not by their rules/ regulations.
- They redefine their clients as customers and offer them choices.
- They prevent problems rather than cure them after they blow out.
- They put their energy into earning money, not simply spending it.
- They decentralize authority, embracing participatory management.
- They prefer market mechanisms to bureaucratic mechanisms.
- They focus not simply on providing public service, but on catalyzing all sectors- public, private, and voluntary- into action to solve community problems.

These features of Entrepreneurial Government yield a multifaceted government system with the following characteristics-

- Catalytic Government
- Community-owned Government
- Competitive Government
- Mission-driven Government

- Results-oriented Government
- Customer-driven Government
- Decentralized Government
- Market-oriented Government

Social Contract

The social contract or political contract is a theory or model, originated during the Age of Enlightenment, which typically addresses the questions of the origin of society and the legitimacy of the authority of the state over the individual. Social contract arguments typically posit that individuals have consented, either explicitly or tacitly, to surrender some of their freedoms and submit to the authority of the ruler or Magistrate (or to the decision of a majority), in exchange for protection of their remaining rights.

In general terms, the social contract states that members of society are accorded certain rights in return for giving up certain freedoms which society's members would otherwise possess in the state of nature (where lawlessness reigns) or by remaining alone. Society (in the sense of a "state") emerges to enforce the rights and responsibilities borne by its members. Because these rights and responsibilities are neither "natural" nor "fixed," they can be altered if a society's members so desire. However, they must remember that exercising additional rights will always entail bearing additional responsibilities, and bearing fewer responsibilities will always entail exercising fewer rights.

The philosophical ideas of the social contract is dated back to Hugo Grotius (1583-1645), Thomas Hobbes (1588-1679), John Locke (1632-1704), Jean Jacques Rousseau (1712-88) and, more recently, John Rawls who wrote in the second half of the 20th Century.

Social Contract Theory- Features

Social contract theory expresses two fundamental ideas to which the human mind always clings-

- The value of liberty; the idea that "will" and not "force" is the basis of government; and
- The value of justice or the idea that "right" and not "might"

The Organizational Apology

At some point, every company makes a mistake that requires an apology – to an individual; a group of customers, employees, or business partners; or the public at large. And, more often than not, organizations and their leaders fail to apologize effectively, if at all, which can severely damage their relationships with stakeholders and their reputations, especially if the incidents become public. Consider L'Affaire de Maggi. For nearly three decades, Nestle's Maggi noodle was the ultimate success story: an unlikely product embraced wholeheartedly by a difficult market. But after the alleged lead adulteration - which later-on turned out to be 'false' and Maggi was allowed to sell its noodles again - it became a case study of an entirely different sort – a textbook example of how not to handle a crisis. In the first few weeks it took for the controversy to spread to social media and grow into a full blown crisis, Nestle chose to remain silent. Whatever side of the story Nestle had at that time should have come out with the same. In today's digital age, a day late is like being a month late.

Companies need clear guidelines for determining whether a mis-step merits an apology and, when it does, how to deliver the message.

Let's recognize two facts about apologies at the outset: First, we are psychologically predisposed to find reasons (or excuses) to delay or avoid saying we're sorry. Apologizing feels uncomfortable and risky. There's a loss of power or face involved – it rearranges the status hierarchy and makes us beholden, at least temporarily, to the other party. Apologies are even more difficult in an organizational context. A company's mistake is often caused by a single division or employee, and a bad situation is frequently made worse by events beyond its control. It can feel unjust for a CEO or an entire organization to have to take responsibility. Second, companies have a strong tendency to evaluate the situation through a legal lens. Corporate counsel may fixate on whether any laws were broken and warn managers that an apology might be construed as an admission of liability (possibly exposing the company to litigation) rather than as an effort to empathize with the wronged party. This is an important distinction, because effective apologies address the recipients' feelings – they don't prove a point.

Once a company has decided that it should apologize, it has to do it the right way. While a good apology can restore balance or even improve relationships, a bad apology can make things much worse. As a framework for getting it right, companies need to think carefully about **who, what, where, when,** and **how**.

Who - The more serious and the more core the violation, the more necessary it becomes that a senior leader – up to and including the CEO – make the apology. In cases where there is a clear transgressor – an employee who made the mistake – there may be merit in involving that person.

What - This is the substance of the apology – the words you say and the actions you take. It's important to keep three goals in mind: candor, remorse, and a commitment to change. Organizations should never sound defensive or as if they're trying to justify a violation.

Where - If a company wants to control the coverage of an apology, the setting can determine how loud – and widely heard – the message will be. Organizations often default to written statements that reach a broad audience, especially when they're published in newspapers. Managers should realize, however, that there are risks to this approach. A live, on-site apology puts a leader in an uncontrolled environment. Apologizing to victims face-to-face can be effective if they accept the apology – but if they don't, the event could turn into a public confrontation. Sometimes public apologies come off as publicity stunts. Social media has changed the calculus for choosing where to make an apology, since now a company's written statement can be shared and re-tweeted, reaching many more people than would typically see an address on the evening news.

When - A good apology arrives quickly. Speed signals sincerity and dispels the idea that executives feel uncertainty or ambiguity about their responsibility. Although sometimes, companies delay apologies for good reasons, while they may be still gathering the facts to understand exactly what took place, but unconditional apology can still be issued in that case.

How - The way an apology is delivered can matter just as much as the content of the apology. Informal language and personal communication can help.

Peter Principle

The Peter principle is a concept in management theory formulated by educator Laurence J. Peter and published in 1969. It states that the selection of a candidate for a position is based on the candidate's performance in their current role, rather than on abilities relevant to the intended role. Thus, employees only stop being promoted once they can no longer perform effectively, and "managers rise to the level of their incompetence".

Parkinson's Law

Parkinson has written satirically on political organisation and public administration and has developed a list of principles-

- Administrators create work for each other by artificial means and swell their rank, irrespective of the volume of work to be done. The empire building tendency prevails in such situations.
- Executives select subordinates who are less smart than themselves with a view to preventing their potential rivals.
- Committees tend to grow in size until they lose their effectiveness.
- In committee meetings, according to the law of triviality, the time spent on subjects varies in inverse proportion to the sum involved.
- Expenditures of an organisation rise to eat up the available money.

is the basis of all political society and of every system of political order.

The theory seeks to explain the formation of societies and governments. It denotes an implicit agreement within a State regarding the rights and responsibilities of the State, i.e. the government and its citizens.

The theory posits that rights of citizens are prior to and more fundamental than the organization of society under the government. The governed, in essence, should be the governors. The idea of self-government is posited as an end in itself. A political order offering opportunities for participation in the arrangement of public affairs should not just be a State, but rather, the formation of a type of society in which the affairs of the State are integrated into affairs of ordinary citizens.

Transparency

Transparency implies openness of decision-making process and freedom of information to the members of the public and media. The people have the right to know how decisions are made on routine as well as on policy matters, whether they are benefited or affected by the decision, how service is rendered or how and when the goods are delivered. What are the work procedures and how are the objectives accomplished?

Transparency is also a moral issue. Lack of transparency is considered to be responsible for making the government slow, inefficient and corrupt. Transparent mechanisms involve the creation of a climate of self-restraint and self-check to avoid irregularity. Transparency can also be seen from following dimensions:

- Ensuring transparency in public dealings is bound to bring about a more careful utilization of public funds.
- Transparency in government functioning will make public servants take decisions more rationally and objectively, forsaking their particularistic bias in favour of any person or caste.
- Transparency in government functioning will hold public servants accountable for their mishandling of public time and money.
- Transparency will help expose counter-productive and inhibiting rules and procedures that make administration more slow.
- Transparency will develop a cordial relationship between the public servants and their clients.

Transparency in government organisations makes them function more objectively, thereby enhancing predictability and accountability. Information about functioning of government also enables citizens to participate in the governance process effectively.

Institutional Means to achieve Transparency in Administration

Following are the institutional means to achieve transparency in the administration-

- Parliamentary Controls- Question sessions, debates, etc.
- Legislative Framework- Right to Information Act, Time bound delivery of goods and services
- Ombudsman- Lokpal and Lokayukta
- Independent Judiciary
- E- Governance
- Free Press

The Age of the Whistle-Blower

Whistleblowing has been on the increase since the 2007-08 financial crisis sparked a crackdown on corporate corruption and collusion. The number of tips received by the "Whistleblower Office" of America's Securities and Exchange Commission (SEC) has risen steadily since it was opened in 2011, to nearly 4,000 a year. "We live in the age of the whistleblower," says Jordan Thomas, a former SEC official now at Labaton Sucharow, a law firm.

Surveys by the Association of Certified Fraud Examiners, a global group for financial sleuths, consistently find tips to be the leading mechanism for unearthing wrongdoing, well ahead of audits or regulatory reviews.

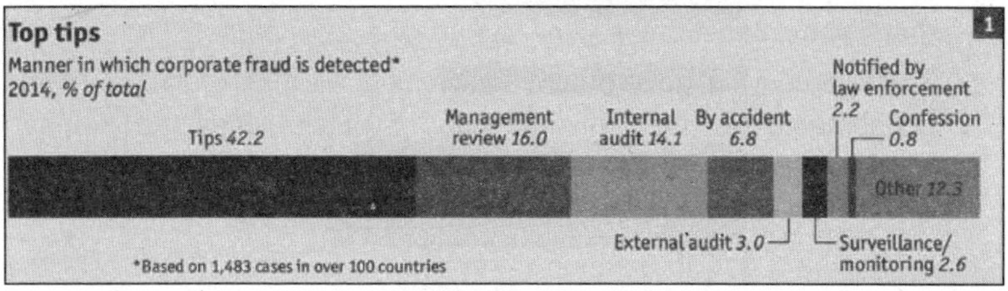

Despite this, companies have often punished rather than praised whistle-blowers. "The institutional equivalent of animal instinct is to strike back," says Tom Devine, legal director of the Government Accountability Project, who has worked with 6,000 whistle-blowers in the public and private sector since the 1970s.

According to one recent study, Britain is the third-best of the G20 large economies in terms of legal protection for whistleblowers (see chart). Enforcement of laws matters, too, of course. Few would say Turkey is a kinder climate for whistleblowers than Canada, which has weaker protections but applies them more assiduously. Europe is "where the action is" when it comes to improving protections, says Mr Devine. What has helped is a strong set of "best practice" guidelines from the Council of Europe, a club of 47 western and eastern European states, as have pro-whistleblower rulings from the council's judicial arm, the European Court of Human Rights. Newer entrants to the 28-country European Union (it would technically become 27 after pro-Brexit voting which would happen from April 2019), such as Romania, had to adopt high standards as a condition of joining. The situation among older members is patchier. Protections are particularly weak in Germany, where whistleblowers who go public after failing to get a response internally face defamation suits, says Anja Osterhaus of Transparency International. Non-EU Switzerland is another with an unforgiving climate.

Protecting the messenger

Rating of private-sector whistleblowing laws
Selected countries, 2014, lowest score = best

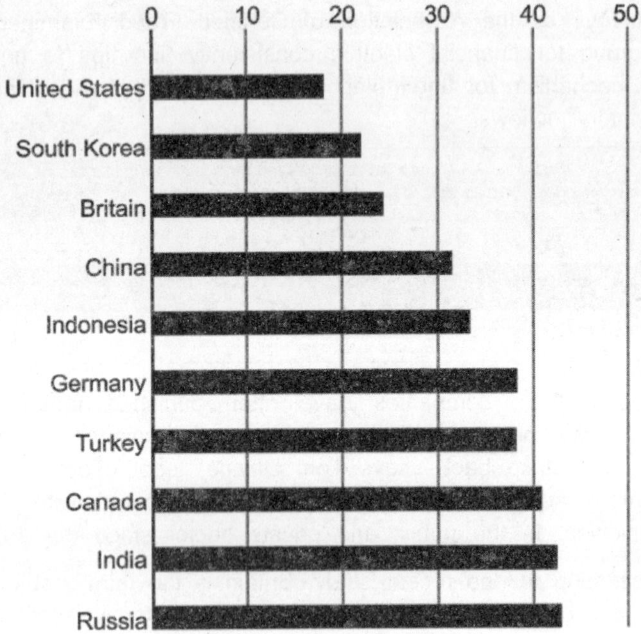

Source: "Whistleblower Protection Laws in G20 Countries", by Simon Wolfe et al, Transparency International Australia, 2014

America is the best place for whistleblowers. The SEC's programme, created by the Dodd-Frank financial-reform act of 2010, is arguably the strongest of the more than 40 federal whistleblower-friendly laws on the books. It rests on three pillars: job protection, anonymity and bounties. It has handed out 22 awards, averaging \$2.5m; these can rise to 30% of any fines that get levied on the employer. Though the programme is not marketed abroad, it has taken on a global hue: tips have come in from 96 countries, and several of the awards have gone to foreigners. In October 2015 a court ruled that whistleblowers can sue individual board members as well as the firm, if these were personally involved in any mistreatment of them.

America is not always kind to whistleblowers. It has given

some public-sector and national-security leakers a torrid time. And it sometimes acts inconsistently. Bradley Birkenfeld, who provided American authorities with vital information about Swiss banks and their tax-evading clients, won a (taxable) $104m award from the IRS. But the Department of Justice prosecuted him. His 66 months of prison and probation ended in November 2016.

Ideally, firms would put in place a formal system for hearing and noting complaints–for their own sake, as well as those of whistleblowers. When people fail to report wrongdoing, the main reason is often not the fear of retaliation but the suspicion that nothing will be done about it. Companies often see whistleblowers as motivated by revenge or greed. But studies consistently show that most are driven to right a wrong. That is why more than 90% of them sound the alarm internally first, rather than running straight to the authorities or newspapers. Given the choice, they would rather warn than accuse.

So, to stifle whistleblowing is to harm the business. Bad news tends to come out eventually, and looks worse if it appears that bosses tried to suppress it. Apart from which, wrongdoing is less likely to occur in the first place if employees know that their bosses are more inclined to hug a whistleblower than to put him in a headlock. India coming in the second last position (as shown in the chart) is certainly a place where bosses dagger the whistleblower without even using a kitchen knife in umpteen number of ways.

Right to Information

The Indian Parliament enacted the Right to Information Act (RTI) in 2005. The Right to Information Act signals the march from darkness of secrecy to dawn of transparency. It opens up government's records to public scrutiny, thereby arming citizens with a vital tool to inform them about what the government does and how much effectively, thus making the government more accountable.

Right to Information (RTI) has been seen as the key to strengthening participatory democracy and ushering in people centric governance. Access to information can empower the poor and the weaker sections of society to demand and get information about public policies and actions, thereby leading to their welfare. Openness in the exercise of public power - Executive, Legislative or Judiciary - is a culture, which needs to be nurtured, with privacy and confidentiality being an exception. The right to information will also be a powerful means for fighting corruption. The effective implementation of the Right to Information Act will create an environment of vigilance which will help promote functioning of a more participatory democracy.

Contest between Official Secrets Act (OSA) and Right to Information Act (RTI)

An 'Official Secrets Act' is a generic term that is used to refer to a law (originally invented by the British, and then exported across the Commonwealth) that is designed to keep certain kinds of information confidential, including, but not always limited to, information involving the affairs of state, diplomacy, national security, espionage and other state secrets.

Criticism of Official Secrets Act

- **Compromises Transparency:** The primary critique of the Act is that it flips the constitutive logic of a democratic republic, where the state is supposed to be transparent to its citizens. The state is given wide powers to place information off-limits to citizens, simply by stipulating that certain documents are secret.
- **Colonial Endowment:** The OSA was enacted in 1923 by the British to keep certain kinds of information confidential, including, but not always limited to, information involving the affairs of state, diplomacy, national security, espionage, and other state secrets.
- **Use of Vague Terms:** OSA has provisions that are vague in nature and can be interpreted arbitrarily, like terms used under Section 2(8)(d) of OSA "prohibited place", "any railway, road, way or channel or other means of communication by land or water..." can be notified by the Central government as a 'prohibited place'.
- **Arbitrary Punitive Action:** It can punish for the communication of any information obtained in contravention of the Act. Therefore, this provision targets whistle-blowing and investiga-

tive journalism, no matter how critically important it might be to have the information public.

Demand for diluting the OSA

- The Law Commission in 1971 observed that "just because a circular is marked secret or confidential, it should not attract the provisions of the Act", though not recommended for any changes.
- 2nd Administrative Reforms Commission (ARC) in 2006, recommended for OSA to be repealed, and replaced with a chapter in the National Security Act containing provisions relating to official secrets, calling OSA incongruous with the regime of transparency in a democratic society".
- A committee constituted in 2015 to review OSA in the light of RTI, recommended that OSA to be made more transparent.

Legal Position of RTI compared to OSA

Introduction of Right to Information Act in 2005 marked a new chapter in transparency and communication between the government and its citizens. The Right to Information Act somewhat diluted the scope of the OSA.

- Section 22 of the RTI Act expressly says - it overrides the OSA. In other words, it is not open to the government to deny access to a document demanded through an RTI question, on the basis that it has been marked secret under the OSA. Rather, the government will have to justify its decision to withhold information under the arguably narrower exception clauses of the RTI Act itself.
- Section 8(2) of the RTI Act, enlists that a public authority may allow access to information covered under the OSA, "if the public interest in disclosure outweighs the harm to the protected Interests".

The very birth of RTI Act was marked for increasing the transparency between government and its citizens. On the other hand, OSA is against the constitutive logic of a democratic republic, where the state is supposed to be transparent to its citizens. The security concerns are justified but when unethical practice assumes the absolute power and tries to curb the voices of the citizens and conceal the information, the OSA comes under the severe criticism and the demand to dilute this act rises.

Code of Ethics

The codes exemplify the fundamental principles and values of a public service. When applied to certain classes of people - public servants, doctors - codes are the ultimate terms of reference. They are the framework upon which professions are built. Often codes are what professionals use to make the claim that they are "professionals" and are often the founding document for a profession, e.g. the Hippocratic Oath. As foundational base, they can provide the framework that public servants - political and civil service - use to carry out their public responsibilities. Codes can clearly articulate unacceptable behaviors as well as providing a vision for which the government official is striving. Therefore, inducing monetary reform, creating democratic institutions or funding economic improvement programs without a professional government workforce can be frustrating, if not counterproductive. A fundamental mechanism for ensuring professionalism is a code of ethics.

Code of Ethics is a written set of guidelines issued by an organization to its officials, to guide their conduct in accordance with its primary values and ethical standards. It ensures that individuals belonging to an organization have a consistent approach in carrying out their responsibilities and making decisions. It may carry general obligations and admonitions, but they are far more than that. They often capture a vision of excellence, of what individuals and societies should be striving for and what they can achieve. A common philosophical definition of ethics is the science of conducts or values of management. Moral values comprise of respect, honesty, fairness, and responsibility and these values are translated into a code of ethics. These values vary between individuals and across cultures.

Hofstede's four value dimensions (1980) help us understand cultural value clashes. Long-term versus short-term values affect many aspects of organizational life. The four key ethical principles are egalitarianism, utilitarianism, individual right and distributive justice. Organizations following the utilitarianism approach in ethics make decisions based on their outcomes and consequences. Ethical behavior is influenced by moral intensity, ethical sensitivity, and the situation.

In India, the current set of ethical norms are the Conduct Rules, contained in the Central Services (Conduct) Rules, 1964 and analogous rules applicable to members of the All India Services or employees of various State Governments. The code of behavior as enunciated in the Conduct Rules, while containing some general norms like 'maintaining integrity and absolute devotion to duty' and not indulging in 'conduct unbecoming of a government servant' is generally directed towards cataloguing specific activities deemed undesirable for government servants. These conduct rules do not constitute a code of ethics.

The 2nd ARC has suggested the inclusion of the following principles in the Code of Ethics for civil servants in India:

- **Integrity:** Civil servants should be guided solely by public interest in their official decision making and not by any financial or other consideration either in respect of themselves, their families or their friends.
- **Impartiality:** Civil servants in carrying out their official work, including functions like procurement, recruitment, delivery of services, etc, should take decisions based on merit alone.
- **Commitment to public service:** Civil servants should deliver services in a fair, effective, impartial and courteous manner.
- **Open accountability:** Civil servants are accountable for their decisions and actions and should be willing to subject themselves to appropriate scrutiny for this purpose.
- **Devotion to duty:** Civil servants maintain absolute and unstinting devotion towards their duties and responsibilities at all times.
- **Exemplary behavior:** Civil servants shall treat all members of the public with respect and courtesy and, at all times, should behave in a manner that upholds the rich traditions of the civil services.

Public Service Bill, 2006

Public Service Bill enumerates fundamental values and a Code of Ethics for public services with the object of developing a professional, politically neutral, merit based and accountable civil service. According to this Bill, the main values by which the Public Servants shall be guided are as follows:

- Allegiance to the various ideals enshrined in the preamble to the Constitution;
- Apolitical functioning;
- Good governance for betterment of the people;
- Duty to act objectively, impartially, honestly and equitably;
- Accountability and transparency in decision-making;
- Act with integrity and in a courteous and just manner;
- Maintenance of highest ethical standards;
- Merit to be the criteria in selection of civil servants, however, it should be consistent with the cultural, ethnic and other diversities of the nation;
- Ensuring economy and avoidance of wastage in expenditure;
- Provision of healthy and congenial work environment;
- Discharge functions with due regard to diversity of the nation/ community and religion but without discrimination of caste, community, religion, gender or class and duly protecting the interest of poor, underprivileged and weaker sections;
- Communication, consultation and cooperation in performance of functions i.e. participation of all levels of personnel in management; and
- Provide honest, impartial and frank advice to political executive.

Second ARC on Ethics

The Second Administrative Reforms Commission (ARC) in its 4th report "Ethics in Governance" has extensively covered the issue of ethics and observes, "The crux of ethical behaviour does not lie in bold words and expressions enshrined as standards, but in their adoption in action, in sanctions against violations, in putting in place competent disciplinary bodies to investigate allegations of violations and to impose sanctions quickly and in promoting a culture of integrity".

In its wide ranging recommendations, it has suggested-

- Partial state funding of elections
- Tightening of anti-defection law
- Code of ethics for ministers, legislatures, judiciary and civil servants

- Tightening the provision of Prevention of Corruption Act
- Making corrupt public servants liable for paying damages
- Confiscation of property illegally acquired
- Speedy trials
- Creation of Lokpal/ Ombudsman at national, State and local level

While recommending a Code of Ethics for Civil Servants the Second ARC has observed: "Civil Service Values which all public servants should aspire, should be defined and made applicable to all tiers of government and parastatal organizations. Any transgression of these values should be treated as misconduct, inviting punishment". In order to create a regime under which quick disciplinary action can be taken against delinquent Government servants, the ARC has recommended deletion of Article 311 of the Constitution, with a proviso that legislation under Article 309 be made to protect public servants against arbitrary action. The Commission has also suggested certain measures to protect honest Civil Servants against malicious complaints. The ARC in its 10th Report on Personnel Administration has re-emphasized the need for prescribing Civil Service Values and laying down a Code of Ethics. The ARC recommended that the Code of Ethics should include: integrity, impartiality, commitment to public service, open accountability, devotion to duty and exemplary behaviour.

Codes of Conduct

A Code of Conduct is a set of rules outlining the expected behaviour from the members of an organisation. The purpose of Code of Conduct is to regulate the conduct of members on various transactions. In India, the Central Government has issued conduct rules for government employees known as Central Civil Services (Conduct) Rules 1964. The rules are more in the nature of "do's" and "don'ts". These Conduct Rules cover matters such as property transactions, acceptance of gifts, joining of non-political organization and host of other issues covering almost every activity which a normal individual undertakes.

Difference between Code of Ethics and Code of Conduct

Ethics codes or codes of conduct are broader sets of principles that are designed to inform specific laws or government actions.

But a code of ethics is different from a code of conduct.

Ethics includes 'the fundamental ground rules by which we live our lives'. As it pertains to business, ethics is generally considered the act of learning what is right and what is wrong in the workplace and then making the decision to do the right thing. The code of ethics for an organization or for a profession are developed more in the form of statement of values and beliefs that defines an organization or a group. Value statements are aspirational while rules or principles are the beliefs that individual members of an organization should subscribe to in order to continue as members of the organization. These are listed in different sections in the code, regarding specific relationships with employees, customers, shareholders, suppliers, and competitors, as well as the society in general. Because of the increasing importance of ethical compliance and public accountability, professional organizations emphasize on imparting training on ethics.

The code of conduct, on the other hand, translates the values (documented in the code of ethics) into specific behavioral standards, keeping in mind the possible reflection on the stakeholders' interest.

It outlines a fundamental set of principles. For example, the Model Code of Conduct for guidance of political parties and candidates during elections is a set of norms, which has been evolved with the consensus of political parties, who have consented to abide by the principles embodied in the said code and also binds them to respect and observe it in its letter and spirit. Codes of conduct for any organization are better understood through the mission statement of the organization.

It helps to explain why members of an organization should behave in a certain way, what actions are prohibited and also how to determine which action is ethical or unethical.

Therefore, the code of ethics covers general guiding principles of good behavior, operational values and governance, while a code of conduct are more specific or formal statements of the values and practices of a business stipulating a list of acceptable and unacceptable behavior and actions.

Political Ethics

Political ethics (also known as political morality or public ethics) is the practice of making moral judgments about political action and political agents. It covers two areas: the first is the ethics of process (or the ethics of office), which deals with public officials and the methods they use. The second area, the ethics of policy (or ethics and public policy) concerns judgments about policies and laws.

Ethics of Process

The Italian Niccolò Machiavelli is heralded as the founding father of the political ethics. He believed that a political leader may be required to commit acts that would be wrong if done by private. In contemporary democracies, this idea has been re-framed as the problem of dirty hands, described most influentially by Michael Walzer, who argues that the problem creates a paradox: the politician must sometimes do "wrong to do right". The politician uses violence to prevent greater violence, but his act is still wrong even if justified. Walzer's view has been criticized. Some critics object that either the politician is justified or not. If justified, there is nothing wrong, though he may feel guilty. Others say that some of the acts of violence that Walzer would allow are never justified, no matter what the ends. Dennis Thompson has argued that in a democracy citizens should hold the leader responsible, and therefore if the act is justified their hands are dirty too. He also shows that in large political organizations it is often not possible to tell who is actually responsible for the outcomes–a problem known as the problem of many hands.

Political ethics not only permits leaders to do things that would be wrong in private life, but also requires them to meet higher standards than would be necessary in private life. They may, for example, have less of a right of privacy than do ordinary citizens, and no right to use their office for personal profit. The major issues here concerns with the conflict of interest.

Ethics of Policy

In the other area of political ethics, the key issues are not the conflict between means and ends but the conflicts among the ends themselves. For example, in the question of global justice, the conflict is between the claims of the nation state and citizens on one side and the claims of all citizens of the world. Traditionally, priority has been given to the claims of nations, but in recent years thinkers known as cosmopolitans have pressed the claims of all citizens of the world.

Political ethics deals not mainly with ideal justice, however, but with realizing moral values in democratic societies where citizens (and philosophers) disagree about what ideal justice is. In a pluralist society, how if at all can governments justify a policy of progressive taxation, affirmative action, the right to abortion, universal healthcare, and the like? Political ethics is also concerned with moral problems raised by the need for political compromise, whistleblowing, civil disobedience, and criminal punishment.

Criminalization of Politics in India

It implies that the criminals entering the election fray and contesting elections and even getting elected to the parliament and state legislature. It takes place primarily because of the nexus between the criminals and some of the politicians. The criminals need the patronage of politicians occupying public offices to continue with their criminal activities and the politicians need the money and muscle power that the criminals can offer to the politicians to win the elections. In course of time, the nexus led the criminals themselves to contest elections. Further, the criminal justice system has inbuilt delays. It takes years for a criminal case to be finally disposed off by the courts.

Under the golden rule of criminal law on which the entire criminal justice system is based, the accused is presumed to be innocent till he is proved to be guilty. Therefore, after the accused is convicted and sentenced by trial court, by going on appeal to higher court, his conviction and sentence are suspended by higher court till it disposes off the appeal. Thus, the convicted person becomes innocent once more in eyes of law and is not prohibited from contesting elections. Moreover, the rate of conviction in the country has been going down which means more and more criminals may go unpunished as their guilt is not proved beyond reasonable doubt in court of law. Thus, the known criminals are not legally prohibited from contesting elections. The criminalization of politics has very adverse consequences on the society as well as on nation.

But this was until July 10th 2013 - the day when the apex court of the nation pronounced a landmark judgement thus changing the horizon of this phenomenon from the electoral process of our country.

The Phenomenal Judgement of SC on Criminal Fighting Elections

In a landmark judgement, the Supreme Court has struck down a section of Representation of the People Act that allows a convicted lawmaker to remain in office while there are still cases pending against them. "The only question is about the vires of section 8(4) of the Representation of the People Act (RPA) and we hold that it is ultra vires and that the disqualification takes place from the date of conviction," a bench of justices A K Patnaik and S J Mukhopadhaya said. In effect, what the Supreme Court order says is that the disqualification of an MP or MLA will come into effect immediately after the representative is convicted by any court. The SC order also says that the representative cannot contest elections again and a representative cannot cast his vote from jail, under any circumstances. However, the court said this order will not have a retrospective effect so that those who have filed appeals in cases pending against them will not be affected. Earlier, the Centre defended an exception carved out to protect convicted MPs and MLAs from disqualification on the ground that their removal would destabilise governments surviving on a "razor edge thin majority". The provision of RPA says that a lawmaker cannot be disqualified in the event of his conviction in a criminal case if he or she files an appeal in the higher court.

The top court's verdict came on the petitions filed by Lily Thomas and NGO Lok Prahari through its secretary SN Shukla who had sought striking down of various provisions of RPA on the ground that they violate certain constitutional provisions which, among other things, expressly put a bar on criminals getting registered as voters or becoming MPs or MLAs. The PILs had said that certain sections of RPA allow convicted lawmakers to continue in office while their appeals are pending and thus those provisions are "discriminatory and encourage criminalisation of politics".

This order is likely to have large repercussions among almost all political parties in the country.

Citizens' Charter

Citizens' Charter is an undertaking a public service organization gives to the citizens, to provide a high level of service while meeting the standards contained in the declaration. It contains specific provisions and set out specific obligations for the public services, the time within which the department would be obliged to provide a service or to respond to a query or complaint.

Citizens' Charter is aimed at demanding from the government and the service organisations (e.g. hospital, post-office, etc.) the fundamentals of accountability, transparency, quality and choice of services supplied to the people. The charter places the citizen at the centre of administration, instead of treating him as a passive recipient of services rendered without regard for quality, cost or timeliness.

The charter is no doubt an innovative device; but its formulation and enforcement are no easy tasks. In order to make these charters effective tools for holding public servants accountable, the Citizens' Charter should contain specific provisions and set out specific obligations for the public services, the time within which the department would be obliged to provide a service or to respond to a query or complaint. They should clearly spell out the remedy/penalty/compensation in case there is a default in meeting the standards spelt out in the charter. Further, there has to be some authority or institution to monitor performance and watch violations and maintenance. The citizens have to play an active role in giving timely and necessary feedback about services rendered by the government agencies. Within the organizations, the employees must be psychologically and infrastructurally well-prepared to serve the public as per the agreed-upon standards.

Principles of Citizens' Charter

The Citizens' Charter is based on the following principles-

- Wide publicity on the standards of performance of public agencies

- Assured quality of services
- Access to information along with courtesy and helpful attitude
- Choice of and consultation with the citizens
- Simplified procedures for receipt of complaints and their quick redressal, and
- Provision of performance scrutiny with citizens' involvement.

Work Culture

Work culture is regarded as a set of practices, values and shared beliefs within an organization and in its employees that arise from what is generally regarded as appropriate ways to think and act. It is the work culture which decides the way employees interact with each other and how an organization functions. The work culture of an organization is a product of its history, traditions, values, and vision.

Desirable work culture includes shared institutional values, priorities, rewards and other practices which foster inclusion, high performance, and commitment, while still allowing diversity in thought and action.

Characteristics of a Healthy Work Culture

Following are the main characteristics of a healthy work culture:

- One respects his fellow workers, i.e., employees are cordial with each other.
- Conflicts are minimum and they are resolved after considering the underlying causes.
- Each employee is treated in alike manner. It is recognized by the employer and managers that partiality leads to dissatisfied employees and eventually an unhealthy work culture.
- Employees are judged only by their work and nothing else.
- Performers are encouraged. And the ones, who have not performed well, are not criticized but are asked to pull up their socks for the next time.
- Employees' participation in decision making and quality suggestion is encouraged.

- There is two way communications. Employees' feedback, negative or positive, is well taken into consideration.
- Workshops, seminars and presentations are frequently conducted to upgrade the existing skills of the employees.

Work Ethics

An important dimension of ethics in public administration is work ethics. It represents a commitment to the fulfillment of one's official responsibilities with a spirit of dedication, involvement and sincerity. It also implies that a government functionary would love his work and not treat it as a burden or a load. And that efficiency, productivity and punctuality will be the hallmark of his administrative behaviour.

Characteristics of Ethical Work/ Organisational Culture

Following are the main characteristics of an ethical work/ organisational culture:

- **Values-** At the center of an ethical organization are its values. To use an organic analogy, an organization's values are its lifeblood. Just as blood nourishes the body, they must flow vigorously through every cell of an organization.
- **Leadership Effectiveness-** The ethical organization will have leaders who both "talk the talk" and "walk the walk" of ethical practice. Leaders must embody the organization's values in their own behaviour and must articulate those values in a compelling way for employees. Leaders set the tone that permeates an organization's culture. If employees perceive that top leaders care more about results than about how those results are achieved, this perception can encourage the bending or even breaking of rules.
- **Stakeholder Balance-** The Ethical Organization Model recognizes that needs and demands of different stakeholder groups frequently exist in tension with one another. Customers want higher quality at a lower price; employees want higher wages and increased benefits; owners/investors want a greater return; suppliers want to be paid more; communities want companies to invest more in them; and competitors want fair competition. The ethical organization recognizes these tensions and works to maintain a balance between them. Focusing too much on

any one stakeholder, whether owners/investors, customers or employees, will create a distortion that can lead to ethical lapses.

- **Process Integrity-** Process integrity is a focus on the systems dimension of organizational life. The ethical organization's values must be built into every operational process. All of its operational systems (e.g., recruiting, hiring, evaluating, compensating, promoting, demoting, firing, marketing, sales, production) need to be aligned with its values. At best, misaligned processes create confusion and poor decision making within the organization; at worst, they create ethical breaches and chaos.
- **Long-Term Perspective-** A fundamental characteristic of an ethical organization is the devotion of its leadership to strategic planning for the long term. This characteristic evokes the question, "What is the purpose of this business?" For some, the answer is to maximize shareholder value, but for others, the goal of business is found in balancing the interests of numerous stakeholders–owner/investors and employees, customers and suppliers, communities and, yes, even competitors.

Significance of Service Delivery

Public service delivery is the most important aspect of good governance because it touches the lives of millions of people. It is through better public service delivery that inclusive and sustainable socio-economic development can be achieved. Public service delivery is also an integral component for achieving growth oriented governance.

Right to Service

The Right to Service legislation is a mechanism to ensure time-bound delivery of services by public officials, prompt solutions to people's grievances and to make public officials punishable for delays. With this legislation, service becomes a right, and no longer remains an act of benevolence.

Right to Service legislation is aimed to reduce corruption among the government officials and to increase transparency and public accountability.

Citizen centricity with the aim of ensuring citizens' welfare and satisfaction is critical for any government- local, state or national- which aims to provide good governance. Therefore, transparency, efficiency and accountability in the public service delivery system that the citizens are most immediately concerned with, is of prime importance.

Challenges in Improving Service Delivery

For several decades, public services have unfortunately been provided with the primary focus on convenience of service providers rather than the service receivers. Various factors like complex regulations, complicated forms, lack of information, absence of performance standards, lack of accountability, corruption and incompetence have left recipients of public services, or ordinary citizens, helpless, dissatisfied and frustrated.

The former Prime Minister of India, Rajiv Gandhi in this context observed "The experiences of the vast majority of our people at the grassroots has been that the interface between the public and the administration is unresponsive, inefficient, unsympathetic, often callous, sometimes even cruel to those whom they are meant to serve". To address these bureaupathologies plaguing the governance, reform initiative has become sine qua non.

We must introspect and recognize that there is a great deal of public dissatisfaction with the functioning of government, at all levels of government. And it is important to realise that the most crucial aspect of governance is improving public service delivery at the grassroots level–the village or Panchayat level. For a common man in a village, a Patwari (or 'Mamladar' as is called in some states) is the biggest and the highest revenue officer; a 'Thanedar' is the biggest police officer; and a forest guard is the biggest forest officer because the peoples' interaction in day-to-day affairs is only with these persons and not with the District Collectors or Superintendents of Police or the Divisional Forest Officers posted at the district level. If the public service delivered through these grassroots level officers is good, the image of the whole government and the administration is good and vice-versa. So, the thrust should be to improve the working of these grassroots and cutting edge level officers having maximum interaction with the common man.

Suggestions for Improving Service Delivery

This is well recognized that there is an imperative need to improve the service delivery mechanism in our country. In this regard, various challenges and constraints being faced by the bureaucracy need to be addressed through multi-pronged strategies. Some suggestions are as follows to create responsive, transparent and accountable systems of public service delivery-

- To place people at the centre of all developmental programmes and activities of the government above all political and administrative considerations, treating people as valued participants, not beneficiaries–enabling them to have alternate choices–and keeping public interest supreme in all governmental policies, programmes and processes;
- To provide services to the people in accordance with specified standards through easily accessible interfaces such as one-stop, single-window, automated service delivery outlets or common civic service centres, devoid of harassment or corruption, minimising waiting time and inconvenience to the public;
- To ensure a minimum tenure for public servants and create a stable and conducive environment for public servants to deliver results based on clarity of vision, mission and objectives, service standards, delegation of authority and responsibility, budgets linked to outcomes, placements on considerations of merit and capability, efficiency and proven track record; and appropriate incentives and disincentives;
- To ensure value for money and cost effectiveness in the provision of services, exploring alternative mechanisms such as outsourcing, public-private-people partnership, public service agreements between policy-makers and service providers, etc. and adopting the most appropriate systems;
- To develop appropriate cost, time and quality benchmarks for service delivery outcomes against which post-implementation evaluation, including citizen report cards needs to be carried out;
- To develop, implement and monitor performance measurement and management systems, developing performance indicators for service delivery-related functions and service providers or functionaries;

- To promote decentralisation and strengthen rural and urban local bodies as grassroots level self-governing institutions, delivering services in accordance with the mandate of the Constitution of India, by empowering them with devolution of functions, finances and functionaries and undertaking capacity building programmes;
- To enable people and their organisations to undertake the delivery of services themselves or assist them in delivering services, wherever feasible and beneficial;
- To strengthen the district administration, including Panchayati Raj Institutions and urban local bodies at the cutting edge level of public administration and clarify the roles and responsibilities of all agencies and functionaries working at the district level;
- To adopt participatory mechanisms in public service delivery, involving the people, peoples' institutions, civil society groups, community based organisations, non-government organisations, self-help groups, in all aspects and stages such as service planning, budgeting, delivery, monitoring, getting feedback, quality benchmarking and assurance, evaluating, undertaking social audit, customer satisfaction surveys, etc;
- To establish independent regulatory mechanisms and effectively implement laws relating to consumer protection to ensure that service standards are adhered to and the citizens get a fair deal from service providers;
- To undertake third party appraisal and objective assessment of programmes, schemes and institutions regarding their functioning and impact by independent professional institutions, citizens' committees, etc. and obtain and use feedbacks to improve policies and implementation mechanisms;
- To firmly establish the Rule of Law and maintain public order at all times as the basic foundation of good governance and provide a safe environment to the citizens and business to pursue their tasks of self-development and nation-building;
- To develop and implement a core governance and core reform agenda covering the key social, economic and human development goals, which are in the supreme interest of the people and social-economic development and which need to be pursued with a vision on a long-term basis;

Utilization of Public Funds

Public fund is used by the government to provide goods and services to the public in general. These funds are generated or acquired by the government. The political nature of public spending decisions means that finance staff can be exposed to difficult ethical situations. The existence of an external ethical framework can be a powerful incentive to behave in accordance with a set of ethical values and to act in the public interest.

Government Budgeting

Government Budgeting is the process of allocating a government's financial resources. Although practical necessity plays a vital role in this process, spending decisions come down to priorities and values, as well. A government which is clear about its ethical directions will approach the budgeting process as a way to make choices that help them to realize its vision and its goals in ways that are also financially sustainable - balancing financial considerations with questions of what makes their citizen's activities meaningful and worthwhile.

Theoretically, it's easy to balance the estimated expenditure and anticipated revenues but when it comes to practical implementation, such balance is hard to achieve. Ethical dimensions of budgeting focuses on the balanced budget, in which, the received revenue neutralizes the expenditure. But, due to dynamism involved in the market, balanced budget is difficult to be maintained. Here the importance of ethical spending rises for judicious utilization of funds that ensures economic stability.

Need of the Government Budget

- **Proper Resource Pool Allocation:** When it comes to budgeting, identifying areas of weakness helps the government to allocate resources in a useful and sustainable manner. This is one of the most fundamental objectives behind framing a government budget. It's important for the government to ensure that funds reach where it's required the most.
- **Ensuring Economic Growth:** A budget allows the government to regulate the imposition of taxes in various sectors. Investment and expenditure are some of the most prominent factors contributing to the growth of a nation's economy.
- **Growth of Business and Trading:** Businesses and enterprises look forward to the government budget as resources being

allocated to various sectors are revealed. The government can encourage business owners to revise their policies accordingly and contribute to the country's economic prosperity.

- **Mitigating Economic Divide:** The government can address economic disparity, inequality and other kinds of threats by introducing public and economic welfare policies for the underprivileged sections of the society through the budget.

Government Accounts

The financial management of any organization must have a prudent financial system backed by sound and effective accounting procedures and internal controls. A well-designed and well managed accounting system helps ensure proper control over funds. Accounts are an integral part of financial management of activities. On the basis of accounts, the Government determines the shape of its monetary and fiscal policies. The accounts of Indian Government are kept in three parts: -

1. Consolidated Fund of India,
2. Contingency Fund of India, and
3. Public Account.

Consolidated Fund of India

All revenues received by the Government by way of taxes like Income Tax, Central Excise, Customs and other receipts flowing to the Government in connection with the conduct of Government business i.e. Non-Tax Revenues are credited into the Consolidated Fund constituted under Article 266 (1) of the Constitution of India. Similarly, all loans raised by the Government by issue of Public notifications, treasury bills (internal debt) and loans obtained from foreign governments and international institutions (external debt) are credited into this fund. All expenditure of the government is incurred from this fund and no amount can be withdrawn from the Fund without authorization from the Parliament.

Contingency Fund of India

Contingency Fund is created as an imprest account to meet some urgent or unforeseen expenditure of the government. Any expenditure incurred from this fund requires a subsequent approval from the Parliament and the amount withdrawn is returned to the Fund from the Consolidated Fund.

Public Account

In the Public Account, the transactions relate to debt other than those included in the Consolidated Fund of India. The transactions under Debt, Deposits and Advances in this part are those in respect of which Government incurs a liability to repay the money received or has a claim to recover the amounts paid. The receipts under Public Account do not constitute normal receipts of Government.

Fund Utilization

The fund utilization marks the concerns the way funds were used in a selected period of time. It shows the amounts issued from a fund selected and how much was paid back or deposited to the fund. The funds are generally used for building the fixed assets as well as current bearing expenses. A proper balance should be maintained while investing in fixed assets and current bearings. Fixed assets involve investment of funds (in land and buildings, plant and machinery, furniture and fittings, office equipment, etc.) over a fairly long period of time.

Importance of Proper Utilization of Funds

Though all the functions of finance management are equally important, special stress is laid on fund utilization because effective and efficient fund utilization enables organizations in profit and wealth/ returns maximization, minimization of the cost of capital, improving savings and bettering its value. Utilization of funds also impacts the liquidity, safety and risk management of the organization. Optimally utilized funds help to grow and flourish in the long-run.

On the other hand, if funds are under or over-utilized or mismanaged, it will be pernicious to the sustainability, viability and growth of the organization. Since, the external sources are key factors for the creation of funds, optimal utilisation of funds and managed balanced sheets will create the confidence in the investors. Also, beyond a certain level, it may not be possible to raise more funding, therefore, optimum utilisation of funds are indispensable.

This cycle in the given figure shows that the efficient public fund management finally leads to the maximizing value of money and building confidence in the investors.

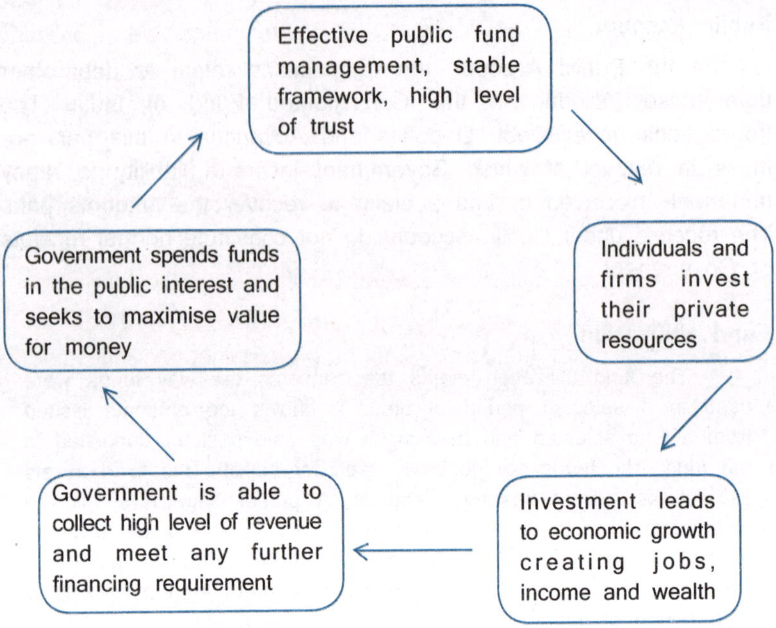

Constituents of the Fund Utilization

- **Investment Decisions:** The investment should be such that there is enough left for the organization to meet its operational expenses and purchase current assets. So, organizations need to properly plan and prioritize the purchase and replacement of the various fixed assets through capital budgeting, profit and loss analysis, opportunity cost analysis, etc.
- **Working Capital and Cash Flow Management:** Organizations need liquidity and cash flow in the short-term in order to meet their operational costs, working capital requirements and emergencies.
- **Utilization of Surplus:** The surplus or profits over and above the fixed costs and tax payments of the organization need to be effectively allocated and utilized for its growth and sustenance.

Under-utilization of Funds and Related Constrains

Several times, the government or any other authority allocates sufficient funds for processing of an event or any scheme, but due to some incompetent measures or inefficiencies, these funds remain idle. The perception dominates that these funds were properly allocated but the outcomes were very low, such situations deems to be under-utilization of funds. There may be many reasons for this like incompetence, lack of interest, limited awareness to the beneficiaries, corruption, myopic vision, and so on. In India, under-utilization of funds can be credited to the institutional and procedural blockages by the States.

Some of the constrains can be marked for the under utilization of funds-

- insufficient and inefficient staff for undertaking activities, inadequate attention to their capacity building and minimal role for community participation,
- shortage of trained, regular staff for various important roles like programme management, finance/accounts, etc.,
- insufficient delegation of financial powers to the lower level authorities and inexperienced decision-making,
- delay in the flow of funds, and in releasing sanction orders for spending, and
- lack of need based budgeting in the schemes, which is often carried out without proper analysis of unit costs on the ground, implied allocations for some of the schemes being decided in a top-down and unrealistic manner.

Mis-utilisation of Funds

Mis-utilisation of funds in government can be defined as spending that involves elements of any of the following like:

1. Illegal Acts

From the perspective of government spending, illegal acts can be defined as acts related to purchasing, contracting, and paying for goods and services that are in violation of governmental laws and regulations, including provisions of the Constitution, charters, legislative acts (laws), resolutions, and other regulatory requirements. Probable instances from the daily government business can be summed up as:

- Using government property or resources for personal or non-public purposes
- Gifting, donating, or loaning public resources to private indi-

viduals, organizations, or corporations without a contract for service

- Accepting gifts or kickbacks for providing favors or special considerations
- Authorizing purchase commitments or contracts in excess of available appropriation or other legal spending limit
- Failing to pay overtime and other compensation to employees in accordance with the requirements of the federal Fair Labor Standards Act, where applicable
- Failing to account for and spend certain restricted resources in separate funds as may be required by law

2. Fraud

Fraud can be broadly defined as an intentional deception or perversion of the truth made for personal gain or to damage another individual. Fraud from the perspective of government spending can be defined as the spending activities or actions that are intentionally designed to deceive another party, and can involve embezzlement of government monies, filing false claims, and contract fraud.

3. Abuse

Abuse involves 'behavior' that is deficient or improper when compared with that of a prudent person would consider, i.e. reasonable and necessary business practice under a given circumstance. Abuse includes misuse of authority or position for personal financial interests or those of an immediate or close family member or business associate. From the perspective of government spending, abuse can involve unreasonable or unnecessary spending or purchases that are extravagant or expensive. Some actions and activities can be considered as abusive although they may not be illegal or fraudulent.

4. Waste

Waste in government spending is much more difficult to define. Identifying wasteful spending involves the application of significantly more judgment than in cases of illegal acts, fraud, and abuse. Often different individuals will have varying perspectives on defining what is wasteful. However, generally government spending waste can be defined as "the inefficient or ineffective use of public resources".

Establishing Key Controls over Wrongful Spending

There are certain broad types of controls (key controls) that should be considered over wrongful spending. These key controls include:

- **Authorization and Approval** - controls over spending that involve delegation of authority with specified limitations and approval requirements (e.g. identifying who is authorized to make certain purchases, setting limits where advance approval is needed, indicating who must review and sign documents for evidence of approval);
- **Security over Access** - controls over access to purchase authorization documents, signature stamps, cash, checks, and computer system processes that safeguard assets from loss or misappropriation;
- **Segregation of Duties** - controls fraud by not putting a single individual in a position to be able to commit a fraud or misappropriate resources and then be able to conceal it;
- **Review and Oversight** - provides sufficient monitoring over spending activities, the reconciliation and investigation of unresolved questions or differences, and the ultimate resolution of those questions or differences (e.g. a timely comparison of budget and actual amounts to look for unexplained variances, and periodic internal audits over spending activities).

Audit of Funds

Unlike the financial auditor or a mere book keeper, the constitutional auditor basically deploys three distinct audit frameworks for auditing the entire gamut of receipts and expenditure at the central, state and union territory levels. Domain of audit of the CAG encompasses all ministries, departments, subordinate offices, autonomous bodies, and organizations, societies which receive substantial public funds in grants or loans, departmental undertakings and central and state public enterprises in the country.

Comptroller of Auditor General (CAG)

In the parliamentary democratic governance framework, the supreme audit institution of India has been conducting three types of audits – **Financial Audit, Compliance Audit and Performance Audit** – and the CAG meticulously uses the benchmarked best practices prevalent in the international comity of audit professionals to capture the totality of transactions, rather than limiting it to verification of arithmetical accuracy and certifying the accounts.

While auditing utilisation of public funds by various agencies, the auditor has no option but to be conscientious about the laid down policy, stated vision, mission along with plan, objectives and targets set by the organization while overseeing planning, implementation, monitoring and reviewing of various schemes, projects, programmes and duly reporting to the Parliament as per the constitutional mandate.

While certification of accounts, financial audit and compliance or regularity audit are based on applicable regulations, procedures and standards, the way performance audit is conducted deserves special mention, due to the methodology and approach.

Equity & Ethics

The auditor conducts in his performance audit using mutually agreed-upon criteria and evaluates the performance of the organization or programme or project in measurable quantitative parameters, as well as qualitative criteria relating to economy, efficiency, effectiveness, ethics and equity in execution of the project or service delivery. The auditor frequently asks the fundamental audit questions: 'Are things being done in the right way?' and 'are the right things being done?'.

The auditor evaluates the performance with reference to the objectives and the means provided for achieving the objectives; assesses the effectiveness of utilization of public funds; compares the impact, outcome and achievements with standards, targets and criteria; analyses the bottlenecks, systemic and procedural deficiencies to suggest improvements.

Besides assessing the results on the basis of value for money based on criteria of economy, efficiency and effectiveness, the performance auditor uses equity and ethics in his auditing framework, because ethics in management of public funds becomes indispensable for public accountability, and infringement of standards of equity and ethics impinges on the achievement of results and adversely affects the outcome. Ethical and equity parameters make the performance auditor duty bound to analyse the outcome of the project, modus operandi of implementation and ethical and equity implications in outreaching the beneficiaries intended, in compliance with the laid-down policy framework and applicable laws, regulations and procedures. Though the auditor is not mandated to discuss the merits and demerits of a programme, his systematic analysis of implementation of a project gives enormous insight to the policymakers to review and improve the systems and procedures for better effectiveness by learning valuable lessons from experience.

Corruption

Corruption refers to deliberate and intentional exploitation of one's position, status or resources directly or indirectly, for personal aggrandizement whether it be in terms of material gain or enhancement of power, prestige or influence beyond what is legitimate or sanctioned by commonly accepted norms to the detriment of the interests of other persons or the community as a whole.

Coercive Corruption

In a vast majority of bribery cases, the citizen is a victim of extortion and is compelled to pay a bribe in order to get a service to which he is entitled.

It is observed that there is a vicious cycle of corruption operating and most citizens often end up losing much more by resisting corruption. Delays, harassment, lost opportunity, loss of precious time and wages, uncertainty and, at times, potential danger of loss of life or limb could result from resistance to corruption and non-compliance with demands. In such cases, the citizen is an unwilling victim of coercive corruption.

Collusive Corruption

There are several cases of collusion between the bribe giver and corrupt public servant. In such cases of collusive corruption, both parties benefit at immense cost to society. Awarding of contracts for public works and procurement of goods and services, recruitment of employees, evasion of taxes, substandard projects, collusive violation of regulations, adulteration of foods and drugs, obstruction of justice and concealing or doctoring evidences in investigation are all examples of such dangerous forms of collusive corruption.

As the economy is freed from state controls, extortionary corruption declines and collusive corruption tends to increase.

Corruption, Ethics and Values

Corruption is an important manifestation of the failure of ethics. The word 'corrupt' is derived from the Latin word 'corruptus', meaning 'to break or destroy'. The word 'ethics' is from the original Greek term 'ethikos', meaning 'arising from habit'. It is unfortunate that corruption has, for many, become a matter of habit, ranging from grand corruption involving persons in high places to retail corruption touching the everyday life of common people.

Anti-corruption interventions so far made are seen to be ineffectual and there is widespread public cynicism about them. The interventions are seen as mere posturing without any real intention to bring the corrupt to book. They are also seen as handy weapons for partisan, political use to harass opponents. Corruption is so deeply entrenched in the system that most people regard corruption as inevitable and any effort to fight it as futile. This cynicism is spreading so fast that it bodes ill for our democratic system itself.

There are two, somewhat contrary, approaches in dealing with corruption and abuse of office. The first is overemphasis on values and character. Many people lament the decline in values and the consequent rise in corruption. The implicit assumption is that until values are restored, nothing much can be done to improve the conduct of human beings.

The second approach is based on the belief that most human beings are fundamentally decent and socially conscious, but there are always a small proportion of people, who cannot reconcile individual goals with the good of society. Such deviant people tend to pursue personal gain at the cost of public good and the purpose of organized government is to punish such deviant behaviour. If good behaviour is consistently rewarded and bad behaviour consistently punished, the bulk of the people follow the straight and narrow path (also refer instrumental conditioning in Unit-2).

In the real world, both values and institutions matter. Values are needed to serve as guiding stars, and they exist in abundance in our society. A sense of right and wrong is intrinsic to our culture and civilization. But values need to be sustained by institutions to be durable and to serve as an example to others. Values without institutional support will soon be weakened and dissipated. Institutions provide the container, which gives shape and content to values. This is the basis of all statecraft and laws and institutions. While incentives and institutions matter for all people, they are critical in dealing with the army of public servants - elected or appointed - endowed with authority to make decisions and impact on human lives and exercising the power to determine allocation of resources. Public office and control over public purse offer enormous temptation and opportunity to promote private gain at public cost. Therefore, creation of institutions and designing of incentives are of utmost importance in promoting ethical conduct of public servants.

Challenges of Corruption

The challenges of corruption manifest themselves in following forms:

- Those who benefit from a corrupt status quo will try to impede reform. Improvements in human well-being seldom occur spontaneously but, instead, require government actions to complement private efforts. Governments that waste resources through malfeasance or inadvertence are a drag on growth and undermine the achievement of other goals.
- High levels of corruption are associated with lower levels of investment and growth and corruption discourages both capital inflows and foreign direct investment.
- Corruption lowers productivity, reduces the effectiveness of industrial policies, and encourages business to operate in the unofficial sector in violation of tax and regulatory laws.
- Highly corrupt countries tend to under-invest in human capital by spending less on education, to over-invest in public in-

frastructure relative to private investment, and to have lower levels of environmental quality.

- High levels of corruption produce a more unequal distribution of Income.
- Corrupt governments lack political legitimacy. In circumstances of low government legitimacy, citizens try to avoid paying taxes, and firms go underground to hide from the burden of bureaucracy, including attempts to solicit bribes.

Moreover, anti-corruption interventions so far made are seen to be ineffectual and there is widespread public cynicism about them. The interventions are seen as mere posturing without any real intention to bring the corrupt to book. They are also seen as handy weapons for partisan, political use to harass opponents. Corruption is so deeply entrenched in the system that most people regard corruption as inevitable and any effort to fight it as futile. This cynicism is spreading so fast that it bodes ill for our democratic system itself.

Ironically, it has also been observed that the people, to a large extent, have accepted corruption as a way of their life and they do not judge it on the grounds of morality and ethics anymore. In other words, the moral threshold of the society has increased and people now consider it as an integral part of the way an administration functions. This is increasingly becoming a major obstacle in fighting with this menace.

Corruption Laws in India

Public servants in India can be penalized for corruption under the Indian Penal Code, 1860 and the Prevention of Corruption Act, 1988. The Benami Transactions (Prohibition) Act, 1988 prohibits benami transactions. The Prevention of Money Laundering Act, 2002 penalises public servants for the offence of money laundering. India is also a signatory to the UN Convention against Corruption since 2005. India ratified the convention in 2011. The Convention covers a wide range of acts of corruption and also proposes certain preventive policies.

Key Features of the Acts Related to Corruption

Indian Penal Code, 1860

- The IPC defines "public servant" as a government employee, officers in the military, navy or air force; police, judges, officers of Court of Justice, and any local authority established by a Central or State Act.

- Section 169 pertains to a public servant unlawfully buying or bidding for property. The public servant shall be punished with imprisonment of upto two years or with fine or both. If the property is purchased, it shall be confiscated.
- Section 409 pertains to criminal breach of trust by a public servant. The public servant shall be punished with life imprisonment or with imprisonment of upto 10 years and a fine.
- In addition to the categories included in the IPC, the definition of "public servant" includes office bearers of cooperative societies receiving financial aid from the government, employees of universities, Public Service Commission and banks.
- If a public servant takes gratification other than his legal remuneration in respect of an official act or to influence public servants is liable to minimum punishment of six months and maximum punishment of five years and fine. The Act also penalizes a public servant for taking gratification to influence the public by illegal means and for exercising his personal influence with a public servant.
- If a public servant accepts a valuable thing without paying for it or paying inadequately from a person with whom he is involved in a business transaction in his official capacity, he shall be penalized with minimum punishment of six months and maximum punishment of five years and fine.
- It is necessary to obtain prior sanction from the central or state government in order to prosecute a public servant.

The Benami Transactions (Prohibition) Act, 1988

- The Act prohibits any benami transaction (purchase of property in false name of another person who does not pay for the property) except when a person purchases property in his wife's or unmarried daughter's name.
- Any person who enters into a benami transaction shall be punishable with imprisonment of upto three years and/or a fine.
- All properties that are held to be benami can be acquired by a prescribed authority and no money shall be paid for such acquisition.

The provisions of the act became more stringent with the coming of the amendments post the amendments inculcated within the act in 2016.

Though the Benami Transactions (Prohibition) Act, 1988 has been on the statute book since more than 28 years, the same could not be made operational because of certain inherent defects. With a view to providing effective regime for prohibition of benami transactions, the said Act was amended through the Benami Transactions (Prohibition) Amended Act, 2016. The amended law empowers the specified authorities to provisionally attach benami properties which can eventually be confiscated. Besides, if a person is found guilty of offence of benami transaction by the competent court, he shall be punishable with rigorous imprisonment for a term not less than one year but which may extend to 7 years and shall also be liable to fine which may extend to 25% of the fair market value of the property. The Benami Transactions (Prohibition) Amendment Act, 2016 came into effect from1st November, 2016. Several benami transactions have been identified since the coming into effect of the amended law.

The Prevention of Money Laundering Act, 2002

- The Act states that an offence of money laundering has been committed if a person is a party to any process connected with the proceeds of crime and projects such proceeds as untainted property. "Proceeds of crime" means any property obtained by a person as a result of criminal activity related to certain offences listed in the schedule to the Act. A person can be charged with the offence of money laundering only if he has been charged with committing a scheduled offence.
- The penalty for committing the offence of money laundering is rigorous imprisonment for three to seven years and a fine of upto Rs 5 lakh. If a person is convicted of an offence under the Narcotics Drugs and Psychotropic Substances Act, 1985, the term of imprisonment can extend upto 10 years.
- The Adjudicating Authority, appointed by the central government, shall decide whether any of the property attached or seized is involved in money laundering. An Appellate Tribunal shall hear appeals against the orders of the Adjudicating Authority and any other authority under the Act.
- Every banking company, financial institution and intermediary

shall maintain a record of all transactions of a specified nature and value, and verify and maintain records of all its customers, and furnish such information to the specified authorities.

Process Followed to Investigate and Prosecute Corrupt Public Servants

- The three main authorities involved in inquiring, investigating and prosecuting corruption cases are the Central Vigilance Commission (CVC), the Central Bureau of Investigation (CBI) and the state Anti-Corruption Bureau (ACB). Cases related to money laundering by public servants are investigated and prosecuted by the Directorate of Enforcement and the Financial Intelligence Unit, which are under the Ministry of Finance.
- The CBI and state ACBs investigate cases related to corruption under the Prevention of Corruption Act, 1988 and the Indian Penal Code, 1860. The CBI's jurisdiction is the central government and Union Territories while the state ACBs investigates cases within the states. States can refer cases to the CBI.
- The CVC is a statutory body that supervises corruption cases in government departments. The CBI is under its supervision. The CVC can refer cases either to the Central Vigilance Officer (CVO) in each department or to the CBI. The CVC or the CVO recommends the action to be taken against a public servant but the decision to take any disciplinary action against a civil servant rests on the department authority.
- Prosecution can be initiated by an investigating agency only after it has the prior sanction of the central or state government. Government appointed prosecutors undertake the prosecution proceeding in the courts.
- All cases under the Prevention of Corruption Act, 1988 are tried by Special Judges who are appointed by the central or state government.

Bringing Probity in Governance- A Multi-pronged Approach

To bring probity in governance and curb corruption we should follow multi pronged approach-

- Accountability through Right to Information Act and transparency through digitization process (e-governance) will curb corruption to certain extent.

Role of Media

A free media has a crucial role in the prevention, monitoring and control of corruption. Such media can inform and educate the public on corruption, expose corruption in government, private sector and civil society organizations and help monitor codes of conduct while policing itself against corruption.

Investigative reporting by media or reporting of instances of corruption as they occur can be a significant source of information on corruption. Timely action should be taken by the authorities to immediately respond to such reports, to appraise the correct facts, to take steps to bring the culprits to book and to keep the press and the public informed from time to time of the progress of such action. It has been the common experience that very often there is no systematic arrangement to take note of these allegations and to follow them up. The collation of reports appearing in different sections of the media and their follow up should be an integral part of complaints monitoring mechanism in all public offices.

It has been observed that sometimes under pressure of competition, the media does not verify allegations and information before putting them in the public domain. Occasionally, such allegations/ complaints are motivated. It is necessary to evolve norms and practices that all allegations/complaints would be duly screened, and the person against whom such allegations are made is given a fair chance to put forth his version.

Further, I would like to say that, owing to the gravity of this topic, more of the same is discussed later-on at an apt place in the book.

- The Bill for time bound delivery of goods and services, if effectively implemented, will increase credibility in government services.
- Strengthening Panchayati Raj Institutions (PRIs) as platform for citizen participation in governance as well as awareness of their rights and duties through various programmes.
- More teeth to grievance redressal system.
- Bringing public participation in service delivery through PPP based system.
- Privatizing certain segments which are better done through private firms reducing cost and faster delivery of service.

- Imparting values based training to public officials.
- Reforms in education system with more emphasis on the equality and morality.
- Electoral reforms and stricter adherence to the guidelines, coalition defiance laws, etc.
- Strengthening of Ombudsman system for independent scrutiny in the high level corruption cases.
- Effective implementation of citizen charters.

Measures to Check Corruption: Brief Comments in the Indian Context

Checking corruption is important for good governance as is the rule of law, citizen-centric administration, effective and vigorous public service delivery and the government's ability and capacity to undertake appropriate mixes of activities and interventions with the help of a competent civil services that would result in the transformation and change of the society, the economy and the polity in desired directions. In a way corruption has become a major threat to good governance the world over; India being no exception.

Corruption can lead to large scale siphoning of public funds meant for government programmes through a combination of bribes and kickbacks whereby the desired objectives are not fully met, or to be specific, making available of government land, or other permissions and allocations at 'concessional' rates to selected individuals or entities - both of which are covered under what today are commonly referred to as scams. Or, it can be 'petty corruption' involving payment of bribes, gratification or considerations in cash or kind for obtaining public (and even, at times, private) services speedily, or evasion of taxes or activities like theft of electricity or potable water and getting the concerned authority to look the other way, or the following of personal or caste and other, non-merit, considerations while taking various decisions regarding public matters. Accordingly, corruption is not limited to government organizations. For example, a private school Principal can use his power to favour someone while granting admission in return for a bribe.

Both the above mentioned types of corruption - large scams or petty corruption - are equally harmful for society, and are equally a threat to good governance. In fact the day-to-day petty corruption faced by the common man is not only harassment for each individual sufferer, but the giver of bribes, gratification, etc., and one who accepts are to blame and they themselves are responsible for the existence of corruption.

Naturally, controlling or checking corruption has to involve a variety of diverse activities which may be preventive, curative, punishmental (or in the form of a deterrence), motivational, procedural and system-changing, and the like. The use of each of these would depend upon the various categories of actors whose behaviour and actions have to be influenced to counter corruption as well as the type of wrong doing that is to be checked.

If one would want to concentrate on the prevention of large scams then politicians, senior bureaucrats (including technocrats) in both government and public sector undertakings, large private companies which benefit from such scams (and their executives), and the "operators" (lobbyists, agents, etc.) who facilitate and become conduits, would all need to be tackled - as would senior functionaries in vigilance and investigating agencies and even the judiciary.

But, when it comes to petty corruption - all sections of society, including middle and lower level government servants, local politicians, the lower judiciary, small and medium manufacturers, businessmen and traders, various professionals like doctors, lawyers, bankers, engineers, chartered accountants, teachers, IT executives, persons from the print and the electronic media, and the farmers and artisans as well as wage earners in both rural and urban settings - each and every person poor or rich - all of whom may be involved as either bribe receivers or bribe givers and as users of influence, would need to be tackled. Of course, not everyone is corrupt - but each category of persons includes a significant number who are willing to undertake corrupt actions.

If everyone in every walk of life is to be reached and influenced to eschew corruption, then education has to be a major means to orient people to avoid undertaking corrupt acts. School and college education, adult and non-formal education, training for government servants, or for corporates in the private sector and by professional bodies, for the various professionals, all have to have a focus on ethics in public life, ethics in social situations, ethics in government, and on the evils of corruption. This would help to create a ground swell, a general climate, that is 'anti-corruption', and which appreciates those who follow ethical norms. Such a general atmosphere in favour of following proper ethics and against corruption can also be positively influenced by campaigns in the mass media.

The preface to the Fourth Report on Ethics in Governance of the Second Administrative Reforms Commission which came out in 2007 asserted that "The Mahatma's vision of a strong and prosperous India - Purna Swaraj - can never become a reality if we do not address the issue of the stranglehold of corruption in our polity, economy and society in general".

In the first chapter of the above mentioned Report of the Second Administrative Reforms Commission, it is pointed out that the setting of standards do not, by themselves, ensure ethical behaviour; that requires a robust culture of integrity. The crux of ethical behaviour does not lie in bold words or expressions enshrined as standards, but in their adoption in action, in sanctions against their violations, putting in place competent disciplinary bodies to investigate allegations of violations and to impose sanctions quickly, and in promoting a culture of integrity.

The Department of Administrative Reforms and Removal of Public Grievances, Government of India, had got a Civil Services Survey conducted through the Centre of Good Governance, Hyderabad, whose report came out in April 2010. Ten Central and All India Services were surveyed with questionnaires being sent to all serving members of the Services concerned. In all about 4800 responses were surveyed.

- The responses in the survey indicate the perception that there are a significant number of cases where anonymous complaints were made in a planned and systematic manner to derail an honest officer and to make him ineffective.
- A number of officers feel that the start of an enquiry on baseless allegations itself is punishment and that it does not matter if the person is finally exonerated at the end.

- Commitment to the job and integrity are not recognized.
- Honest and upright officers are sidelined or harassed.
- There is no incentive to remain honest, and the system is so designed that an officer entering service is forced to adapt to this corrupt system.
- A majority of the respondents felt that corrupt officers get away without being punished.
- In fact corrupt officers are able to get the most sought after postings.
- The Civil Service Survey Report also indicate that 40% of the respondents felt that a majority of officers uphold ethics, rules, etc. inspite of the personal risks involved, while 23% of the respondents felt that such officers who are willing to uphold ethics or rules despite the risks were only "few" or "very few".

T.S.R. Subramanian, a former Union Cabinet Secretary and former Chief Secretary of Uttar Pradesh - recently also chaired the commission which gave its report in 2016 to the MoHRD about New Education Policy, wrote a book **'GovernMint in India: An Inside View',** which was published in 2008. He has pointed out with examples that those civil servants who were willing to adjust their attitudes and behaviour and to break existing norms found it extremely satisfactory, rewarding and lucrative while others more able, conscientious and honest were condemned to sit out in a corner in insignificant postings. The weapons used for subjugation included frequent transfers, start of an interminable departmental enquiry, malicious character roles in performance appraisal reports, and the like. For assignments from the Secretary level down to Deputy Secretary in Central Ministries, one often had to be demanded by the Minister concerned, who had his own reasons for inducting 'cooperative' officials into his Ministry.

Example of a Public Sector Corporation

T.S.R. Subramanian gives an example from the early 1970s. Sadly many more such example may be found now-a-days. A young officer working as Managing Director of a State Public Sector Corporation discovered that the State political leadership was negotiating a kickback in a foreign purchase deal. He cautioned the potential suppliers against it and negotiated a price that did not contain any "cushion" for gratifying the political leadership. They in turn blocked official approval of his recommendations. He recorded the details of the matter in internal files notings and was promptly transferred to an insignificant assignment. Hearing of his plight, the Central Government arranged a decent posting for him on deputation in Government of India. Promptly, the State Government informed the Centre that such a good officer could not be spared for the Central assignment and that the State Government needed to retain him in the State. But, in the State he continued to be sidelined. He took voluntary retirement and joined a private company. The politicians in the State Government did not let go and pressurized the private company to fire him, which it did. Luckily for him he later got a job in a national concern whose boss was willing to ignore the strong hints from the aforesaid State politicians not to hire him. It is another matter that the said officer later happened to prosper as a private businessman, but his harassment had been total and sustained. Obviously a message was being sent to all others to toe the line in future.

Subramanian points out that many a times an initially idealistic administrator loses his intellectual integrity within 15 to 20 years of joining service, and in many cases also loses his financial integrity. To quote Subramanian "Sadly, many of the middle level officers with growing children to educate, elderly parents to look after, cannot bear the constant pressure and buckle, they either switch off or become irrelevant to the system; or they join the politicians, and all is well thereafter".

It may be added that it is not just politicians, but some senior bureaucrats, technocrats, members of investigating agencies, even of the judiciary and the media, and NGOs and public businessmen, have been known to exert pressure to get wrong decisions or actions undertaken for personal gain.

What can be done to check corruption and to encourage honesty in all government activities and transactions?

- Measures to protect honest persons, who refuse to indulge

in corruption, from malicious enquiries, prosecutions and harassment need to be strengthened. Procedures need to be continually evolved and improved to ensure the speeding up and early completion of enquiries (and where necessary court trials) so as to ensure that the guilty are determined and punished and the innocent are exonerated. For this, the investigating and enquiring agencies need strengthening and capacity building, as also to be manned by honest personnel. Simultaneously, we need to vigorously ensure that each accused gets full opportunity to defend himself or herself so as to establish his or her innocence. But once guilt is established the punishment should be swift and effective so as to act as a deterrent.

- In addition, work procedures and processes have to be regularly reviewed and it needs to be ensured that such procedures are strictly followed in a systematic manner to make corruption difficult and thus act as preventive measures. In this context, the system of office inspections also needs to be revitalized.
- The audit system can be an effective tool to suggest systemic improvements and changes in the working procedures of government so that chances of corruption diminish. Effective monitoring and supervision can also reduce corruption, particularly petty corruption. The Right to Information Act, though not an unmixed blessing since its provisions can be misused to harass officers, has demonstrated the potential to place a check on corruption or to expose corrupt acts.
- Some of the causes of corruption also need to be identified so as to work out solution. For example, it is suggested by many that the electoral system has become one where vast amounts of money are required to contest elections and that unless appropriate electoral reforms are thought of and implemented, corruption cannot be eliminated.
- The honest also need to be encouraged and incentivized in some way or the other. However, determining who is honest may prove to be even more difficult than establishing guilt beyond doubt in corruption matters.
- For Government agencies and departments an 'Integrity mark scheme' on the lines of Britain's 'Charter mark Scheme' for

good public service delivery and effective implementation of citizen charters could be thought of. However operationalizing such an 'Integrity mark Scheme' may prove difficult since it would involve conclusively identifying departments and agencies where by and large there is such corruption.

- In fact, none of the measures attempted to check or prevent corruption is likely to be easy to implement.
- What Constitutes quality governance is contextual in terms of time and place. What was required as good governance in India at the time of Independence in 1947 is quite different from what would be deemed to be good governance today. Similarly, what is good in terms of governmental practices in one country or in one region of a country may differ from what is required at another place. What works at one place at one point of time due to the context cannot be transplanted unchanged to another place to control or check corruption. It can be first adapted and then could be emulated at other places. At least nuances if not more substantive elements may need to be modified when these gets implemented in a different contextual environment. Thus what worked, or did not work, in checking corruption in different places should be documented and written about extensively, so that it could lead to better understanding, followed by suitable adaptation and adoption at other places.
- As already indicated above, corruption is not limited to persons having authority and power within the government. In the private sector also persons can misuse their power and authority - for example, granting or refusing admission to a patient in a private hospital or a student in a private school or college based upon receipt of a bribe or recommendations from members of one's own caste or relatives or of an influential politician, businessman or bureaucrat. The approach suggested and discussed above in the context of government activities could be emulated for corruption in private and non-governmental institution.
- One should not be enamoured of comparative rankings of countries or States based upon a corruption index. What matters is not whether a country is more or less corrupt than certain other countries. If the situation in our country is

unsatisfactory from the point of view of corruption, then we need to take steps to rectify the situation regardless of our comparative position or rank as per any corruption index.

Rationale Behind This

We all are aware how such indices are made. Based on various indicators, mostly decided by western research Institutions/ Universities/NGO, they present a subjective perception of corruption. Can we say what it means to be corrupt in Nordic nations – having different set of social and demographic realities – can be copied for India?

Further, a major strength of the India's national movement was that countless individuals decided each in his or her own way, and as per his or her capabilities or abilities, to do something to serve the country and to work towards independence.

If in every walk of life, from each section of society, ordinary people, each man and woman, young and old, decide that they will each take a personal step, however small it may be, to improve some aspect of life in our country about positive and creative and tangible individual actions then the overall impact may be stupendous. If each and every individual were to decide to eschew corruption - corruption would cease to exist.

Canons of Financial Propriety

Every officer incurring or authorizing expenditure from public money should be guided by high standards of financial propriety. Every officer should also enforce financial order and strict economy and see that all relevant financial rules and regulations are observed by his own office and by subordinate disbursing officers. Among the principles on which emphasis is generally laid are the following:-

- Every officer is expected to exercise the same vigilance in respect of expenditure incurred from public money as a person of ordinary prudence would exercise in respect of expenditure of his own money.
- The expenditure should not be prima facie more than what the occasion demands.
- No authority should exercise its powers of sanctioning ex-

penditure to pass an order which will be directly or indirectly to its own advantage.

- Expenditure from public money should not be incurred for the benefit of a particular person or a section of the people, unless -
  - a claim for the amount could be enforced in a Court of Law, or
  - the expenditure is in pursuance of a recognized policy or custom.
- The amount of allowances granted to meet expenditure of a particular type should be so regulated that the allowances are not on the whole a source of profit to the recipients.

The Legislative Control over Administration

In India the legislature, the representative body of the people exercises control over the administration. The administration cannot act contrary to the guidelines laid down by the legislature. It lays down the broader policy of administration. The legislature not only defines the functions of the government but also provides the finance for its various programmes. The control over financial matters is exercised through the various committees established by the legislature. The administration cannot spend a single rupee without the sanction of legislature. The administration is expected to keep the accurate account of all financial transactions and submit the reports of such transactions to the legislature.

The legislature also deals with the matter related with public personnel. The manner of recruitment of the public personnel, their number, their duties and powers, their service conditions, rules of procedure, code of conduct, etc. are determined by the legislature. The failure to adhere to those rules accounts for the disciplinary action against the administration. Further the public personnel are held responsible for their official acts. They are supposed to keep the proper records of their official acts and submit the reports to the legislature at least once a year, when called upon by the legislature giving a full account of their acts. The legislature may also conduct the special investigation or inquiry of the manner in which administrative affairs have been conducted. The legislature has the general power of direction, supervision and control over administration.

The Means of Legislative Control

The opportunity to exercise control over the administration assumes several forms such as questions, resolutions, Zero-Hour Discussions, Adjournment Motions, Vote of Censure, Budget and the Parliamentary Committees. The various means are discussed below:

- The President's Speech
- Discussion on Budget
- Question Hour
- Adjournment Motions
- Censure Motion
- Debates on the Legislations
- Parliamentary Committees
- External Audit

Budget

Budget is a statement of estimated revenues and expenditures. It is a comparative table giving the amounts of the receipts to be realized and of the expenses to be incurred.

In a way, the Budget is a forecast and an estimate of all the public receipts and expenses and an authorization to incur them and to collect them. The Budget, thus, is something much more than a mere estimate of revenues and expenditures. It is a plan of government action from the financial point of view. It is an instrument for the articulation of government programmes which have ramifications in the entire national economy. Thus considered, the Budget has tremendous social and economic implications in a genuine welfare state.

Importance of Budgeting

When public money is sent for public purposes, the important task before public administration is to have efficient management of public money. Budgeting is one of the major processes by which the use of public resources is planned and controlled. Its importance can be understood from following:

- It helps administrative management and co-ordination.
- It is an instrument of social and economic policy.
- Budgetary system is the most important technique of parliamentary control over administration.

- It ensures the financial and legal accountability of the executive to the legislature.

Auditing

Audit is one of the most important instruments of parliamentary control over the finances of the country. Independent audit is a very important safeguard of the public money. Auditing is a systematic examination of the books and records of a business or other organisations in order to ascertain or verify and to report upon the facts regarding its financial operations and the results thereof. Audit of government money in a democratic country is done by an independent officer, who performs this duty on behalf of the legislature. It is his duty to see that money has been spent economically and honestly.

Parliamentary Committees

The Parliamentary committees act as a tool of effective control over the administration. The financial committees of the Parliament such as Committee on Public Undertakings exercise detail and substantial control over the financial matters. The Committee on Assurances reports on as to what extent the assurances given by the ministers on the floor of the House are implemented in a specified time limit required for the purpose. Such enquiry makes ministers more responsible and careful and administration to take quick action on the given promises.

Politicisation of Bureaucracy

Politicisation of bureaucracy is not a new phenomenon in democracy. However, the intensity of application and reasons for politicisation vary from country to country. There are some levels of political involvement in personnel matters in all countries.

The Indian bureaucracy is both celebrated and criticized, the opinion changing its shades according to context. Jawaharlal Nehru once said the Indian Civil Service was "Neither Indian, nor Civil, nor a Service". However, his Deputy, Sardar Patel considered the civil service "the steel frame of Government machinery". Later the institution was also derided as 'babudom'.

Politicisation of bureaucracy refers to undue political influence in the governance due to nexus between bureaucracy and politics resulting on one hand - government appointing their own people to senior and sensitive public service positions, and defaming politicization and on the other hand - it refers to the substitution of political criteria for merit based criteria.

For instance, after so many political scams of 2G spectrum, Coal allocation (Coalgate) scams, etc. The Supreme Court of India even called Central Bureau of Investigation (CBI) as "Caged Parrot" which speaks for its masters. There is also a perception in the country that CBI has become a tool of political vendetta of government to suppress voice of opposition.

In fact, politicisation of civil service has become institutionalised in such a way that the government thinks seriously about the composition of Commissions, who recruits the civil servants. This is done with the expectation that the Commission would recruit supporters of the ruling party.

Consequences

If unqualified candidates get recruited in the civil services and elevated to different significant positions, they won't be able to give quality administration to the state. A conspicuous outcome is that bureaucracy is getting inefficient and ineffective in the absence of professionalism, decency and unbiasedness. The most compromising thing is that a large number of splendid brilliant civil servants have been punished now and again for the sake of their "loyalty". Such a circumstance will unquestionably discourage qualified and talented graduates from competing for the civil services.

Improvements Required

In a democracy, it is essential that the politicians play the role of masters assisted by the civil servants. The political leaders should be able to spell out their requirement to the bureaucracy and distinguish the jurisdiction of the bureaucracy in the affairs of the state. Only then will the bureaucracy remain confined within their jurisdiction and consider themselves as the servants of the people.

- The government will have to take necessary initiative to recruit competent graduates at the entry level. The Public Service

Commission should be constituted with qualified persons who would be allowed to work without any interference.

- The government will have to refrain from the policy of politicisation, meaning that recruitment and promotion would be made on the basis of merit.
- The government will have to take initiative to train our bureaucrats for increasing their efficiency.
- The commitment of the political parties is an utmost necessity since they form the government every five years.

Bureaucratisation of Politics

Bureaucrats need to maintain political neutrality and impartiality to ensure the triumph of democracy. Politicisation of Bureaucracy and Bureaucratisation of politics are the grey areas to interpret.

In the last couple of years, numerous bureaucrats and civil servants have joined the political arena. This phenomenon cuts across over various parties, be it in the largest party of India, Bharatiya Janata Party (BJP), Indian National Congress (INC), National Conference, and so on.

It is important to perceive this trend, not for any individual or the parties but from the larger perspective of the politics of India as a country. Additionally, analyzing the process of switching of bureaucrats into politics and how this process is converting into a nexus.

India saw huge number of civil servants diving into Indian Politics. For instance, former Indian Prime Minister Dr. Manmohan Singh had served as Governor of RBI before becoming Finance Minister during Narsimha Rao' regime. Similarly, numerous civil servants joined as ministers in the present government - S. Jaishankar (former Foreign Service diplomat) recently became Minister of External Affairs of India. Some other Union Ministers holding important profiles in the government who are bureaucrat turned politician: R K Singh, Hardeep Singh Puri, Alphons Kannanthanam, etc.

Also, there are some examples of bureaucrats - Arvind Kejriwal, Shah Faesal, O.P. Chaudhary and others, who prima facie resigned from their service and joined politics to bring change in the society.

But in any case, the civil service pre-requirements that they should be unprejudiced and unbiased towards political outfits. But the civil service requisite doesn't talk about their voluntary retirement or resignation, and also there is no bar on bureaucrats resigning early to join politics or joining after their retirement.

Since bureaucracy, still constituting an important part of state functionaries, it has its own powers and functions within the state structure. Therefore, the factor must be realized that they own role to play for the society and pre-mature resign to join politics or even just after retirement may degrade their stature as well as the morale of the coming generations to join the services and serve the nation as a bureaucrat.

As an equality of opportunity, provides for any citizen to be an active politician, the consideration and sensitivity of the matter must be taken in to account by the lawmakers and bureaucrats so that the goal of dignity and the authenticity of the nation are not bargained.

Judicial Control over Public Administration

Public administration exercises a large volume of power to meet the citizens' needs in modern democratic welfare state. Today, administration is not concerned with only pure administrative functions but also involved with a large number of quasi-legislative and quasi-judicial functions. In this respect, they have a number of chances to become arbitrary or master of the citizens. So, it is very necessary to control them. One of the ways for controlling the administrative actions is control through judiciary. Here, judicial control means the power of the courts to examine the Legality of the officials act and thereby to safeguard the fundamental and other essential rights of the citizens.

The role of judiciary in protecting the citizens against the excesses of officials has become all the more important with the increase in the powers and discretion of the public officials in the modern welfare states. But, the courts cannot interfere in the administrative activities on their own accord. They can intervene only when they are invited to do so by any person who feels that his rights have been abrogated or are likely to be abrogated as a result of some action of the public official.

Secondly, the courts cannot interfere in each and every administrative act, as too much of Judicial action may make the official too much conscious and very little of it may make them negligent of the rights of citizens.

Forms of Judicial Control over Administration

- Judicial Review
- Statutory Appeals
- Criminal and Civil Suits against Public Officials
- Extraordinary Remedies (prerogative writs)

Judicial Review

The judicial review implies the power of the courts to examine the legality and constitutionality of administrative acts of officials and also the executive orders and the legislative enactments. This is very important method of judicial control.

The statutes made by Parliament and State Assemblies itself provide that in a particular type of administrative action, the aggrieved party will have a right of appeal to the courts or to a higher administrative tribunal. Sometimes, legislative enactment itself may provide for judicial intervention in certain matters.

Ombudsman

The traditional democratic avenues of accountability through parliamentary controls have become increasingly inadequate with the growth of state activities in a democratic welfare state. Not only has government bureaucracy expanded, so have the points of contact between citizens and the state. Because of this, some disputes inevitably occur, and often on a scale and complexity which renders traditional avenues of redress largely inappropriate. To resolve such disputes numerous mechanisms have been adopted worldwide through which the decisions and actions of public authorities can be challenged. Four main avenues can be identified:- the courts; statutory inquiries; administrative tribunals; and ombudsman.

Ombudsman as a control mechanism aims at restricting administrative excesses and ensuring fair play in the exercise of administrative powers. An ombudsman is an officer of state appointed to provide a check on the rights of the citizens against government actions. Ombudsman, in the words of Cutchin, is a respected, apolitical individual outside the bureaucracy who is empowered to investigate citizens' complaints about government services and recommend rectification. Usually he has the power to investigate, criticize, and publicize administrative actions, but cannot reverse them. In principle, it enables a citizen who feels that he/she has been the victim of mal-administration to make a complaint to the ombudsman office.

The ombudsman serves three related purposes:

- Redressing individual grievances;
- Improving the quality of administration; and
- Helping the legislature to supervise the bureaucracy.

The very existence of an ombudsman improves the general climate of public opinion towards government. The citizens who secure redress are generally gratified. Others may become reconciled by the ombudsman's explanation of the basis for agency actions. Moreover, the ombudsman encourages the administration to explain to the citizen why it acts as it does and to include in any adverse decision clear information as to the possible right of appeal. More generally, the populace gains a sense of security in knowing that there is someone to whom they can turn.

Indian Ombudsman- Lokpal and Lokayukta

Lokpal at the central level and Lokayukta at the state level refer to an independent body which is empowered to enquire into cases of corruption against public functionaries, with a mechanism for filing complaints and conducting inquiries. The Lokpal is enacted to act as a watchdog over the integrity of Ministers, Members of Parliament and the senior civil servants.

In December, 2013 the Parliament passed the historic Lokpal Bill that provides for formation of an anti-graft ombudsman to fight corruption in public offices and ensure accountability on the part of public officials, including the Prime Minister, but with some safeguards.

Following are some important features of the Lokpal and Lokayuktas Bill, 2011, passed by Parliament.

- Lokpal at the Centre and Lokayukta at the level of the states.
- Lokpal will consist of a chairperson and a maximum of eight members, of which 50 per cent shall be judicial members.
- 50 per cent of members of Lokpal shall be from SC/ST/OBCs, minorities and women.
- The selection of chairperson and members of Lokpal shall be through a selection committee consisting of Prime Minister, Speaker of Lok Sabha, Leader of Opposition in the Lok Sabha, Chief Justice of India or a sitting Supreme Court judge nominated by CJI, eminent jurist to be nominated by the President of India on the basis of recommendations of the first four members of the selection committee.
- Prime Minister has been brought under the purview of the Lokpal.
- Lokpal's jurisdiction will cover all categories of public servants.
- All entities receiving donations from foreign source in the context of the Foreign Contribution Regulation Act (FCRA) in excess of Rs 10 lakh per year are brought under the jurisdiction of Lokpal.
- Provides adequate protection for honest and upright public servants.
- Lokpal will have power of superintendence and direction over any investigation agency including CBI for cases referred to them by Lokpal.
- A high powered committee chaired by the Prime Minister will recommend selection of the Director, CBI.
- Directorate of Prosecution headed by a Director of Prosecution under the overall control of Director.
- The appointment of the Director of Prosecution, CBI on the recommendation of the Central Vigilance Commission.
- Transfer of officers of CBI investigating cases referred by Lokpal with the approval of Lokpal.
- The bill also incorporates provisions for attachment and confiscation of property acquired by corrupt means, even while prosecution is pending.

- The bill lays down clear time lines for preliminary enquiry and investigation and trial and towards this end, the bill provides for setting up of special courts.
- A mandate for setting up of the institution of Lokayukta through enactment of a law by the State Legislature within a period of 365 days from the date of commencement of the Act.

Social Audit

Social Audit is a process in which the details of the resources, financial and non-financial, used by the public agencies for the development initiatives, are shared with the people, often through a public platform. It allows people to enforce transparency and accountability, thereby providing the ultimate users an opportunity to scrutinize the development initiatives.

Social audit can also be defined as a tool with which government departments can plan, manage and measure non-financial activities and monitor both internal and external consequences of the department/ organisation's social and commercial operations. It is an instrument of social accountability for an organisation. In other words, Social Audit may be defined as an in-depth scrutiny and analysis of the working of any public utility vis-à-vis its social relevance. Social Audit gained significance especially after the 73rd Amendment of the Constitution relating to Panchayati Raj Institutions.

The purpose of conducting Social Audit is not to find fault with the individual functionaries but to assess the performance in terms of social, environmental and community goals of the organisation. It is a way of measuring the extent to which an organisation lives up to the shared values and objectives it has committed itself to. It provides an assessment of the impact of an organisation's non-financial objectives through systematic and regular monitoring, based on the views of its stakeholders.

E-Government

E-Government is defined as the application of Information and Communication Technology (ICT) by government agencies to improve the efficiency, effectiveness, transparency and accountability of government. E-Government aims to make the interaction between government and citizens, government and business enterprises, and inter-agency relationships more friendly, convenient, transparent, and cost-effective.

E-Governance

The impact of information technology on Indian Administration finds manifestation in the Electronic governance, i.e. E-Governance. E-G is the application of ICTs to the processes of government functioning to accomplish simple, accountable, speedy, responsive and transparent governance. It aims to steer society and promote public interest. The essence of E-governance is to reach the beneficiary and ensure that the services intended to reach the desired individual has been met with. The E-Governance envisages multiple way transactions through widest networking between diverse social entities and all political and administrative activities.

E-G is not about simply automating their current ways of doing business. With the new tools of a networked society, government is not merely computerising existing government; it is transforming the existing government. E-G is the ICT enabled route to achieving good governance. It integrates people, processes information and technology for meeting governance goals. E-G represents a journey from passive information giving to active citizen involvement: Informing the Citizen; Listening to the citizen; Representing the citizen; Consulting the citizen and Engaging the citizen.

Case Study I

Mrs. X has recently cleared a central government exam and joined her dream job. During her first year, she began to notice that funds allocated to her department is being mismanaged and misallocated.

However, Mrs. X was most shocked by the hiring practices she witnessed at the office. Prospective applicants were supposed to take exams that were monitored by government employees. The results of these exams determined whether or not the applicants were appointed and what they were hired for. Mrs. X began to notice that those monitoring the exam were allowing applicants to cheat in the tests because the applicants had already been chosen for the job. Many of these pre-chosen applicants were friends of current employees.

Mrs. X reported what she witnessed to Mr. Y, the department's assistant secretary, who was second-in-command to the department head. Mr. Y told Mrs. X, "You heard nothing, you saw nothing, you do as you are told and you'll get your reward." Mrs. X was absolutely shocked; not only by the corruption, but that it was deliberately being swept under the carpet.

Mrs. X felt trapped. She really needed the job to take care of her parents, and she loved the job she was doing. On the other hand, she felt extremely uncomfortable in her work environment due to the culture of corruption.

Analyse the situation and different options available to Mrs. X. What should Mrs. X do to come out from this ethical dilemma?

Premise: The case presents an example of dilemma faced by Mrs. X along with the challenges posed by the mismanagement and misallocation of public funds, corruption and nepotism in hiring of employees.

This case comes under the following topic:

- Ethical Dilemma
- Challenges of Corruption
- Conscience as a Source of Ethical Guidance

Answer: Mrs. X is facing an ethical dilemma where she has to choose between being a woman of integrity having respect for professional ethics or she should go for her socio-economic well being and fulfil her responsibility towards the family.

The people who are involved in this situation and will be affected by the decision of Mrs. X are Mrs. X herself, her family, organisation in which she's working and candidates which have given the recruitment exam. Government and society at large will also be affected in the long run.

The different courses of action which Mrs. X can go for are:

- Leave the organisation and look for some other job.
- Adapt to the organisation by changing her moral system.
- Secretly leaking the information with the proof of corruption to the press.

- Try to change the malpractices in the organisation through legitimate means.

The first option that is leaving the organisation and get into some other job may be an easy way out for Mrs. X but is definitely not the right one. By doing this, she will run away from the problem instead of solving it. There is also no guarantee that she will not find corruption in the next organisation she will join. Such action will further encourage corrupt officers to indulge in nepotism as any voice against them can be easily curbed into silence. Such action will also go against the professional values of taking responsibility of changing the system for good and putting national interest over her personal interest. Such action will also go against the virtues of courage, patriotism and dedication towards her organisation and society at large. The present job is the dream job of Mrs. X and leaving it will not be that easy due to emotional attachment. Such action may also impact the resume of Mrs. X as she will not be able to give a valid reason for leaving the previous job.

The second option that is adapting to the organisation by ignoring or changing her moral values may work in the short run by giving financial benefits and job assurance but can be disastrous in the long run. Moral values take long time to integrate themselves with one's personality. It is not easy to change them in the short period of time. Thus, the present morals of Mrs. X i.e. honesty, loyalty, truthfulness, integrity and commitment towards the organisation will often come in conflict with the corrupt behaviour of Mrs. X. This will further lead to dissonance and unrest as incongruence will be there in thought and action.

Such transformation of Mrs. X will be harmful for the organisation and the society as it will lead to corruption and nepotism. Such action will violate the Fundamental Right of Equal Opportunity in employment to every candidate under Article 16 of our Constitution. It will also go against the spirit of Article 39(c) which calls for action to avoid concentration of wealth in few hands. Such action will be harmful for the majority of the people in the organisation as well as in the society as it will only benefit few corrupt officers and their political bosses. Thus, both utilitarianism and rights perspective go against this option of adapting to the corrupt activities of the organisation.

Such action will also lead to injustice to the candidates and the society as equal distribution of benefits and burdens in equal circumstances is not there. Benefits will be enjoyed by corrupt officials and rich candidates but the burden will fall upon those candidates who are honest or are not able to bribe the officials. Such action will further lead to social instability as people will discard public institutions as unfair and discriminatory.

Credibility and trustworthiness of government organisations among the citizens is a common good which is beneficial to everyone. Once it is destroyed, it will lead to chaos and anarchy in the society. Such action of adapting to the corrupt activities will also go against the ideals set by Mrs. X in her endeavour of life.

The third option that is secretly leaking the information to the press may solve the problem but will also have certain negative repercussions. Job of Mrs. X will remain safe without making any compromise on her part but it will be against the professional values of secrecy and loyalty towards the organisation. Secondly, it will bring criticism to the organisation as whole and will reduce the confidence of people in the recruitment process.

The fourth and the last option i.e. making efforts to remove malpractices in the organisation through legitimate means seem to be the most appropriate one. The government has enacted many laws like:

- The Right to Information Act (2005) and equivalent Acts in the states that require government officials to provide information requested by citizens or face punitive action.
- Indian Penal Code, 1860
- Prosecution Section of Income Tax Act,1961
- The Prevention of Corruption Act, 1988
- The Benami Transactions (Prohibition) Act, 1988 to prohibit benami transactions.
- Prevention of Money Laundering Act, 2002

These laws have considerably reduced corruption or at least have opened up avenues to redress grievance.

Through the inaction of the Whistle Blowers Protection Act, 2011 it establishes a mechanism to receive complaints relating to disclosure on any allegation of corruption or wilful misuse of power or wilful misuse of discretion against any public servant. It also seeks to inquire into such disclosure and provides adequate safeguards against victimization of the person making such complaint.

The Lokpal And Lokayuktas Act, 2013, received the assent of the President on the 1st January, 2014, which provides for the establishment of a body of Lokpal for the Union and Lokayukta for States to inquire into allegations of corruption against certain public functionaries. Whereas, India has ratified the United Nations Convention Against Corruption and the Government's commitment to clean and responsive governance has to be reflected in effective bodies to contain and punish acts of corruption; therefore, Parliament have enacted these laws for more effective implementation of the said Convention and to provide for prompt and fair investigation and prosecution in cases of corruption to ensure transparency and probity in governance.

The Directorate General of Income Tax Investigation, Central Vigilance Commission and Central Bureau of Investigation are certain organisations which deal with anti-corruption initiatives. Every department has its own internal mechanism to check corruption.

Thus, Mrs. X can also take help of these internal mechanisms to fight against corruption in her organisation. At first, she can approach to the head of the department along with the proof. If he also does not listen to the genuine complains then she can approach other anti-corruption agencies in the government.

Even if she just refuses to take bribe and stay firm on her decision, it will create fear in the mind of the wrong doers and it will force them to rethink their actions. She can also act as a whistleblower but only as a last resort because this will bring the incident in the open.

Though working on this option will not be easy for Mrs. X as she'll face hostile environment in her own organisation. But in the long term, this is the only way through which some concrete changes can be made. The success of Mrs. X will finally depend upon her courage, integrity and dedication towards a corruption free society.

Case Study II

Mr. X is the board member of State Industrial Development Corporation (SIDC). The organization is responsible for allotment of industrial plots and functions under the supervision of Managing Director (MD). The demand for plots far exceeds supply and offers scope for corruption. The chairman of SIDC is an influential politician who wants to gain from the situation. Unfortunately, MD decides to go along with the chairman, and enters into a nexus with him. To further their purposes, they create an opaque system for the allotment. Outwardly, the allotment of plots was based on first-come-first served basis, but there was no system of promptly recording the date and time of receipt of applications, especially using tamper proof computer software. The chairman assumed the power of discretionary allotments under the pretext of helping highly deserving or hard pressed entrepreneurs. By making arbitrary allotments of industrial plots and through other means the chairman and the MD made money. As a result, plots have been allotted to non-industrialists. Most of the out of turn allotments went to influential individuals. Many plots were much larger than the permissible size. No reliable records were available to show the application dates, or any reliable queue system for making allotments. Many allotments were made without consulting the Board. Mr. X is aware of all these developments. Under these circumstances, what course of action will be taken by Mr. X to check the ongoing corrupt practices?

This case comes under the following topics:

- Challenges of Corruption
- Transparency and Accountability
- Morality
- Ethical Concerns in Public Administration

Premise: The given case exemplifies the nexus between two highest officials of the organization. It highlights the corrupt practices adopted by them in order to make personal gain. Hence, the first and foremost question arises is that of transparency and accountability. Moreover, it highlights the dilemma of a board member to deal with the situation. Even after being aware of the corrupt practices adopted by the organizational heads, he is unable to take any direct action in the lack of evidence.

Answer: SIDC is an organization that creates industrial estates in acquired land by providing infrastructure such as roads, water supply, drainage, power, waste disposal, transport, parking lots, and bank branches and so on. Since there is a high demand of plots in comparison to the supply, the corruption is bound to happen. In this case also, MD and Chairman has entered into nexus and manipulated the allotment process for personal gains. Although Mr. X is aware of the corrupt practices ongoing in the organization, he is unable to intervene directly in lack of evidence.

It is quite natural that both the heads of the organization would resist the attempts of board members to introduce a system for plot allotment through public auctions. Under these circumstances Mr. X can take following actions:

- He should call the urgent meeting of all the board members and discuss the issue with them and arrive on a plan to tackle the issue, based on consensus.
- In order to gather the evidence, he along with the other Board members should meet some of the applicants who were denied plots. He should ask the applicants to seek information regarding allotment process and the name of those allotted the plots, by using Right to Information.
- With the help of these applicants Mr. X should instigate some dummy applications in order to reveal the truth. Once these applicants are allotted with the plot, the board members should immediately report the matter to the CVO (Chief Vigilance Officer) of the department concerned.
- He should recommend to CVO, an inquiry against the various irregularities that have been taken place in the organisations.
- In the meanwhile, he should also report the matter to anti-corruption police and conduct the raid in the residences of the chairman and MD. As most of the money earned by them is unaccounted, they must have been kept in cash. A raid by police may help in recovering large amounts of cash collected through unfair means.
- Once all this is over, as a long term measure Mr. X should recommend the government to empower the board members to make recommendation for removal of MD and Chairman, if found engaged in unfair practices, so that the issue can be dealt effectively if occurs in future again.

9

CONFLICT OF INTEREST & CONFLICT IN ADMINISTRATION

The Issues Discussed in this Unit

- Conflict of Interest in Government
- Office Duties
- The Virtue of Selfishness "The Objectivist Ethics"
- Conflict in Administration
- Spirit of Service
- Conflict of Interest in Overlapping & Intersectional Roles
- How to Resolve Conflict of Interest

Conflict of interest is an important concern which sometimes becomes the root cause for many of the ethical dilemmas as far as public life and government service is concerned. Though, Conflict of Interest has been discussed in other Units of this book but this Chapter is exclusively devoted for this aspect.

Conflicts of Interest in Government

What are Conflicts of Interest?

An individual play multiple roles in his life, they inherently possess many different interests and loyalties. At any given time, these interests may compete with each other. Such conflicts are a part of life and are unavoidable. Public officials, as stewards of the public trust, are required to put the public's interest before their own. Impropriety occurs when an officeholder, faced with conflicting interests, puts his or her personal or financial interest ahead of the public interest. In the simplest terms, the official reaps a monetary or other reward from a decision made in his or her public capacity.

The most common conflicts in local government happen when office-holders face a vote on real property/land use issues that affect their own holdings. Other examples include voting to grant a benefit to a company in which the officeholder owns stock or even to a non-profit organization on whose board the officeholder may sit.

When a conflict of interest is possible, an officeholder is expected to abstain from the discussion and the vote.

What do Conflicts of Interest have to do with Ethics?

Public service is always about protecting the common good, which may be defined as the common conditions that are important to the welfare of everyone-police, fire, parks, libraries, and other services. A public servant must always put the common good ahead of any personal, financial, or political benefit they might receive from a decision about such matters as where to situate a park or who should collect the garbage.

Also, conflicts of interest interfere with the basic ethical principle of fairness-treating everyone the same. A public official should not take unfair advantage of his or her position by voting on a matter that could benefit them at the expense of others.

Finally, conflicts of interest undermine trust. They make the public lose faith in the integrity of governmental decision-making processes.

Guidance

Conflicts of interest can occur in teaching, in research, in clinical practice and while in Public office. They may be obvious (and for that reason comparatively easy to identify and avoid) or extremely subtle. No code of ethics or brief "Issues in Ethics" statement can be framed that will specifically identify all of the forms such conflicts can take.

This Issues in Ethics statement attempts to do two things in a fairly general way: (1) give some guidance in identifying conflicts of interest and (2) suggest what should be done when a conflict is identified.

Identifying Conflicts of Interest

Since many conflicts of interest involve commercial interests or financial arrangements, all business practices, even commonly occurring business practices, should be evaluated to be sure that they will not introduce biases or preferences into the professional's clinical judgments or research interests. Generally, if a professional enjoys any unearned financial benefit, even a benefit as minor as a free box of lunch, conflict of interest may be suspected.

Personal and family relationships always arrange themselves along a continuum from the very close and intimate to the distant and detached, so it can be particularly difficult to recognize conflicts of interest that arise from personal friendships. Any time a pattern of preference emerges that cannot be explained on the basis of shared assessments, proven competence, or empirical facts, a conflict of interest may exist. Such patterns may occur in referrals, in the evaluation of employees, or in the assessments of students and fellow faculty members.

What to do about Conflict of Interest?

The proper responses fall into three categories: avoid, disclose, and recuse. Obviously, the best thing to do is avoid situations that give rise to conflicts of interest or that even appear to give rise to such conflicts. In commercial and financial matters, avoidance is by far the best strategy. This does not mean that absolutely no non-wage benefits may be accepted, but it does mean that some are prohibited and that all should be carefully scrutinized. Speech-language pathologists and audiologists should not accept gifts or benefits unless it can be clearly demonstrated that such gifts or benefits primarily contribute to the welfare of persons served professionally; do not reasonably appear to bias professional judgment; enhance one's professional knowledge and skills do not diminish the dignity or autonomy of the professions.

Disclosure is often associated with recusal. When one sits on a committee or a board that makes decisions about the advancement of others or about the distribution of resources and benefits to others, a conflict of interest may require that the professional withdraw or recuse herself or himself from a particular consideration or decision. This may occur because of the professional's financial interests in or personal ties to one or more of the parties being considered. By disclosing the nature of the association and by stepping out of the decision-making process, the professional ensures that any personal preferences or biases she or he may have will not unfairly influence the deliberations in favor of one candidate and against others.

Conflict of Interest Vis-a-Vis Morality

Is conflict of interest a governance issue or moral issue? Let's start at the beginning. What is a conflict of interest? It is defined as 'a conflict of interest occurs when an individual or organisation is involved in multiple interests, one of which could possibly corrupt the motivation for an act in the other.' Is this an accurate description?

Arguably, it is unwise to attempt to define a conflict of interest in absolute terms, for like many things in life, there is more than one definition. What is deemed to be a conflict of interest in one social or cultural context may be entirely appropriate in another. The same decision can be interpreted as entirely legitimate in a different setting. Take the example of nepotism in Africa. In Africa, where family bonds are highly valued, nepotism is a common practice, and an employee may face ostracism for not hiring a relative for a position at the firm. However, most Western-based multinationals actively discourage allowing personal relationships to influence an employee's business judgment.

Who decides what constitutes a conflict of interest in a business context? A company's board directs the policy, actions and affairs of the organisation. The UK Corporate Governance Code (2010) (formerly the Combined Code) states that corporate governance is about what the board of a company does, including how it sets the values of the company: "the board should set the company's values and standards and ensure that its obligations to its shareholders and others are understood and met." The most common way that a large corporate set out the company's values and standards is through an ethics policy and/or a code of ethics, which aims to govern employees' day-to-day conduct. Frameworks for dealing with a conflict of interest are normally included in such guidance documents.

It is without doubt that guidance for employees is necessary, especially since the definition of a conflict of interest will vary with context. Thus, providing a framework based on the company's ethical values for employees to refer to, will help to ensure consistency in employee's decision-making across the organisation when it comes to dealing with a conflict of interest. And it goes without saying that training for staff on the framework (and the company's values) is required to help them identify, manage, and resolve potential conflicts of interest. This should be coupled with a broader awareness of why it is important to manage those conflicts.

But no framework and no amount of training can cover every potential conflict of interest or guarantee that every employee will make the 'right' decision, by the company's standards.

Are Conflicts of Interest Not Moral Dilemmas? And Are People's Morals Not Inherently Different?

There is often an expectation by senior management that many conflicts of interest are avoidable; an expectation that is not shared by experience. Conflicts of interest are not necessarily of our own creation. It could be argued that in fact the conflicts that employees encounter is the product of the structures implemented at a more senior level. Normal human relationships can be transformed by individuals' professional roles into a source of conflict, regardless of whether they do in fact influence the individual, or just create the perception of influence. But we are very often influenced, and driven to act in certain ways, unconsciously.

Having a framework to govern employees behaviour when it comes to conflict of interests shouldn't stifle people's ability to make their own decisions. But trusting the ethical judgement of employees may not fit well with effective governance of a company. The middle ground is hard to find. Perhaps conflicts of interest are such a moral maze that it cannot be governed with a framework. A supportive and open culture, which encourages employees to understand how their relationships may be perceived so that they may be transparent about their interests, may be the middle ground we are striving for.

Conflict of Interest Vis-a-Vis Ethicality

Conflict of interest is a complex issue that reflect structural problems of any uncivilized society. It relates with several facets including socio-cultural, political, and administrative. If government officials lack ethical immunity in enhancing values and cultural systems then they lost consciences to protect public interest. This creates an ethical issue. When government officials lack in ethical standards, it creates shortcomings in performance and services to the citizens.

The common phenomena are the abuses of power for interfering in development policies, projects and economic activities. The abuses of political and administrative power for self-interest whether for individual, group or party, have damaged public and private sector organizations, public and society. It also destroys future opportunities for sustaining long-term socio-economic development.

Thus, it is prime time to raise public awareness among agencies concerned, both local and international communities and to seek mutual efforts to prevent and protect the negative impacts arising from the conflict of interest. It is, indeed, an urgent task of policy makers, government leaders, advocates, and all partners to rethink and renovate our consciousness with new values and cultural framework. Enhancing governance system of political and administrative organizations and promoting ethical standard among key actors to ensure their transparency and accountability for the sake of public interest is on top priority. Agendas with public forum both at national, regional and global level are necessary inputs for improving better understanding on conflict of interest. Policy measures on values and cultural reform, and specific laws should be seriously addressed through close collaboration among public, private and civil sectors.

Michael McDonald defines the term "conflict of interest" as "a situation in which a person, such as a public official, an employee, or a professional, has a private or personal interest sufficient to appear to influence the objective exercise of his or her official duties."

Based on McDonald, there are three key elements: 1) a private or personal interest–often a financial interest; 2) official duty--quite literally the duty you have because you have an office or act in an official capacity; and 3) conflicts of interest interfere with professional responsibilities in a specific way, namely, by interfering with objective professional judgment. He emphasizes that conflict of interest is an ethical issue.

Whenever the official lacks ethical standard there is potential risk for underlying conflict of interest.

Conflict of interest typologies can be considered the work of Canadian political scientist Ken Kernaghan and John Langford in their book, 'The Responsible Public Servant'. They list seven categories:

- **Self-dealing:** Using official position to secure a contract for a private consulting company of your own. Another instance is using government position to get a summer job for your daughter.
- **Accepting benefits:** Bribery is one example; substantial [non-token] gifts are another. For example, you are the purchasing agent for your department and you accept a case of liquor from a major supplier.
- **Influence peddling:** The professional solicits benefits in exchange for using her influence to unfairly advance the interest of a particular party.

- **Using your employer's property for private advantage:** This could be as blatant as stealing office supplies for home use. Or it might be as a bit subtler, say, using software which is licensed to your employer for private work of your own.
- **Using confidential information:** While working for a private client, you learn that the client is planning to buy land in your region. You quickly rush out buy land in your region.
- **Outside employment or moonlighting:** An example would be setting up a business on the side that is in direct competition with your employer. Another case would be taking on so many outside clients that you don't have time and energy to devote your regular employer. In combination with influence peddling, it might be that a professional employed in the public service sells private consulting services to an individual with the assurance that they will secure benefits from government: "if you use my company, I am sure that you will pass the environmental review."
- **Post-employment:** A person who resigns from public or private employment and goes into business in the same area. For example, a former public servant sets up a practice lobbying the former department in which she employed.

The factors contributing to a conflict of interest can be considered as five main components. First, the individual factor which comprises of personal values, belief, attitudes and behaviour. Second, the economic factor which involves official's incomes and indebtedness. Third, the social factor such as societal values, moral and ethical framework, position, patronage system and nepotism, and roll model of top leaders and supervisors. Fourth, legal factor including rules and procedures: some pitfalls are outdated laws with legal loopholes, lack of rules of law and auditing system. Fifth, the environmental factors, such as organizational culture, expectations and traditional practices of government officials encapsulating the phenomenon of Conflict of Interest.

What Ethical Dilemmas Do Conflicts of Interest Present?

Many times, government officials honestly believe that they are not being unduly influenced by their personal stake in an issue.

They may feel, to the contrary, that their interest in the matter gives them special insight into the subject. A city council member who ran on a platform of revitalizing the city market, for example, may feel entirely justified in supporting measures to improve the area, even if part of the benefit of such improvement might go to their own business. They might argue that they understand the problems of a market because they own one. They might claim, further, that their constituents elected them specifically to represent this interest.

But conflict of interest laws prevents such partiality. First, it's almost impossible for individuals to determine whether they are being fair when their self-interest is involved. Also, as the Institute for Local Self-Government puts it, "The law is aimed at the perception, as well as the reality, that a public official's personal interests may influence a decision." Even the appearance of impropriety undermines the public's faith that the process is fair.

Another common misconception about conflicts of interest is that officeholders are absolved of their responsibility merely by being transparent about their stake in the issue. It is not sufficient for government officials to make conflicts public. They must take themselves out of the decision-making process altogether.

This includes discussion and debate as well as actual voting. Abstention is only half the requirement. A public official is also expected to refrain from public pronouncements and private arm twisting on decisions in which he or she has an interest.

Note, also, that the interest may be personal as well as financial. Helping one's fraternal order to obtain rent-free space in a public building is a form of conflict of interest, especially if it improves one's standing in the organization. Being elected president of a community group because of such favors might prove to be in an officeholder's personal and political interest when the next election rolls around. Conversely, public office should not be used to punish one's personal and political enemies. Voting no on your annoying neighbor's reasonable zoning waiver request is another form of putting private ahead of public interest.

Ethics, Morality and Conflict of Interest

What is the relation between Ethics, Morality and Conflict of Interest? We will talk about how Ethics, Morality and Conflict of Interest are interlinked.

Bandfield (1967), in his work on The Moral Basis of a Backward Society, studied the cultural conditions and moral standard then concluded that individual may not lose his morality when household or institution uphold public spiritedness or enlightened self-interest. He also pointed out that amoral society member tend to neglect public interest and always seek for self-interest.

In Moral Hazards of an Executive, Norris (1989) addressed on ethics and morality of executive and emphasized that integrity and loyalty are preamble for organizational achievement. One key issue is whether the executive's decision is made for the sake of public or of inner group. This reflects the principles of democratic morality which is in practice that executive must be strongly concerned about public values. It also involves the moral control of reality and justice in decision-making in particular situation. The protection of truth is an indicator testing integrity of any executive. As for utilitarianism, the principle "the greatest good for the greatest number" may or may not be responsive to people's expectations. Executive often face moral hazards with ethical issues and conflicting circumstance. At least one might be concerned on people awareness and take actions for maintaining common benefits for the public.

Conflict of interest is one type of corruption when we consider corruption as an action which violates rules of law, loss of loyalty and integrity, and lack of moral standard. It is the abuse of public office for private gain and it generates social equity problems that imply inequality so-called distributive justice (White, 1993).

Thai political scientist Somporn Saengchai (1985) classified corruption based on Heidenheimer (1978) into three main types:

1. **White corruption-** Corruption which the public visualizes as a common thing and allows it to happen since it has no serious effect to society.
2. **Grey corruption-** In this type of corruption the public is still

unclear about its processes and impacts. Academics think it is a serious issue but the public seems to be reluctant.

3. **Black corruption-** This type of corruption society and all parties concerned judge a wrong conduct that requires to be punished in accordance with legal framework.

Conflict of interest, thus, lies in the gray area of corruption (Anechioco and Jacobs). It relates with ethical standard and social values. Each society has different values system in judging human actions. Some people may not perceive conflict of interest as a misconduct action but for civilized society one could not bear for a violation of moral and ethical behavior.

Conflict of interest also arises when an individual has to decide between official duties, public interest, and personal or self-interest. When this conflict arises in ethical terms, then the individual must resolve the conflict depending on the situation he/she is in.

First, we will understand the various facets of conflicts- Official duties, Public interest and personal interest.

Official Duties

Official Duty Activities are those activities performed by an employee as part of, or an extension of, regular official responsibilities.

Principles of Ethical Conduct While Enacting Official Duties -

- To ensure that every citizen can have complete confidence in the integrity of the Government.
- Each employee shall respect and adhere to the fundamental principles of ethical service as implemented in regulations.
- Public service is a public trust, requiring employees to place loyalty to the Constitution, the laws, and ethical principles above private gain.
- Employees shall not hold financial interests that conflict with the conscientious performance of duty.
- Employees shall not engage in financial transactions using nonpublic Government information or allow the improper use of such information to further any private interest.

- An employee shall not, except pursuant to such reasonable exceptions as are provided by regulation, solicit or accept any gift or other item of monetary value from any person or entity seeking official action from, doing business with, or conducting activities regulated by the employee's agency, or whose interests may be substantially affected by the performance or nonperformance of the employee's duties.
- Employees shall put forth honest effort in the performance of their duties.
- Employees shall make no unauthorized commitments or promises of any kind purporting to bind the Government.
- Employees shall not use public office for private gain.
- Employees shall act impartially and not give preferential treatment to any private organization or individual.
- Employees shall protect and conserve Federal property and shall not use it for other than authorized activities.
- Employees shall not engage in outside employment or activities, including seeking or negotiating for employment, that conflict with official Government duties and responsibilities.
- Employees shall disclose waste, fraud, abuse, and corruption to appropriate authorities.
- Employees shall satisfy in good faith their obligations as citizens, including all just financial obligations, especially those such as Federal, State, or local taxes that are imposed by law.
- Employees shall adhere to all laws and regulations that provide equal opportunity for all Americans regardless of race, color, religion, sex, national origin, age, or handicap.
- Employees shall endeavor to avoid any actions creating the appearance that they are violating the law or the ethical standards promulgated pursuant to this order.
- Employees are expected to work cohesively with one another. Numerous policies at all agency levels prohibit harassment, sexual harassment, corruption, and violations of common personnel policies.
- Some government functions have a higher threshold of duty due to the importance placed on the activity. For instance, the fiduciary duty of fiscal officers creates a higher level of

responsibility to protect funds and assets of a government department from unnecessary loss and to make sure assets are used for the right purpose. This role includes oversight and reporting problems found with budgeting, accounting, procurement and contracting.

- Managers also carry more responsibility with the duty to manage their staff and be responsible for their actions and output. And they are expected to be the daily control points for leadership, implementing broad policy on a regular basis.

Every government employee is expected to maintain the honesty, integrity and impartiality of programs. The last element in particular may be a harder challenge at the higher levels due to the influence of politics. However, all government employees are still required to maintain a truthful operation in their particular function.

There is also a common ethics expectation that employees avoid and do not involve themselves in fraud or abuse of government programs, criminal activity, or felony activity in their personal life. If discovered, many policies authorize employee demotion or termination from the organization.

Government employees are held to specified standards that are common in all government agencies, regardless of government level. This expectation for good behavior and cooperation is critical to protect the agency and the government taxpayer funds used for operations. Failure to follow such duties and responsibilities interferes with the organization function of agencies and, when discovered, the employee involved is corrected or removed. All employees, whether management or staff, are expected to adhere to these rules.

Before going to terms like 'Personal interest' and 'Public interest', it is important for us to know, what exactly is 'interest'? How does interest characterize the personal and public persona of an individual?

The Virtue of Selfishness "The Objectivist Ethics"

The term "interests" is a wide abstraction that covers the entire field of ethics. It includes the issues of: man's values, his desires, his goals and their actual achievement in reality. A man's "interests" depend on the kind of goals he chooses to pursue, his choice of goals depends on his desires, his desires depend on his values–and, for a rational man, his values depend on the judgment of his mind.

Desires (or feelings or emotions or wishes or whims) are not tools of cognition; they are not a valid standard of value, nor a valid criterion of man's interests. The mere fact that a man desires something does not constitute a proof that the object of his desire is good, nor that its achievement is actually to his interest.

To claim that a man's interests are sacrificed whenever a desire of his is frustrated–is to hold a subjectivist view of man's values and interests. Which means: to believe that it is proper, moral and possible for man to achieve his goals, regardless of whether they contradict the facts of reality or not. Which means: to hold an irrational or mystical view of existence. Which means: to deserve no further consideration.

Public Interest

Discussions of public interest in public administration have generally been concerned with efficiency and economy. The underlying idea has been to see that administration becomes result-oriented and productive by spending least resources.

Alongside this efficient approach, there has been a growing concern about what may broadly be called 'morality' or 'ethics' in public administrative governments having a universalistic character. It has to serve the common good without making any sort of distinction between man and man. Efficiency in governments has thus a moral tone. It is against this background that a general framework for the functioning of public administration is formulated.

The concern for public interest in public administration can be traced to a variety of reasons.

Indeed, the members of the bureaucracy constitutes a power elite. They are likely to take decision in self-interest or under pressure from powerful interest groups. In either case, public interest may be in jeopardy. Another argument has been that the bureaucracy is a mindless machine that turns out decisions mechanically. The rule-bound administration may look very neat and tidy, but it may not be able to serve the winder cause of public interest in public administration. Still another argument can be derived from Herbert Simon's discussion on administrative decision making.

According to Simon, administrative decision is often based on ground other than those of efficiency and economy. Social and psychological factors greatly influence the way decisions are taken by the decision-makers. The importance of sense of public interest as an ethical commitment in public administration assumes significance in this context.

As it has been very aptly commented upon:

"The most frequently hidden agenda in the deliberations of public servants is the effects of substantive or procedural decision upon the personal lives and fortunes of those deliberations and yet the very call to serve a large public often evoke a degree of selflessness and nobility on the part of public servants beyond the capacity of cynics to recognize or to believe. Man's feet may wallow in the bog of self-interest, but his eyes and ears are strangely attuned to calls from the mountaintop. As moral philosophy has insistently claimed, there is a fundamental moral distinction between the propositions: 'I want this because it serves my interest' and I want this because, it is right.

Philosophies of public interest in public administration fall broadly into four classes:

- The very intuitionist philosophy seeks to justify existing practices by pointing out that in conflicting situations; the administrative chooses an alternative by intuition. In other words, what the administrative actually does is an intuitionist solution which seems to him the right course of action under given circumstances. This philosophy does not provide any guideline for action, nor does it spell out an explicit theory of public interest in public administration.
- Perfectionism, the second philosophical school, views public interest from the standpoint of promotion of excellence in all spheres of social activities. Public resources, according to this school of thought, should be spent in such a way that the best members of the society benefit most from the expenditure. Thus conceived, perfectionism is an elitist philosophy and obviously anti-egalitarian; as such it is not compatible with democratic theory.

- Utilitarianism, as propounded by Jeremy Bentham and John Stuart Mill, has been the most influential school of thought in the determination of public interest in public administration. According to utilitarian philosophy, the public interest is served when a public policy makes everyone slightly better off even though it makes a few individuals slightly worse off. Under the utilitarian calculus, public interest is judged by the augmentation of the net balance of social satisfaction.
- The fourth major ethical framework for public interest in public administration can be derived from the Theory of Justice as propounded by the philosopher, John Rawls, in this monumental work on the subject. Rawls's principles are essentially an elaboration of the Anglo-Saxon concept of fairness and these come close to what is called in economics 'Pareto optimality'. Rawls suggests two basic principles of justice to test public interest in public administration. One of these is that "each person is to have an equal right to the most extensive basic liberty compatible with a similar liberty for others".

The other principle postulates that social and economic inequalities are to be arranged so that they are both

(a) reasonably expected to be to everyone's advantage and

(b) attached to positions and offices open to all.

In case of conflict between these two principles, the second principle is expected to prevail and give way to the first. Rational decision-making in public administration has to have an ethical framework. The principles of John Rawls provide an operating logic for the determination of public interest by the decision-makers.

The intuitionist philosophy justifies status quo and is of very little help in actual administrative situations. The perfectionist philosophy favours excellence at the expense of social equality. it is patently anti-democratic. Utilitarian calculus has the merit of emphasizing total social good but it also accepts the position that few may be worse off. Compared to all these philosophical positions, the formulation of Rawls seems much more balanced and, as rightly observed by Nicholas Henry, it represents a workable way for determining the public interest by public administrators.

Components of Public Interest

Acting in the public interest has two separate components:

Objectives and outcomes – that the objectives and outcomes of the decision-making process are in the public interest, and

Process and procedure – that the process adopted and procedures followed by decision-makers in exercising their discretionary powers are in the public interest, which would include:

1. Complying with applicable law (both in letter and spirit)
2. Carrying out functions fairly and impartially, with integrity and professionalism
3. Complying with the principles of procedural fairness/natural justice
4. Acting reasonably
5. Ensuring proper accountability and transparency
6. Exposing corrupt conduct or serious maladministration
7. Avoiding or properly managing situations where their private interests conflict or might reasonably be perceived to conflict with the impartial full-filment of their official duties, and
8. Acting apolitically in the performance of their official functions (not applicable to elected public officials).

What is Not in the Public Interest?

In some ways, it is easier to distinguish the public interest from what is not. For example, the "public interest" can be distinguished from:

- **Private interests** – of a particular individual or individuals (although there are certain private 'rights' viewed as being in the public interest)
- **Personal interests** – of the decision-maker (including the interests of members of their direct families, relatives, business associates, etc) – public officials must always act in the public interest ahead of their personal interests and must avoid situations where their private interests conflict, might potentially conflict, or might reasonably be seen to conflict with the impartial fulfilment of their official duties
- **Personal curiosity** – i.e., what is of interest to know, that which gratifies curiosity or merely provides information or amusement

(to be distinguished from something that is of interest to the public in general)

- **Personal opinions** – for example, the political or philosophical views of the decision-maker, or considerations of friendship or enmity
- **Parochial interests** – i.e., the interests of a small or narrowly defined group of people with whom the decision-maker shares an interest or concern, and
- **Partisan political interests** – for example, the avoidance of political/government or agency embarrassment.

These can be categorised as motivation type issues that focus on the private, personal or partisan interests of the decision-maker (and possibly also those of third parties).

Personal Interest

Personal interest can also be called as self-interest. Self-interest generally refers to a focus on the needs or desires (interests) of the self. A number of philosophical, psychological, and economic theories examine the role of self-interest in motivating human action.

In philosophy, Philosophical concepts concerned with self-interest include:

- **Enlightened self-interest,** a philosophy which states that acting to further the interests of others also serves one's own self-interest.
- **Ethical egoism,** the ethical position that moral agents ought to do what is in their own self-interest.
- **Hedonism,** the school of ethics which argues that pleasure is the only intrinsic good.
- **Epicureanism,** a philosophical system related to hedonism.
- **Individualism,** a philosophy stressing the worth of individual selves.
- **Rational egoism,** the position that all rational actions are those done in one's self-interest.

One general challenge is getting people to act properly. What counts as proper behavior is, of course, a rather contentious matter. However, it seems reasonable to believe that at the most basic level harming others is not proper behavior.

It can be argued that personal interest will motivate people to act properly. The stock argument (which is based on Hobbes, Locke, and Smith) is that a rational person will realize that behaving badly is not in his personal interest because the consequences to him will be negative.

Naturally, a person might be tempted to act badly if she thinks she can avoid these consequences, which is why it is rather important to make sure that these consequences are rather difficult to avoid. In addition to this concern, there are also other concerns about personal interest or self-interest as a regulating factor on bad behavior.

First, for self-interest to be a regulating factor, a person's self-interest must coincide with acting correctly. If a person's self-interest (or what he believed is his self-interest) goes against acting correctly, then he will be inclined to act incorrectly. Not surprisingly, various philosophers have tried to argue that what is truly in a person's self-interest is to act correctly. While there are some good arguments (such as those presented by Socrates) for this view, there are also good arguments that this is not the case. Naturally, from a purely practical standpoint the trick is to get people to believe that their self-interest coincides with not acting badly.

Second, even if it is assumed that it is in a person's interest to act correctly this will not motivate a person to act correctly unless a person knows what is in her self-interest. While it is tempting to assume that a person automatically knows what is in her self-interest, this need not be the case. After all, a person can think that something is in her best interest, yet be mistaken about this. A person might be misled by his emotions, confused or wrong about the facts (to give but a few examples).

Third, even if it is assumed that a person knows what is in her self-interest and that it is in her self-interest to act correctly, there is still the question of whether the person will choose to act in accord with her self-interest or not. To use a simple example, a person might know that exercising is in her self-interest, but be unable to stick with exercising. Roughly put, a person might have knowledge but lack the will or motivation to act on this knowledge.

Thus, self-interest can play a role in regulating behavior- provided that it is in accord with correct behavior, the person has knowledge and the will to act on this knowledge.

Conflict in Administration

Conflict in administration is arising due to changing dynamics in Public Administration. Public Administration must deal with many issues as the political, social and economic face of the country changes. Because administration of public programs requires attention to the ethics and culture of society, it must change as the government policies change. Here are six issues that create conflict in administration:

1. Political Environment

In India, there are three tier systems of government- Central, State and Local government. Public Policy is mainly formulated at the Central level. With many States enacting their own laws according to their own requirements, these rules and regulations comes into conflict with each other if they happen to impinge on each others domain.

2. Contracting / Networked Governance

Responding to a demand for more frugality in programs, administrators have turned to private contractors. That change has had the opposite effect in many cases. Services that are part of the governance tend to be more responsible toward its policies and limitations. Private contractors have tended to "play by other rules." This has resulted in numbers of problems such as exemption to auditing by the private players. Also, in name of providing contracts, tender is given to one's own relatives or family members.

Also, contracting has resulted in budget over-runs and in outrageous user charges. Still, the theory that competition may spur some more efficient use of resources may prove true in some instances. The challenge seems to be in deciding which things to privatize.

3. Technology

With the advent of technology, the administration too had to revamp itself to encourage more accountability and transparency. Even if public services did not want to implement technology, they would have no choice. Every other sector has turned to data-oriented operations and public service and non-profits must as well in order to interface with them. The issue is with organizational and personal security. In order to maintain a secure database someone must have the expertise to administer the computer programs and that demands additional and more specialized personnel.

4. Social Equity

The challenge presented by this issue is to make public organizations representative of the social and cultural environment in which they exist. In simpler terms, public housing organizations in minority areas must include a proportionate number of minority members in the administration. That not only applies to racial issues, but to gender and to sexual orientation. However, organizations founded in this manner may encounter conflicts between members and cultural groups. In each case, while recognizing the rights of the majority, organizations must protect minorities.

5. Transparency

Politicians and Public administrators must have a personal and a public opinion. That is, there are times when administrators of public programs act contrary to their own convictions for the good of the organization. There are also times when organizations are not forthcoming about some actions because programs deemed necessary would not be well received or understood by the public that is funding the organization. The trend toward transparency means that administrators must walk a thin line between full public disclosure and having some clandestine policies. This transparency also affects other issues like the contracting problems and the inclusion of minorities in appropriate numbers.

Of course, there are other issues to be dealt with, but these are representative of the difficulties governments face in implementing civil programs for the benefit of the public. The face of Public Administration must always change to mirror the government and culture that houses it.

6. Inhouse Conflicts

Conflict may arise as a result of different needs and interests of service users and public administration as their provider. When customers wish to achieve their goals, and note that service provider (civil servant) stands in the way, it usually leads to conflict. Such conflicts can be personal (disagreement between the user and service provider), communicational (language difficulties) or organizational (blurred boundaries of service responsibilities). Conflicts within the organizational units in the public administration can have short and long-term consequences for the whole administration.

Dissatisfaction and emotional exhaustion of employees, increased stress, poor working environment, reduced creativity and service efficiency are just some of the symptoms that occur when the conflict is not managed properly. The consequences of conflicts with service users can also have a bad effect on the organizational units of public administration (departments, divisions, departments).

If we are not ready to adequately respond to these conflicts, or stop them before they fully develop, this will decrease performance and service delivery. To be able to efficiently respond to conflicts, employees need essential new knowledge and access to helpful new tools.

The key question is whether conflicts are desirable or not. The answer depends on how individuals react when they find themselves in a conflict situation. It can be both positive and negative. The misconception is that conflict is always anegative but properly managed conflicts can often result in positive outcomes.

Conflict Management

Conflict management in administration is an arduous process. When different stakeholders are involved in conflict in a dynamic environment then the decision maker should evolve itself to resolve the differences. When implementing new solutions, it is important to be careful not to build walls among employees and employees in public administration and the users of its services. Efficiency of public administration depends on the approach and efficiency of conflict management. The prevailing view is that conflicts are neither good nor bad. However, their effects can be good or bad depending on the knowledge about managing conflict situations.

There are different approaches to conflict management that result in different effects. In order to effectively manage conflicts in the public administration, it is necessary to know the conflict situation, related parties to the conflict, to know the time when the conflict arose and the time available for conflict resolution. The best way to manage conflicts is avoiding them if at all possible.

The most difficult thing is to manage conflict in which both the sides are by no means giving up their positions, convinced that they are absolutely right. One needs to know about communication methods and how to stop the escalation of the conflict. One needs to know how to intervene in crisis situations and how to manage conflict.

The knowledge base about conflicts that we here propose and new software tools that can help all employees and all those who participate in resolving conflicts. If we effectively resolve conflict situations, we will have a reduction in the effects of stress and overcome unpleasant situations.

A good preparation and training are necessary for efficient conflict solutions in the service process. The new software tools based on the knowledge bases and the Semantic Web can enable a simpler and more effective training and better knowledge of conflict resolution. If one does not possess adequate knowledge or if one cannot quickly find them to efficiently respond to the conflict, one will face obstacles.

Consequently, the conflict can be painful or even devastating for the participants in the service system. The most that can be provided is that the public administration is seen as a chance for better service and on the positive side of conflict management. In order to efficiently manage a conflict, one should be able to: identify the causes of conflict, recognize and manage their emotions in a conflict situation, to achieve compliance with different interlocutors, take multiple perspectives in order to gain a better overview of the situation. To effectively manage conflict, one must know the very process of conflict. Dealing with the management of conflicts begins from the moment it has been noticed. Noticing, requests information on the cause of the conflict, the participants, their experiences, beliefs, behaviors and perceptions. The analysis afterwards should give a clearer picture of the conflict situation and all its elements. The key role of conflict management in public administration is in the hands of its managerial staff. The behavior of the participants in the conflict depends on knowledge of all the necessary information. Conflicts are a natural part of every work or service environment and their appearance results in reduced labor productivity.

Thus, it is better for an individual to resolve conflicts rationally, observing all the situations and analyzing all the alternatives. Decision makers should choose the best possible alternative which minimizes the conflict and keep all the parties involved in the conflict satisfied.

Spirit of Service

Dr. Martin Luther King, Jr. once said: "Everyone can be great because everyone can serve. You don't have to have a college education to serve. You don't even have to make your subjects and verbs agree to serve. You only need a heart full of grace."

Social service does not mean merely going out into the streets and cleaning them. Whatever work you are engaged in, whatever duties you have to perform as an official or an employee, to do your duties efficiently and with diligence and devotion is also Seva (social service).

Those in authority who discharge their functions well enough to justify the salary they receive are rendering real service. But such persons are rare. Employees agitate for more wages but do not render commensurate service to justify the incomes they receive. Disinterested service will ennoble man and raise his stature. It endows man with the intelligence and the skills required refining human nature. Doing one's duty diligently is not enough. Men have to cultivate other qualities like love, sympathy, fairness, compassion and forgiveness. Only when one has these qualities will he be able to render dedicated service. It is the sense of dualism---of "mine" and "thine"--which accounts for all the joys and sorrows, likes and dislikes experienced by man. This dualism is rooted in selfishness, which makes one think that as long as he is all fight, it does not matter what happens to the world. Such a self-centered person, who regards his body, his wealth and his family as all that matter to him, looks upon truth as untruth and the false as true. To get rid of this deep-seated malaise, men have to engage themselves in service. They have to realise that the body has been given not to serve one's own interests but to serve others. Service is an expression of gratitude to society. Service should not be done in a spirit of condescension or to achieve some ulterior selfish objective. Not recognising the sacredness and purifying power of service, people hesitate to embark on social service.. It should not be imagined that one is promoting the well-being of the nation by one's service. One should realise that he is bettering himself by rendering service. Service should proceed from an awareness of what one owes to society. One's name and fame, all the comforts one enjoys, are derived from society. One finds full-filment in society. That being the case, if one does not serve society, whom else can he serve? Sheer gratitude demands that one should serve society which is the source of all benefits enjoyed by man. Men without gratitude are worse than wild animals. What are required for service are not money and materials. A loving heart is the first requisite. All service done without a love-filled heart is as dry as dust. Fill your hearts with love. When you are filled with conceit, everything looks out of shape. When you are immersed in the Spirit, everything looks good and beautiful. Forgetting this higher destiny of man, people are ceasing to be human.

Example of Spirit in Service in Indian Context

The esoteric teaching about the true nature of the jivatma and its eternal relationship with the Lord as that of servant and master is skillfully interwoven in the Ramayana. The jivatma who realises the significance of this bond is inspired with the yearning to serve the Lord who is the embodiment of all auspicious qualities that the human mind can recognise – perfection, compassion, prowess, goodness, etc, and even much more beyond all these. Lakshmana, Vibhishana and Bharata, for instance, seek Rama's feet knowing that their true worth is fully realised only when involved in selfless service to the Lord.

Each of them desires this cherished reward of acceptance by the Lord to serve Him in their respective subservient roles. The spirit of service inherent in Lakshmana is revealed when he literally clasps Rama's feet and seeks permission to serve Him and

Sita during their stay in the forest. He promises that by doing so there will be no taint to the dharma He upholds. His desire to serve Rama will be fulfilled and He will also benefit by his service. The way shown by Vibhishana is also somewhat similar. He is frank about his position. "Ravana treated me as a vile slave and put me to shame before all. His sharp words pierced my heart through and through. So, I have cast behind me wife and child, wealth and luxury, and sought refuge with Rama."

Vibhishana teaches the way by which the hurdles that prevent one's efforts from seeking refuge with the Lord have to be overcome. Bharata, in his state of total renunciation, is the very embodiment of nobility and is steadfast in his service to the Lord in thought, word and deed. The privilege to serve the Lord has to be diligently earned by each one through selfless love, devotion and admiration for Him.

These characters truly imbibe the spirit of service. To serve their Lord, they sacrificed their own happiness, wealth and luxury. The spirit of service was performed, not to attain any material gains but to achieve fulfillment and self-actualization.

Conflict of Interest in Overlapping & Intersectional Roles

This topic has been discussed in a question format.

The Question:

In today's world there are complexities of 'cross-holdings' and different roles played by a single organization/person. This results in conflict of interest becoming a regular phenomenon. Discuss this with live and real-life scenarios. Elaborate on the ways to negotiate with such happenings.

Can moral dilemmas arising out of such indispensable conflict of interest could ever be resolved on the canvass of consciousness of human soul?

Conflict of interest can be seen in varied fields and professions. It has pervaded most aspects of the society. For us to understand, what is conflict of interest we will try to understand that with some live examples. These examples will show us how conflict of interest has permeated, either in an exposing or subtle manner.

Conflict of Interest in Providing Justice

In USA, before the Supreme Court returned from its summer break, Justice Neil Gorsuch, the court's newest member, attended a luncheon at the Trump International Hotel, where he was to give the keynote address. The location of the speech attracted the attention of dozens of protesters and a number of ethics watchdogs, who noted the apparent conflict of interest posed by Justice Gorsuch–a Trump nominee–keynoting an event at a hotel whose revenue goes in part to President Trump. That arrangement was bad enough on its own. But there was another potential conflict of interest created by Justice Gorsuch's speaking engagement–and it highlights the ongoing ethical issues that threaten the credibility of US's highest court.

That same morning that Justice Gorsuch gave his speech, the Supreme Court announced that it would hear Janus v. AFSCME. This is a case that would have determined whether public sector unions–which represent teachers, nurses, firefighters and police in states and cities across the country–can collect fees from all employees in the workplaces they represent. Justice Gorsuch was widely expected to deliver the court's deciding vote to strip unions of this ability. A decision along these lines would seriously undercut workers' freedom to have a real voice to speak out and fight for higher wages, better benefits and improved working conditions.

Here's the rub. Justice Gorsuch's speech at the Trump hotel was hosted by the Fund for American Studies. And who funds the Fund of American Studies? It is the Charles Koch Foundation and the Bradley Foundation. The Charles Koch Foundation is dedicated to promoting limited government, free markets and weaker unions; and the Bradley Foundation has worked for decades to, in their own words, "reduce the size and power of public sector unions." In fact, the Bradley Foundation helped pay the litigation expenses for Janus–the case in which Justice Gorsuch is likely to be the deciding vote. Think about that: Just as the ink was drying on the court's announcement that it would hear Janus, Justice Gorsuch was off to hobnob with some of the biggest supporters for one side of this important case–the side that wants to deny workers the freedom to build a future that doesn't hang by a thread at the whim of a few billionaires.

The Code of Conduct for United States Judges requires judges to recuse themselves when certain potential conflicts arise, such as in cases in which the judge, the judge's spouse or the judge's minor children have a financial interest or in cases in which the judge has a "personal bias or prejudice" against or for any party in the case. But those rules don't apply to Supreme Court justices.

In fact, Supreme Court justices are the only federal judges who are not bound by a formal code of conduct. The reason is that the Supreme Court of United States is the only court created under Article III of the Constitution of the US's while the lower courts are created by Congress. Thus, it's sufficient that the justices consult the code when determining their ethical duties and voluntarily abide by rules on a case-by-case basis.

But the argument is exactly backward. When an ethical cloud hangs over the court, its fundamental integrity is compromised. At a time when polls have found that fewer than half of Americans approve of the way the court is handling its job, the justices ought to be making every effort to show that their personal integrity is above reproach.

To begin rebuilding American's confidence in the court, it is time to establish a formal code of conduct. As the nation's highest court, the Supreme Court has an even greater duty to set the example for courts around the country and demonstrate that its decisions are based on a fair and unbiased assessment of the facts and the law, not personal biases or their own financial interests. Eliminating ethical questions and conflicts of interests should be the starting point.

Federal judges are not supposed to be politicians or advocates. They are supposed to rise above the political winds of the day and demonstrate a single-minded commitment to one promise: equal justice under law. As judges of the nation's highest court, it is important for Supreme Court justices to demonstrate that they can meet that standard.

Conflict of interest interlinking Think Tank and Government Policy

An alleged conflict of interest has been witnesses in the case of the National Security Advisor's son in think-tank. The alleged conflict of interest was uncovered by a newspaper. It states that NSA's son who is a CA by profession, and is a founder of private equity firm has close underlying links with the government.

The firm merged the company with another foreign company whose chairman is one of the Princes of the Saudi royal family. The association is problematic because the advisor's son also heads a think-tank that allows corporates and businessmen to interact with Ministers for discussing government policies. Further, it receives sponsorship from private and government establishments whose names are not made public.

If we connect the two, the foundation wields power to influence government contracts and policy decisions. The powerful influence of the think-tank can be gauged from the fact that some of its major proposals have been accepted by the government. The other members of the foundation are drawn from Central government's inner circle. It includes the party's national general secretary and Rajya Sabha members among others. The influence is such that it yields and engages with government's policy, which is being formulated with foreign funds. Also, the source of the funds remains unknown.

Another example can explain the conflict of interest

The CBI has been pursuing a case against civil aviation company Boeing for selling passenger planes at inflated prices, causing the government a loss. Now, Boeing also sponsored an India foundation event that had MoS Civil Aviation as a director. This raises suspicion about the likelihood of the investigation being influenced in Boeing's favor.

Conflict of Interest in Media

Drug companies have been promoting their views on the nation's op-ed pages via commentary writers who come across as neutral-sounding experts, and editors don't always call out these industry mouthpieces for what they are.

Pharma-friendly guest columns have appeared on editorial pages around the country without disclosure of the authors' drug industry ties.

Sometime ago, a news agency retracted a commentary praising drug industry sales reps after the physician whose byline it contained was found to be on the pharma payroll. The physician, a board member of the industry-funded Alliance for Patient Access (AfPA), also admitted that it was ghostwritten. Another commentary, which praised drug ads, was written by a patient who said a PR firm employed by a drug company helped her write it.

But while the News Organisation has taken a lot of heat for the lack of transparency, it's clear other publications aren't informing readers about conflicts of interest on their op-ed pages?

There had been dozens of examples with some connection. A writer's affiliation was sometimes disclosed, but with no mention of the organization's financial backing. In some cases, physician writers had personally accepted pharmaceutical money that was not disclosed. This is a sharp contrast to transparency standards for news reporting. These organisations have even been described as "ethical bordellos," where editors in need of content are sometimes complicit in concealing the connections between a writer and the subject of a column. Editors aren't always open about their practices. Efforts to find out how these commentaries ran without mention of the drug industry ties of their authors met with limited success.

Shouldn't editors offer some information about little-known groups to help readers evaluate arguments they put forth? Frankly, it's not easy to make a hard distinction between outright front groups and industry-backed fellow-travelers and think tanks – and what difference it should make if one could make that distinction. Publications have limited incentive to promote disclosure.

Unfortunately, there's not always an incentive for editors to probe. Commentaries by outside writers constitute free content and fulfill the mission of providing diverse voices. With media organizations cutting editorial staffs, special-interest groups are happy to step in and fill the content void.

Conflict of Interest in Climate Change Treaty

According to a report, fossil fuel companies are undermining

Paris agreement negotiation. Report says outcomes of climate negotiations have been skewed to favour biggest corporate polluters. Global negotiations seeking to implement the Paris agreement have been captured by corporate interests and are being undermined by powerful forces that benefit from exacerbating climate change. The report, co-authored by Corporate Accountability, uncovers a litany of ways in which fossil fuel companies have gained high-level access to negotiations and manipulated outcomes.

It highlights a string of examples, including that of a negotiator for Panama who is also on the board of a corporate peak body that represents carbon traders such as banks, polluters and brokers. It also questions the role of the world's biggest polluters in sponsoring the meetings in return for access to high-level events. The report argues that as a result of the corporate influence, outcomes of negotiations so far have been skewed to favour the interests of the world's biggest corporate polluters over those of the majority of the world's population that live in the developing world. It finds that influence has skewed outcomes on finance, agriculture and technology.

It comes as the 2018 deadline approaches for member countries to finalise the rule book that guides the implementation of the Paris Agreement. That rule book will determine things such as how compliance will be monitored and enforced and how the developing world will receive finance and support.

The UNFCCC's Climate Technology Network, which advises on how to develop and transfer green technology to the developing world, includes a member of the World Coal Association, and its board has included managers at Shell and EDF - one of the world's biggest electricity producers.

A negotiator for Panama is currently a board member of the International Emissions Trading Association (IETA), and was previously its president for several years. IETA was set up by the fossil fuel companies including BP and Rio Tinto in order to make sure climate action caused "minimal economic harm". Today its members include Chevron, BHP, Dow, Duke Energy, Repsol, Xcel Energy, Veolia and Statoil.

Sponsorship of the COP21 meeting in Paris gave fossil fuel companies access to the "communications and networking area" inside the rooms where the negotiations were taking place.

Big agricultural corporations such as Monsanto, Syngenta and Yara have been lobbying heavily at UNFCCC meetings, with Monsanto even co-chairing the World Business Council on Sustainable Development's Climate-Smart Agriculture working group.

The report argues this access has influenced outcomes at the UNFCCC, undermining the Paris agreement in the following ways:

- Market-based solutions to climate change have become dogma at UNFCCC meetings, despite many developing world countries urging alternative mechanisms such as direct regulation, and despite studies suggesting they can allow big polluters to continue polluting, according to Corporate Accountability.
- The US and Canada have adopted agricultural corporations' approach to "climate-smart agriculture", and argued against regulation of non-CO2 emissions from agriculture.
- Most of the funds from the Green Climate Fund have so far been allocated to private sector projects.
- The report argues that if the UNFCCC process results in a rulebook being developed in line with what the world's biggest polluters want, then the Paris agreement is doomed to failure.

Momentum has been building over the past couple of years to have an official conflict-of-interest policy agreed on at the UNFCCC.

However, Australia's delegation has argued that "there is no clear understanding of what a conflict of interest is and it means different things to different people" and that fossil fuel companies were "the providers of the biggest and best solutions".

Conflict of Interest in Policy Making

Several public health and nutrition advocates and pediatricians had written to the Niti Aayog Vice Chairman regarding the conflict of interest of non-governmental officials in the Aayog's constituted working group on nutrition.

They pointed out that members included food company lobbyists, people on the boards of multinational food companies and founders of startu-ps selling nutritional supplements. They expressed concern over non-availability of information about how these members were selected.

The letter referred to Niti Aayog's own National Nutrition

Strategy (NNS) guiding principles on ensuring that there was no conflict of interest. The NNS guiding principles state: "An underlying principle of action is that policy development and programme implementation must be transparent, open to public scrutiny and kept free from conflict of interest, with requisite safeguards. (This includes ensuring that representation on policy, technical advisory groups and various management committees at different levels is free from conflict of interest.)" It also sought inputs on monitoring, effectively implementing and scaling up existing government schemes in the nutrition sector.

The public health advocates pointed out that the expert group included representative of International Life Sciences Institute (ILSI). "It is a lobbying arm of the food industry globally. ILSI's member trustees include Nestle, Hindustan Unilever, Abbott Healthcare, Mars, Ajinomoto and Mondelez Foods," they added.

Including such parties or individuals in the working group would "negatively influence the policy, programme, decisions taken" and "may hamper public interest," stated the letter.

Leading government institutions which have done extensive work on nutrition policy, including the Central Food Technological Research Institute in Mysore, AIIMS Delhi, Indian Academy of Pediatrician's nutrition chapter and MS University of Baroda are not represented on the working group.

Conflict of Interest in Appointments

Questions were recently raised on the conflict of interest when a celebrated actor was appointed as the Film and Television Institute of India (FTII) Chairman. The students' association at the institute alleged that there was a "conflict of interest" as the actor ran his own acting school in Mumbai.

The FTII Students' Association (FSA) also raised objections over the statements made by the actor during the debate over intolerance in the country and his attempts at "advertising certain ideas of the government".

The question is how can a person, who heads a private enterprise can also be asked to head a government institute?

Conflict of Interest in Health Care

The IVF industry has been accused of increasingly placing profits over patients, with a new study suggesting that some doctors are offering women more treatment cycles than appropriate or necessary.

A team of Australian bioethicists has found that conflicts of interest are leading to fertility doctors making decisions that financially benefit them and their employer, at the expense of their patients.

As some IVF clinics became more corporate, there are growing concerns that professionals put profit before patients. The study by Macquarie University and Sydney University researchers and published in the journal Human Fertility was based on interviews with eight professionals in the IVF industry, including counselors and clinical specialists.

They said most participants believed commercial interests had some impact on a doctor's commitment to their patients, and was "particularly true of doctors working for corporations".

In Australia, most clinics are privately run. The two major players, Virtus Health and Monash IVF, were floated on the stock exchange in 2014, both raising more than $300 million.

The study noted that the move was welcomed by the financial sector, with one analyst declaring that "people will pay almost anything to have a baby".

Lead author Dr Brette Blakely from the Australian Institute of Health Innovation at Macquarie University said there was evidence that conflict of interest changed clinical practice. She said there was concern that financially motivated clinicians were offering IVF to patients who may actually achieve success with cheaper and less invasive treatments. "This was, in turn, seen to not only place current patients at risk, but also to mislead future patients who might be tempted to seek unwarranted treatment by high-reported success rates based on women who do not represent the average IVF patient," the study said.

The study also suggested profit-driven businesses were exploiting Medicare. At present, there is no Medicare limit to the number of cycles that can be reimbursed or the age of the woman receiving treatment.

Dr Blakely said conflict of interest could result in financial, physical and emotional harm to women." This is because ovarian stimulation and egg retrieval may be harmful in the short term and potentially the longer term," she said.

"Moderate to severe ovarian hyperstimulation syndrome may occur in one to five per cent of treatment cycles and this may result in significant morbidity and can, in rare cases, be fatal."

Conflict of Interest in Sports

It seems India is afflicted with a 'conflict of interest' disease. A disease that apparently plagues everything from Indian cricket to Indian companies to Indian journalism. A commentator managing a cricket player to a chairman of a conglomerate handing out contracts to family entities to media houses indirectly controlled by business interests are all termed instances of conflict of interest. Is there a standard definition of conflict of interest and does it apply equally across all facets of society?

An official cricket commentator is also the head of an agency that manages players of the Indian cricket team. Is this a conflict of interest? It is beneficial and makes commercial sense for a player management firm to contract a player only if he continues to be selected to the Indian national team. A player can be in the national team only if he scores runs or takes wickets consistently for India at the international level. A commentator extolling the greatness of his contracted player on air has no influence on that player's abilities to score runs or take wickets. Merely commenting about a player does not enhance that player's cricketing prowess, which alone can ensure the player's sustained place in the national team. In a brutally competitive and meritocratic profession such as sports and Indian cricket in particular, a player cannot continue to hold his place despite a dismal performance in front of hundreds of millions of discerning fans. If performance alone matters and no outsider can influence that player's performance on the ground, then does the commentator or his firm really stand to gain personal benefit from this perceived conflict? The same logic can be extended to mentors and coaches of players who are accused of conflicts of interest but it is very hard to impute a direct personal benefit from their official capacities. The sheer meritocracy of Indian cricket, with every game judged acutely by millions of devout fans, acts as a natural antidote to inordinate personal benefits being reaped due to perceived conflicts of interest. But, can the same be said about other professions?

But, one can also take the view that sports oozes idealism and should be pristine. After all, there is a reason why we have the word 'sportsmanship' but not 'businessship' or 'bankership'. Sports will be held to higher standards than other professions. Sporting heroes are role models for entire societies and generations. Sports is as much about ethics as it is about skill. We expect more from our sports heroes because we do not view them as one of us. They are deservedly placed on a higher pedestal than other mere mortals simply because we judge their success as true success achieved with extraordinary skill and talent that others lack. It is, thus, incumbent upon sportspersons even after they have long given up their profession to continue to hold such high standards in public life. They will be held to higher standards than others, however harsh and unfair it may sound.

Other Varied Examples

Often times, at greater intensity than the Minister himself or the MP herself, the corporation Chairperson, the District Commissioner or the Police Officer in-charge–in happenings that hurt the government, the administration and the party in power- the spouse, the children, the nephews and the nieces, the uncles and the aunts, the PS, the APS, the PS to the APS and the driver, who in varying styles execute such clout (read "power") that it is not clear whether they know of the actual authority whose name is being sold.

- For example, if an MP is chairing a school/college board and the MP's daughter or a distant relative is a student therein, it is possible that some in the school, headmaster/principal, will orchestrate academic and extra-academic advantages for the child. These may include, but is not restricted to, awarding extra marks in examinations, being selected to present a wreath to the chief guest (daughter garlanding father), undeserved inclusion in the institution's cultural programme, and no queries about absenteeism without rhyme or reason.

- For example, a government corporation has called a tender for supply of thousands of office supplies. However, there is a genuine office supplier with experience as well but if the party happens to be related by blood or otherwise to the chairperson or the chief engineer or the CEO, there will be murmurs about "fowl" play.
- For example, an architect has designed a building. According to the morals of architectural practice, the construction of the building should be carried out by some other entity, known as a contractor. This division of work protects the architect from being suspected by the building owner of gleaning surplus financial benefits when the architect proposes changes, additions and deletions to the design after he assumes the auxiliary role of constructing the building or that of supplying building materials. Engineers could be entangled in similar conflicts. On that count, developer firms owned by or employing architects/engineers harbour conflict of interest if design and construction of a building is accomplished in-house under a single decision-maker.
- For example, imagine an interview board. The father-in-law of a candidate is on the board. Why? He was nominated by the candidate's father, the chairman of the institution. The boy was among the top of his class. Perhaps he would have got the job without the need of his father sitting across the interview table. But, soon after his appointment, tongues will begin to wag that the selection was a crude specimen of nepotism, and a result of complicity by the in-laws.
- For example, a man has been charged with criminal charge sheet, and lands in a court. Is it possible that the judge would be his father or uncle or grandfather or a distant relative? If it does by sheer coincidence, that is when conscientious judges use the armor "feeling embarrassed" and opt out of that court, or the case is transferred to a different and neutral court of law.
- For example, a journalist has unearthed a factory of spurious drugs, and finds that his own uncle is involved in the unscrupulous production. What does he do? If he shelves the scoop, he would be guilty of letting his uncle off the hook, and doing disservice to the nation. If he breaks the story, even if he

covers all the details, the skeptic would pounce back that he has been easy on his uncle. The only noble option for him is to pass on the story to a colleague and move on.

- For example, a government officer was elected president of an association of professionals. That's great and well-deserved! The conflict emerged when as a public servant he was party to implementing a national project–cutting down dozens of ageing trees. Many members of his association and others objected to the degradation of the environment, but the president could not express due solidarity. Nor could he join the rally at the grounds where the trees were being felled. The president too felled his association because of a conflict of interest.
- For example, a cricketer cannot expect his father to be one of the umpires, or even the third umpire.
- For example, lottery organisers bar employees of the organisation and their families from participating.

These examples show how conflict of interest has become an issue of concern. Thus, ways and solutions have to be formulated to assuage this problem.

Conflict of Interest too is Corruption

The massive success of the Aam Aadmi Party (AAP) in Delhi in the 2015 assembly election has brought the issue of corruption back into focus. The anti-corruption drive, however, seems limited to bribery and processes involving financial transactions. One dominant form of corruption governments appear to overlook is 'conflict of interest'.

It is high time we recognise that conflict of interest needs to be tackled through tough rules and laws. Conflict of interest occurs when an individual or entity indulges in multiple roles, one affecting the other. The occurrence of conflict of interest in policy making, regulation, rule-making and setting of standards has serious implications for the public.

This is why India Needs a Law on Conflict of Interest

India's political class has set for itself such questionable standards of behaviour that a lot of what politicians do here would be outrightly declared as criminal misconduct in another democracy. The Lalit Modi controversy, Nirav Modi, Mehul Choksi fraud cases controversy, etc. acted as an instigator for this call on the conflict of interest vexatious issue - has brought into sharp focus the absence of legal-ethical conduct among public persons and Parliament must take up the issue urgently. These issues are so sensitive, as some of the Members of the Parliament (MPs) are also alleged for forming the nexus with the private industrialists. The priority must be to frame a modern law relating to conflict of interest, along the lines of what exists in the statute of the other countries like the United States.

> A US Code provides the basic criminal conflict of interest statute in that country and "prohibits an executive branch employee from participating personally and substantially in a particular Government matter that will affect his own financial interests, as well as the financial interests of:
>
> - His spouse or minor child
> - His general partner
> - An organization in which he serves as an officer, director, trustee, general partner or employee, and
> - A person with whom he is negotiating for or has an arrangement concerning prospective employment.

If such law, covering criminal conflicts of interests had existed in India, the fugitive offenders, businessmen and political nexus (like controversy on the issues of Gujarat Gas pipelining, Finance Minister Arun Jaitley and Vodafone case controversy, etc.), ongoing continous frauds in banks with political approaches (Nirav Modi and his revelations about the political linkages) and others could have been curbed and if not curbed then accusations may have been proven and due punishment must have been awarded.

Recently, a beedi manufacturer from Uttar Pradesh, Shyama Charan Gupta, was on a Parliamentary Committee which postponed the requirement for a more prominently displayed pictorial warning on cigarette packets even as Gupta waxed eloquent about how beedis were not such a big health hazard and that western research was biased against the Indian product. There could not have been a more obvious case of conflict of interest.

Thus, the moral of the story is we urgently need laws to

tackle such widespread violations of ethics and morality, which in current circumstances invite no punishment at all.

For the time being, though, this area of conflict of interest has also become the favourite hunting ground for questions - whether that be theoretical or case study based - coming in the GS Paper IV.

Rigged Panels

Conflict of interest assumes great significance when it comes to statutory regulatory bodies that deal with public health and food safety issues. Vested interests are always working to get rules or standards that work in their favour. This is what happened when the Food Safety and Standards Authority of India (FSSAI) was set up to act as an 'independent' food safety regulator more than six years ago.

Industry representatives were nominated to scientific committees to set standards for a number of parameters ranging from pesticide content to food labelling. The membership of these panels read like Who's Who of food industry - Nestle, Pepsi, Coca Cola, Britannia, Marico, ITC, GSK, Hindustan Lever and so on. It was only after being exposed in the press that the Supreme Court took note of it and directed FSSAI to purge its panels. Till then the Authority did not even have a rudimentary conflict of interest policy in place.

Like the Environment Ministry, the FSSAI too has not learnt any institutional lessons. Industry consultants and scientists working on industry projects continue as members of its scientific panels. The same is the case with the regulatory process for genetically modified food crops.

Scientific panels are infested with scientists working on seed industry projects or enjoying their grants and at the same time regulating projects of the same sponsors. In one case, a scientist in the regulatory body approved a research project proposed by his wife. Another recent case is of the expert panel that the Health Ministry set up to decide follow-up action after a damning parliamentary report on human clinical trials. The Ministry chose an expert who is head of clinical trials division of a corporate hospital.

Serious Implications

Conflict of interest can be particularly dangerous in the health sector. The case of HPV vaccine trials probed by the Parliamentary Standing Committee on health clearly showed how vested interests in collusion with scientists can influence public policy. The same interests are in play outside the government.

The Indian Academy of Paediatrics is a body of doctors which recommends vaccine schedules for paediatricians and participates in government vaccine policy making. Its annual report in 2012 made a shocking revelation that IAP's Committee of Immunisation was almost fully funded by vaccine makers – Sanofi Pasteur, GSK, Merck, Pfizer and Serum Institute. In such a situation, can thousands of paediatricians who depend on the academy's wisdom really go by what it recommends? How can hapless parents know these schedules are not influenced by vaccine makers?

Parliamentary Panels

The malaise extends to our parliamentary panels too. We have Sachin Tendulkar – who endorses a computer security product – as member of the Standing Committee on IT. We had Vijay Mallya (the disgraced former Rajya Sabha MP) – whose UB group had a sizeable stake in a fertiliser firm – as member of the Standing Committee on Fertilisers. The Prime Minister appointed an empowered Group of Ministers on pictorial warnings for tobacco products, which had among its members a Cabinet Minister who is better known as 'beedi king'.

The time has come to put an end to such misuse of public policy and regulatory instruments and to codify a stringent legal framework to govern 'conflict of interests'. Taking a bribe is a criminal act, but acting in ways that undermine public interest is a more serious crime.

How to Resolve Conflict of Interest?

This is an interesting concept. When a conflict of interest does occur, how should we negotiate our path so that it can be sidelined?

A conflict of interest can occur in business or in public life. This happens when a person has a divergence between what she might gain on a personal, perhaps financial level, and her professional responsibilities. If this potential for conflict is disclosed and dealt with correctly, no serious repercussions will follow. However, if it is not properly addressed, a conflict of interest has the potential to damage the people involved and also the whole organization.

- A recognition of the potential for conflict of interest is crucial. All too often these issues erupt when something goes wrong -- when the outside world becomes aware of the conflict of interest and the worst is assumed.
- Develop a clear policy on disclosure, so that all employees or board members know what outside interests must be divulged. Sometimes these issues are suppressed not because of ill-intent but because the person either did not recognize the conflict or did not fully disclose it in good time.
- Disseminate this policy and information to all relevant parties. If appropriate (perhaps in the case of a public body), also make this information available to the world at large. This encourages openness and minimizes the chances of later misunderstandings.
- Keep the policy proportionate. For instance, it may be that a person who has a conflicting interest should just withdraw from particular meetings or decision-making processes. There may be no problem with the person dealing with other issues within the organization.
- Develop a clear policy to deal with situations where a person does not disclose conflicting interests. This can be a serious issue, and a disciplinary procedure may need to be instigated. It may be necessary to act swiftly and decisively in this situation, as allegations of corruption can be extremely damaging and can tarnish the reputations of others who may not even have been involved.

Managing Conflicts of Interest

The following are indicative of the range of different approaches a board has available to manage the various risks associated with conflicts of interest.

Policies and Procedures

Well-designed policies and procedures will help boards and their members identify and deal with conflicts of interest. These can provide clear guidelines for simple and predictable situations and establish a process for dealing with the more difficult ones. The seriousness of some situations will be a question of degree or materiality and not easily managed by a 'hard and fast' rule. For example, sometimes the existence of a conflict of interest will not outweigh the value of an, at least, partial contribution by the conflicted individual to the board's deliberations.

Determination of the Desired Board Culture

There is value in a board engaging explicitly in the deliberate development of a desired board culture. An effective governance culture is likely to be based on characteristics such as professionalism, capability, accountability, independence, trust, diligence and candor. Candor and trust are particular characteristics of the context within which conflicts of interest need to be handled.

Induction

The effective induction of new board members is an important adjunct to the development of appropriate policies and procedures. New board members must be under no misunderstanding about the organisation's expectations of how its governors will behave when their personal interests may conflict with those of the organisation. Ideally, an existing conflict or potential for a conflict of interest should be declared and the ramifications discussed prior to election or appointment to the board. In some cases, the appointment should not proceed.

Ongoing Training and Development

It is also important for existing board members to have an opportunity to update their knowledge and understanding of matters like the handling of conflicts of interest. Thinking about the best way to handle conflicts of interests is constantly changing as a consequence of public controversies, judicial decisions and statements of best practice released by regulators and professional associations.

Disclosure and Recording

Having an effective process of disclosure is central to any board's ability to continuously assess the seriousness of an actual or potential conflict of interest. Each board should have an interest register, updated at least annually and as necessary (as a result of changes in directors' circumstances) during the year. Depending on the agenda to be covered at each board meeting directors should make further declarations about possible conflicts that might arise during the meeting. A potential conflict may also arise between meetings. The director concerned should raise this with an appropriate person (often the chairman, or possibly the chief executive) as soon as the risk is identified.

The onus of declaration is on the individual. It is invariably awkward and embarrassing when a board has to 'call' one of its members on a failure to declare an interest. A declaration should be made as long as possible before the matter in which a director has an interest, is discussed. If any doubt remains, the matter should be treated as a conflict. If necessary, legal advice should be taken and all disclosures should be recorded in writing. Disclosure should be thorough enough to allow the board to make an informed decision when assessing an actual or perceived conflict of interest.

How to Resolve Moral Dilemmas Arising in Our Consciousness Or Can it Ever be Resolved: Strong institutions are not those that are entirely free of conflicts of interest but those that acknowledge such conflicts and address them transparently. Casting aspersions on people and personalities unilaterally just because they are in positions of potential conflict is an unending endeavor. If one were to accept the 'six degrees of separation' doctrine, then almost everything in this world will be riddled with such conflicts of interest. Every adult subconsciously accepts this inevitability of an interest conflict and deals with it in the realm of her own principles and priorities.

In this context, when conflicts of interest are ubiquitous in all walks of life and it is almost impossible to draw a direct link between deriving personal benefits arising out of a conflict of interest in any profession, who is accused and who is a victim has become a significant problem. This problem cannot be eliminated entirely. To say that conflict of interest can be annihilated is a naive statement. It is going to remain with us for a long time. And thus, thoughts should be directed to, how to allay this problem.

Mitigation Options in an Organization

Simply declaring a conflict of interest is unlikely to be sufficient in many situations. The action required should be determined by the board of that profession. It should assess the substance and seriousness of the conflict of interest and the practicability of any options for avoiding or mitigating the conflict. Typically, mitigation options involve some degree of withdrawal or exclusion of a conflicted director. For example, the conflicted director has restrictions placed on his/her access to information (e.g. does not receive relevant board papers) is excluded from a committee or working group dealing with the issue prior to the board's consideration; withdraws from discussing or voting on a particular item of business at the board meeting; has certain tasks or duties reassigned to another person (e.g. to another director if the chair is the director conflicted) relinquishes the interest that creates the conflict; or takes leave of absence from the board for the period while the conflict exists.

When in doubt, the default position should be that a director interested in a decision or transaction is completely removed from discussion, deliberation and decision making in relation to the matter.

If the board's decision making has already been compromised by a director's failure to declare a conflict, it may be necessary to abort a decision or restart a process (e.g. a tendering process).If none of these steps are sufficient, protect both the director and the organization or a resignation from the board may be the only remaining option. Ethical obligations and good practice require directors to ensure that the board is informed of any dealings that could give rise to perceptions of preferential treatment or misuse of position. While the onus is on the individual director to declare his or her interests this does not, however, absolve a board from the broader obligation to be vigilant and proactive. Boards should be asking: How well do our policies and practices for conflict of interest disclosure and management meet 'best practice' standards? If there appears to be a shortcoming in how we approach conflict of interest matters, is that justified by our situation, or are we running unnecessary risks?

An individual can also reduce his moral dilemma to resolve the conflict of interest by following ways-

Recognising Conflicts of Interest in an Individual

There is a variety of pragmatic tests that can be used by individuals to identify potential conflicts or perceptions of conflicts. For example:

- **The 'sniff test'** - does this 'smell' right?
- **The 'trust test'** - would others trust your judgment and have confidence in your integrity if they knew you were in this position?
- **The 'headline news test'**- how readily would you be able to defend your position confronted by media and public scrutiny?

The answers to these types of questions should help alert those concerned to whether...

... a reasonably informed objective observer would infer from the circumstances that the individual judgment is likely to be influenced to the detriment of the company's best interests.

Whenever in doubt, apply this principle to resolve the issue of conflict of interest. This test can tell us that whether we are right or wrong, the path that we have chosen to do not lead us astray or betray our position, credibility and profession in any other manner.

US Supreme Court Justice Louis Brandeis in 1913 said: "Sunlight is the best disinfectant". Transparency is the best remedy for conflict of interest.

Case Study I

You are a District Administrator. One day you got the information that a mob has gathered in huge force near a village in your area. On gathering more information, you find that mob has tied two people on the suspicion that they are child kidnapper. Both of them have sustained injuries and if not helped could die.

The police force too is gathered there but is finding themselves helpless on the face of a large mob. One of the policemen gathers courage and rescues both the people. An FIR has been registered against the mob who had participated in it and arrest have been made.

You get a call from local MLA that arrested people should be let free as they belong to his religion. The MLA is a powerful person and he has strong hold in the region. What do you think should be your action? As an administrator, how do you think should mob lynching be prevented?

This case comes under the following topics:

- Ethical Dilemma
- Conflict in Administration
- Impartiality
- Non-partisanship
- Objectivity
- Dedication to Public Service

Premise: In this situation, as an administrator you face an ethical dilemma. You are being asked to turn a blind eye to the crime and culprits in question. Your job as an administrator requires you to practice integrity, impartiality, equality to law and equity. If you let the culprits free then it lead to jungle raj. But also, if you disobey the MLA, it might lead to some other problems in the form of riot, chaos or penalty in your workings. Thus, you have to choose which way you should go.

Answer: Everyone is equal in the eyes of law. I cannot favor someone and leave the rest. Equality of law for an administrator is one of the code of conduct in this line of duty. So, I will choose the way which will bring harmony in the society and also justice in the system.

The course of action that I would take is to talk to the MLA and let him know that my job as an administrator do not allow me to act in such a manner. Also, make him understand that he is the MLA of whole community and do not represent handful of people. Thus, when one sees him acting in such a manner will lead to resentment by others. Those people committed an act of crime and thus should be punished accordingly.

As a preventive measure i.e. in future such type of accidents do not incur, I will make certain guidelines.

From the outset, one must note that social media platforms like Facebook, Twitter and WhatsApp aren't the problem. They are just mediums of disseminating information, false or not. The problem lies in the action of people who don't verify the news they receive through these mediums and then proceed to take the law into their own hands and lynch whoever they suspect.

The advent of social media has indeed hastened the dissemination of false information. Fake news does pose one of the most significant challenges before India's law enforcement apparatus.

Here are the methods that I will implement to prevent mob lynching:

1. I will assign villages to constables, who will not only visit the village once a week, spreading awareness on critical social issues, but will also develop networks with community leaders. I will myself will speak the village Sarpanches on a variety of topics. What these local networks will help the police, is to nip WhatsApp rumours in the bud.

2. I will also kick-start an extensive community outreach campaign against the spread of fake news, local troupes performed in these villages, singing, preaching or enacting skits about the dangers of fake news.

3. I will start a drive where teachers from government schools will teach students how to recognise fake news and rumours, deal with sensational news stories and how to break out of their "filter bubbles". The teachers will try to inculcate the spirit of Article 51 (A) (h) of the Constitution (develop the scientific temper, humanism and the spirit of inquiry and reform), in school kids.

4. I will establish State police units which will have their own dedicated IT cells that monitor content on social media.

Case Study II

Supposedly, you are the administrator of your district. The district administration had received multiple complaints regarding food adulteration, scarcity of resources and unhygienic practices. There is a strong lobbyist of hotel owners who have pressurized government to turn a blind eye to their working. Anyone who takes action or warns them is transferred. This has made anyone too reluctant to act. The local MLA's nephew is the head of the group of hotel owners. He had even threatened previous Food, Inspector.

Thus, nothing was done about it since the post of Food Inspector (FI) has remained vacant (due to the lack of administrative capacity). What will be the course of action that you will take?

This case comes under the following topics:

- Ethical Dilemma
- Conflict of Interest & Conflict in Administration
- Dilemmas in Government and Private Institutions
- Quality of Service Delivery

Premise: Food adulteration is the process in which the quality of food is lowered either by the addition of inferior quality material or by extraction of valuable ingredient. As an administrator it is your duty that people are provided with good quality food products. Here is an ethical dilemma faced by you that if you take action, you run the risk of angering nephew of a local MLA and crony hotel lobbyists. On the other hand your inaction may take dangerous turn in the form of casualty.

Answer: Here are the steps that I will follow -

1. To overcome the scarcity of resources I will adhere to the due procedure, I will take along with me army of government officials on raids starting where videography evidence will be collected.
2. In the first instance, if I find that vendors are not regulating and practicing hygienic practices, I will seal the hotels for want of necessary documentation and not adhering to food standards. The administration will also serve show-cause notices on the spot.

3. Till the time, a food inspector is posted at the district, I will constitute a special team consisting of deputy chief medical officer and deputy magistrate of the collectorate which will regularly visit these establishments, maintaining continuous vigilance based on the procedure for food safety norms prescribed by the State government. This special team will operate as a force multiplier to the efforts of the food safety officer:

4. There is a gross lack of awareness among hotel owners and shopkeepers with regards to licensing norms and food safety criteria as enunciated in the Food Safety and Standards Act, 2006. Moreover, lack of enforcement and non-imposition of penalties in the past made the owners complacent. Responding to these concerns, I will initiate a special enrolment drive for new registrants with restaurant owners and food safety officials coming together under one roof to process applications online.

5. Meanwhile, an awareness camp will be conducted for the district chamber of commerce and restaurant owners regarding FSSAI licensing norms. In other words, the administration will build the food safety ecosystem from the ground up.

6. Food vendors in the district will be directed to sign an affidavit stating that they would maintain specific conditions of safety and hygiene. Once they do so, the business can re-start. These food vendors will be warned that if they violate the conditions stated in the affidavit they would be booked under criminal sections of Indian Penal Code, which could mean jail term.

7. I will also take a meeting with hotel owners to inform them that such practices will not be tolerated and substandard food products should not be used. Keeping with law practices, if it is found that any hotel have been using adulterated food products, a strict action will be taken against them.

10

ETHICAL ISSUES

The Ethical Issues Discussed in this Unit

- Society and Social Issues
- Science & Technology
- Public Administration & Governance
- Environment
- Economy
- International
- Security
- Disaster Management

We find some ethical lapses in our daily life in almost every dimension that needs some immediate attention. Every day in the newspapers, we find news related to corruption, cheating scandals, doping in sports, crimes, etc. Such events are so common in their occurrence that now it is being questioned – does anyone act ethically? Studying ethics can help you arrive at clearer positions and arguments on real life issues – and can help you apply them, too. In fact, thinking more about ethical theory may even change your mind about issues in today's world.

In this chapter, we are providing some of the common ethical issues related to our daily lives as well as the global ethical concerns. Such issues will give some greater knowledge and understanding about applied ethics in different fields.

Society and Social Issues

Lynching and Intolerant Society

Lynching means punishing (or may be killing) someone for alleged offence without any legal trial or due procedure. In India, lynching generally arises due to tensions between two cultural groups. But, in recent years, cow protection and beef ban has become a major issue for mob lynching (especially after 2015 mob lynching of Dadri, UP).

Ethical Issues Involved in Lynching

- **Creates Intolerance in the Society:** Such acts make absence of resilience in the society and individuals are influenced by prejudices, etc. Such events also add fuel to fire in case of communal tension in a region (if inter-religious confrontation occurs).
- **Violation of Law:** Any group or mobs have no privilege to take any action against individual, even if he is convicted or found guilty of a crime (like cow smuggling, etc.). Only legitimate authority can punish such person after due legal process. Voluntary mass punishment will create chaos in the society.
- **Right to Life:** Often mob violence results in death; this violates natural human right of the individual's right to life.

- **Trust Deficit:** Many accused of lynching are roaming freely and government still not taking serious action against them and causing trust deficit in the government. This also questions about the government's integrity, compassion, etc.

With the Mahatma Gandhi's Non-violence ideology, now it is the time when we have to inculcate these ideologies and make our society ethically strong.

Sexual Harassment at Workplace

In India, Sexual Harassment of Women at Workplace (Prevention, Prohibition and Redressal) Act was passed in 2013. The Act has adopted the definition of 'sexual harassment' from Vishakha case, a Judgment and the term 'sexual harassment' includes -

- any unwelcome acts or behaviour (whether directly or by implication) such as physical contact and advances,
- demand or request for sexual favours,
- making sexually coloured remarks,
- showing pornography, or
- any other unwelcome physical, verbal or non-verbal conduct of sexual nature.

The Act provides that no woman shall be subjected to sexual harassment at any workplace.

Ethical Issues Involved in Sexual Harassment

- **Discouragement of Women Participation:** The consequences of sexual harassment to a working women or even as a group has a cumulative, demoralizing effect that discourages women from asserting themselves within the workplace, while among men it reinforces stereotypes of women employees as sex objects. Such incidences demoralize the women from entering into the work environment and also family members stop them due to such fear.
- **Degraded Ethical Working Environment:** Whenever the harassment happens, the unwelcome sexual conduct of co-workers make the working conditions hostile for women and unpleasant - putting indirect pressure on her to leave the job. These

whole events make the office environment bitter from the ethical perspectives. Sexual harassment can have a demoralizing effect on everyone within range of it, and it often negatively impacts company's productivity on the whole.

- **Very Low Impact of Legal Action**: It is seen that the legal system alone is not an adequate mechanism for reducing or preventing sexual harassment. The legal requirements are necessary but not sufficient to drive the change needed to address sexual harassment. The codes of ethics are truly necessary for the ethical conduct in a working environment.

Marginalized Sections

1. Ethical Issues Involved with the Old Age People

Increased life expectancy, rapid urbanization and lifestyle changes have led to an emergence of varied problems for the elderly in India. It must be remembered that comprehensive care to the elderly is possible only with the involvement and collaboration of family, community and the Government. India should get prepared to meet the growing challenge of caring for its elderly population.

- **Insufficient Focus on Elderly Care:** Emphasis on geriatrics in the public health system is limited with few dedicated geriatric services. The other issues of the public health system are lack of infrastructure, limited manpower, poor quality of care, and overcrowding of facilities due to insufficient focus on elderly care.
- **Changing Family Structure:** The traditional norms and values of Indian society also laid stress on showing respect and providing care for the elderly. However, with the emerging prevalence of nuclear family set-ups in recent years, the elderly are likely to be exposed to emotional, physical and financial insecurity in the years to come.
- **Lack of Social Support:** The elderly in India are much more vulnerable because of the less government spending on social security system. The elderly in urban area rely primarily on hired domestic helps to meet their basic needs in an increasingly-chaotic and crowded city. Social isolation and loneliness has increased.
- **Social Inequality:** Elderly are a heterogeneous section with an urban and rural divide. They are less vulnerable in rural areas as compared to their urban counterparts, due to the still hold-

ing values of the joint family system. All the elderly are not seen in the same view as the needs and problems of elderly are rejected to a vast extent as government classifies these people based on caste and other socio cultural dimensions.

- **Economic Dependency:** The elders living with their families are largely contingent on the economic capacity of the family unit for their economic security and well-being. Elderly often do not have financial protection such as sufficient pension and other forms of social security in India. Being financially dependent, they are most vulnerable to infections and have low priority for own health.

2. Ethical Issues Involved with Children

- **Inadequate Nutrition:** In India, millions of children suffer from acute malnutrition due to famines, droughts, calamities, government policy failures, and other reasons with many more suffering from chronic malnutrition. There are many concerns like the quality of school meals produced in government schools, too many children are living in the families below the poverty line, etc. Such status of children is totally unethical for any nation and as India claims to have highest number of demographic dividends, it must strengthen its children.
- **Bonded Child Labour:** There is increasing concern in a variety of areas about the use of bonded child labour, i.e. children effectively sold into slavery. In India, child labour is predominant and has become an acceptable feature for our society. Serious concerns have been voiced about the use of bonded child labour in textile, manufacturing, restaurants, vender shops, etc. Such child labour is pathetic and unethical for the little children; therefore it is not only government's duty but our involvement to eliminate this activity from India.
- **Risks to Child Safety and New Digital World:** New digital world resulting from the growth of the internet offers new opportunities for child entertainment and education, but they also raise questions of child safety on the internet and mobile phones through potential contact from undesirable people. Children and young people, inadvertently or deliberately accessing either illegal or inappropriate sexual or violent material. This kind of new world is unethical and disastrous for children who don't have acumen of what is right or wrong.

3. Ethical Issues Involved with Women

Several ethical issues are faced by women in their daily life and in their working environment. Everyday women are dealing with harassment from mild to extreme forms on our streets, workplaces, public transportation, and even at homes. It is evident that despite significant progress in female participation in industry in last many years, pervasive and persistent gender differences have been documented in both developed and developing countries.

- **Organisational Subjugations:** Females often view themselves as treated worse than males in the workplace. Males show higher reactivity towards organization, revenge, and interpersonal violence and females are more sensitive on ethical issues.
- **Lack of Parity:** In the working place women encounter with the disparity in pay structure in comparison to their male counterparts. On the ethical context, such type of differences make women discouraged for joining organizations.
- **Apathy:** A few organizations provide for the relocation or transfer facility for post-marriage women. The business and work ethics demands the management to have some empathy towards the women and their place in the society and also the customs followed. Therefore, the availability of relocation and transfer benefits must be easily provided to the women after marriage.
- **Unethical Violence:** Cultural and household stress factors contribute to the prevalence of domestic violence, and it has been argued that these factors need to be thoroughly addressed through such channels as the institutionalization of routine screening for warning signs of domestic violence by health professionals, legislation (along with feasible mechanisms for enforcement), and support and empowerment stemming from women's groups.

4. Ethical Issues Involved with LGBTQ

Homophobia and transphobia affect workers all over the world. In many societies around the world, lesbian, gay, bisexual and transgender (LGBT) people are subject to abuse and attacks. Gender and sexual minorities are excluded and stigmatised because of who they are, and alarmingly, many countries still have laws and policies that specifically make homosexuality a crime. In a landmark judgement, the honourable Supreme Court of India in 2018 scrapped section 377 of the Indian Penal Code (IPC) that criminalised homosexuality.

- **Discriminated Everywhere:** LGBT employees are more than twice as likely to be bullied and discriminated against as heterosexual employees in the workplace; and nearly half of trans- people are not living permanently in their preferred gender role - for fear it might threaten their employment status. They are not accepted in the working organizations, societies, families, friends, and so on.
- **Lack of Acceptance:** The LGBTQ community is always disrespected in the society and the society members have no empathy towards them as low awareness exists in the society. Many people are not able to understand that the sexual orientations are naturally endowed to them. Even after the Indian Supreme Court has decriminalized such acts, socially it is yet to get accepted.
- **Unequal Healthcare:** The LGBT community continues to fight for better access to healthcare, and for equal treatment by doctors and health insurance companies that can block individuals' access to care they need. LGBT youth are more likely to have health issues because of substance abuse and mental health issues, and 'trans' individuals can face discrimination from health insurers simply for identifying as 'trans'.

5. Ethical Issues Involved with Differently-Abled

Persons with disabilities are considered as one of the marginalized groups in the whole world. They have the same kind of health needs like non-disabled ones - for health screening, immunization, etc. They may even experience a narrower health margin, both because of social exclusion and poverty, and even because they can be vulnerable to the secondary conditions like urinary tract infections or pressure sores.

- **Psychological and Infrastructural Barriers:** A large number of persons with disabilities remain out of school due to lack of institutional infrastructural support for differently-able persons. Also, the family members of them are not in favour of sending them schools or colleges as they have the mindset that they will not be able to compete with the outer world.

- **Unequal Opportunity for Employment:** Though many persons with disabilities are capable of productive work, they remain unemployed or under-employed. Forget about the private sector offering employment to these people, even the public sector hardly does.
- **Large Attitudinal Barriers:** Persons with disabilities also encounter with the attitudinal barriers from the social elements. Many people actually look them as differently-abled and not equal to themselves, which is very disappointing for the persons with disability. The ethical principles clearly provide them an equal status in the society. India looks at disability from medical or pathological angle only, not from social angle.

Health and Healthcare Ethics

- **Privatization and Corporatization of Healthcare:** At present doctors are attracted towards private practice rather than public sector hospitals. Doctors form nexus with the drug and pathology industries and refer the patient to such places to earn profit.
- **Pricing of Medicines:** Due to privatization of health system, medicine costs are too high and out of pocket expenditure is unaffordable to lower and middle class. No issue raises more ethical considerations in the emerging markets (or in the developed ones), than pricing. Ethical issues in pricing cluster around two poles:
    - providing access to existing medicines for those that cannot pay, and
    - maintaining the incentive to continue to develop medicines that address unmet needs. In Indian perspective, first reason is dominant.
- **Depriving Population in Rural and Remote Areas:** Health facility related infrastructure is very low in the rural areas. There is unwillingness among doctors to work in such remote areas due less availability of civic amenities and hard conditions to survive on.
- **Responding to the Threat of Infectious Diseases:** Efforts to contain the spread of infectious diseases raise difficult ethical questions, about the appropriateness of restricting individual choices to safeguard other people's welfare. Examples include

- the use of isolation and quarantine for tuberculosis and pandemic influenza.

- **Participation, Transparency, and Accountability**: As an ethical matter, the process by which decisions are made is as important as the outcome of the decisions. But several recent incidents (like malpractice in recruitment of doctors, corruption in the medical boards, etc.) raises question about the accountability of the medical associations.
- **Disparities in Health Status, Access to Health Care and to the Benefits of Medical Research**: There is rampant practice of unequal distribution of medical resources. Resource allocation depends in part on value judgments about the relative importance of small improvements in quality of life for a large portion of the population as compared with a life-saving intervention that would benefit only a few people.

Education & Ethical Issues

- **Corruption in Education Sector:** The major cause of ethical degeneration in education system is rapidly spreading corruption. Corruption in the education sector can be defined as "the systematic use of public office for private benefit, whose impact is significant on the availability and quality of educational goods and services as a consequence on access, quality or equity in education". Corruption in education sector can include bribes and illegal fees for admission and examination; academic fraud; withholding teacher's salaries; preferential promotion and placement; charging students for "tutoring" sessions to cover the curriculum needed to pass mandatory examinations which should have been taught in the classroom; teacher absenteeism; and illegal practices in textbook procurement, meal provision, and infrastructure.
- **Lack of Value Education in Curriculum:** Imparting value education was the main aim of the teachers of the ancient age. Present school curriculum lacks emphasize on value education. Although value education is included in the primary education curriculum, at the adolescent or adult stage, which are the most sensitive stages to build the character of the youth, the curriculum finds no space to value education.
- **Educator's Pedagogy:** The present age does not engage

proper teaching methodologies. Evaluation stresses on routine remembrance. Curriculum design is done by the university and little collection of topics and subjects out of the syllabus. The accumulation or presentation of data is not enough to decide the criteria for quality education.

- **Guru-Shisya Bonding Going Away:** Students should learn to respect Guru (Teacher), and a guru should selflessly teach his Shishya (Student), these days the bonding between Guru-Shishya is going away, there is no respect on guru. Education is now becoming a business rather than a media to change the society.
- **Privatization of Educational Institutes:** Privatization of educational institutes is a major cause for the declining ethical values in education system. Privatization of education has emerged in several forms in the recent decade in India. The Government has allowed opening of self-financed private institutions with recognition, which may be termed as commercial private education institutions. With the mushrooming of these private institutes in the modern era, the education has acquired the status of a marketable commodity, where educational institutes are the traders and students are the customers. Universities award degrees and certificates without ensuring the related quality.

Science & Technology

Genome Editing

Genome editing (also called gene editing) is a group of technologies that give scientists the ability to change an organism's DNA. These technologies allow genetic material to be added, removed, or altered at particular locations in the genome. It also raised the ethical question of whether human should alter the genetic material or not.

Arguments in Favour

- **Potential Treatment of Genetic Diseases:** Genome editing is of great interest in the prevention and treatment of human diseases. It is being explored in research on a wide variety of diseases, including single-gene disorders such as cystic fibrosis, hemophilia, and sickle cell disease.

- **Equity and Well-being:** It holds promise for the cheaper and equitable access to treatment and prevention of more complex diseases, such as cancer, heart disease, mental illness, and human immunodeficiency virus (HIV) infection, which are beyond the reach of poor people.
- **Parental Rights and Duties:** For the parents watching their child suffering from painful genetic disorder, gene editing is a ray of hope, which can ameliorate the suffering of their child.
- **Human Life & Dignity:** Germline gene editing can ensure dignified life to a new born by saving her/him from a crippling genetic disease like sickle cell anemia, HIV or mental illness.
- **Justice:** Every year an estimated 6% of total births worldwide - are born with a serious birth defect of genetic or partially genetic origin. For them, just as justice delayed is justice denied, so therapy delayed is therapy denied.
- **Rationality:** "Serious and unquantifiable" safety issues feature in all new technologies like nuclear fusion, space exploration and artificial intelligence. So, it's better to regulate gene editing instead of banning it. E.g. Three parent baby in United Kingdom.
- **Reproductive Autonomy:** Genetic modifications would fall under individual right for autonomy and thus should not be prohibited. 'My body, my life, my decision'.

Ethical Issues

- **Scope and Scale of Editing:** Even though we have been enhancing our biological functioning through various means like caffeine and supplements, the question arises as to what is the limit of such enhancement.
- **Safety:** The possibility of any off-target consequences and mosaicism (when some cells carry the edit but others do not) after editing the genes is real and disturbing.
- **Social Justice and Equity:** The technology might be used for enhancing certain human characteristics like mental capacity, strength and stamina. Additionally, it might reinforce the idea of perfect bodies and perfect personalities and pressurize people to opt for gene editing for the utopian physical characteristics. However, the question arises as to who would have access to such technology? Will it widen the gap between the haves

and have-nots and create a chasm between the rich and the poor not only in monetary terms but also across social, cultural and physical aspects.

- **Patient's Ill-informed Consent:** When doctors offer gene editing alternatives to patients, they put them in the way of risk as long term consequences of modifying genes are not yet fully comprehended. The inability to obtain the consent of future generations also forbids the use gene editing.
- **Issues of Human Nature and Identity:** The social consequences emanating from gene editing might push human beings to question the sense of self and human nature. This idea of changing the human nature and characteristics is problematic at all levels of rationality.
- **Commercial Aspect:** The race for offering on-demand specification in human body has brought various commercial entities into the field of gene therapy and editing with full force. The profit motive overrides the idea of finding genuine solutions for various crippling genetic disorders.
- **Medical Ethics:** Should patients be treated as guinea pig for the experimental studies? Should there be a moratorium on such activities until we completely understand the effects of the process in totality? The ethical grey area regarding the responsibility of medical fraternity regarding the checks and balances that they must impose on themselves before venturing into the unchartered waters of gene therapy is an extremely contentious issue, which impinges on the principles of medical ethics.

Three-Parent Baby

The process of 'three-parent' baby encompass mitochondrial replacement therapy (MRT), a procedure that allows women with mitochondrial disease to give birth to unaffected children by inserting a nucleus from one of her eggs into an enucleated egg from a woman with healthy mitochondria, followed by in vitro fertilization.

Arguments in Support

- **Right of Mothers to have Healthy Babies:** It can give women the chance to have a healthy child without the fear of passing on the painful and debilitating condition of mitochondrial diseases to their babies.

- **Right to have a Dignified and Disease-free Life of New-Born:** Prevention of transmission of serious mitochondrial disease will try to ensure a dignified life for a new-born. Faulty mitochondria can cause catastrophic organ failure in children and lead to severe epilepsy or conditions such as muscular dystrophy. Children often die in an agony that can't be alleviated.
- **Minuscule Contribution of Mitochondrial DNA:** Mitochondrial DNA represents less than 0.054 per cent of the total DNA, and is not part of the nuclear DNA, which determines our personal characteristics and traits such as personality, hair, and eye colour.
- **Alleviation of Human Suffering:** Embryo research is permissible if it's undertaken to alleviate human suffering.
- **Right to Parenthood:** Infertile couple have right to have parenthood which is unattainable in case of pregnancy complications due to faulty mitochondrial DNAs.
- **Rationality:** 'Three-parent' baby is virtually similar to IVF (In-Vitro Fertilization) and sometimes called as 2.01 IVF and have difference of 37 genes only out of total 23000 genes. If IVF is allowed, then rationally MRT should be allowed too.

Ethical Oppositions

- **Embryo has Personhood:** It is unethical to destroy the unwanted embryos generated during research; as an embryo has personhood, and has equal rights as an adult.
- **Risk vs. Compensation:** Egg donation requires powerful hormone therapy, stoppage of normal ovarian functions, super ovulation for the woman to provide eggs, hormones to release matured eggs from the ovaries and minor surgery to remove them from the body. The financial compensation offered will always be less than the risk undertaken. The process may even lead to death, which cannot be compensated for.
- **Precautionary Principle:** MMT could have uncontrollable and unforeseeable consequences, affecting future generations and modifying genetic heritage in an irreversible way, inevitably affecting the human species as a whole.
- **Informed Consent:** It violates the right of informed consent of future generation.

- **Psychological / Emotional Well-being of Child:** It can affect the child's sense of identity and psychological / emotional well-being, when compared to two-parent babies.
- **Access to this Technology**: Its high cost may exclude poor parents and if the access to this technology is not fairly distributed, then economically disadvantaged women may be at risk of exploitation because of the excessive compensation paid to mitochondrial donors.

Ethical Issues in Artificial Intelligence

The term "artificial intelligence" (AI) was mentioned for the first time in 1956 by **John McCarthy** and is usually defined as the capability of a computer program to perform tasks or reasoning processes that we usually associate to intelligence in a human being. Often it has to do with the ability to make a good decision even when there is uncertainty or vagueness, or too much information to handle.

Arguments in Support

- Brings **precision** and **accuracy** along with increase in productivity.
- Intelligent machine systems are transforming our lives for the better. As these systems become more capable, our world becomes more efficient and consequently richer.
- AI systems can potentially be used to help discover insights to treat disease, predict the weather, and manage the global economy.
- The ability of AI systems to transform vast amounts of complex, ambiguous information into insight has the potential to reveal long-held secrets and help solve some of the world's most enduring problems.
- Including **algorithmic accountability** in any AI system is to manage the potential for bias in the decision-making process. Non human interferences can usher in objectivity and rationality.
- 24*7 working, non-stop monitoring effectively with less error and theft control can improve security scenario of the world.
- Right now experts say that current AI technology is not yet capable of achieving this extremely dangerous feat of self-awareness.

- The point at which technology growth surpasses human intelligence is referred to as **"technological singularity"** but it is a hypothesis and current level of sophistication has not reached that level.

Ethical Concerns

- **Unemployment:** What happens after the end of jobs due to automation?
- **Inequality:** How do we distribute the wealth created by machines?
- **Humanity:** How do machines affect our behaviour and interaction? E.g. Rights of robot as Sophia has got citizenship of UAE.
- **Artificial Stupidity:** How can we guard against mistakes? E.g. the training phase cannot cover all possible examples that a system may deal with in the real world.
- **Racist Robots:** How do we eliminate AI bias? For example bias associated with algorithm or data.
- **Security:** How do we keep AI safe from adversaries? E.g. Sophisticated AI technology in the hand of terrorists.
- **Evil Genies:** How do we protect against unintended consequences? For example a rogue robot.
- **Singularity:** How do we stay in control of a complex intelligent system? Dominance of human on earth is due to his intelligence.

Data Privacy and Protection

Data privacy involves the right of any individuals to expect that personal information collected about them will be processed securely and will not be disseminated in any form without their written consent. **Data protection** consists of a framework of security measures designed to guarantee that data are handled in such a manner as to ensure that they are safe from unforeseen, unintended, unwanted or malevolent use. Data protection is the technical mechanism to ensure data privacy.

Ethical Concerns

- Issue of **legitimacy**, **necessity** and **proportionality** related to the collection of data.

- Is it legitimate to collect the data?
- Is it necessary to collect the data?
- How much data will be sufficient?

- Lack of **clear and unambiguous definition** of private data. Wider interpretation of vague definition creates space for coercion and exploitation.
- Categorization of data in different segment and provide differential treatment and protection. Example: Children's data and sensitive data.
- Right to **autonomy** and **self-determination** in respect of one's personal data i.e. **Informed consent.** It means respecting individuals and their rights regarding privacy and the use of information about them.
- Is data collection process is **transparent**? Is associated person aware about its intended use and subsequent repercussions?
- **Improper use and data protection**
  - Does the collected data will be used for intended purpose only?
- **Anonymisation** and respect for the **right to be forgotten.**
- Balancing of the requirements of privacy coupled with other values which the protection of data sub-serves together with the legitimate concerns of the State i.e. security and efficient governance of country.

Guidelines to Resolve the Dilemmas

- Data protection law should have clear and unambiguous definition of personal data.
- **Data Collection and Purpose Principle:**
  - Personal data must be collected in a lawful and fair way for a purpose directly related to a function/activity of the data user (i.e., those who collect personal data).
  - Data subjects (i.e., individuals from whom personal data are collected) must be notified of the purpose and the classes of persons to whom the data may be transferred.
  - Data collected should be necessary, but not excessive.
- **Informed and free consent** is the pivotal principle for legitimate processing.

- **Appropriate use of consent:** The use of consent **'in the right context'** is crucial.
- **Absence of bias:** Data is employed in a way that promotes fairness rather than perpetuating racial, gender or other kinds of bias.

Public Administration & Governance

Indian Journalism and Indian Media

Ethical Issues Involved in Indian Media and Journalism

- **Paid News:** The origin of the unethical practice of paid news goes back to the liberalisation of the Indian economy in 1991. With market forces at play and public investment in private companies, journalists found it sometimes lucrative to write only partially true stories of companies waiting to list on the stock exchanges. This started the race for creation of money to compete in the market and journalism, and news media started political coverage and candidates' praise/criticism on the television for gaining higher monetary benefits. This started the deterioration of ethical standards of many news agencies at present.
- **Negative Nexus with Media:** Often not only the government, but also the opposition parties and other industrial gainers form the nexus with media to create a buzz in the media about certain issues and malign the sitting government. For example, in October 2008, in the midst of stiff opposition to the government granting permission to trial runs of genetically-modified crops a reputed national daily **ran a story about how no farmer suicides were reported from two villages that had switched to GM seeds. However, viewers** were unaware of any idea about such nexuses.
- **Fake News:** Social networking sites like Facebook, Instagram, and Twitter, etc. at present are highly used for circulating fake news. But, on the ethical testing platforms it is found that the authenticity, transparency, etc. are not confirmed and the people's mindsets at present doesn't enquire about such posts but believe and proliferate. Such compromised attitudes towards social ethics are disastrous for the society.

- **Menace of Social Media:** Social Media platforms are now being utilized to mobilize the mass for political and personal benefits. In many events, it is found that social media news spreads like a fire and the mass gets mobilized and results in lynching, communal and caste-based violence, etc. Much of the people are not aware of emotional intelligence and therefore these posts poses a threat to society in large.

Administrative Discretion

In public administration, administrative discretion refers to the flexible exercising of judgment and decision making allowed to public administrators. Regulatory agencies have the power to exercise this type of discretion in their day-to-day activities, and there have been cases where regulatory agencies have abused this power. Administrative law can help these agencies get on the path of following regulations, serve the public, and in turn, a reflection of the public's values and beliefs.

Ethical Issues Involved in Administrative Discretion

- **Ethical Unsoundness:** Public bureaucrats frequently make decisions relating to the lives of citizens, like, for taxes, survival and the dismissal of people. In doing so, the bureaucrats use their discretion according to the incumbent situation and availability of resources. The main concern is that they should make decision to avoid ethical dilemmas. But due to lack of trainings and preparedness provided in the public service, they lack such ethical character to use this discretion in an appropriate manner.
- **Conflict:** There has been a constant conflict between the claims of administration to an absolute discretion and the claims of subjects to a reasonable exercise of it. Discretion is necessary not only for the individualization of the administrative power but also because it is humanly impossible to lay down a rule for every conceivable eventuality in the complex art of modern government. But it is equally true that absolute discretion is a ruthless master. The ethically weak administrator uses such tools for personal benefit than that of for the larger mass.
- **Discretion Utilized with Myopic View:** It is factual that within the rules and regulations laid down by legislature and within

the prescribed procedures, there is plenty of opportunity for the public official to use his discretion. When faced with alternatives the choice of the public official poses an ethical problem, the choice may be acceptable to only a small section of society. The problem is that the selection of one path of action from among several alternatives is often made on the basis of personal preference, political or other associations, or even personal embellishment, thus ignoring identified facts and thus the possibility of rational decision making.

Corruption in Administration

Corruption is a complex social, political and economic phenomenon that affects all countries and hinders the rule of law. It undermines democratic institutions, erodes economies and contributes to political instability. Corruption is the greatest ethical challenge in the world today and we need to combat it.

We must say no to corruption, face it and fight it! It is corrupt individuals that make corrupt government. So, to fight corruption, there is an urgent need for good values to be inculcated in people. Confucius said, "The strength of a nation is derived from the integrity of a home". Charity begins at home. It is the duty of parents to teach their wards good values. Campaigns and enlightenment programs should be conducted to stir up the awareness that values are still as important as they were in the past. The failure of some parents to instill good values in their offspring has affected national development. Children need to be properly trained in order for them to say no to corruption when they are of age. In the past, corruption and other crimes were minimal in society because values were instilled.

A.P.J Abdul Kalam said, "If a country is to be corruption free and become a nation of beautiful minds, I strongly feel there are three societal members who can make a difference: the father, mother and teacher."

Ethical Issues Involved in Corruption

The ethical dilemma that faces the public officer with regard to corrupt practices as result of private interests primarily concerns his reaction to the situation. If a corrupt practice or an attempt to corruption is exposed, it is quite possible that the official's personal loyalties or his political relationships may be in conflict with his official responsibilities.

- **Hindrances for Development:** Corruption leads to loss of wealth and prosperity which is a great loss for the future of India. For the past ten years, India has shown growth in corruption rate, where the country has lost billions and billions dollars of money in various scams, which are tax payer's money. Many developmental projects are taking unnecessary delay for their completion due to corruption. This leads to backwardness in every field like sports, technology, medicine, research, economy, defence, and infrastructure.
- **Obstacles for Business:** Corruption in public services sector carries high risks for conducting good businesses. Companies are likely to perform unintentional red tapism, petty corruption, bribes for finalizing any procedures or deals. Payments to expedite public services, such as police protection, water supply, and government assistance became a headache.
- **Backwardness and Poverty:** Due to corruption in India, the Indian government is unable or lacked the will to eradicate poverty. While the rich are becoming richer, the poor are becoming poorer. Despite the announcement of rehabilitation and monetary packages, corrupt people in various government departments and contractors, suck the fund through various means leaving very little for the end users.
- **Brain Drain and Loss of Talent:** Corrupt government employees and mediators offer jobs to unskilled and incapable candidates by taking bribe leaving the management with poor decision making. When good employees in private sectors also face harassment due to government policies and corruption in India, they move to foreign countries.
- **Loss of Faith in Judicial System:** There is a high risk of corruption in India while dealing with India's judiciary, particularly in lower court levels - put the common man in great stress. With bribes often exchanged in return for favorable court decisions leads to people to lose faith in judiciary.

Whistle-blowing

With the rise of nexus and wrongdoing activities in organizations today, it has become essential for employers to have a mechanism in place that encourages and protects employees who report wrongdoing within the organization. A person who raises concerns and reveals information about such cases is a "whistle-blower." Whistle-blowers may make their allegations internally (to other people within the organization) or externally (to regulators, law enforcement agencies, media, etc.). The law on whistle-blowing in the Indian public sector is primarily covered under the Whistle Blowers Protection Act, 2014, which details a process for receiving complaints relating to allegations of corruption or willful misuse of power against a public servant.

Ethical Issues Involved in Whistle Blowing

- **Fear of Social Stigma:** The fear of social stigma and losing job makes it difficult for even those who are aware of such frauds to come up. Many a times, even though an officer has a character of identifying the malign activities in the organization, he refuse to make complain internally or externally due to social pressure of being defamed.
- **Occupational Hazards:** Whistleblowers are shunned by management and as such, it becomes very difficult for them to make a choice between personal responsibility, professional responsibility and organizational responsibility. Whistle-blower complaints against the employees of an organisation or the employers cause a violation of occupation agreements. Breaching such a confidentiality agreement can make the whistle-blower liable, so these kinds of agreements can put the burden of liability of sanctions on them. Whistleblowers bear the fear of their superiors that if they are also involved in wrongdoings then they will have to face the adverse actions even their suspension at extremes.
- **Lack of Ethical Compliance:** In many organizations, there are less practice of ethical compliance sessions and promotion of activity of vigilance and whistle blowing, so that the wrong practices in the organizations must not be revealed.
- **Security Issue:** Although, in the eyes of codes of conduct as well as in the code of ethics the whistle-blowers act in a righteous manner by revelation of any malign activity but, such act put him and his/her family in danger. Even after the enactment of several acts (like Whistle-blower Act), many

incidents witnessed the vulnerability of job security and their life, etc. of the whistle-blowers, and no one is held responsible and accountable to such incidences (for example Vyapam case in Madhya Pradesh).

Nepotism

Nepotism can be defined as 'the act of using power or influence to get unfair advantages for members of one's family'. As a consequence, such instances of overlooking merit principle, may lead to the declining of the quality of the public service. Indian politics has seen the most of nepotism in its history, despite ours being a democratic country. Also, it is very common practice in government offices.

Ethical Issues Involved in Nepotism

- **Trust Deficit:** The act of nepotism upsets the trust and resulting in unethical management, owing to the ability of a select few to weaken control measures on account of their personal relationship with the policy-maker, and by reason of their not being easily dismissed or replaced by others.
- **Issue of Competence:** When nepotism is dominant in any organization or in public services, the energy level and morale of the employees degrades and as an outcome it reduces their performance. Workforces may stop giving their best and accept a career at their current level. Such incidences of nepotism has potential to dilute the talent pool by inserting less-qualified personnel into positions that suit others better.
- **Incite Violent Activity:** Nepotism also causes the lopsided development as the benefit of growth not reached to the lower strata in the similar manner as it reached to the upper strata. Such nepotism also causes certain prominent security predicaments for the nation. Rise of Left Wing Extremism (LWE) is empirical evidence in this regard.

Other Ethical Problem Areas

- **Public Accountability:** Public officials have great responsibility to implement key public policies. They ought to be accountable for their official actions to their superiors, the courts and the public. It is however, possible for them to hide behind prescribed procedures, the cloak of competence and even political office-bearers.

- **Policy Dilemmas:** Policy makers in government bodies are often challenged by conflicting responsibilities. They have definite loyalties to their bosses, but also to society. They have liberty to act on behalf and in the interest of others, but they must be answerable to others, their superiors and society for their actions. The official's obligation to respect the political process may conflict with his view on how the objects of policy making are treated. It can be understood that the dilemma of the public official is the clash between his opinion of the public interest and the requirements of law.

Environment

Inter-Generational Equity

Inter-generational equity in economic, psychological, and sociological contexts is the concept or idea of **fairness** or **justice** between generations. The concept can be applied to fairness in dynamics between children, youth, adults and seniors, in terms of treatment and interactions. It raises the ethical dilemma of striking balance between the rights of present and future generations.

Arguments in Support

- **Gandhian Ethics:** Gandhiji's idea that "nature has enough to satisfy every one's needs, but not to satisfy anybody's greed" became one line ethic to modern environmentalism. It is for this reason that taking more than the required resources is seen as theft.
- **Accountability to Future Generation:** We do not inherit the Earth from our ancestors; we borrow it from our children. So we are accountable to their need and want.
- **Informed Consent:** We cannot take decisions for future generations without their consent that what will be good for them.
- **Distributive Justice:** Present generations may be said to exercise power over (remote) future generations when, for example, they create conditions that make it costly for future generations to decide against continuing to pursue present generations'

projects. In this way, present generations effectively manipulate interests of future generations, and can successfully achieve the intended result of having their projects continued.

- **Responsibility:** Future people's existence, number, and specific identity depend (are contingent) upon currently living people's decisions and actions. As with greater control, comes greater responsibility, so it is the responsibility of present generation to ensure inter-generational equity.

Arguments in Opposition

- **Positivist Thought:** No exact quantification of future population hinders rational decision making in terms of conservation of resource. How much is sufficient for how many people?
- **No Rights for Future Population:** The future generation by definition, do not exist now. They cannot now be the present bearer or subject of anything, including rights.
- **No Morality can be Attached to Future Generations:** Some people doubt whether intergenerational relations can be evaluated in moral terms at all. That fundamental doubt pertains particularly to actions that affect persons in the far future, such as the disposal of radioactive waste that remains hazardous for millennia.
- **Denial of Application of Distributive Justice:** Considerations of justice do not apply to intergenerational relations, because there is a lack of direct reciprocity between generations of people who are not contemporaries. Among non-contemporaries, there is no mutual cooperation and there are no exchanges in kind.

Climate Refugees

Environmental migrants or climate refugees are people who are forced to leave their home region due to sudden or long-term changes to their local environment. These are changes which compromise their well-being or secure livelihood. Their migration raised the ethical question about their acceptance and rehabilitation and denial by some countries in the name of security and other concerns.

Arguments in Support

- **Humanitarian Support:** Being human they have the right to live a dignified life. UN charter also supports it. So, it is the responsibility of every nation to help climate refugees.

- **Historical Principle and Concept of Justice:** The historical principle is based on the "polluter pays" notion. It takes historical wrongs into account and bases justice claims not only on unfair distribution at the current point in time but also on what has been done in past decades and centuries. More developed countries (MDCs) in general and the U.S. in particular, have built their wealth and prosperity by means of fossil fuel combustion and have enjoyed the benefits that these developments bring with them.
- **Common But Differentiated Responsibility with Respective Capability (CBDR-RC):** CBDR-RC principle acknowledges all states have shared obligation to address environmental destruction but denies equal responsibility of all states with regard to environmental protection. Based on its development and coping capacity, every country should help climate refugees.
- **Egalitarianism and Shared Prosperity:** All people are equal and deserve equal rights and opportunities and hence climate refugees should be treated fairly.
- **Conflict and Violence:** Inhumane treatment to climate refugees will breed disaffection, discontent and may usher in violence and conflicts, which will hamper the lasting peace of the world.

Arguments in Opposition

- **Violation of State Sovereignty:** Every sovereign country has right to take decision without any external pressure or coercion. They are the sole arbiter on the issue of immigration of climate refugees.
- **Citizen's Hardship:** Migrants can put extra pressure on the resources, jobs, depress wages and marketplace competition of a nation and may compete aggressively with natives. It may result in the hardship for native population.
- **Vicious Cycle of Pollution:** Immigration of climate refugees in developed country will result in their acceptance of materialism of developed nation which will set vicious cycle of pollution and ecological degradation across the globe.
- **Right Not to Associate:** State's right to limit immigration as an instance of its more general right to freedom of association.

The right to freedom of association includes the right not to associate and even the right to disassociate.

- **Environmental Degradation:** Immigration would conflict with the interests of non-human beings since it results in large ecosystem and habitat destruction.

Issue of Man-Animal Conflict & Culling of Vermin Species

Vermin are pests or nuisance animals that spread diseases or destroy crops or livestock. Disease-carrying rodents and insects are the usual case, but the term is also applied to larger animals–especially small predators–typically because they consume resources which humans consider theirs, such as livestock and crops. In the wake of rising Man-Animal conflict and crop destruction, from time to time governments issue notifications for their killing and population control. Example: Nilgai in Bihar, Monkey in Himachal Pradesh and wild boar in Uttarakhand. But, is it right to cull animals? Or do we have the right to cull wild animals?

Arguments in Favour of Culling

- **Gandhian Ethics:** Gandhiji's vision of Sarvodaya implies a healthy development and environment that can be evolved by man to ensure his harmonious existence with nature and other living beings. Regarding the law of species Gandhi believed that without the cooperation and sacrifice of both human and non-human beings, evolution is not possible. Being rational human beings, we are the custodians of the rest of creation and should respect their rights and cherish the diversity.
- **Biospheric Egalitarianism:** The "**deep ecology movement**", endorses "**Biospheric egalitarianism**", the view that all living things are alike in having value in their own right, independent of their usefulness to others. The deep ecologists respect this intrinsic value, taking care, for example, when walking on the mountainside not to cause unnecessary damage to the plants.
- **Animal Right's Perspective:** Animal Rights theorists, such as the philosopher Tom Regan, maintain that humans and certain other animals share critical similarities (such as being able to feel pain and having desires about their future). These shared capacities, on this view, underpin the **possession of moral rights of animals.** In the case of wild animals, we should not

kill, confine, or otherwise interfere in their lives. It is neither our right, nor our duty, to cull, nor in other ways to manage wild animals.

- **Respect for Nature Perspectives:** "Respect for nature" refers to views, concerned with values other than those possessed by individual sentient living beings. It focuses on protecting the value of naturalness itself, preservation of whole species, on protecting the "integrity" of species, and biodiversity conservation.

Arguments against Culling

- **Anthropocentric Perspective:** It puts man at the centre while deciding any environmental conflict and hence subjugates the rights of animal with respect to the right of man. Therefore, vermin species can be culled for the benefit of human i.e. saving standing crops.
- **Utilitarian Perspective:** Utilitarianism theory is based on the idea that we should aim to bring about the best outcome overall, taking into account everyone affected by the decision. Suppose a deer population has grown so large that there is insufficient food to support it, causing all the deer to suffer and starve. In this case, culling some deer as painlessly as possible is likely to reduce animal suffering overall.
- **Contractarian Perspective:** Contractarianism is an influential group of ethical approaches which maintain that morality has emerged – or should emerge – from humans making agreements or contracts among themselves. But animals can't make contracts. Thus, from a Contractarian perspective, wild animals fall outside the ethical sphere and are, essentially, a resource for human use.

Environment vs. Development Debate

The genesis of **Environment vs. development debate** lies in the conflicting need of environmental conservation and social justice for poor.

Arguments in favour of Environment

- **Intrinsic Value of Nature:** This theory implies a kind of respect for the whole environment as an entity with its own intrinsic value, just because it exists and it's not an object made for our exploitation.

- **Consequentialism & Concept of Responsibility and Intergenerational Equity:** Consequentialism talks about the consequences that we generate with our actions in the present but mostly in the future, for next generations. Here we find the concept of responsibility that's a basis of ethical arguments and finally equity, related to the present society, the future being and all the components of the environment (inter-generational equity).
- **Deep Ecology Movement and Biospheric Egalitarianism:** The **"deep ecology movement"**, endorses **"Biospheric egalitarianism"**, the view that all living things are alike in having value in their own right, independent of their usefulness to others. So other animals have equal claim over environment.
- **Moral rights of animals and Environmental Justice** affirms the sacredness of Mother Earth, ecological unity and the interdependence of all species, and the right to be free from ecological destruction.
- **Strong Sustainability:** Natural capital comprises of all natural occurring organic and inorganic resources including genetic information, biodiversity, life-support systems and sinks. Strong sustainability stipulates an undiminished bequest of natural capital.

Arguments in favour of Development

- **Right to LIfe with Dignity:** Poor people have right to live with dignity and in the garb of environmental conservation, denial of their legitimate basic need tantamount to tyranny.
- **Responsibility of State:** A sovereign state has responsibility to uplift the living standard of deprived people and usher in intra-generational equity in society. State cannot shed its responsibility in the name of environmental protection.
- **Democracy vs. Elltes:** In democracy, it's the need of the majority that apparently counts, not a few elite conservationists.
- **Anthropocentrism and Equity**, Fairness and Justice to deprived people.

- **Weak Sustainability:** Human-made capital comprises of all attributes including human and social capital i.e., people, their skill, intelligence, virtues, and institutions. Weak sustainability stipulates an undiminished capital bequest irrespective of how it is composed.

Economy

Wealth Maximization & Equal Distribution of Wealth

To most people who are not economists, the word "wealth" suggests money. But to an economist, it refers to weighting preferences for the things that people want, either by willingness to pay for a thing, if you do not own it or by unwillingness to part with it voluntarily, if you do own it.

Arguments in favour of Wealth Maximization

- Wealth maximization does not depend on profits. Profit maximization presents a shorter term view as compared to wealth maximization. Short-term profit maximization can be achieved by the managers at the cost of long-term sustainability of the business.
- The wealth maximization is based on **cash flows** and not on profits. Unlike the profits, cash flows are exact and definite and therefore avoid any ambiguity associated with accounting profits.
- Wealth maximization is superior to profit maximization. Profit can easily be manipulative, if there is a change in accounting assumption/policy, there is a change in profit.

Disadvantages of Wealth Maximization

- Wealth maximization is a perspective idea and not a descriptive idea.
- The objectives of the wealth maximization are not clear.
- When ownership and management are separated, difficulties arise.

Ethical Issues Involved in Wealth Maximization

- **Invisible Hand & Visible Consequences:** The apparent "moral neutrality" of maximization of wealth is the ultimate corporate objective in the first place. But at the same time they are focused to evade the moral accountability in their actual professional pursuit of wealth. The real workplace realities betray the utilitarian assumption (produce the greatest good for the greatest number) - of the 'invisible hand' of free market exchange.

- **Valuing Human Resources:** There are no easy institutional or legal fixes to the problem of unethical behavior in the pursuit of maximization. Ethics is about hard choices, and the decision to forgo a measure of wealth in order to pursue a right course of action may prove anything but easy for a corporate manager. Nevertheless, there seem to be some means available for smoothing the transition to an ethically oriented approach.

Ethical Issues in Farmers' Distress

Farmer's distress is a typical situation of Indian farmers, having low income and minimal level of survival amenities due to low agricultural income. Agrarian problems, in the present context, are mainly in terms of low agricultural prices and, consequently, poor farm incomes. Low productivity in agriculture and related supply side factors are equally important. An issue that is connected is the declining average size of farm holdings and the viability of this size for raising farm incomes.

Ethics forms an important part of farming. There is a growing need in agriculture for farmers and the industries that serve them to reflect on the morals that underpin their actions. Progress begets progress. Innovation begets innovation. We barely have time to stop and think about things like far-reaching consequences. The continuous farmers' distress is a major reason for increased farmers' suicide.

Ethical Issues

- **Politicization of Farmers' Issue:** The poor Indian farmer has rarely become a national issue before elections. Politicians have often worried about their vote during individual state elections, but even there, farmer or agricultural concerns have rarely been a big, decisive factor. The other problem is that in terms of vote banks, even in most states, politicians woo specific castes instead of the farming/agricultural community as a whole. The empathy and other basic ethical standards are missing with the political leaders for diluting the farmer's distress.

- **Minimum Support Price (MSP) and Loan Waiver:** The MSP creates the ethical tension for the farmers as its price are low and the distributions are also very inconsistent. There were few takers among traders who would be willing to pay MSP and MSP could not help every farmer - it would be of little use for farmers, who grew a lot of vegetables, etc.
- **Loan Waivers Create a Moral Hazard:** A farmer who has seen his loan waived once would tend to wait and delay repayment in anticipation that the government would announce a waiver again. Similarly, those who have managed to pay off their loans on time would feel cheated.
- **Moneylender's Dominance:** For cultivators who have taken land on rent, it does not work - they typically borrow from moneylenders, not banks. The farmers always bear the burden of such moneylenders. The behaviour of such lenders is generally harsh and unethical to them.
- **Sustainability:** Agricultural businesses that ruin the land have chemical run-off in local water sources and inadvertently harm wildlife and don't help to sustain the business or the environment. Such event causes adverse situation for farmers to grow and earn and the industrial developments are unethically using the lands for their personal benefits and the farmer's stake are at risk. This results in an unhealthy environment for farmers and also future of food productions.

Ethics & Corporate Social Responsibility

The concept of Corporate Social Responsibility (CSR) is underpinned by the idea that corporations can no longer act as isolated economic entities operating in detachment from broader society. Although there is no fixed definition, the concept revolves around that fact that corporations need to focus beyond earning just profits and work for the betterment of the society. Under the Companies (amendments) Act, 2013, CSR (2 per cent of the companies' profit) is made mandatory in India.

Arguments in Favour of CSR

- **Improves the Image of Company:** CSR activities reflect positively on the image of a company. When you implement CSR policies in your company, it increases your goodwill. Consumers will be more willing to avail your products/services because of the clean image of your company.

- **Satisfied Employees:** Employees want to feel proud of the organization they work for. An employee with a positive attitude towards the company is less likely to look for a job elsewhere.
- **Overall Improvements:** Since the company is working on the ground therefore it knows the situation of its surroundings and the adversities faced by the society members and hence can work better for the overall development of the society.
- **Long Term Future for Business:** CSR is not something for the short-term. It's all about achieving long-term results and business continuity. Large businesses refer to: "shaping a more sustainable society".

Ethical Issues Involved in CSR

- **Lack of Empathy and Community Participation:** CSR, the term is a combination of 'Corporate' and 'societies' responsibility together. However, there is a lack of interest of the local community in participating and contributing to CSR activities of companies. No serious efforts have been made to spread awareness about CSR, earn participation from the locals and to know about the local's problems that need to be addressed.
- **Lack of Leadership and Management at the Ground Level:** There is a lack of capacity building of the local non-governmental organizations and local leaders that can effectively contribute to the ongoing CSR activities initiated by companies. This seriously compromises scaling up of CSR initiatives and subsequently limits the scope of such activities.
- **Issues of Transparency:** Lack of transparency is one of the key issues found in several CSR activities. There is an expression by the companies that there exists lack of transparency on the part of the local implementing agencies as they do not make adequate efforts to disclose information on their programs, audit issues, impact assessment and utilization of funds.
- **Low or No Accountability:** The Company Act doesn't penalize

a defaulter and just allows them to walk away with an explanation regarding their failure on CSR activities. Therefore, the CSR enablers do not show any responsibility or accountability towards the law for its spirits and merely tries to avert the adverse actions of the government. This results in high corruption, low levels of public confidence, low development and weak institutions.

- **Visibility Factor:** The role of media in highlighting good cases of successful CSR initiatives is welcomed as it spreads good stories and sensitizes the local population about various ongoing CSR initiatives of companies. This apparent influence of gaining visibility and branding exercise often leads many non-governmental organizations to involve themselves in event-based programs; in the process, they often miss out on meaningful grassroots interventions.
- **Narrow Perception towards CSR Initiatives:** Nongovernmental organizations and Government agencies usually possess a narrow outlook towards the CSR initiatives of companies, often defining CSR initiatives more donor-driven than local in approach. As a result, they find it hard to decide whether they should participate in such activities at all in medium and long-run.

Ethics and Corporate Governance

Corporate Governance in India is a set on internal controls, policy and procedures which form the framework of a company's operations and its dealings with various stakeholders such as customers, management, employees, government and industry bodies.

Ethical Issues Involved in Corporate Governance

- **Ethical Issues and Business:** The objective of any business is to make and supply goods or services to customers, which will lead to prosperity of the economy. Businesses, which make goods like - alcohol, cigarettes, drugs, etc., are in ethical dilemma for business, as society sees these products as goods that are not good for the society. The contradiction is - these companies offer employment opportunities to many people in the society.

- **Moral Rights Between Company and Stakeholders:** To keep the stakeholders happy, companies indulge in various unethical activities like - manipulating the book of accounts to show higher profits, reducing the work force to show higher earnings.
- **Ethical Issues Relating to Relationship Between Companies:** In business, takeover is acquisition of one company by another. In case of hostile takeover, the company acquires a target company without the willingness of the target company board. The contradiction here is, the company might have indulged in hostile takeover which can result in higher profits for both the business, hence more employment opportunity in the society. Industry espionage refers to the activities such as theft of trade secrets, bribery, blackmail, spying on commercial organizations to increase their profits, or for their survival.
- **Political Contribution Made by Companies:** In a country like India, corporate groups contribute a part of their profit to the political parties and in return they expect that the sitting government to frame policies which will help grow their business. The contradiction is that the companies contribute funds towards the growth of the political parties but that may not reflect towards the growth of people and the society.

International Ethics

Ethics of Developmental Assistance and Conditionalities

Development assistance include grant and loan assistance within and across sovereign territorial limits by governmental and non-governmental actors and agencies. But the associated conditionalities with loans have raised the ethical question on the intent and action of donor countries.

Arguments in Favour

- **Altruism and Humanitarian Support:** According to this argument donor assistance is motivated by altruistic and humanitarian considerations.
- **Risk Minimization:** It is used to advance wide-ranging objectives such as efficiency, equity of the public sector, overcoming infrastructure deficiencies, promoting growth, facilitating poverty

alleviation and good governance that result in minimising risks for loan repayment.

- **Contractualism**: Conditions are imposed as part of lending or grant assistance unilaterally or by mutual agreement of the donor and the recipient. It is transparent and informed.
- **Realism:** Realist arguments also support the conditionalities in developmental assistance, as every has right act in its best interest.

Ethical Concerns

- **Irrational**: A case is often made that conditionality of assistance is required to ensure that the project is implemented as agreed to ensure that the donor gets repaid according to the terms of lending. This is a **weak argument** as repayment of loans would depend critically upon a recipient's credit worthiness rather than any loan conditions. In addition, sovereign default on international borrowing has serious economic and fiscal consequences for the defaulter and as a result is relatively rare.
- **Coercion**: Conditionality often forces a recipient to make political choices on reform options and to commit to specific policy prescription. It amounts to violation of sovereign rights of nation due to their compulsion and moribund situation.
- **Paternalism**: The donor knows best what is good for the recipient. Donor conditions frequently embody an implicit judgment that the recipient lacks the knowledge to pursue economic policies that serve its best interest and donor agencies have better knowledge as to what would work best. The "**Washington Consensus**" and the "**Modified Washington Consensus**" are examples that shaped loan conditions in the 1980s and 1990s. Such policies, however, do not safeguard for aid dictum of "**do no harm**", as the consequences of failure of lending operations are only borne by the recipient.
- **Cultural Relativism and Ethnocentric Act**: Donor evaluates the socio political set up of recipient from his own world view. So, conditionalities amount to imposing of socio-political norms of the donor on the recipient country.
- **Economic and Political Imperialism:** Sometimes aid is used to advance wide-ranging objectives such as support for a specific

ideology, influence peddling, and economic and political imperialism. It violates the **cosmopolitan** principles of engagement between two countries and **pacifist ideals**.

- **Asymmetry in Negotiation**: Even though contractual obligation are transparent and informed, they are negotiated by two parties which are standing at totally different pedestal and hence the terms of negotiation are nor fair and equitable.

Humanitarian Intervention

Humanitarian intervention is a means to prevent or stop a gross violation of human rights in a state, where such state is either incapable or unwilling to protect its own people, or is actively persecuting them. But there is ethical debate on the vested interest, intent and sanction of Humanitarian Intervention.

Arguments in Favour

- **Cosmopolitan Perspective:** Sovereign states have the responsibility to protect the human rights of people as sanctioned by UN charter.
- **Moral Duty:** Moral duty is the complimentary part of respect for sovereign rights of nation. In this way it is an obligation on other states to protect human right of people in a rogue state.
- **Sanctity of Life:** Human intervention is essential to restore sanctity of human life by protecting civilians from human right abuse.

Arguments in Opposition

- **Sovereignty and Right of Self Government:** Humanitarian intervention violates the sovereign right of a state.
- **Against the Norms of International Order:** Permitting humanitarian intervention creates a chaotic condition and may lead to other type of interventions. E.g. Regime change in the garb of humanitarian intervention.
- **Futile Exercise:** Majority of human interventions have failed to achieve their objectives. Conversely they have accentuated the plight of native people. Example: Yemen and Somalia.
- **Vested Interest and Hegemony:** Sometime world power use intervention as a policy to assert its hegemony or promote vested interest. Example: Gulf oil and intervention in Iraq.

WTO Norms of International Trade and Interest of LDCs (Least Developed Countries)

Duty free trade policies of WTO have been criticized for their undue tilt in favour of developed countries. In this scenario different arguments in its favour and opposition are following:

Arguments in Favour

- **Global Prosperity:** Duty-free trade will usher in efficiency and boost global prosperity in long-term. Fruits of prosperity will also seep into least developed countries.
- **Free Market Liberal Perspective:** Government should not interfere with free trade and market, and forces of globalization will adjust accordingly.

Arguments in Opposition

- **Humanitarian Perspective:** Legitimate developmental needs of poor countries like subsidized food to hungry people should not be seen as distortion of trade and market.
- **Exploitation of LDCs:** Asymmetric trade potential and weak economic development of LDCs hamper their negotiation capability and leads to economic exploitation.
- **Inequality:** Prosperity in the absence of credible distribution will further increase inequality.
- **Absence of Fair and Equitable System:** Free trade without any safeguards to nascent industries of LDCs is unfair and in long-term hurt the interest of LDCs.
- **Protectionism:** Rising protectionism in developed countries in the garb of various non-tariff barriers such as phytosanitary standards has diminished the export potential of LDCs.

Manipulation of Currency

Recently USA labeled China as a currency manipulator and to countries that engage in a certain degree of currency intervention, a monetary policy in which a central bank buys or sells foreign currency in exchange for domestic currency, generally with the intention of influencing the exchange rate and commercial policy.

Arguments in Favour

- **Sovereign Right:** It is the sovereign right of a nation to take decision free from external coercion and pressure.
- **Realism and National Interest:** In the international arena every country tries to maximize the gains for its citizen and from this perspective 'it's absolutely fine to enhance export and trade by manipulation of currency'.
- **Legal Perspective:** There is no legal binding treaty on exchange rate managing. Further there isn't any mechanism to determine when and how much exchange can be changed. So manipulation of currency is not reprehensible.
- **Invisible Hand of Market:** Market will adjust and wipe out the negative outcome of currency manipulation.

Arguments in Opposition

- **Liberal Perspective:** It violates the principle of free and fair trade across the world. It will aid undue advantage to the exporter of currency manipulator and violate the principle of fairness and equity.
- **Institutional Arrangement:** The aggressive tricks like currency manipulation will violate the institutional arrangement for free flow of trade and may leads to trade wars. It will dismember the world trade flow and in long term will reduce the efficiency of trade and prosperity of the world.
- **Discriminatory:** It will be discriminatory to other nations who are not manipulating their exchange rates. Further, it will set the trend and provide undue incentive for currency manipulation by other countries.
- **Exploitation of LDCs:** Developed countries have deep pockets to bear the repercussions of currency manipulations but LDCs will suffer disproportionately.

Security

Human Rights of Terrorists

Terrorism is the most serious violation of human rights and human rights violation is a major causative factor of terrorism. In this emotional and passionate matter the relevant question is about safeguarding the human rights of people and usher in humane counter terrorism operation. In this light the ethical question is about the human rights of terrorists. Do they have human rights?

Arguments in Favour

- **Inalienability**: Human rights are inalienable rights and act of terrorism cannot separate it from human beings.
- **Human Dignity**: Human rights are neither a gift nor a commodity that can be given or taken away. Instead human rights are underpinned by the notion of human dignity and it means that every individual has rights regardless of where that individual is geographically positioned in the world (even if state is not a liberal democracy) and regardless of any atrocities they may commit e.g. act of terrorism. A failure to respect human rights is a failure for humanity.

Arguments in Opposition

- **Non-Existence of Human Right:** Human rights are a human construct and therefore exist only where they are enforceable. So, in case where means of enforcement are not available (terror infested disturbed areas or liberated zones), talking about human rights is absurd.
- **Alienability of Human Rights**: Human Rights are mere human concepts and their existence depends on their enforceability. So, the absence of mechanism of implementation dilutes the concept of inalienability, ultimately neutralizing the very concept of Human Rights.

Disproportionate Use of Force by Government against Civilians

Recent cases of use of pellet guns against protesting civilian population in China and India has raised the ethical question of how much force a state can use against civilians? Is it ethical that an entity, which derives its legitimacy from people, can use excessive force against people?

Arguments in Support

- **Law and Order:** State has legitimate right to uphold law and order and any form of violence is condemned. If it continues even after the warning and harms the symbol of state, tantamount to challenging the authority of state and warrants strong action from state.

- **Right to Defence of Security Personnel:** Security personnel have the right to defend them in case of violence. But it should be used with due care and constraint.
- **Violation of Fundamental Duties by People:** Constitution prescribes certain duties for citizen which is counter part of their right. They should uphold it and avoid violence in any form.

Arguments in Opposition

- **Humanitarian Ground:** It's illegitimate to use disproportionate force against an unarmed civilian. Dissent is the hallmark of democracy and it is totally uncivilized to use pellet guns against them.
- **Social Contract:** State derives its legitimacy from people and should not use excess repression against them.
- **Democracy:** Democracy represents the will of the people and dissent is its hallmark. So democratic states should detest from using excessive force against civilians.

Arrest of Fishermen Straying into Foreign Waters

Arrest of fishermen straying into foreign waters has raised the ethical issue of territorial rights of countries and humanitarian rights of fishermen.

Arguments in Support of Fishermen

- Violation of their right to livelihood and dignity.
- It's inhumane on the part of arresting country that denies poor people from their livelihood.
- It's the failure of fishery policy of government to ensure ample catch in native waters.
- It can be an unintentional straying or trespassing in case of wandering or failure in identifying the state boundary in open sea.
- Root causes of decline of fish population are different. These are
    - Climate change.
    - Mechanized trawling.
    - Overexploitation and lack of time for recuperation of fishing zones.

Arguments in Favour of State

- Legitimate right of the state to arrest foreign fishermen as per the international law.
- Protection of fishing rights of native fishermen.
- If it is a deliberate action of breach or stealing of catch then state should arrest them to uphold the general law of land.
- Safety and security of nation - as terrorist sometimes try to enter in the garb of fishermen.

Nuclear Weapons and Disarmament

Is using a nuclear weapon morally permissible under some circumstances? Is it ethical to implement nuclear deterrence (threatening to use atomic weapons) as a self-defense strategy? These are some of the eminent questions on which hinges the fate of humanity.

Ethical Concerns with Nuclear Weapons

- **It is immoral because of what it means.**

The current paradigm is immoral primarily because it promotes the idea that, in order to resolve conflict, it is ethically acceptable and practically feasible to destroy others, in terrible pain, forgetting that we belong to a common human family.

- **It is immoral because of what it has done.**

Nuclear weapons were first conceived and then used in Hiroshima and Nagasaki which resulted in widespread mortality and suffering of future generations suggest that it was a case of disproportionate use of force which has no place in a civilized society.

- **It is immoral because of what it continues to do.**

It creates an unequal order on nuclear haves and have-nots. Those responsible for nuclear weapons, proactively maintain a mindset based on the assumption that "national security" is the supreme good, an end in itself. Therefore, any sacrifice, including human sacrifice, is more than justified, even if it leads to the extinction of the entire human race, a phenomenon more prevalent since Hiroshima and Nagasaki. Despite witnessing the atrocities, the unspeakable suffering and the damage projected into future generations ever, more powerful nuclear tests and devastating weapons manufacturing continues.

- **It is immoral because of what it is prepared to do.**

In spite of the threats of nuclear holocaust, ever complex and expensive nuclear systems are getting created. If terrorist will get nuclear weapon by chance, it will be an unimagined catastrophe for mankind.

- **Anthropological Perspective**
    - How has it been possible for a small group of the nuclear elites to prevail over the survival instincts of an entire species?
    - How is it that even though 90% of the global population is in favour of the complete elimination of nuclear weapons, the nuclear weapons continue to be manufactured?

Arguments in Favour of Nuclear Weapons

- **MAD (Mutually Assured Destruction) and Nuclear Peace:** Critics usually justify their position with reference to MAD and the Cold War, claiming that a "**nuclear peace**" was the result of both the U.S. and the U.S.S.R. possessing mutual second-strike retaliation capability.
- **Deterrence to Aggression:** Some critics say that disarmament would undermine the ability of governments to threaten sufficient retaliation upon an attack to deter aggression against them.
- **Nuclear Ban will be Ineffective:** Nuclear ban will be ineffective and send the transparent regime of nuclear framework underground and usher in clandestine nuclear activity across the world.

Disaster Management Ethics

Disasters are unpredictable, acute situations which cause extensive damage, destruction, and suffering, and which often cannot be dealt with by the local community on its own. The people responding to disasters (victims, health care personnel, humanitarian aid workers or military personnel) often record disillusionment and a kind of ethical frustration with making ethical decisions during disasters. Ethical practices help to provide stability for organizations in a rapidly changing and increasingly complex world.

A typical disaster management continuum comprises six

elements; the pre-disaster phase includes prevention, mitigation and preparedness, while the post-disaster phase includes response, rehabilitation, reconstruction and recovery.

This substantial and complex task requires significant funding - both internally and externally. Such funding is seldom immediately available hence disaster fund raising is in itself a complex task that poses unique ethical dilemmas.

Utility of Disaster Management

- **Prevent Disaster:** Disaster management teams can help to prevent the disasters before its arrival. The Disaster management team may examine the possible causes of disaster, and may take appropriate measures to avert a disaster.
- **Post-disaster Rescue Operations:** Disaster management personnel can undertake rescue operations effectively. Trained disaster management personnel can rescue people effectively at the time of floods, major fires, building collapses, and so on.
- **Post-disaster Relief:** To reduce the misery of the disaster victims, disaster management team is responsible to provide relief measures to the victims. For instance, the team ensures arrangement for food, clothing, and relief camps, medicines, etc.
- **Rehabilitation Programmes:** Disaster management team can work effectively to undertake rehabilitation programmes in the affected areas.
- **Provide Collaboration:** The disaster management team undertakes collaborative works relating to the disaster. Such collaborations are required with various agencies-private and government (including hospitals) in order to obtain funds and donations, and other resources or services so as to manage and overcome the disaster.
- **Environment Protection:** Disaster management team can help to protect and preserve the environment. For example, a disaster management team can plan pre-emptive action to avert forest fires, etc.

Ethical Issues Involved in Disaster Management

- **Crisis of Funds and its Utilization:** The response to any disaster, to provide safety, food, shelter, clothing, and security for the victims of the tragedy requires substantial and complex task i.e., significant funding - both internally and externally. Such funding is seldom immediately available hence disaster fund raising is in itself a complex task that poses unique ethical dilemmas.

- **Public Authorities' Attitude:** Disaster management team many a times faces ethical issues like deficit of trust; public authorities usually neither like to share information nor authorize operations where they think it is inconvenient, such as in refugee camps.
- **Media Mindset:** The mass media sometimes spreads unverified information and rumors during and post-disaster events; under political pressure, they may hide the truth intentionally and even spread misleading news, which is completely unethical. Images of dead and wounded people might be published without any respect to personhood rights.
- **Insufficient Guidelines and Regulations:** Professional guidelines and regulations for disaster management do not provide enough guidance in disaster settings. The application of general guidelines might be contradictory to local values and conditions. Therefore, it is the ethical duty of the personnel that on the ground level there must be appropriate rules and guidelines to follow and do not harm the locals.
- **Professional Competence:** Concern of medical competence has potential source of ethical problems. Sometimes the team has limited disaster training on medicine mainly through short theoretical lectures during their undergraduate education. Therefore, it a moral duty of the management to provide ethical standards during medication.
- **Mismanagement due to Unpreparedness:** One of the main reasons for mismanagement is stated as the lack of rapid health assessment to determine actual needs, which can cause misallocation of resources while excessive and useless resources pile up in one place, but no care in another, eventually leading to preventable suffering and death. Incorporating ethical principles into practice basically depends on the effectiveness of humanitarian aid management.

◆♦□□♦◆

11

QUOTATIONS & SAYINGS

Golden-Rules Includes Section From

- Indian
- Western
- Global/Universals
- Sayings on Values
- Jottings on Morality
- Philosophical Ponderings on Power
- 'Catchy Lines' on Corruption

In this section, a collection of quotations & sayings are given.

Allocated to famous philosophers, thinkers and leaders; and perpetually pertinent, I can strongly say that questions which come in GS Paper IV, from this domain, would certainly move in and around from the ethical statements replicated here.

Now, a relevant question that must arise in your mind regarding the utility of studying this Unit if one can easily make out the moral and question of virtue raised in the saying.

If one knows the sayer of a particular saying; then the start/introduction which she can give to that question would be of an excellent style. Add to this, the temporal framework in which that statement was made which one can easily make out if one knows the person who said it. This information would add a new and certainly a novel dimension to your answer.

Having said that, I would also add the importance or shall I say the indispensability of this chapter for other compulsory papers - in-particular GS Paper II and Essay - and also for Paper II of certain optional papers of Humanities.

INDIAN

Buddha

- Three things cannot be long hidden: the sun, the moon, and the truth.
- No one saves us but ourselves. No one can and no one may. We ourselves must walk the path.
- You will not be punished for your anger, you will be punished by your anger.
- Better than a thousand hollow words, is one word that brings peace.
- What we think, we become.
- A jug fills drop by drop.
- Virtue is persecuted more by the wicked than it is loved by the good.
- Hatred does not cease by hatred, but only by love; this is the eternal rule.
- To live a pure unselfish life, one must count nothing as one's own in the midst of abundance.

Swami Vivekananda

- Arise! Awake! and stop not until the goal is reached.
- You cannot believe in God until you believe in yourself.
- Where can we go to find God if we cannot see Him in our own hearts and in every living being.
- Truth can be stated in a thousand different ways, yet each one can be true.
- All differences in this world are of degree, and not of kind, because oneness is the secret of everything.

Mahatma Gandhi

- Your beliefs become your thoughts,
  Your thoughts become your words,
  Your words become your actions,
  Your actions become your habits,
  Your habits become your values,
  Your values become your destiny.
- Corruption and hypocrisy ought not to be inevitable products of democracy, as they undoubtedly are today.
- You must not lose faith in humanity. Humanity is an ocean; if a few drops of the ocean are dirty, the ocean does not become dirty.
- The weak can never forgive. Forgiveness is the attribute of the strong.
- You must be the change you wish to see in the world.
- An eye for an eye only ends up making the whole world blind.
- I object to violence because when it appears to do good, the good is only temporary; the evil it does is permanent.
- Power is of two kinds. One is obtained by the fear of punishment and the other by acts of love. Power based on love is a thousand times more effective and permanent than the one derived from fear of punishment.
- Live as if you were to die tomorrow. Learn as if you were to live forever.
- The best way to find yourself is to lose yourself in the service of others.

- Non-violence is the greatest force at the disposal of mankind. It is mightier than the mightiest weapon of destruction devised by the ingenuity of man.
- A nation's culture resides in the hearts and in the soul of its people.
- Strength does not come from physical capacity. It comes from an indomitable will.
- There is a higher court than courts of justice and that is the court of conscience. It supercedes all other courts.
- An ounce of practice is worth more than tons of preaching.
- Truth stands, even if there be no public support. It is self-sustained.
- It is the quality of our work which will please God and not the quantity.
- Self-respect knows no considerations.
- Religion is a matter of the heart. No physical inconvenience can warrant abandonment of one's own religion.
- Man is supposed to be the maker of his destiny. It is only partly true. He can make his destiny, only in so far as he is allowed by the Great Power.
- Capital as such is not evil; it is its wrong use that is evil. Capital in some form or other will always be needed.
- The good man is the friend of all living things.
- Non-cooperation with evil is as much a duty as is cooperation with good.
- To believe in something, and not to live it, is dishonest.
- All the religions of the world, while they may differ in other respects, unitedly proclaim that nothing lives in this world but Truth.
- The greatness of a nation can be judged by the way its animals are treated.
- A man is but the product of his thoughts what he thinks, he becomes.
- Even if you are a minority of one, the truth is still the truth.
- A 'No' uttered from the deepest conviction is better than a 'Yes' merely uttered to please, or worse, to avoid trouble.
- Morality is the basis of things and truth is the substance of all morality.

- I reject any religious doctrine that does not appeal to reason and is in conflict with morality.
- Non-violence and truth are inseparable and presuppose one another.
- When restraint and courtesy are added to strength, the latter becomes irresistible.
- Freedom is not worth having if it does not connote freedom to err.
- Purity of personal life is the one indispensable condition for building up a sound education.
- Satisfaction lies in the effort, not in the attainment, full effort is full victory.

Jawaharlal Nehru

- Culture is the widening of the mind and of the spirit.
- What we really are matters more than what other people think of us.
- Action to be effective must be directed to clearly conceived ends.
- The only alternative to coexistence is codestruction.
- Democracy and socialism are means to an end, not the end itself.
- Failure comes only when we forget our ideals and objectives and principles.
- Citizenship consists in the service of the country.
- Ignorance is always afraid of change.
- The forces in a capitalist society, if left unchecked, tend to make the rich richer and the poor poorer.
- The policy of being too cautious is the greatest risk of all.
- The purely agitational attitude is not good enough for a detailed consideration of a subject.

Mother Teresa

- Loneliness and the feeling of being unwanted is the most terrible poverty.
- Peace begins with a smile.
- The hunger for love is much more difficult to remove than the hunger for bread.

- The biggest disease today is not leprosy or tuberculosis, but rather the feeling of being unwanted.

Dr. B R Ambedkar

- I like the religion that teaches liberty, equality and fraternity.
- I measure the progress of a community by the degree of progress which woman have achieved.
- Cultivation of mind should be the ultimate aim of human existence.
- Sincerity is the sum of all moral qualities.
- We are Indians, firstly and lastly.

A.P.J. Abdul Kalam

- Educationists should build the capacities of the spirit of inquiry, creativity, entrepreneurial and moral leadership among students and become their role model.
- If you want to shine like a sun, first burn like a sun.
- If a country is to be corruption free and become a nation of beautiful minds, I strongly feel there are three key societal members who can make a difference. They are the father, the mother and the teacher.
- Teaching is a very noble profession that shapes the character, calibre, and future of an individual. If the people remember me as a good teacher, that will be the biggest honour for me.
- Let me define a leader. He must have vision and passion and not be afraid of any problem. Instead, he should know how to defeat it. Most importantly, he must work with integrity.
- Educationists should build the capacities of the spirit of inquiry, creativity, entrepreneurial and moral leadership among students and become their role model.
- Man needs his difficulties because they are necessary to enjoy success.
- Real education enhances the dignity of a human being and increases his or her self-respect. If only the real sense of education could be realized by each individual and carried forward in every field of human activity, the world will be so much a better place to live in.

- Don't take rest after your first victory because if you fail in second, more lips are waiting to say that your first victory was just luck.
- Those who cannot work with their hearts achieve but a hollow, half-hearted success that breeds bitterness all around.
- India should walk on her own shadow - we must have our own development model.
- While children are struggling to be unique, the world around them is trying all means to make them look like everybody else.
- Where there is righteousness in the heart, there is harmony in the house; when there is harmony in the house, there is order in the nation; when there is order in the nation, there is peace in the world.
- One lesson that every nation can learn from China is to focus more on creating village-level enterprises, quality health services and educational facilities.
- Ultimately, education in its real sense is the pursuit of truth. It is an endless journey through knowledge and enlightenment.
- When a nation is surrounded by weaponized nations, she has to equip herself.
- Small aim is a crime.
- To become 'unique,' the challenge is to fight the hardest battle which anyone can imagine until you reach your destination.
- Poetry comes from the highest happiness or the deepest sorrow.
- Without your involvement you can't succeed. With your involvement you can't fail.

Deen Dayal Upadhayaya

- "It is essential that we think about 'Our National Identity' without which Independance has no meaning."
- "Independance can be meaningful only if it becomes instrument for expression of our Culture."
- "The fundamental characteristic of Bhartiya Culture is that it looks upon life as an integrated whole."
- "Strength lies not in unrestrained behaviour but in well-regulated action."

- Education is an investment. An educated individual will indeed serve society."
- "Religion means a creed or a sect and it does not mean Dharma."
- "Society must enable the individual to carry out his obligations towards the society by properly educating him."
- "God has given hands to every man but hands by themselves have a limited capacity to produce. They need the assistance of capital in the form of machines."
- "To educate a child is in the interest of society itself."
- "When nature is channelled according to the principles of Dharma, we have culture &civilisation."
- "Human nature has both tendencies--Anger & Greed on the one hand and Love & Sacrifice on the other."

Atal Bihari Vajpayee

- Empowering the individual means empowering the nation. And empowerment is best served through rapid economic growth with rapid social change.
- No guns but only brotherhood can resolve the problems.
- Terrorism has become a festering wound. It is an enemy of humanity.
- Our words, actions, and diplomatic efforts should be aimed at trying to achieve pragmatic goals rather than creating rhetorical effect.
- India was secular even when Muslims hadn't come here and Christians hadn't set foot on this soil. It is not as if India became secular after they came. They came with their own modes of worship, and they, too, were given a place of honor and respect. They had the freedom to worship God as per their wish and inclination.

Western

Kant

- I had therefore to remove knowledge, in order to make room for belief.

- In law, a man is guilty when he violates the rights of others. In ethics he is guilty if he only thinks of doing so.
- He, who is cruel to animals becomes hard also in his dealings with men. We can judge the heart of a man by his treatment of animals.
- Two things awe me most, the starry sky above me and the moral law within me.
- Even philosophers will praise war as ennobling mankind, forgetting the Greek who said: 'War is bad in that it begets more evil than it kills.'
- Religion is the recognition of all our duties as divine commands.
- Live your life as though your every act were to become a universal law.
- Morality is not the doctrine of how we may make ourselves happy, but how we may make ourselves worthy of happiness.
- Always recognize that human individuals are ends, and do not use them as means to your end.
- To be is to do.

Socrates

- A system of morality which is based on relative emotional values is a mere illusion, a thoroughly vulgar conception which has nothing sound in it and nothing true.
- He is richest who is content with the least, for content is the wealth of nature.
- The unexamined life is not worth living.
- He is a man of courage who does not run away, but remains at his post and fights against the enemy.
- Worthless people live only to eat and drink; people of worth eat and drink only to live.
- False words are not only evil in themselves, but they infect the soul with evil.

Plato

- Human behavior flows from three main sources: desire, emotion, and knowledge.
- Courage is knowing what not to fear.

- The measure of a man is what he does with power.
- He who commits injustice is ever made more wretched than he who suffers it.
- One of the penalties for refusing to participate in politics is that you end up being governed by your inferiors.
- The most virtuous are those who content themselves with being virtuous without seeking to appear so.
- All men are by nature equal, made all of the same earth by one Workman; and however we deceive ourselves, as dear unto God is the poor peasant as the mighty prince.
- Virtue is relative to the actions and ages of each of us in all that we do.
- Justice in the life and conduct of the State is possible only as first it resides in the hearts and souls of the citizens.
- The greatest wealth is to live content with little.
- There are three classes of men; lovers of wisdom, lovers of honor, and lovers of gain.
- Courage is a kind of salvation
- Honesty is for the most part less profitable than dishonesty.

Aristotle

- Quality is not an act, it is a habit.
- We are what we repeatedly do. Excellence, then, is not an act, but a habit.
- At his best, man is the noblest of all animals; separated from law and justice he is the worst.
- The worst form of inequality is to try to make unequal things equal.
- Good habits formed at youth make all the difference.
- We make war that we may live in peace.
- The law is reason, free from passion.
- The greatest virtues are those which are most useful to other persons.
- All human actions have one or more of these seven causes: chance, nature, compulsions, habit, reason, passion, desire.
- Those that know, do. Those that understand, teach.

- The least initial deviation from the truth is multiplied later a thousand-fold.
- Moral excellence comes about as a result of habit. We become just by doing just acts, temperate by doing temperate acts, brave by doing brave acts.
- The virtue of justice consists in moderation, as regulated by wisdom.
- Persuasion is clearly a sort of demonstration, since we are most fully persuaded when we consider a thing to have been demonstrated.

Hume

- Nothing is more surprising than the easiness with which the many are governed by the few.
- The rules of morality are not the conclusion of our reason.
- The law always limits every power it gives.
- The corruption of the best things gives rise to the worst.
- Custom is the great guide to human life.
- The whole is more than the sum of its parts.
- Fear is pain arising from the anticipation of evil.
- All virtue is summed up in dealing justly.
- The gods too are fond of a joke.

Thomas Aquinas

- Law is nothing other than a certain ordinance of reason for the common good, promulgated by the person who has the care of the community.
- Good can exist without evil, whereas evil cannot exist without good.
- Reason in man is rather like God in the world.
- Perfection of moral virtue does not wholly take away the passions, but regulates them.
- Happiness is secured through virtue; it is a good attained by man's own will.

Jeremy Bentham

- It is the greatest good to the greatest number of people which is the measure of right and wrong.

- The greatest happiness of the greatest number is the foundation of morals and legislation.

John Stuart Mill

- A person may cause evil to others not only by his actions but by his inaction, and in either case he is justly accountable to them for the injury.
- One person with a belief is equal to ninety-nine who have only interests.
- All action is for the sake of some end; and rules of action, it seems natural to suppose, must take their whole character and color from the end to which they are subservient.
- I have learned to seek my happiness by limiting my desires, rather than in attempting to satisfy them.
- Pleasure and freedom from pain, are the only things desirable as ends.
- It is not because men's desires are strong that they act ill; it is because their consciences are weak.
- The creed which accepts as the foundation of morals, "utility", or the "greatest happiness principle", holds that actions are right in proportion as they tend to promote happiness; wrong as they tend to produce the reverse of happiness. By happiness is intended pleasure and the absence of pain; by unhappiness, pain and the privation of pleasure.
- The idea that truth always triumphs over persecution is one of those pleasant falsehoods, which most experience refutes. History is teeming with instances of truth put down by persecution. If not put down forever, it may be set back for centuries.
- The love of power and the love of liberty are in eternal antagonism.

Friedrich Nietzsche

- Morality makes stupid-- Custom represents the experiences of men of earlier times as to what they supposed useful and harmful - but the sense for custom (morality) applies, not to these experiences as such, but to the age, the sanctity, the indiscussability of the custom. And so this feeling is a hindrance to the acquisition of new experiences and the correction of customs: that is to say, morality is a hindrance to the development of new and better customs: it makes stupid.

- Whoever has overthrown an existing law of custom has always first been accounted a bad man: but when, as did happen, the law could not afterwards be reinstated and this fact was accepted, the predicate gradually changed; - history treats almost exclusively of these bad men who subsequently became good men!
- What is new, however, is always evil, being that which wants to conquer and overthrow the old boundary markers and the old pieties; and only what is old is good. The good men are in all ages those who dig the old thoughts, digging deep and getting them to bear fruit - the farmers of the spirit. But eventually all land is depleted, and the ploughshare of evil must come again and again.
- Suspicious-- To admit a belief merely because it is a custom- but that means to be dishonest, cowardly, lazy! - And so could dishonesty, cowardice and laziness be the preconditions for morality?

Soren Kierkegaard

- People demand freedom of speech as a compensation for the freedom of thought which they seldom use.
- Life is not a problem to be solved, but a reality to be experienced.
- If I were to wish for anything, I should not wish for wealth and power, but for the passionate sense of the potential, for the eye which, ever young and ardent, sees the possible. Pleasure disappoints, possibility never. And what wine is so sparkling, what so fragrant, what so intoxicating, as possibility!
- The proud person always wants to do the right thing, the great thing. But because he wants to do it in his own strength, he is fighting not with man, but with God.
- If anyone on the verge of action should judge himself according to the outcome, he would never begin.

Global/Universals

Confucius

- He who speaks without modesty will find it difficult to make his words good.
- I hear and I forget. I see and I remember. I do and I understand.
- Everything has beauty, but not everyone sees it.
- If I am walking with two other men, each of them will serve as my teacher. I will pick out the good points of the one and imitate them, and the bad points of the other and correct them in myself.
- He that would perfect his work must first sharpen his tools.
- Virtue is more to man than either water or fire. I have seen men die from treading on water and fire, but I have never seen a man die from treading the course of virtue.
- Be not ashamed of mistakes and thus make them crimes.
- Isn't it a pleasure to study and practice what you have learned?
- Isn't it also great when friends visit from distant places? If one remains not annoyed when he is not understood by people around him, isn't he a sage?
- It is not possible for one to teach others who cannot teach his own family.
- Education breeds confidence. Confidence breeds hope. Hope breeds peace.
- Without feelings of respect, what is there to distinguish men from beasts?
- It is not possible for one to teach others who cannot teach his own family. He who excels in study can follow an official career.
- He who excels in study can follow an official career.
- Forget injuries, never forget kindnesses.
- Things that are done, it is needless to speak about...things that are past, it is needless to blame.
- Learn as though you would never be able to master it; hold it as though you would be in fear of losing it.

- Do not be desirous of having things done quickly. Do not look at small advantages. Desire to have things done quickly prevents their being done thoroughly.

Abraham Lincoln

- When I do good, I feel good. When I do bad, I feel bad. That's my religion.
- I never had a policy; I have just tried to do my very best each and every day.
- I never had a policy; I have just tried to do my very best each and every day.
- Freedom is the natural condition of the human race, in which the Almighty intended men to live. Those who fight the purpose of the Almighty will not succeed. They always have been, they always will be beaten.
- Nearly all men can stand adversity, but if you want to test a man's character, give him power.
- There are no bad pictures; that's just how your face looks sometimes.
- Be sure you put your feet in the right place, then stand firm.
- I am not bound to win, but I am bound to be true. I am not bound to succeed, but I am bound to live up to what light I have.
- You can fool some of the people all of the time, and all of the people some of the time, but you cannot fool all of the people all of the time.
- Character is like a tree and reputation its shadow. The shadow is what we think it is and the treeis the real thing.
- I have been driven many times upon my knees by the overwhelming conviction that I had nowhere else to go. My own wisdom and that of all about me seemed insufficient for that day.

Dalai Lama

- Happiness is not something ready made. It comes from your own actions.
- Our prime purpose in this life is to help others. And if you can't help them, at least don't hurt them.

- Love and compassion are necessities, not luxuries. Without them humanity cannot survive.
- Be kind whenever possible. It is always possible.
- We can never obtain peace in the outer world until we make peace with ourselves.
- In the practice of tolerance, one's enemy is the best teacher.
- A lack of transparency results in distrust and a deep sense of insecurity.
- Where ignorance is our master, there is no possibility of real peace.

Martin Luther

- Forgiveness is God's command.

Martin Luther King, Jr.

- The function of education is to teach one to think intensively and to think critically. Intelligence plus character - that is the goal of true education.
- We must accept finite disappointment, but never lose infinite hope.
- Love is the only force capable of transforming an enemy into friend.

After having been through sayings coupled with its propounder; in the following section some more have been given together with the person who made them.

Sayings on Values

- "It is no measure of health to be well adjusted to a profoundly sick society". **– Jiddu Krishnamurti**
- "Possessions, outward success, publicity, luxury - to me these have always been contemptible. I believe that a simple and unassuming manner of life is best for everyone, best for both the body and the mind". **– Albert Einstein**

- "I think honesty is the most heroic quality one can aspire to". **– Daniel Radcliffe**
- "Money is only a human invention". **– Vanna Bonta**

Jottings on Morality

- "Wisdom, compassion, and courage are the three universally recognized moral qualities of men". **– Confucius**
- "I am not interested in power for power's sake, but I'm interested in power that is moral, that is right and that is good". **– Martin Luther King, Jr.**
- "Happiness and moral duty are inseparably connected". **– George Washington**
- "In many countries today, moral and ethical norms are being reconsidered; national traditions, differences in nation and culture are being erased". **– Vladimir Putin**
- "Moral values, and a culture and a religion, maintaining these values are far better than laws and regulations". **– Swami Sivananda**

Philosophical Ponderings on Power

- "Knowledge is power". **– Francis Bacon**
- "Power tends to corrupt and absolute power corrupts absolutely". **– Lord Acton**
- "Nothing strengthens authority so much as silence". **– Leonardo da Vinci**
- "Knowledge will give you power, but character respect". **– Bruce Lee**
- "When the whole world is silent, even one voice becomes powerful". **– Malala Yousafzai**
- "He who wishes to be obeyed must know how to command". **– Niccolo Machiavelli**

- "The power to question is the basis of all human progress".
  – Indira Gandhi
- "The greater the power, the more dangerous the abuse".
  – Edmund Burke

'Catch-the-Lines' on Corruption

- "It is not power that corrupts but fear. Fear of losing power corrupts those who wield it and fear of the scourge of power corrupts those who are subject to it". **– Aung San Suu Kyi**
- "A man who has never gone to school may steal a freight car; but if he has a university education, he may steal the whole railroad". **– Theodore Roosevelt**
- "Power-lust is a weed that grows only in the vacant lots of an abandoned mind". **– Ayn Rand**
- "Keep in Mind to be Kind." **– A. Volta**

◆◆❑❑◆◆

GLOSSARY

A

Absolutism: Absolutism as an ethical theory in contrast to relativism. The belief in a value or good that always holds its value. It is expressed by the ancient stoics as "Let justice be done though the heavens fall".

Accountability: A situation in which someone is responsible for things that happen and can give a satisfactory reason for them. It is the readiness or preparedness to give an explanation or justification to stakeholders for one's judgments, intentions and actions.

Administrator: A person responsible for carrying out the administration of a business or organization.

Admire: It is defined as regard with respect or warm approval. If you hold someone in high esteem or look up to someone, you admire that person.

Afflictions: Affliction denotes a cause of persistent pain or distress. In ethics, it is something which causes physical or mental sufferings (either by wrongdoing or undoing).

Agitation: It is a state of anxiety or nervous excitement. Agitation is to argue forcefully, especially in public, in order to achieve a particular type of change.

Ahimsa: Ahimsa means 'not to injure' and 'compassion' and refers to a key virtue in Hinduism and Jainism. The word is derived from the Sanskrit root hims - to strike (himsa is injury or harm); a-himsa is the opposite of this, i.e. cause no injury, do no harm. Ahimsa is also referred to as nonviolence.

Altruism: In ethics altruism can be contrasted with selfishness or egoism. It is acting out of selfless concern for others.

Alienation: It is the state or experience of being alienated. The concept of alienation identifies a distinct kind of psychological or social ill; namely, one involving a problematic separation between a self and other that properly belong together.

Ambiguity: It is the quality of being open to more than one interpretation. It is best to avoid ambiguity in action in public service. When the actions are ambiguous, it is not possible to persuade to others and action will be unpredictable in nature.

Anchor: In ethics, anchor is someone or something that is strong and reliable, and so makes people feel safe and confident.

Animal Welfare: Animal welfare is the well-being of non-human animals. The standards of "good" animal welfare vary considerably between different contexts. These standards are under constant review and are debated, created and revised by animal welfare groups, legislators and academics worldwide.

Anthropocentrism: It refers to a human-centered, or "anthropocentric," point of view. In philosophy, anthropocentrism can refer to the point of view that humans are the only, or primary, holders of moral standing.

Anxiety: Anxiety is an emotion characterized by an unpleasant state of inner turmoil, often accompanied by nervous behaviour such as pacing back and forth, somatic complaints, and rumination, etc.

Apathetic: Apathy is a state of indifference, or the suppression of emotions such as concern, excitement, motivation, or passion. An apathetic individual has an absence of interest in or concern about emotional, social, spiritual, philosophical, or physical life and the world.

Applied Ethics: Applied ethics refers to the practical application of moral considerations. It is ethics with respect to real-world actions and their moral considerations in the areas of private and public life, the professions, health, technology, law, and leadership.

Appreciation: It is the act of recognizing or understanding that something is valuable and important. Ethical appreciation, is a way to review a piece of literary art to instill and embrace the moral, cultural, and humane elements of literature like sympathetic and emotive attitude, rich morals, and role of man in the human world.

Aptitude: Aptitude is our potential to learn skills, the abilities we develop and perfect over time. Aptitudes may be physical or mental. Aptitude is not knowledge, understanding, learned or acquired abilities (skills) or attitude.

Atheism: The belief that God does not exist. Philosophers who were atheists include Karl Marx, Friedrich Nietzsche, Bertrand Russell, and Jean-Paul Sartre.

Attitude: Attitude is related to kind of behavior at work or outside depending upon the attitude. Attitude is either positive or negative or indifferent feeling towards a person, object, event or idea.

Authoritarian Style: An authoritarian style is exemplified when a leader dictates policies and procedures, decides what goals are to be achieved, and directs and controls all activities without any meaningful participation by the subordinates.

Awareness: Awareness is a knowledge or perception of a situation or fact. It means looking for patterns in the way we tend to think about and perceive what happens to, how we explain things to ourselves and make sense of the world around us.

B

Behaviour: Behaviour is the way in which one acts or conducts oneself, especially towards others. It is the way person behaves in response to a particular situation or stimulus.

Belief: A belief is an opinion or supposition. It can mean "know", or "think" (I believe you are telling the truth) but is more usually associated with religious doctrines or dogmas and sometimes philosophical and ethical positions.

Benevolence: Benevolence indicates a charitable disposition to do 'good' in regard to others, and to act with genuinely compassionate and kind considerations of their needs and desires. It is embraced as a vitally important ethical virtue in most human societies, religions, philosophies and cultures.

Bhagvad Gita: 'Gita' is a Sanskrit scripture and is set in a narrative framework of a dialogue between Pandava prince Arjuna and his guide and charioteer Krishna. It presents a synthesis of Hindu ideas about dharma, theistic bhakti, and the yogic ideals of moksha.

Biocentrism: Biocentrism is an ethical point of view that extends inherent value to all living things. It is an understanding of how the earth works, particularly as it relates to biodiversity.

Bona fide: The meaning of bona fide is 'in good faith' or without deception. Bona fide denotes the mental and moral states of honesty and conviction regarding either the truth or the falsity of a proposition.

Bona fide Mistakes: Bona fide mistake is defined as an honest mistake that when rectified quickly requires no punishment. Bona fide mistake is a legal term referring to an unintentional mistake or oversight that may be corrected promptly to avoid exposure to legal action.

Bureaucratic Attitude: Bureaucratic attitude means the behaviour or attitude of an officer, who believes in the infallibility of the rule book, on the basis of that belief and attitude.

Business Ethics: The application of ethics to the roles and responsibilities of persons connected to the modern business corporation.

C

Caste System: A caste system is a class structure that is determined by birth. In India, caste system divides Hindus into rigid hierarchical groups based on their karma (work) and dharma. Caste system in Hindus divides them into four main categories - Brahmins, Kshatriyas, Vaishyas and the Shudras.

Capital Punishment: The use of the Death penalty as a punishment determined by a legally empowered Court.

Character: Character is one of the attributes or features that make up and distinguish an individual. Character is the combination of personal qualities that make each person unique. Character deals with how people think and behave related to issues such as right and wrong, justice and equity, and other areas of human conduct.

Charisma: It is a special power that some people have naturally that makes them able to influence other people and attract their attention and admiration. It is a personal magic of leadership, arousing special popular loyalty or enthusiasm for a public figure (such as a political leader). It creates persuasion and inspiration to others.

Chauvinism: Chauvinism is a form of extreme patriotism and nationalism and a belief in national superiority and glory. It is an irrational belief in the superiority or dominance of one's own group or people.

Checks and Balances: Checks and balances usually ensure that no one person or department has absolute control over decisions; clearly defines the assigned duties, and forces cooperation in completing tasks. The term is most commonly used in the context of government.

Citizen's Charter: Citizen's Charter is a document which represents a systematic effort to focus on the commitment of an organisation towards its citizens in respect of Standard of Services, Information, Choice and Consultation, Non-discrimination and Accessibility, Grievance Redress, Courtesy and Value for Money.

Civic Responsibilities: Civic Responsibility is defined as the "responsibility of a citizen". It is comprised of actions and attitudes associated with democratic governance and social participation.

Civil Servant: Civil servants are the actual makers of Indian law and policy. They work on behalf of the elected government and cannot publicly show their disinterest or disapproval for it. It is mandatory for them to form certain rules and policies according to the government's views and interests. They, during their service, have to follow the code of conduct, civil service code and code of ethics for the benefit of the larger mass.

Civilized: Civilized is an adjective that describes the very opposite of barbarity. Civilized - shows an advanced stage of social and cultural development. A civilized person is ethical, polite and courteous.

Climate Change: Climate change occurs when changes in Earth's climate system result in new weather patterns that remain in place for an extended period of time. This could be a change in Earth's usual temperature. Earth's climate is getting warmer as per scientists and global warming is increasing due to anthropogenic activities.

Codes of Conduct: A code of conduct is a set of rules outlining the norms, rules, and responsibilities of, and or proper practices for, an individual. An ethical culture is created by the organization's leaders who manifest their ethics in their attitudes and behavior.

Codes of Ethics: A code of ethics is a guide of principles designed to help professionals conduct business honestly and with integrity.

Cognitive: Cognitive means relating to the mental process involved in knowing, learning, and understanding things. These skills are used to comprehend, process, remember and apply incoming information.

Cognitive Dissonance: Cognitive dissonance is the mental discomfort (psychological stress) experienced by a person who holds two or more contradictory beliefs, ideas, or values. A classic example of this is "explaining something away."

Cohesion: Cohesion means sticking together. Social cohesion involves the internalization of social ethics and constitutes the level of realized propensity among citizens to engage in virtuous behavior for the common good.

Collusive Corruption: Prior agreement between the parties involved in corruption making corruption a voluntary act. In India, it is described as the phenomena where executives from corporations dishonestly collude with government officials for a mutual unlawful benefit.

Communal Riots: A riot is "a violent disturbance of the peace by an assembly or body of persons". It becomes a communal riot if disturbance of peace is caused by distinct community (ies) and is aimed at other distinct community (ies).

Compassion: Compassion motivates people to go out of their way to help the physical, mental, or emotional pains of another and themselves. It is a strong feeling of sympathy and sadness for the suffering or bad luck of others and a wish to help them.

Complacent: The literal meaning of this word's Latin root is "very pleased". A complacent person is happy with one's self and unconcerned. He is contented, yet unconcerned, and uneager to improve or change.

Concupiscence: Concupiscence is often defined as an ardent, usually sensual, longing. The concept is most commonly encountered in Christian theology, as the selfish human desire for an object, person, or experience.

Conflict of Interests: A conflict of interest is a situation in which an individual has competing interests or loyalties. Conflicts of interest involve a person who has two relationships that might compete with each other for the person's loyalties.

Conscience: A conscience is a built-in sense of what's right and what's wrong. It denotes the inner self of a person. It is the part of oneself that judges how moral one's own actions are and makes them feel guilty about bad things that may have done or things feel responsible for.

Constitutional Law: Constitutional law is a body of law which defines the role, powers, and structure of different entities within a state, namely, the executive, the parliament or legislature, and the judiciary; as well as the basic rights of citizens.

Corporate Governance: Corporate governance is the system of rules, practices, and processes by which a firm is directed and controlled. It is the technique by which companies are directed and managed. It means carrying the business as per the stakeholders' desires.

Corporate Social Responsibility (CSR): CSR is how companies manage their business processes to produce an overall positive impact on society. It covers sustainability, social impact and ethics about core business - how companies make their money - not just add-on extras such as philanthropy.

Corruption: Corruption is the abuse of entrusted power for private gain. It can be classified as grand, petty and political, depending on the amounts of money lost and the sector where it occurs.

Crisis of Conscience: A situation in which someone feels worried or uncomfortable because they have done something which they think is wrong or immoral. Crisis of conscience is a situation in which it is very difficult to decide 'what is the right thing to do'.

Crony Capitalism: It is an economic system characterized by close, mutually advantageous relationships between business leaders and government officials. In such a system, the false appearance of "pure" capitalism is publicly maintained to preserve the exclusive influence of well-connected individuals.

Cynicism: It is an attitude of suspicion where one believes that the future is bleak and people are acting only out of self interest. Cynicism is the feeling of distrust or that something isn't going to work out well.

D

Decision Making: Decision making is the thought process of selecting a logical choice from the available options. An effective decision-making helps to achieve the desired goals or objectives by solving such problems.

Denial: Denial is refusal of something requested or desired. Many a times this denial is a refusal to acknowledge an unacceptable truth or emotion or to admit it into consciousness, used as a defence mechanism.

Deontology: Actions are intrinsically right or wrong. They are right or wrong in themselves and irrespective of their consequences. They are traditionally associated with Kantian duty but can also be linked to ethical systems which uphold absolute moral norms and human rights.

Deprived Sections: The section of society those who have not having the things that are necessary for a pleasant life, such as enough money, food, or good living conditions. In Indian perspective, social deprivation is the reduction or prevention of culturally normal interaction between an individual and the rest of the society.

Determinism: The doctrine that all events, including human action, are ultimately determined by causes regarded as external to the will. Some philosophers have taken determinism to imply that individual human beings have no free will and cannot be held morally responsible for their actions.

Dictatorship Government: A dictatorship is a form of government characterized by the absolute rule of one person or a very small group of people who hold all political power and little or no toleration for political pluralism or independent programs or media.

Dilemmas: Dilemma originated from a Greek word meaning

"double proposition." A dilemma is a difficult situation in which one has to choose between two or more alternatives.

Diligence: Diligence is the quality of working carefully and with a lot of effort.

Dimensions of Ethics: Ethics, as a branch of Philosophy, has multi-dimensions. It can be applied in many fields like environment, cyberspace, public sphere, international relations and so on. Ethics is divided into four main branches. They are: Meta-Ethics (Ethics about Ethics), Prescriptive Ethics (Normative Ethics), Descriptive Ethics, Applied Ethics.

Disaster Management: Disaster Management can be defined as the organization and management of resources and responsibilities for dealing with all humanitarian aspects of emergencies, in particular, preparedness, response and recovery in order to lessen the impact of disasters.

Doctrine: Doctrine is a codification of beliefs or a body of teachings or instructions, taught principles or positions, as the essence of teachings in a given branch of knowledge or in a belief system. There are many practical doctrines evolved in ethics.

Doctrine of Double Effect: This doctrine says that if doing something morally good has a morally bad side-effect; it's ethically OK to do it providing the bad side-effect wasn't intended. This principle is commonly referred to in cases of euthanasia.

E

Economic Offences: Economic offences cover fraud, forgery and counterfeiting, offences against the legislation governing cheques (in particular forgery or use of stolen cheques), forgery or use of credit cards, undeclared employment, offences against companies, etc.

Effectiveness and Efficiency: Efficiency means whatever you produce or perform; it should be done in a perfect way. Although, Effectiveness has a broader approach, which means the extent to which the actual results have been achieved to fulfill the desired outcome i.e. doing accurate things. These are the metrics used to gauge the performance of an employee in an organization.

Egalitarian Society: An egalitarian is a person who believes in the equality of all people, and an egalitarian society gives everyone equal rights. This is a word that means something close to equality and has to do with fairness.

Egoism: A moral theory that commonly states that each person ought to act in his or her own self-interest.

Ego Defensive Mechanism: Like body's defenses against physical wounds and injuries, ego defence mechanisms is to protect the mind/self/ego from anxiety, emotional shocks or social sanctions or to provide a refuge from a situation with which one cannot currently cope. These mechanisms are called "Ego Defense Mechanisms" or "Unconscious Defense Mechanisms".

Embarrassment: It is a feeling of self-consciousness, shame, or awkwardness.

Eminent Domain: Eminent domain is the Right a government or state has to take property away from someone so it can be used for a public purpose. When a new highway is built, some people often lose part of their land by eminent domain.

Emotional Intelligence (EI): It is the capacity to be aware of, control, and express one's emotions, and to handle interpersonal relationships judiciously and empathetically.

Emotional Quotient (EQ): It is a measure of one's EI i.e. through a standardized test, one's awareness of emotions in relation to self and others is known.

Empathy: Empathy is the capacity to understand or feel what another person is experiencing from within their frame of reference, that is, the capacity to place oneself in another's position.

Ends and Means: Some moral systems evaluate the goodness and badness of actions solely by examining their means (actions), while others examine the consequences, the ends produced by those actions.

Environmental Ethics: Environmental ethics is a branch of ethics that studies the relation of human beings and the environment and how ethics play a role in this. Environmental ethics believe that humans are a part of society as well as other living creatures, which includes plants and animals.

Equality: Equality is the Right of different groups of people to have a similar social position and receive the same treatment. Equality really means equal opportunities for development.

Equality before Law: "Equality before law" implies the absence of any special privileges in favour of individuals and the subject of all classes to the ordinary law and equal protection of the law which implies "Equal Treatment in Equal Circumstances".

Espirit de corps: Esprit de corps is a French phrase that translates into 'group spirit'. Esprit de corps is a feeling of loyalty and pride that is shared by the members of a group who consider them to be different from other people in some special way.

Ethical Failures: An ethical failure is a bad decision that intentionally or unintentionally breaks a law, transgresses a compliance mandate or violates an organization's code of conduct.

Ethical Governance: Ethical governance in business is more than 'regulatory compliance'. Ethical governance is an umbrella concept. It is not a utopian concept. It does not only involve governance and good governance but also nurtures self reliance, integrity and hope for a better future.

Ethical Guidance: Ethical guidelines or codes are used by groups and organizations to define what actions are morally right and wrong.

Ethical Issues: Ethical issues occur when a given decision, scenario or activity creates a conflict with a society's moral principles. Both individuals and businesses can be involved in these conflicts, since any of their activities might be put to question from an ethical standpoint.

Ethical Management: Ethical management refers to corporate management that not only fulfills economic goals and legal responsibilities, but also meets the ethical expectations imposed by social norms in conducting business.

Ethical Obligations: Ethical obligations are a set of "ought to" standards that define a moral course of action and draw a line between right and wrong.

Ethnic Community: Ethnic community is a stable grouping of people that has developed historically, such as a tribe, a nationality, or a nation. The members of an ethnic community share a common sense of identity, in which the notion of a common origin plays an important role.

Ethos: An ethos is a set of ideas and attitudes that is associated with a particular group of people or a particular type of activity. Ethos is a rhetorical device that includes any content in an argument that is meant to appeal to ethics.

Euthanasia: Euthanasia, also called mercy killing, act or practice of painlessly putting to death persons suffering from painful and incurable disease or incapacitating physical disorder or allowing them to die by withholding treatment or withdrawing artificial life-support measures.

F

Fantasy: A fantasy is a pleasant situation or event that anyone thinks about and that they want to become in reality, especially one that is unlikely to happen.

Fatalism: Fatalism is a philosophical doctrine that stresses the subjugation of all events or actions to destiny. It is the belief that people cannot change the way events will happen and that events, especially bad ones, cannot be avoided.

First-come-first-served: This is the system to indicate that a group of people or things will be dealt with or given something in the order in which they arrive.

Forgiveness: Psychologists generally define forgiveness as a conscious, deliberate decision to release feelings of resentment or vengeance toward a person or group who has harmed, regardless of whether they actually deserve forgiveness.

Fortitude: Fortitude comes from the Latin word “fortis”, meaning “strong,” and in English it is used for strength of mind that enables a person to encounter danger or bear pain or adversity with courage.

G

Gender Equality: According to UNICEF, gender equality means that "women and men, and girls and boys, enjoy the same rights, resources, opportunities and protections. It does not require that girls and boys, or women and men, be the same, or that they be treated exactly alike".

Gender Sensitization: Gender sensitization is the process in which the people of all genders are taught to respect everyone irrespective of gender while acknowledging the differences. This can be achieved by conducting various sensitization campaigns, training centres, workshop, programs, etc.

Generosity: Generosity is a quality that's a lot like unselfishness. A generous person is ethical, selfless, polite and ready to help others with either cash or kind.

Gesture: Gesture is a movement of part of the body, especially a hand or the head, to express an idea or meaning. It is a type of non-verbal interpersonal communication.

Global Ethics: Global ethics is an area of critical ethical enquiry into the nature and justification of values and norms that are global in kind and into the various issues that arise such as world poverty and international aid, environmental problems, peace and security, intervention, and human rights.

Gratitude: Gratitude, thankfulness, or gratefulness come from the Latin word "gratus" - is a feeling of appreciation felt by and/or similar positive response shown by the recipient of kindness.

Greed: Greed is an extreme or excessive desire for resources, especially for property such as money, real estate, or other symbols of wealth.

Grudge: It is a persistent feeling of ill will or resentment resulting from a past insult or injury. It is a strong feeling of anger and dislike for a person who has been treated badly.

H

Hedonism: The belief that pleasure is the chief "good."

Holistic Approach: A holistic approach means taking care of something totally in all aspects. This approach denotes all encompassing views based on the ethics, knowledge of the nature, functions, and properties of the components, their interactions, and their relationship to the whole.

Human Values: Human values are the virtues that guide us to take into account the human element when we interact with other human beings. Human values are, for example, respect, acceptance, consideration, appreciation, listening, openness, affection, empathy and love towards other human beings.

Humanitarianism: Humanitarianism is an active belief in the value of human life, whereby humans practice benevolent treatment and provide assistance to other humans, in order to better humanity for moral, altruistic and logical reasons.

Humility: Humility is the quality of being humble. Humility comes from the Latin word humilis, which literally means low. If you feel humility in front of someone, you feel small in the scheme of things – that you are just a simple, insignificant person.

Hypothetical Situation: It is a situation that is something assumed or based on theory. The ethical solutions are based on hypothetical situations and that change according to the need of the reality.

I

Ideals: An ideal is a principle or value that one actively pursues as a goal. Ideals are particularly important in ethics, as the order in which one places them tends to determine the degree to which one reveals them as real and sincere.

Illusion: Illusion is some instance of a wrong or misinterpreted perception of a sensory experience. The understanding of ethics clarifies the illusion and directs towards the reality.

Immoral: Immoral directs to a person who is not adhering to ethical or moral principles. It is also deliberately violating accepted principles of right and wrong. Such person is described as unethical.

Impartiality: Impartiality (also called evenhandedness or fair-mindedness) is a principle of justice holding that decisions should be based on objective criteria, rather than on the basis of bias, prejudice, or preferring the benefit to one person over another for improper reasons.

Inclusive Growth: Inclusive growth is a concept that advances equitable opportunities for economic participants during economic growth with benefits incurred by every section of society. The ethical dimensions of inclusive growth led its emphasis on inclusiveness–especially on equality of opportunity in terms of access to markets, resources, and an unbiased regulatory environment–as an essential ingredient of successful growth.

Inequality: Inequality is the unfair situation in society when some people have more opportunities, such as social disparity, disparity of distribution or opportunity, lack of evenness, the condition of being variable, etc.

Influence: Influence is the power to have an important effect on someone or something. In ethics, this influence is utilized in the concept of leadership management, persuasion, etc.

Information Sharing: Information sharing describes the exchange of data between various organizations, people and technologies.

Integrity: Integrity is the practice of being honest and showing a consistent and uncompromising adherence to strong moral and ethical principles and values. In ethics, integrity is regarded as the honesty and truthfulness or accuracy of one's actions.

Interpersonal Communications: Interpersonal communication is defined as all the interactions between two people. Any interaction between two persons, as long as one of them has a good purpose, it will be considered as ethical interpersonal communication.

Intrinsic Value: Intrinsic value of something is said to be the value that thing has "in itself," or "for its own sake," or "as such," or "in its own right. It has traditionally been thought to lie at the heart of ethics.

Introspect: The term "introspection" literally means "looking within". Introspection is the process by which someone comes to form beliefs about her own mental state.

Intuition: It is the ability to understand something instinctively, without the need for conscious reasoning. Intuition enables the discovery of the basic moral truths, and everyday moral decision-making then involves thinking about the choices available and making moral judgements in an ordinary sort of way.

IQ (Intelligence Quotient): An intelligence quotient (IQ) is a total score derived from several standardized tests designed to assess human intelligence. IQ scores are used for assessment of intellectual disability, educational placement and other areas.

J

Justice: Justice is concerned with the equitable distribution of benefits and burdens to individuals in social institutions, and how the rights of various individuals are realized. The principle of justice could be described as the moral obligation to act on the basis of fair adjudication between competing claims.

Judicial Activism: Judicial activism is a legal term that refers to court rulings that are partially or fully based on the judge's political or personal considerations, rather than existing laws.

Judicial Restraint: Judicial restraint is commonly considered to be the opposite of judicial activism. Judicial restraint embraces the belief that judges should narrowly interpret existing law and constitutional interpretations, adhering to prior interpretations in making decisions.

L

Law and Order: It is a situation in which the laws of a country are being obeyed, especially when the police or army are used to make certain of this. It is assumed that if laws are generally accepted and obeyed, society functions normally.

Lax: If you say that a person's behaviour or a system is lax, you mean they are not careful or strict about maintaining high standards.

Leadership: Leaders who lead ethically are role models, communicating the importance of ethical standards, holding their employees accountable to those standards, and crucially designing environments in which others work and live.

Legal Framework: The rules, rights and obligations of companies, governments, and citizens are set forth in a system of legal documents called a legal framework. Ethical framework goes beyond the legal frameworks.

LGBTQI: LGBTQI stands for Lesbian, Gay, Bisexual, Transgender, Queer or Questioning, and Intersex that refer to people's sexual orientation.

Loyalty: Loyalty, in general use, is a devotion and faithfulness to a nation, cause, philosophy, country, group, or person. Loyalty is one of the most controversial issues in ethics, especially because it can cause so many problems in practical situations.

M

Maladaptive Behaviour: The term "maladaptive behavior" is used to describe types of behaviors that inhibit one's ability to adjust to situations. It is a series of behaviors that react and behave inappropriately to internal or external stimuli. Maladaptive responses can be seen in people of all ages, nationalities, socio-economic statuses, and backgrounds.

Malfeasance: Malfeasance is an intentional conduct that is wrongful or unlawful, especially by officials or public employees. The term is used especially of an act in violation of a public trust.

Management Ethics: 'Management Ethics' is related to social responsiveness of a firm. It is "the discipline dealing with what is good and bad, or right and wrong, or with moral duty and obligation. It is a standard of behaviour that guides individual managers in their works".

Materialism: It is a tendency to consider material possessions and physical comfort as more important than spiritual values. This concept directly contrasts with idealism, where mind and consciousness are first-order realities to which matter is subject and material interactions are secondary.

Maxim: A moral rule which according to Kant was the subjective rule that an individual uses in making a decision.

Meditation: Meditation is a practice where an individual uses a technique - such as mindfulness, or focusing the mind on a particular object, thought or activity - to train attention and awareness, and achieve a mentally clear and emotionally calm and stable state.

Mental State: A mental state is a mental condition. Several of these states are a combination of mental representations and propositional attitudes. There are several paradigmatic states of mind that an agent has: love, hate, pleasure and pain, and attitudes toward propositions such as: believing that, conceiving that, hoping and fearing that, etc.

Meta-ethics: Meta-ethics is the branch of ethics that seeks to understand the nature of ethical properties, statements, attitudes, and judgments. Meta-ethics deals not with the substantive content of ethical theories but with questions about their nature that explores the status, foundations, and scope of moral values, properties, and words.

Misinformation: Misinformation is false or inaccurate information that include false rumors, insults and pranks, while examples of more deliberate disinformation include malicious content such as hoaxes, spear phishing and computational propaganda.

Moral Certitude: It is a confident assent concerning human conduct based on people's certain needs, abilities, and motivations. Moral certitude is a degree of certitude, based on currently available limited knowledge, sufficient to act in good conscience, i.e. without actual sin.

Moral Intellectualism

Moral intellectualism or ethical intellectualism is a view in meta-ethics according to which genuine moral knowledge must take the form of arriving at discursive moral judgements about what one should do. One way of understanding this is that if we know what is right, we will do what is right.

Moral Quotient (MQ): The concept is evolved from Intelligence Quotient (IQ). MQ is the ability to know when one is or is not acting morally; moral intelligence means knowing how to lead with these traits.

Moral Standards: A moral standard refers to the norms which we have about the types of actions which we believe to be morally acceptable and morally unacceptable. Specifically, moral standards deal with matters which can either seriously harm or seriously benefit human beings.

Morality: Morals refer to an individual's own principles regarding right and wrong. Morality is a code of behavior usually based on religious tenets, which often inform our ethical decisions. Morals come from within.

Motivation: Motivation is one's direction to behaviour, or what causes a person to want to repeat a behaviour, a set of force that acts behind the motives. An individual's motivation may be inspired by others or events (extrinsic motivation) or it may come from within the individual (intrinsic motivation).

N

Negative Repercussions: Repercussions can be thought of as ripple effects occurring because of an incident or action. Negative repercussions are usually bad effects of an event, action, or decision. An unethical conduct results into such repercussions.

Negative Rights: A negative Right is a Right not to be subjected to an action of another person or group; negative Rights permit or oblige inaction. A positive Right is a Right to be subjected to an action or another person or group; positive Rights permit or oblige action.

Neo-bureaucracy: The term 'neo-bureaucracy', denotes a model that retains classical bureaucracy's focus on rules, but places rather less emphasis on a unified hierarchy as the means of enforcing such rules.

Nepotism: It is a practice of appointing relatives and friends in one's organization to positions for which outsiders might be better qualified. It is an unethical conduct and unfair use of power.

Netiquettes: "Netiquette" refers to Internet etiquette. This simply means the use of good manners in online communication such as e-mail, forums, blogs, and social networking sites to name a few. It is an ethical use of internet.

Non Partisanship: The literal meaning denotes a person without any bias. This non-partisanship ensures a neutral approach in politics and a solid commitment to the government. It is regarded as an ethical virtue of a public servant.

Normative Ethics: Normative ethics is the study of ethical action. It is the branch of philosophical ethics that investigates the set of questions that arise when considering how one ought to act, morally speaking.

O

Objectivity: Objectivity is a concept of being true independently from individual subjectivity caused by perception, emotions, or imagination. According to the ethical objectivist, the truth or falsehood of typical moral judgments does not depend upon the beliefs or feelings of any person or group of persons.

P

Pathos: Pathos or the emotional appeal means to persuade an audience by appealing or stirring up people's emotions. It includes appeals to people's pity, anger, fear, hope, and the like.

Patriarchal Culture: It is a culture or form of social organization in which the father is the supreme authority in the family, clan, or tribe and descent is reckoned in the male line, with the children belonging to the father's clan or tribe.

Peer Pressure: Peer pressure (or social pressure) is the direct influence on people by peers, or the effect on an individual who gets encouraged to follow their peers by changing their attitudes, values or behaviors to conform to those of the influencing group or individual.

Personal Ethics: Personal ethics is a category of philosophy that determines what an individual believes about morality and right and wrong. These personal ethics can differ widely from person to person.

Persuasion: Persuasion is an umbrella term of influence. Persuasion can attempt to influence a person's beliefs, attitudes, intentions, motivations, or behaviors. Persuasion is a process aimed at changing a person's attitude or behaviour toward some event, idea, object, or other person(s) or a combination thereof.

Philanthropy: Philanthropy is an idea, event, or action that is done to better humanity and usually involves some sacrifice as opposed to being done for a profit motive. Philanthropy has some distinguishing characteristics that separate it from charity; not all charity is philanthropy, or vice versa.

Philosophy: Philosophy is a way of thinking about the world, the universe, and society. It is the study of the fundamental nature of knowledge, reality, and existence, especially when considered as an academic discipline.

Phronesis: According to Aristotle, 'Phronesis' is practical wisdom, the ability to make the right decision in difficult circumstances.

Political Attitude: Political attitudes are the approaches of people to the areas of public life covered by political psychology such as views on nationalism, political conservatism, political liberalism, and political radicalism.

Positive Attitude: Positive attitude is the guide to leading a positive life. Positive attitude is a state of mind that envisions and expects favorable results.

Pragmatism: Pragmatism is solving problems in a sensible way that suits the conditions that really exist now, rather than obeying fixed theories, ideas, or rules. It emphasizes the practical application of ideas by acting on them to actually test them in human experiences.

Prejudices: Prejudice is an affective feeling towards a person based on that person's perceived group membership. Practically, it is an unreasonable dislike for a particular group of people or things, or a preference for one group of people or things over another.

Probity: Probity refers to adherence to the highest principles and ideals that is utmost honesty. Probity is the evidence of ethical behavior, and can be defined as complete and confirmed integrity, uprightness and honesty in a particular process.

Professional Ethics: Professional ethics are principles that govern the behaviour of a person or group in a business environment. Like values, professional ethics provide rules on how a person should act towards other people and institutions in such an environment.

Public Administration: Public administration is the implementation of government policy and also an academic discipline that studies this implementation and prepares civil servants for working in the public service.

Public Funds: Public fund refers to the funds of every political division of a state wherein taxes are levied for public purposes.

Public Interest: Public interest is 'Welfare of the general public', in which the whole society has a stake and which warrants recognition, promotion, and protection by the government and its agencies.

Q

Quality of Service Delivery: Quality service delivery is a comparison of expectations with performance. A customer's expectation of a particular service is determined by factors such as personal needs and past experiences. The expected service and the perceived service sometimes may not be equal.

R

Rationality: Rationality is the habit of acting by reason, which means in accordance with the facts of reality. Rationality implies the conformity of one's beliefs with one's reasons to believe, and of one's actions with one's reasons for action.

Realistic Utopia: A utopia is commonly understood as a desirable yet unachievable - impossible - future state, e.g. of a society. The meaning of "utopian realism" is an attitude to the state of the world that is realistic in the long term. In the short term, a state closely resembling status quo is typically what is most likely to occur. In the long term, which we regard as totally unrealistic today, are often more likely to materialize in the long term than is the status quo.

Renounce: Renounce is defined as to give up a claim, belief, a practice, or to refuse further association with someone. In religion, renunciation often indicates an abandonment of pursuit of material comforts, in the interests of achieving spiritual enlightenment.

Repression: Repression is an unconscious defense mechanism employed by the ego to keep disturbing or threatening thoughts from becoming conscious. Thoughts that are often repressed are those that would result in feelings of guilt from the superego.

Right to Equality: The Constitution of India grants Fundamental Rights to all the citizens of India, irrespective of race, place of birth, religion, caste or gender. Right to Equality is one of the six Fundamental Rights provided in the Constitution of India.

Righteousness

Righteousness is defined as "the quality of being morally correct and justifiable." Such behavior is characterized by accepted standards of morality, justice, virtue, or uprightness. It is a concept that can be found in Indian religions as a theological concept.

Role Model: Role model is someone who inspires others to imitate his or her good behavior. In ethics, role models are key to persuasion and influencing.

S

Saint: A saint is a person who is recognized as having an exceptional degree of holiness or likeness or closeness to God. However, the use of the term "saint" depends on the context and denomination.

Scrupulous: Scrupulous means very careful to do things properly and correctly, such as paying friends back for money borrowed right away. Someone who is scrupulous takes great care to do what is fair, honest, or morally right.

Self-regulation: Self-regulation in the most basic sense involves controlling one's behavior, emotions, and thoughts in the pursuit of long-term goals.

Sensationalisation: It is the method to present information in a manner intended to arouse curiosity or broad interest, especially through the inclusion of exaggerated or lurid details.

Seven Sins: Originating in Christian theology, the seven deadly sins are pride, envy, gluttony, greed, lust, sloth, and wrath. These sins are often thought to be abuses or excessive versions of one's natural faculties or passions.

Sexual Ethics: Ethical issues related to sex including pre-marital sex, extra marital sex, homosexuality, contraception, masturbation, etc.

Sexual Harassment: Sexual harassment is defined as unwelcome sexual advances, requests for sexual favours and other verbal or physical conduct of a sexual nature. It is unethical and disapproved in every manner.

Sexual Violence: Sexual violence is any sexual act or attempt to obtain a sexual act by violence or coercion, acts to traffic a person or acts directed against a person's sexuality, regardless of the relationship to the victim.

Social Harmony: Social Harmony is defined as a process of valuing, expressing, and promoting love, trust, admiration, peace, harmony, respect, generosity and equity upon other people in any particular society regardless of their national origin, weight, marital status, ethnicity, colour, gender, race, age and occupation, etc.

Social Stigma: Social stigma is the extreme disapproval of a person or group on socially characteristic grounds that are perceived, and serve to distinguish them, from other members of a society.

Social Well-being: Social wellbeing is the extent to which one feels a sense of belonging and social inclusion; a connected person is a supported person in society. Lifestyles, ways of living together, value systems, traditions and beliefs are all important to our social well being and quality of life.

Soft Power: Soft power is the ability to shape the preferences of others through appeal and attraction. A defining feature of soft power is that it is non-coercive; the currency of soft power is culture, political values, and foreign policies.

Spiritual Awareness: Spiritual awareness or spiritual awakening is the process by which we begin to explore our own being in order to become whole and reunite our spirits with our physical bodies in a commonality of purpose.

Stereotype: A stereotype is a mistaken idea or belief many people have about a thing or group that is based upon how they look on the outside, which may be untrue or only partly true.

Subconscious Mind: 'Subconscious' is defined as all reactions and automatic actions we can become aware of if we think about them. The subconscious mind stores all of our previous life experiences, our beliefs, our memories, our skills, all situations we've been through and all images we've ever seen.

Sympathy: Sympathy is a feeling of pity or sense of compassion – it's when we feel bad for someone else who's going through something hard.

T

Teleological Ethics: Ethical theories which establish the rightness or wrongness of a given act by consideration of the consequences.

Tenderness: Tenderness is a feeling of concern, gentle affection, or warmth. It's the quality of a person who cries when he/she sees someone get hurt or who gently picks up a tiny kitten.

Tolerance: Tolerance is being patient, understanding and accepting of anything different. It is the ability or willingness to tolerate the existence of opinions or behaviours that one dislikes or disagrees with.

Torch Bearer: Torch bearer is a leader. He is a person who leads or inspires others in working towards a valued goal.

Total Quality Management (TQM): It is a system of management based on the principle that every member of staff must be committed to maintaining high standards of work in every aspect of a company's operations.

U

Uncooperative Behaviours: Behaviours that marked by an unwillingness or inability to work with others. This denotes no cooperation with others. This is against the common ethical standards or unethical.

Unethical: Something that does not get considered as right in society or an act that may create confrontation among people is known as unethical.

Universal Values: A value is a universal value if it has the same value or worth for all or almost all people. Spheres of human value encompass morality, aesthetic preference, human traits, human endeavour, and social order.

Universal Welfare: The perception of government responsibility for universal welfare is defined as the sense that welfare should not be aimed at the poor but rather based on citizenship regardless of income and other conditions and publicly provided to all citizens regardless of their ability to pay.

Uprightness: Uprightness is defined as the quality of being honest, responsible, and moral in the perspective of ethics.

Utilitarianism: It is the doctrine that focuses on actions that are right if they are useful or for the benefit of a majority. It also describes an action is right in so far as it promotes happiness, and that the greatest happiness of the greatest number should be the guiding principle of conduct.

Utility: Utility is a term in economics that refers to the total satisfaction received from consuming a good or service. Economic theories based on rational choice usually assume that consumers will strive to maximize their utility.

V

Value System: A fixed set of ethical and moral beliefs and practices usually associated with a world view of truth, life and death. It may be part of a religious belief system or a secular ideology.

Veracity: Veracity is the quality of an ethical person; it is the quality of being true, honest, or accurate. An example of veracity is the historical correctness of a biography; the veracity of the story.

Vigilance: In modern psychological terms, vigilance, also termed sustained concentration, is defined as the ability to maintain concentrated attention over prolonged periods of time. But its literal meaning is the action or state of keeping careful watch for possible danger or difficulties.

Vindictiveness: Vindictiveness is a strong desire to get back at someone. People who hold grudges and seek revenge are full of vindictiveness.

Virtue Ethics: Virtue ethics is 'person' based rather than action based: it looks at the virtue or moral character of the person carrying out an action, rather than at ethical duties and rules, or the consequences of particular actions.

W

Well-being: Well-being is the experience of health, happiness, and prosperity. It includes having good mental health, high life satisfaction, and a sense of meaning or purpose. Well-being emerges from our thoughts, actions, and experiences – most of which we have control over.

Whims and Fancies: Whims are sudden decisions to do something, on impulse, with no particular reason and fancies are in the same vein, a sudden liking expressed for something or someone. Therefore "Whims and fancies" refers to these sudden, impulsive even irrational actions; chopping and changing with no real reason.

Whistleblowers: A whistleblower is anyone who reports insider knowledge of illegal activities occurring in an organization. Whistleblowers can be employees, suppliers, contractors, clients, or any individual who become aware of illegal business activities.

Willpower: 'Will' is the ability to make conscious choice. Willpower is the motivation to exercise will. A person with strong willpower will assert decisions even in the face of strong opposition or other contradictory indicators.

Wisdom: Wisdom is "the ability to think and act using knowledge, experience, understanding, common sense, and insight". Wisdom is knowledge of how to live well, and the disposition to act appropriately on that knowledge.

Work Culture: Work culture is a concept that, as a whole, deals with the elements that make up an organization. It is a study of how the interactions among employees at your workplace affect the way the organization functions.

Work Ethics: A work ethic is a set of moral principles an employee uses in his or her job and it encompasses many of these traits: reliability/dependability, dedication, productivity, cooperation, character, integrity, sense of responsibility, emphasis on quality, discipline, teamwork, professionalism, respectfulness, determination, accountability, humility, passion, communication skills, being goal oriented, having organizational skills, creativity, and being adaptable and flexible.